D1458367

Philippe Legrain is an independent writer, commentator, consultant and public speaker. In February 2011, European Commission president José Manuel Barroso appointed him as a principal adviser and head of the analysis team at the Bureau of European Policy Advisers, which provides strategic thinking and policy advice to the president and the Commission. Before that, he was a visiting fellow at the London School of Economics' European Institute, a senior fellow at the Lisbon Council, a contributing editor at *Prospect* magazine and a commentator on global economic issues for publications such as the *Financial Times*, the *Guardian* and *The Times*, as well as for BBC TV and radio. He blogs at www.philippelegrain.com and on his Facebook author page, and tweets as @plegrain. He is also the author of *Open World: The Truth About Globalisation* (Abacus, 2002) and *Immigrants: Your Country Needs Them* (Little, Brown 2007), which was shortlisted for the 2007 *Financial Times* Business Book of the Year Award. In 1999, he was highly commended as Young Financial Journalist of the Year in the Harold Wincott Press Awards. Previously trade and economics correspondent for *The Economist* and special adviser to World Trade Organization director-general Mike Moore, he has a first-class honours degree in economics and a master's in politics of the world economy, both from the London School of Economics. Philippe is thirty-seven and lives in London.

Aftershock

Reshaping the World Economy
after the Crisis

Philippe Legrain

ABACUS

First published in Great Britain in 2010 by Little, Brown
This paperback edition published in 2011 by Abacus

A CIP catalogue record for this book
is available from the British Library.

ISBN 978-0-349-12275-5

Typeset in Sabon by M Rules
Printed and bound in Great Britain by
Clays Ltd, St Ives plc

Abacus
An imprint of
Little, Brown Book Group
100 Victoria Embankment
London EC4Y 0DY

An Hachette UK Company
www.hachette.co.uk

www.littlebrown.co.uk

To David

Contents

Acknowledgements

Writing a book is a huge task and it would not have been possible without many people's help and support. I am extremely grateful to Jonny Geller, my agent at Curtis Brown, and Tim Whiting, my editor at Little, Brown, with whom I have worked on all three of my books. Thanks too to everyone else at Curtis Brown and Little, Brown who has helped in any way. My good friend Martyn Fitzgerald provided invaluable research assistance. My father gave lots of useful comments and suggestions that greatly improved many chapters. Simon Long very kindly suggested many contacts in Asia and also read through the final manuscript.

Researching this book involved lots of reading, many discussions and interviews, and a gruelling trip around the world. Many of the people I spoke to are quoted in the book, but others deserve particular mention. Richard O'Brien and Alasdair Keith stimulated lots of interesting ideas. Razeen Sally and Fredrik Erixon were extremely supportive and provided many helpful contacts. Mark Kobayashi-Hillary was a mine of useful information on outsourcing. Gernot Wagner helped clarify my thoughts on emissions trading. Kristinn Hrafnsson introduced me to many interesting people in Iceland. In Sweden, Tove Lifvendahl, Kirsten Åkerman and Johan Norberg were very helpful. In Denmark, Stefan Kumarage Schou was tireless in his efforts to help me. Thank you too to Jill Farrelly in Dublin, Cristina Niell in Barcelona, Michael Pettis in Beijing, Alex Capri and David Zweig in Hong Kong, and Manu Bhaskaran and Stella Jiang in Singapore. Big thanks to Bron Sibree in Perth. In

Miami, I owe many thanks to the lovely Cathleen Farrell and to Joe Garcia for his unforgettable tour of the city. In Silicon Valley, I owe special thanks to Paul Fox. Patrick Collison in Vancouver is a fantastic talent and great company.

I would also like to thank many people for their support throughout my career. I was honoured to be a visiting fellow at the LSE's European Institute and am particularly grateful to Nick Barr for everything he has done for me over the years. The LSE library has also been a very useful resource. Mike Moore has always been a good friend to me. I still have many fond memories of my time at *The Economist* and of many people there. A special thank you to Bill Emmott, Edward Lucas and Iain Carson. Pam Woodall, who was among the first to warn of the dangers of America's bubble economy, has always been lovely to me. Thanks too to Gideon Rachman, Tim Harford, James Crabtree and Martin Wolf at the *FT*, David Goodhart at *Prospect*, Matt Seaton at the *Guardian*, Oliver Kamm at *The Times*, Evan Davis and Stephanie Flanders at the BBC, Marco Visscher at *Ode* and everyone else in journalism who has supported me. Jonathan Rauch is a good friend and an exceptional journalist. Thanks too to Claire Fox, Ceri Dingle, Austin Williams and everyone at the Institute of Ideas. In the think-tank world, thanks to Jessica Asato, Olaf Cramme, Alasdair Murray, Philip Booth, Jacob Arfwedson, Sarah Mulley and everyone on the IPPR's immigration team, Danny Sriskandarajah and everyone else who is on the right side of the immigration debate. Kenan Malik is also a great guy. Jean-Pierre Lehmann of the Evian Group has been very supportive. All the best to Rajat Nag, Giovanni Capannelli and everyone else I have worked with at the Asian Development Bank. Thank you to Claire Szabó at English Language Partners New Zealand and everyone at the Office of Ethnic Affairs who made my trip to New Zealand in 2009 such a huge success; I have made many new friends there. Thank you too to everyone around the world who has invited me to speak and contribute articles over the past few years; you know who you are.

A big thank you to my friends and family for their love and support. My brother Pierre designed my website and has also helped me in lots of other ways. Lots of love to Mum, Dad, Pierre, Gabe, Milli, Elizabeth and Morag, as well as to Patrick and all the Fairweathers.

I am blessed with many good friends, not all of whom I can mention here, but I want to thank in particular Allison Gallienne, Asma Bashir, Chris and Emily Foges, Chris Wilks, Colin and Shirley Iles, Daniele Deiana, Dusch and Rebecca Atkinson, Frank Paget, Frank Smith, Gary Cox, Gideon Lichfield, Harry Rich, Hugo Macgregor, Jo Malvisi, Joe Marci, Johan Nordin, John Cormack, Kelly McSherry, Kevin Goatcher, Lee Freeman, Linda Pearson, Mark Alefounder, Mark Westhenry, Nick Morton, Nick Tulk, Paul Bates, Paul Richardson, Raffaele Orsini, Richard Scandrett, Rob Gunns, Sandra Carter, Simon Sadler, Sophie Pittaway, Tashi Mannox, Tim Laxton and William Devine. Peter and Marion Doyle are incredibly special to me. Last but not least, thank you to David Sanderquist, to whom this book is dedicated.

Preface to the
Paperback Edition

The world has moved on since the first edition of *Aftershock* was published in May 2010. Britain has dumped Gordon Brown for a coalition between the Conservatives and the Liberal Democrats. They have opted for an unprecedented austerity drive and pledged to reform the economy, but their willingness to shake up the financial system and the housing market is doubtful. Barack Obama has enacted limited healthcare and financial reforms, but he must now deal with a hostile House of Representatives run by resurgent Republicans. Ireland has followed Greece into the care – or should that be clutches? – of the International Monetary Fund and the European Union. Across the world, the issue of how to build a fairer, richer, more stable and greener economy – the central theme of *Aftershock* – remains at the top of the agenda.

The good news is that the recession is over for now in the United States and most of Europe. Some advanced economies, notably Sweden and Australia, are booming. Stock markets are rebounding. China, India, Brazil and other emerging economies are spurting ahead. As a result, the world economy as a whole is now growing nearly as quickly as it was before the crisis and the gap between rich countries and poor ones is narrowing.

The bad news is that the recovery looks fragile, unemployment across America and Europe remains painfully high, many economies are still weighed down by huge personal, bank and government debts, and many governments are embarking on painful austerity measures that will limit growth, cost jobs and slash services, with the poor bearing the brunt of the cuts. In fast-growing emerging economies, the new fears are inflation and bubbly asset markets. The two are connected: with near-zero interest rates in America and the US Federal Reserve printing dollars with gay abandon, money is gushing out of the US and into emerging economies with better growth opportunities, sounder finances and higher interest rates.

Thus in place of 1930s-style trade protectionism, we have twenty-first-century 'currency wars': countries conspiring by different means to hold down their currencies and thus keep their exports competitive. The Bank of England talks the pound down, the Fed engages in 'quantitative easing', China limits the renminbi's rise, Japan and Switzerland try to curb their currencies' strength, Brazil, South Korea and other emerging economies (understandably) try to stem the huge inflows of hot money that send their currencies soaring. The euro, meanwhile, weakens of its own accord, as panicky traders question its member governments' ability to pay off their debts.

The key issue for Britain is whether, in the face of an unprecedented public-sector squeeze, with consumers weighed down by huge debts, business investment and exports can drive growth forward and reduce unemployment. One risk is that the economy will stagnate. Another is that an unreformed economy will fall back into its bad old bubble ways, with growth driven by debt-fuelled consumption, housing and finance. If the UK economy is to recover strongly, it needs to break these habits and tap into the fast-growing markets of China and other emerging economies.

For the seventeen economies that share the euro – hello Estonia, which traded in its kroon in January 2011 – the immediate issue is how to arrest the financial panic that has dragged down Greece and Ireland, and which threatens to sweep through Portugal and Spain to Belgium, Italy, France and eventually even Germany.

At heart, the 'euro crisis' is a wrestling match over who will ultimately bear the huge losses incurred by European banks on their dodgy loans during the bubble years. So far, EU governments have decided that banks' bondholders must be protected at all costs, preferring to impose losses on taxpayers instead – even if this stretches governments' solvency to breaking point. Yet because voters' tolerance for bank bailouts has worn thin, governments are acting covertly: lending huge sums to Greece and now Ireland so that they can repay German, French and UK banks in full – all under the pretence of 'defending the euro'.

This strategy is not just unfair, costly and dangerous; it is ineffective. Governments are burdening taxpayers with huge bills that will impede future growth; Ireland's 'bailout' is actually a high-interest loan of €20,000 per Irish person. They are inviting a populist and extremist backlash; witness Sinn Fein's recent success. They are corroding support for both the euro and the EU: prudent Germans rage against bailing out profligate Greeks and reckless Irish, the Irish against EU-imposed 'reparations', when their anger ought to be directed at the banks that ultimately benefit. They are encouraging financial speculation, not least by distressed banks – heads they win, tails taxpayers lose. And by guaranteeing banks' debts, all EU governments are risking their credibility and ultimately their solvency.

Bond markets are now testing governments' promises: you bailed out holders of Greek government bonds and Irish bank bonds, what about Portuguese, Spanish and other debt? This is a self-fulfilling prophecy: even a sound credit is in trouble if markets refuse to lend. And whereas Greece's bailout cost €110 billion and Ireland's €85 billion, Spain's could top €400 billion – and then, who knows? At some point the cost of bailing out banks would prove unbearable – there is a limit to Germany's ability and willingness to borrow – and the euro could needlessly fall victim to the resulting political and financial turmoil.

Even if EU governments' ability and willingness to bail out banks is not tested to destruction, the strategy remains misguided. Instead of sacrificing taxpayers to protect bondholders, watching the sovereign dominoes fall and failing to tackle the underlying banking problem, what is needed is an EU-wide solution that forces banks to recognise their losses and bondholders to recapitalise them if necessary. This is a decisive moment for the EU. Will the narrow interests of financiers prevail or those of society as a whole?

As I write in January 2011, two of the bright spots of the global economy, Australia and Brazil, are suffering terrible floods. But while these natural disasters are causing death and destruction, they have not derailed their economies' success, which has a lot to do with exporting nature's bounties to China, the new locomotive of the global economy. Germany too is doing surprisingly well by selling capital goods to the Middle Kingdom. As China's and India's middle classes swell, their demand for the premium consumer goods and sophisticated services that advanced economies excel at will soar. Britain, America and others need to emulate Australia and Germany and plug in to the boom of the century.

These are difficult times for the world economy. The four big dangers identified in *Aftershock* – financial collapse, debt crises, protectionism and climate change – loom large. Enlightened leadership, bold reforms, international cooperation and a bit of luck are desperately needed to see us through. But it isn't all bleak. Even for Ireland, catastrophically mismanaged and betrayed by its political leaders, the future can be bright. Its people still have plenty to offer the world – as do those in other angst-ridden advanced economies. *Aftershock* sets out what needs to be done.

Introduction

Back from the Brink

*But the world economy
is still in danger*

Is my money safe? Will my credit card work? Will my wages get paid? Will I even have a job? What about my pension? What is my home really worth? Where will it all end? What if the economic system around us actually collapsed? Such questions had never even crossed the minds of most people in Britain, America and other rich countries until the recent financial crisis. Economic meltdown might strike poorer places such as Argentina, Asia or Africa. It may feature in the history books: remember the soup kitchens and dole queues of the Great Depression of the 1930s. But it did not happen – surely could not happen – nowadays in supposedly advanced economies. Or so we thought – until September 2008, when banks were suddenly falling like ninepins, markets were plummeting and governments seemed overwhelmed. Was everything we took for granted falling apart around us?

For a while, it seemed like it was. It was a terrifying mix of panic, bewilderment and powerlessness. It seemed surreal. How could everything just seize up like that? Suddenly, seemingly out of nowhere, our jobs, savings and hopes for the future were in jeopardy. Eventually, though, governments and central banks managed to quell the panic by conjuring up incredible sums – hundreds of billions, then trillions – to prop up the banks. Even so, they could not prevent the financial meltdown becoming an economic one: factories ground to a halt, trade slumped, unemployment soared. But again the authorities rode to the rescue – slashing official interest rates to zero, flooding the economy with money, pumping out huge fiscal stimulus packages and providing open-ended guarantees to the banking sector. It worked: a depression has been avoided. But huge dangers still lurk ahead.

As I write, in October 2009, the panic already seems like an age ago. Our brains conspire to black out such a traumatic experience. All the talk is of recovery, even as unemployment remains high. China's economy is growing in leaps and bounds, India's almost as fast. Brazil is bouncing back. Other emerging economies in Asia and Latin America are back in business too. For once, the developing world is leading the way. World trade is recovering. America, Britain and the rest of Europe are twitching too. They could hardly fail to show signs of life after the huge shot of monetary and fiscal adrenaline that the authorities have administered. Stock markets are surging ahead, as is the price of oil. House prices show signs of picking up. Bankers are back to gambling at public expense. Politicians are patting themselves on the back for saving the world. But while the terror has passed, the aftershocks endure – dreams dashed, jobs gone, futures mortgaged.

By the time you read this, the economy may be growing at a fair clip – or the recovery may have fizzled out. But irrespective of the immediate outlook, is the recovery really sustainable? Is the world economy back on the right track? Have we learned the correct lessons from the crisis? Have governments done enough to prevent such a cataclysm happening again? Or might we actually be even more vulnerable to a bigger crisis over the next decade or so?

Powerful voices argue that little needs to change. The financial system may need a few tweaks here and there, but otherwise the world should go back to business as usual. The faster economies recover, the stronger such siren voices will grow. Others feel that everything must change. Global capitalism is a giant wrecking ball that crushes the poor, destroys jobs and is killing the planet; such a dangerously unstable and destructive force needs to be tamed. Many people aren't quite sure what to make of it all. Angry but confused, they lash out at all and sundry – greedy bankers, conniving politicians, dastardly foreigners. Unfortunately, this debate is generating more heat than light and too little action where it is needed, too much where it isn't.

Heed the warning

We have been here before. The global financial crisis that began in 2007 was preceded by one a decade earlier. That tsunami kicked off in Thailand in the summer of 1997 and soon engulfed much of Asia and then Russia too. By 1998 stock markets everywhere were tanking and when LTCM, an American speculative fund – sorry, 'hedge fund' – sank in September its huge debts threatened to drag down the international financial system with it. For a few weeks that October the world economy seemed on the brink of meltdown. I remember it vividly: I was an international economics writer at *The Economist* at the time. Suddenly, all my friends in London were interested in what I had to say. (It didn't last long.) This is how I wrote about it in my first book, *Open World*:

> The US Federal Reserve bailed out LTCM and made emergency cuts in American interest rates to try to calm panicky investors' nerves. The world waited anxiously to see if the medicine

would work. The fear everywhere was of recession, depression, slump. But fortunately the storm abated. Europe and North America emerged shaken, but relatively unscathed. Soon it was back to business as usual. Grand talk about rebuilding the world's financial architecture proved to be hot air. All the blueprints for reform gathered dust. Investors found new games, like punting on glorified get-rich-quick pyramid schemes known as internet start-ups ... American multi-millionaires like LTCM's John Meriwether were bailed out. Ordinary Americans and Europeans were saved by interest-rate cuts. People in poor countries bore the brunt of the financial storm.

How quickly we forget! Yet add ten years to the dates and uncanny similarities emerge. The most recent crisis also started in a seemingly unimportant part of the global financial system – America's market for 'subprime' mortgages (housing loans for risky borrowers) – in the summer of 2007. It soon spread to Britain, causing a run on Northern Rock bank in September, and to much of Europe. By 2008 stock markets everywhere were plunging and when Lehman Brothers, an American speculative 'investment bank', collapsed in September, its huge debts and other commitments threatened to drag down the international financial system with it. The US Federal Reserve and other central banks slashed official interest rates to try to calm panicky investors' nerves – and the world economy fell off a cliff. It seems the fire-fighters have lost some of their potency.

That Europe and North America have not emerged unscathed from the most recent crisis is not the only difference from 1997–8. For a start, the crisis began in the United States, which supposedly has the world's most advanced financial system, rather than in a developing country with a less sophisticated one. It soon also gripped Britain and much of Europe, which have highly developed financial systems too. So it cannot be blamed on the shortcomings of particular economies with underdeveloped financial sectors.

Rather, it shreds the foundations of modern globalised finance. As I argued in 2001 in *Open World*, financial markets are inherently unstable. They are prone to *Manias, Panics and Crashes*, the title of a classic history of financial crises by Charles Kindleberger. And that instability can have devastating consequences for people's jobs and the economy as a whole. Reforms that were shelved a decade ago must not be ducked now.

Alarmingly, governments appear to be failing to heed the lessons of the latest crisis. They are instead perpetuating past mistakes and compounding them with new ones. Insiders increasingly claim that the crucial difference between 1998 and 2008 is that whereas the Fed organised a rescue of LTCM, the Bush administration decided to let Lehman go bust. In their view, a deep recession could have been avoided if Lehman had been bailed out. But the real mistake was not allowing Lehman to fold; it was letting it collapse so chaotically, as I shall explain in Chapter 1. Unless the right action is taken now, we risk an even greater catastrophe within the next decade or so – when, hamstrung by huge debts, policy-makers in mighty America, let alone not-so-mighty Britain, would be almost powerless to respond. Life could become as chilly as it is now in Iceland for Thorvaldur Thorvaldsson, whom we will meet in Chapter 1. An even more devastating crisis would not only cause untold misery to billions of people. It could also finish off our Open World – and with it countless opportunities for progress.

But perhaps the most striking contrast between the earlier crisis and the recent one is the very different role played by emerging economies – poorer countries that are developing fast. In 1997–8 – and in earlier crises, such as the Latin American debt crisis of the early 1980s – emerging economies were hit first, hardest and longest. This crisis hit them last, least and shortest. Very quickly the big emerging economies (BEEs) bounced back, with China leading the way, India close behind and Brazil following on. These buzzing BEEs are leading the global recovery, not following it. 'Investors and political leaders are looking at us differently,' Luiz Fernando Furlan, a Brazilian businessman whom I interviewed for *Open World* and who served as his country's trade, industry and development minister from 2003 to 2007, proudly remarks. 'For the first time we are part of the solution, not part of the problem.'

Buzzing BEEs

The crisis has highlighted and accelerated a historic shift in the world economy: the amazing rise of the BEEs – China, India and Brazil – not to mention that of smaller emerging economies, such as South Korea, Turkey, Indonesia, Chile and perhaps one day South Africa too. As recently as 2003 only thirty-one of the world's five hundred largest companies by revenues were from emerging economies. By 2010 China alone had forty-six companies in the Fortune Global 500, South Korea ten, India and Taiwan eight each, Brazil seven, Russia six, Mexico and Singapore two each and Malaysia, Saudi Arabia, Thailand, Turkey and Venezuela one each. That's ninety-four in total.[1] The change has been particularly dramatic in finance. In September 2009 four of the world's top ten banks by market value were Chinese; in 2006 none was. The Industrial and Commercial Bank of China holds more deposits than any other. In the world's biggest-ever share sale, Petrobras, Brazil's oil giant, raised $27.5 billion from investors in 2010.

By some measures, emerging economies already account for half of the world economy. More significantly, over the next decade (and beyond) they are likely to account for the bulk of economic growth in the world.[2] This has huge implications for everything from global energy use to how the world economy is run, as will be discussed in Chapter 5. Inexorably, the centre of gravity of the world economy is shifting east (and south).

Emerging economies' growing prosperity is incontrovertible evidence of the immense benefits of freer trade, investment and people flows. For sure, poverty remains extreme for the bottom billion – mostly in Africa – who live in states that are incapable of providing for their basic needs, let alone reaping the benefits of globalisation. The World Bank reckons that the crisis has pushed another 90 million people into the extreme poverty of surviving on less than $1.25 a day. Those tragedies urgently need addressing. But life is looking up for most of the developing world. In less than a generation, poverty in what was once known as the Third World has been slashed. Whereas in 1990 nearly two-thirds (63.4 per cent) of people in developing countries lived on less than $2 a day, by 2005 fewer than half (47 per cent) did.[3] (Remember that $2 stretches much further in rural India than it does in London or New York.) The ranks of the middle classes – those living on between $2 and $13 a day – swelled from 1.4 billion to 2.6 billion people over the same period. Half of the developing world is now middle class. In India, average incomes doubled between 1994 and 2008.[4] Astonishingly, average incomes in China multiplied tenfold between 1980 and 2008, doubling since the turn of the century alone.[5] Annual income per person has soared to $6,000 (£3,750) a year, allowing for differences in purchasing parity. If living standards in China and India – which together account for three in eight people on the planet – continue to grow at 8 per cent a year, they will double every nine years and quadruple in eighteen. By 2025 1.3 billion Chinese – many of whom were starving as recently as the 1970s – could be as prosperous as the Portuguese are today. And by 2035 so could 1.5 billion Indians.

This ought to be cause for celebration, not just in emerging economies but also in the West. Primarily, in my view, because it offers unprecedented opportunities for billions of people to enjoy a better life: first to escape poverty, then to enjoy the comforts of middle-class life and eventually to achieve the living standards that are taken for granted in the West. Anyone who has a shred of concern for their fellow human beings should rejoice, not try to impede it. It will make the world a much fairer place – and a safer one. Emerging economies' growth can also make people in rich countries better off – by creating new jobs, new businesses and new technologies, as well as by providing a wider choice of cheaper and better imports. In the decade before the crisis, American consumers' free-spending ways helped power the world economy. Since then governments have stepped in. But a sustainable and balanced global recovery will depend increasingly on demand from China and other emerging economies, as will be discussed in Chapter 4.

China's investment needs are already boosting growth in Australia, Germany and across the emerging world – and it is also the world's fastest-growing consumer market. Any company that taps into it can prosper, as Darius Stenberg, a young Swedish entrepreneur whom we shall meet in Chapter 4, can testify. He is minting it by helping Chinese people to obtain a nicer smile. China is also, increasingly, a land of opportunity for Westerners – dare I call them immigrants? – who are moving to Shanghai, Beijing and Shenzhen for the buzz and the chance to get rich. Gary Speed, who left London for Shanghai in 2005, will tell us his story in Chapter 8. As India's entrepreneurial companies become world-beaters, they are snapping up and turning around Western ones, creating new jobs and better products for Westerners. In Chapter 5 we will meet Baba Kalyani, an Indian industrialist whose father was a penniless peasant, whose company probably supplied some of the parts for your car. Many of the companies developing new clean-tech solutions to the problem of climate change are based in China or India, or rely on Chinese and Indian brainpower. Last but not least, cheaper and better imports from emerging economies help the money in people's pockets to stretch further, which is particularly welcome in these straitened times. Brazil, in particular, could help feed the world, as I will argue in Chapter 9, where we will also meet Kitty de Kock, who picks fruit for Tesco in South Africa.

Yet the rise of the BEEs is often seen as a threat, particularly in angst-ridden advanced economies (the As) – America, Europe, Japan, Canada, Australia and New Zealand. China, in particular, has become the lightning rod for many people's fears about the global economy. Many Americans and Europeans worry that Chinese exports threaten their jobs, especially now unemployment is so high. Joe Fehsenfeld, a mild-mannered gentleman who makes printed circuit boards in America's Midwest, thinks it is time we tamed the Chinese dragon, as we shall see in Chapter 6. Generally happy-go-lucky Australians are getting anxious about Chinese investment, as Chapter 7 will explain. Some, particularly in America, even blame China for the financial crisis. The broader fear is that emerging economies' increasing energy use will cause an already overheating planet to fry. The BEEs feel it is unfair that they should compromise their chances of development now to solve a problem caused primarily by the As, but unless everyone eventually reduces their carbon emissions, climate change could have catastrophic consequences, as will be discussed in Chapter 10. Politicians in America and Europe are upping the ante by threatening to tax imports from countries that they feel are not doing enough to curb their carbon emissions. This has the makings of a huge trade war that could hammer the fragile world economy and shatter the chances of countries cooperating to limit global warming.

The stakes are huge. Our relatively Open World has delivered – and can continue to offer – immense benefits to both rich and poor. New freedoms, new opportunities, new ideas, greater variety and diversity, better lives in the broadest sense – in other words, unprecedented progress. But it now faces four huge challenges: making global finance safe; reshaping the world economy along healthier and more balanced lines; keeping the global economy open as it emerges from the crisis and adjusts to emerging economies' rise; and coping with climate change. Failing to fix the flaws in global finance risks an even bigger crash. Failing to shake up the world economy could lead to stagnation, political tensions, economic instability and a nasty debt crisis. Succumbing to protectionism and prejudice could throttle everyone's future prosperity. Failing to address climate change properly could pose even greater dangers to the planet. In short, our Open World is threatened by crash, crisis, closure and a climate catastrophe.

But it's not all doom and gloom. Each of these challenges also contains an opportunity. Put global finance right and a safer world beckons. Reshape the world economy and a stronger, more stable world is in prospect. Open up the global economy further – free up farm and services trade, allow people to move more freely – and a fairer and richer world is in sight. Embrace a low-carbon future and a cleaner, sustainable and more secure world is possible.

The future of the global economy hangs in the balance. What happens next is up to us. Decisions taken (or not) now could shape it – for good or ill – for a generation or more. It is vital that the right choices are made. Worryingly, though, governments are already making big mistakes.

Risky moves

The world came perilously close to financial Armageddon in 2008–9. Next time we might not be so lucky. Governments were right to rescue the banking system – on which the rest of the economy depends – but their misguided efforts to prop up existing banks are storing up huge problems for the future. They missed an opportunity to reshape global finance while it was on its knees. Now that it is resurgent, pumped up with public money and guarantees, the big danger is that its awesome lobbying power and sway over policy-makers' thinking will block much-needed changes.

Contrary to those who argue that global finance should be left largely intact, it requires radical reform. Yet the changes that policy-makers are considering are too timid; some are irrelevant, others wrong-headed. The understandable furore about bankers' bonuses is diverting attention from much more important issues, not least the unacceptable notion that some banks are 'too big to fail' and so have a licence to gamble at public expense – heads they win, tails taxpayers lose. Economists call this 'moral hazard'. But that is a huge understatement – it is a racket. Capitalism without risk of failure is like power without account-ability – it corrupts absolutely.

Fixing global finance is a precondition for a healthy and bal-anced recovery. Righting the policy mistakes that sowed the seeds for this crisis is also essential. So too is avoiding new errors. As economies struggle to their feet, many weighed down by huge household debts, governments need to tread a delicate course between nurturing the recovery while it remains weak and supporting it for too long on an unsustainable path. The big danger is that they will seek to postpone the much-needed adjustment rather than easing it – or even try to relaunch the world economy along the old, unbalanced, unsustainable lines. They must not flinch in the face of tough decisions – such as allowing yesterday's industries to fail or tilting currencies in the right direction – that are needed for a strong and sustainable recovery, as I shall discuss at length in Chapter 4.

Protectionism in all its ugly forms must be resisted. Contrary to those who claim that globalisation in general has failed, free trade, foreign investment and the free movement of people are all overwhelmingly forces for good. The crisis represents a failure of finance, not of markets in general. It is sloppy thinking to suggest otherwise. Just because Royal Bank of Scotland (RBS) failed does not mean Tesco has stopped delivering the goods.

Citibank's collapse does not detract from Google's genius. Even in a crisis, companies are vying to better Apple's iPhone. The only migrants that ought to be blamed for the crisis are international bankers. So while bankers need caging, businesspeople and workers need freeing.

Politicians protest that they will not repeat the protectionist mistakes of the past. But their actions belie that. Even in the boom years, suspicion of foreign investment, products and workers was often strong. The Doha Round of trade talks at the World Trade Organization (WTO), launched in 2001, has been deadlocked for years, while a thicket of rules prevents most people from working where they want to. But now that times are tough in America, Europe and elsewhere, the temptation for governments to hit out at all things foreign may prove irresistible. Victor Fung, chairman of the International Chamber of Commerce (ICC), which represents world business, says he is 'extremely worried' about protectionism. 'Leaders still pay lip service to the idea that we should not be protectionist, but we've seen a lot of backsliding since the last G20 meetings.'

When leaders of the Group of Twenty (G20) major advanced and emerging economies met in Washington DC soon after Barack Obama's election in November 2008, they pledged to resist protectionism. 'We underscore the critical importance of rejecting protectionism and not turning inward in times of financial uncertainty,' their joint statement said. Yet by September 2010 the world's governments had implemented 638 beggar-thy-neighbour measures – and G20 members were responsible for imposing 395 of them, according to Simon Evenett of the University of St Gallen in Switzerland, who coordinates a website called Global Trade Alert (GTA) that provides independent monitoring of policies that affect world trade.[6]

China was the biggest target of protectionist measures. Among the worst offenders were Russia, India, Indonesia, Ukraine, the European Union and the United States. And despite all the talk about boosting green jobs, innovation and industries of the future, most of the measures (outside of finance) seek to protect sectors such as agriculture and smokestack, lower-end manufacturing. 'Only the most cavalier observer could dismiss the harm being done to exports and its possible contribution to economic recovery,' Evenett concludes.

On the positive side, Mexico has opened up many of its markets unilaterally. China and, to a lesser extent, India have also abolished many export taxes. Sweden has bucked the global trend by allowing in foreign workers more freely. But in general the omens aren't good. Around the world, protectionism is rising in a variety of guises. Government-supported banks are directed to keep their lending national; US ones have been forced to rescind job offers to foreign graduates. Politicians are urging people and businesses to keep their spending local; the US fiscal stimulus package contains explicit 'Buy American' provisions. Asian countries are responding with their own 'buy local' campaigns. Anti-dumping investigations against imports that are deemed too cheap are proliferating (albeit from a low base). America is lashing out at Chinese tyres[7] and steel pipes; China responds by targeting American poultry. The EU is keeping out Chinese steel pipes on the basis that they *might* harm European companies. America is banishing Brazilian orange juice. Mexico has announced sanctions against a variety of US imports in retaliation for Congress keeping Mexican trucks off American roads. Russia has raised a host of import tariffs. Indonesia has introduced a swathe of import licensing schemes, Argentina a host of protectionist reference prices. Japan is rewriting sanitation policies in a way that will restrict food imports. India has banned imports of Chinese toys and mobile phones altogether. 'Hit by a tide of imports?' asks an ad by India's customs service depicting a crashing wave. 'Safeguard duty may be your lifeguard.'

Bailouts for car companies – more than $50 billion for

General Motors (GM) and $7 billion for Chrysler in the US, €4.5 billion of loan guarantees from the German government for Opel, GM's European subsidiary – threatened an all-out subsidies war. In September 2010 Brazil's finance minister, Guido Mantega, warned that an 'international currency war' had broken out. The US accuses China of giving its exports a competitive edge by keeping its currency too cheap. At the same time, the US Federal Reserve is printing money with gay abandon, driving the dollar down and other currencies up. Other countries have also sought to push their currency down; the governor of the Bank of England has tried to talk down sterling.

EU members are not only taking aim at America and Asia; they are increasingly falling out among themselves too. Left unchecked, this could cause the EU to unravel. In breach of Europe's single market and stringent rules against state aid, President Nicolas Sarkozy called on French car makers to 'repatriate' their production from Czech assembly plants. Germany's subsidies to Opel seek to prop up domestic factories at the expense of more productive ones in Britain and Spain.[8] In Britain, strikes against foreign workers have targeted Italian, Portuguese, Polish and other EU workers who have a right to work there freely. Around the world, immigration rules are being tightened and foreign workers urged to leave. What a terrible irony – capital fails, workers pay.

The longer the pain lasts, the bigger the risk of a major rollback. With unemployment high, corporate profits depressed and America's trade deficit gaping, support for protectionism is growing. The crisis has also heightened fears about immigrants taking jobs and draining public finances, and amplified the voices of those whose real objection to immigration is cultural. But the danger is more than just cyclical. The crisis has also hammered Americans' and Britons' self-confidence and exacerbated the prevailing pessimism in much of continental Europe. Gripped by fear of decline, Americans and Europeans increasingly see the rise of China and other emerging economies as a threat. Those who think they can't compete will be tempted to try to hobble their perceived rivals. 'Green protectionism' also enjoys a new legitimacy. Smokestack industries have suddenly become greener than thou: keep out Chinese steel to save the planet. Overnight the US Congress flipped from opposing curbs on America's carbon emissions to bashing those who refuse to toe its line. (However, with the election of a Republican majority in the House of Representatives in November 2010, the chances of US action against climate change appear dead for now.) Last but not least, the crisis has undermined faith in free markets, while the bank and car bailouts have made government support for other industries seem more acceptable. With the intellectual climate more inclined towards government intervention than at any time since the 1970s and powerful interests lining up to lobby for help, even liberal-minded politicians may struggle to hold the line.

It is complacent to think that globalisation is a technological inevitability – a fact of life – and that global businesses are too entrenched and economies too intertwined for the world to change course. Globalisation is neither uniform nor universal and will always be incomplete. Clearly, then, it is also reversible. Politicians have put an end to globalisation before and they could do so again. While the chances of a return to the wholesale protectionism of the 1930s remain remote for now, the risks of reverting to the 1970s – a decade marked by creeping protectionism in trade, the slamming shut of borders to migrants and rising xenophobia – are far greater. Another crisis could turn that drift into a rout.

The logic behind all this protectionism is simple but misguided: if the economic pie has shrunk, all the more reason to ensure that the remainder goes to hungry local workers and businesses. But if everyone fights to keep more of the scraps for themselves, there ends up being even less to go around. Why? Because protectionism is a tax on trade, which depresses global demand further. By raising the cost of imports, it reduces people's purchasing power, hitting the poor hardest. And since one country's imports are another's exports, it also reduces demand for traded goods more generally. Higher taxes and lower exports are a sure-fire way of stunting growth. To put it another way, while governments have been boosting spending and cutting taxes to bolster the economy, protectionism acts like the opposite of a fiscal stimulus.

Because protectionism depresses demand, it also costs jobs. For every job preserved in sectors that compete with imports, others are lost in export industries and throughout the rest of the economy. Making US steel more expensive, for instance, may protect some steelworkers' jobs at the expense of workers in viable American companies such as Caterpillar that rely on affordable steel. Likewise, making it harder for foreigners to come and work in a country – or worse, expelling those already working there – reduces demand for the goods and services they consume (and thus employment for those who make those products) as well as demand for labour in complementary lines of work. Fewer foreign builders would mean fewer jobs for those selling building supplies as well as for local interior designers.

Protectionism doesn't just reduce demand; it also adds to the economy's dislocation. The last thing that a credit-starved high-tech company needs is to be deprived of valuable foreign workers too – especially since their brainpower will help drive the eventual recovery. Protectionism obstructs the world economy from adjusting, rather than encouraging it. Delaying the day of reckoning prolongs the pain at huge expense. There is, for instance, huge overcapacity in the US and European car industries. But despite the collapse in sales, not a single factory closed in Europe in the year after Lehman's collapse. If each country acts to prop up domestic car makers, none will thrive. Only if the least efficient shrink can the car companies that produce the vehicles people actually want to buy do well. Ford stands a better chance of surviving if Chrysler and GM are not propped up by government subsidies. Europe's car industry would be in better shape if the German government had allowed Italy's Fiat to take over Opel and restructure it. If America and the EU keep out foreign cars, India's Tata Motors and South Korea's Hyundai, Daewoo and Kia will all suffer too. What's more, if American and European governments subsidise gas-guzzlers, the development of greener hybrid and electric cars will be stunted.

Economic growth increasingly relies on tapping into dynamic global networks that develop and transfer new ideas, technologies and businesses. These require products, investment, ideas – and people – to move as freely as possible. Cutting ourselves off from these networks would be more damaging than simplistic economic models allow for. It would be tragic if our Open World fell victim to a mixture of atavistic prejudice, outdated economics and crisis-inspired protectionism. Fear of the future and the failings of global finance should not blind us to the huge opportunities for greater freedom and prosperity that globalisation offers.

In the longer term, climate change poses perhaps the biggest global challenge. Doing nothing would be a reckless gamble. If the climate scientists' predictions are correct, a hotter planet could cause polar ice caps to melt, sea levels to rise, coastal areas to flood, deserts to expand and weather patterns to become more extreme. Many species could die out and many people suffer. Hundreds of millions could lose their homes and their livelihoods, creating a stampede of environmental refugees. While people in rich countries might be able to afford to adapt, the poorest would doubtless be hardest hit.

Most people now agree that something must be done. But they disagree as to how and who should pay for it. Certainly, slashing global carbon emissions requires a shake-up of the world economy. But done the right way, it could cost surprisingly little – and bring many additional benefits, not least an end to dependence on oil-producing countries with nasty regimes and the resulting wars. In Chapter 10 we shall visit innovative 'clean-tech' companies that are developing electric cars, eco-friendly housing and renewable energy solutions that could make a world of difference – and who knows what wonderful new technologies could emerge over the next few decades? But trying to tackle climate change in the wrong way would not only be hugely costly. It could also be ineffective or even counterproductive. One example: the German government has, at vast expense, subsidised covering a cloudy country with solar panels, causing a shortage and higher prices in sunny countries where they could be of much greater benefit. Nor are America and Europe wise to be threatening a trade war with China and India over their carbon emissions when their cooperation is needed to solve the problem.

Some environmentalists argue that economic growth in general and globalisation in particular are incompatible with saving the planet. Better to consume less and produce what we need locally, they say. The ostensible aim is to curb carbon emissions, but their real target seems to be capitalism itself, with global warming a convenient lever to force people to abandon their wicked materialistic lifestyles. From the comfort of middle-class Europe and America, they decry the fact that people in China, India and other poorer countries aspire to the lifestyles that Westerners enjoy. Some even object to their sheer numbers, arguing that the world would be a better place if there weren't so many (other) people around. Watered-down versions of such views now permeate many rich-country societies. Sadly, many on the left who used to believe in progress have now become reactionary.

Ultimately, the only sustainable solution is to develop new clean technologies. Tap the limitless energy of the sun, the wind and the atom and the false choice between growth and greenery is removed. The surest way to get there as quickly and cheaply as possible is to keep markets open and allow people, new ideas and new technologies to spark off each other. Globalisation can help save the planet; localism could kill it.

The power of positivity

Globalisation is a confusing and often-misused word that describes a simple concept: the world is increasingly interconnected. Thanks to distance-shrinking technologies and market-opening government policies, global connections are – for the most part – cheaper, faster and more pervasive than ever. Our lives are increasingly intertwined with those of people from far-off places. Shop in Tesco, Wal-Mart or IKEA and your spending decisions affect the Chinese migrant worker or the South African fruit picker who played a part in producing what you buy. Put money in a pension fund and its investment decisions impact on whether a new mine is opened in Chile, another is closed in Australia or a company drills for oil in Nigeria. Your vote decides whether people from Mexico, Morocco or Myanmar (Burma) get a chance of a better life in your country. It's not only our actions that affect others: theirs affect us too. Your job may depend on selling to foreigners – or be threatened by what they sell. Your employer may be foreign-owned or depend on loans from an international bank. You might want to move to America, Australia or China but not be able to. Increasingly we are involved in collective experiences that transcend national boundaries. People around the world join forces to campaign for action against climate change or poverty. When Americans elected their new president, the rest of the world watched with anticipation – and when Obama won, millions cheered. When national football teams competed for the World Cup in South Africa in 2010, our eyes and our emotions responded together. In our world of Facebook, foreign holidays and fusion food, many of the barriers that once kept us apart are falling.

This is my third book. My first, *Open World*, addressed many of the big debates about globalisation. Is trade responsible for the shrivelling of manufacturing jobs in the West? In some cases, yes, but for the most part the culprit is technology, which allows us to produce more with fewer workers. This not only boosts wages, it frees up workers for more productive uses. Does trade harm developing countries? On the contrary: just look at China's and India's rise. Africa's huge problems are due to a variety of problems: for the most part, Africans are victims not of globalisation, but of a lack of it. Do big companies run the world with their seemingly all-powerful brands? No, governments with the power to tax, regulate and fight wars do. But Chapter 1 will argue that, in finance, big banks have got too powerful and need to be cut down to size. Are global markets so powerful that governments are being forced to shrink? Hardly. Even posing the question now seems ridiculous, though people such as Naomi Klein, the author of *No Logo* and more recently *The Shock Doctrine*, and Thomas Friedman, author of *The World Is Flat*, thought so then.

Is the WTO a new world government? Are you serious? It can't even reach agreement on an ever-shrinking Doha deal. Is farm protectionism justified? Not at all, and I shall revisit this issue in Chapter 9. Are globalisation and greenery incompatible? Not if a global carbon tax (or cap-and-trade scheme) is introduced. Are global patent laws justified? No. Just as one size doesn't fit all in terms of labour and environmental standards, countries at different stages of development should not have identical intellectual-property standards imposed on them. Is global finance dangerous? Most definitely. Is globalisation Americanising culture everywhere? Not really: it tends to make culture within countries more diverse, although that may make countries seem more alike. This book will touch on some of these debates in passing, but it will not rehash what I have already written. If you are interested in my detailed thinking on these issues, please pick up a copy of *Open World*.

My second book, *Immigrants: Your Country Needs Them*, looked at the most controversial dimension of globalisation, the movement of people. It argued that immigration controls were economically stupid, politically harmful and morally wrong. It looked at the humanitarian cost of border controls – the deaths and the suffering – and made the economic case for all kinds of migration, of highly skilled workers as well as less qualified ones. It emphasised the often-underappreciated dynamic gains from diversity and the long-term boost to economic growth it can produce. It showed that migrants do not cost jobs or burden the welfare state. It pointed out the huge benefits to developing countries from the money migrants send home, the new skills and connections they bring back with them, and the diaspora networks they create. It considered cultural fears about immigration such as the perceived threats to national identity and social solidarity and looked at how diverse people can learn to live together well. It examined American fears about Latino migrants and European concerns about Islamic ones. This book will look at how the crisis is affecting global migration and highlight new trends in global mobility. But it will not delve into all the issues that are comprehensively covered in *Immigrants*.

The focus of this book is forward-looking. It examines the three big forces that will shape the global economy over the next decade: recovering from the crisis, adjusting to the ongoing rise of emerging economies, and coping with climate change. What it is not is an attempt to predict the future. The future is unknowable: forecasting what will happen next year, let alone in twenty years' time, is a mug's game. In 1988 nobody foresaw that the Berlin Wall would fall the following year, still less that 2008 would witness the part-nationalisation of the Western banking system and the election of a non-white US president. Caution, scepticism and, above all, humility are essential in seeking to peer into a murky future.

Aftershock is aimed at a global audience, but in particular at people in rich countries who are fearful about the future. The pain now is real and unavoidable – jobs lost, homes repossessed, mountains of debt to pay off. A home that was once a cash machine is now a millstone. Pessimism is the order of the day.

'When I meet Europeans, they think the sun is shining here in Brazil while the sky is dark in Europe,' Luiz Fernando Furlan remarks. 'And they don't know how to reverse the situation.' This crisis of confidence is dangerous. When people feel threatened, they tend to hunker down and turn inwards. But trying to shut out the world would make us all poorer. Far from making us safer, it would jeopardise our security. In particular, treating the rise of emerging economies as a threat could in part be a self-fulfilling prophecy. It could prompt nationalist and protectionist responses. It would encourage the development of new relationships and institutions that exclude the West. It would undermine chances of securing their cooperation in tackling climate change. Trying to swat away the buzzing BEEs could end up stinging us badly.

The overarching challenge is to rediscover optimism about the future. It is still in our hands – and it need not be bleak. If companies are to invest in tomorrow's technologies, people to embrace change and policy-makers to make difficult reforms, a positive outlook is essential. Gloomy Americans and Europeans should visit Asia or Brazil and allow themselves to be carried away by their refreshingly positive vibe. Delight in their success and view their growing prosperity as an opportunity, not a threat.

The aftermath of the crisis also opens up huge opportunities to reshape the world economy for the better. As Rahm Emanuel said when he was Barack Obama's chief of staff, 'Never allow a serious crisis to go to waste.' A fairer, richer, greener and more stable global economy is possible. But to achieve it we need to rediscover the virtues of open markets, open societies and open minds that go hand in hand with progress: greater opportunities for everyone to chase their dreams and fulfil their potential. We must not allow another financial collapse, a debt crisis, a closing of borders, a climate catastrophe or a corrosive pessimism to destroy that huge promise.

1

Meltdown

Bubble and bust

When the capital development of a country becomes a by-product of the activities of a casino, the job is likely to be ill-done.

> John Maynard Keynes, *The General Theory of Employment, Interest and Money,* 1936

I [suspect] we are throwing more and more of our resources, including the cream of our youth, into financial activities remote from the production of goods and services, into activities that generate high private rewards disproportionate to their social productivity. I suspect that the immense power of the computer is being harnessed to this 'paper economy', not to do the same transactions more economically but to balloon the quantity and variety of financial exchanges . . . I fear that, as Keynes saw even in his day, the advantages of the liquidity and negotiability of financial instruments come

at the cost of facilitating nth-degree speculation which is
short-sighted and inefficient.

                                James Tobin, Nobel laureate, 1984

The real housing bubble in America and Britain is . . . the
growth in mortgage debt, which is at record levels in
relation to incomes . . . At the very least, households
hoping that ever-rising house prices will provide generous
nest eggs are likely to be disappointed. At worst, the risk
is that prices in many countries may take a tumble.
Falling house prices, massive debts and low inflation: now
that really would be an unpleasant cocktail to
contemplate.

                    Pam Woodall, economics editor, *The Economist*,
                                                  August 2002

There is growing recognition that the dispersion of credit
risk by banks to a broader and more diverse group of
investors, rather than warehousing such risk on their
balance sheets, has helped make the banking and overall
financial system more resilient . . . Consequently the
commercial banks may be less vulnerable today to credit
or economic shocks.

                IMF, *Global Financial Stability Report*, April 2006[1]

When the music stops, in terms of liquidity, things will be
complicated. But as long as the music is playing, you've
got to get up and dance. We're still dancing.

                Chuck Prince, chief executive of Citigroup, July 2007

Thorvaldur Thorvaldsson is an unlikely property speculator. A
bust of Lenin is proudly displayed in his home and he refers regularly to the Russian revolutionary's famous analysis of global
capitalism, *Imperialism: The Highest Stage of Capitalism*. His

shirt and T-shirt – even his hair – are red. Yet this sombre, apparently unexcitable forty-one-year-old with a deep, almost lugubrious voice got carried away by the collective financial frenzy that gripped Iceland in the years before the crisis. A carpenter since the age of sixteen, he took out a big mortgage in 2005 to buy a new flat and workshop in the centre of Reykjavik, the Icelandic capital, while keeping his old flat in the suburbs.

'I thought that buying property wasn't that risky,' he says. 'That property was much more stable than, say, the stock market. I thought that some structures in society would not let anything terrible happen because even the banks and the authorities had an interest in stability. Also in our history housing prices had always gone up – sometimes faster than inflation, sometimes slower, but we had never seen falling prices before.' Thorvaldur's reasoning goes a long way towards explaining why not just Icelanders but also Americans, Australians, Britons, Irish, Spaniards and many other people got caught up in an unprecedented global property bubble.

An insatiable demand for property was one side of the story; the other was a massive expansion in the supply of credit. This happened particularly suddenly in Iceland, after the country's state-owned banks were privatised around the turn of the century. 'I was totally against the privatisation of the banks,' Thorvaldur interjects excitedly, briefly breaking out of his monotone. The biggest, Landsbanki – literally 'the national bank', which until the 1960s had issued the country's banknotes, as the Bank of Scotland and RBS still do in Scotland today – was sold off between 1998 and 2003. Set free from government control, Iceland's banks soon outgrew their tiny domestic market of 320,000 people by expanding overseas. They took advantage of cheap money and globalised finance to borrow massively from international markets, funding not just a domestic property boom but also a foreign acquisition spree. Icelandic raiders snapped up swathes of Britain's high street – including the Oasis group and stakes in Debenhams, House of Fraser and Hamleys – as well as West Ham football club and Saks Fifth Avenue, an upmarket American retailer. By offering high-interest online savings accounts, Landsbanki's Icesave hoovered up cash from British and Dutch savers, while Kaupthing Edge garnered money in eleven countries. As Kaupthing's loan book swelled, its assets grew thirtyfold between 2000 and 2008. All together, the loans and other assets of Iceland's banks expanded until they were nine times greater than the country's national income.

The banks were run almost like cults to their superstar bosses. 'We were told we had to be "all in",' explains one young banker, who was persuaded to tie his fortunes to the bank's mast. 'The bosses said, "If you're not all in, it means you don't believe in what you're doing – and if you don't, you're not right for the job." They were played videos with loud music to whip them into a frenzy. 'I borrowed 5 million Icelandic krónur in foreign currency, around my annual salary at the time, from the bank to invest in its shares.' This gave the bank a double boost: it expanded the bank's lending and ramped up its share price. Like a chain letter, people were convinced to spread the word to others. 'The guy you went to school with would convince you to put your savings into banks' bonds because they're safe,' the banker explains. 'Young women would call up old people to convince them to invest. All the loans were guaranteed by housing and other collateral.'

The banks encouraged customers to take out loans in foreign currencies; the interest rates were much lower, they pointed out. Many Icelanders bought houses and cars with loans denominated in Japanese yen, Swiss francs and euros. 'We thought it was normal,' says Inga Jessen, a chirpy thirty-two-year-old who worked as an office manager for an Icelandic bank. 'My husband and I both had good salaries. We had enough money to buy shares and travel after the monthly repayments on our loans. We didn't think we were taking too many risks.'

Reykjavik, a chocolate-box town of 120,000 people where everyone seems to know everyone else, became a global financial centre. Everyone wanted to become a banker. 'My generation lived all our adult lives like this,' Inga says. 'Everything was always going up. We thought it was normal. There was so much money floating around in the bank. You could almost see it in the air.' Property developments sprouted all over the place, the streets clogged up with fancy sports cars and SUVs, designer stores and restaurants mushroomed. Inflows of foreign cash kept the Icelandic króna strong, making imports cheap. On paper, Iceland, an economy traditionally based on fishing, became one of the richest countries on earth.

'Everybody thought, It's a bit weird; where is the money coming from?,' says a young, well-dressed former estate agent. 'The banks made out that they were the best and the smartest. It was like a collective delusion. Icelanders weren't thinking for three years. People just believed it – or wanted to believe it – and did it.'

But disaster struck in September 2008. As the global financial crisis swept around the world, Iceland's overextended banks collapsed and were renationalised. The currency lost half its value, the housing market froze and the economy went into freefall. 'I first realised things might go wrong a few weeks before the crash,' the banker says. 'But we were assured the system would stand the storm. A few days before the bank collapsed, we were told we had six months' funding. But we had no real money left, just lines of credit from other banks. When they pushed a button, all our liquidity [cash] was gone.' Gordon Brown played his part when the British government misused anti-terrorism laws to seize Kaupthing's UK assets, precipitating its downfall. Reverberations from Iceland's crash were felt around the world. German savings banks racked up big losses, a Californian property developer went bust, British charities, local councils and even the National Audit Office lost money. Eventually, the

International Monetary Fund (IMF) stepped in with a huge emergency loan. Among its conditions: raising interest rates to an eye-watering 18 per cent.

'When things fell apart, we thought, What's going to happen? Where do we stand?,' says the former estate agent. 'The government and the central bank had no clue what to do; what were the people supposed to think? When the prime minister said, "God bless Iceland," people thought, It's over. People didn't know what would happen to them. Would they have jobs? Personally, I was in shock. I thought it was a dream. Lots of people thought that it would take a while and then it would all be OK. Now we realise we need to start again and do something new. Who do I blame? The previous government and the central bank for letting the bankers do it. The bankers themselves: they have no morality. And yes, we Icelanders are also responsible. We took the decision to buy houses and cars and to believe all this crap. We were all caught up in it.'

As the house of cards collapsed, the banker, Inga and Thorvaldur were toppled in quick succession. The banker who went 'all in' is now all out. 'The shares are now worthless, and my debt has doubled to 10 million krónur because of the króna's collapse,' he explains. 'Everything I have is invested in this garbage. Now I'm just trying to survive month by month. But when the loan comes due in three years' time, I'll be bankrupt.' The banker is thirty, with a wife and two young children. 'If I go bankrupt, so will my mum and dad, because my loan is guaranteed against their home, as will my brother and sister.' The chain letter has become a chain gang. The banker does not try to pass the buck. 'I'm responsible for what I did,' he says. 'I could have said no. I don't blame the system. I put my money and my reputation on the line. I even convinced a very good friend to go all in too. He doesn't blame me. Most of us were acting in good faith.'

Inga, like many Icelanders, was hit by a triple whammy. Her

house halved in value, her debts more than doubled – and she lost her job too. 'During the boom we had even applied to build our own house.' She points to the ghost town on the barren hill opposite her flat, a graveyard of half-built property developments. 'Thank goodness we didn't do it.' She pauses. 'When you come to Reykjavik now, it looks like there is a lot of money here. People drive great cars and there are large houses everywhere. But we are prisoners,' she says. 'We can't sell our cars or houses. We can't afford to buy food and clothes for our children.' So far, though, the nationalised banks have not repossessed many homes, although that may change. 'I feel betrayed,' she says. 'I had my dreams.' But she is picking herself up. She writes a blog (atvinnulaus.blog.is), has launched a website that suggests things to do for free in Reykjavik (freecitytravel.com) and is helping her mother publish a book. 'I've changed, I don't think so much about money any more.'

When demand for his carpentry work dried up, Thorvaldur converted his workshop into a flat and moved in, renting out the flat that overlooks it. Since February 2009, he has been unemployed. He has no savings, and even with the rental income from his two flats and Iceland's generous unemployment benefit he cannot afford the mortgage. He feels trapped, as many people around the world do, by huge debts that exceed the value of his assets and from which he cannot walk away. Even bankruptcy is not a way out in Iceland, because under its moralistic laws bankrupts are still stuck with their debts until they die. Thorvaldur has set up a group to lobby for a change in the law, so that – as in America – property owners could hand over their keys to the bank and be free. 'I don't think I have been so irresponsible,' he says. 'Lots of ordinary people own two apartments.' He says he was planning to sell the one in the suburbs before the crisis hit, but that it proved difficult to shift. 'This is not an individual problem, it's a social problem. It must be solved collectively.'

A financial collapse like the one Iceland has experienced

undermines your trust in everything. One day you think that the company that you work for is secure, its profits are real, your currency has value, the government is overseeing things properly and will protect you if things go wrong – and then suddenly all those beliefs are shattered. According to the September 2009 economic survey by the Organisation for Economic Co-operation and Development (OECD), domestic demand in Iceland will slump by almost 30 per cent between 2007 and 2010. By September 2009, the stock market was down 94 per cent from its peak.[2] 'We have to look to the future and think it will be better,' Inga insists.

Icelandic taxpayers are lumbered not just with their own debts, but also with many of those incurred by their reckless bankers. The Icelandic government has pledged to repay British and Dutch savers' deposits in Icesave. The amount owed to Britain (£2.3 billion) and the Netherlands (€1.2 billion) is equivalent to half of Iceland's national income, or £11,000 for every one of its people. Icelanders complain that they have become 'Iceslaves'. A further $2.1 billion (£1.3 billion) – £4,000 per person – is owed to the IMF. Government spending is set to be slashed by 20 to 30 per cent, while taxes will soar. In effect, a handful of foolish financiers and careless politicians have all but bankrupted the country.

Thorvaldur is adamant that he should not pay for the Icesave debacle. 'Iceland is such a small society and the financial sector was so overwhelming. It shouldn't be possible for a small group of oligarchs [as Iceland's bankers are known] to take on such huge debts. I'm not saying the British people should pay my debts because there are more of them. But I don't consider these my debts. I didn't sign anything.' I put it to him that he could escape the crippling taxes that will be needed to pay off the banks' debts by emigrating. 'I have thought about it,' he replies. 'I have contacts in Denmark.' But his sense of collective duty intrudes. 'More empty houses would make matters even worse.

We need massive immigration, not emigration, to make use of all these newly built houses.'

Thorvaldur thinks the way forward is a return to a simpler life. 'We must live cheaply, produce and export, and earn our own money. Not just take out new loans to pay off old loans.' And the banks should remain state-owned. 'Now that we have experienced the biggest period of corruption in our history, primarily linked to the privately owned financial sector, I think the main lesson from the crisis is that financial systems should all be collectivised or socialised because privately owned ones do not produce any value. They only take value from other sectors instead of spreading it to productive areas of the economy. We need a complete change of direction.'

Not a world away

In many ways, Iceland is a charming oddity. It is a remote volcanic island perched in the North Atlantic where the North American and Eurasian tectonic plates meet. (While Reykjavik is culturally European, it is geographically in North America.) The land seems to have a life of its own: the earth frequently quakes, geysers spurt and hot sulphurous water bubbles up from the ground. (This provides ample geothermal power, as well as fantastic outdoor spas.) The sky is bright at midnight in mid-summer – which, in my case, provoked a kind of insomniac loopiness – and oppressively gloomy in winter (so I'm told). Nature is wildly beautiful. Iceland is a country of epic waterfalls, snow-capped mountains and vast glaciers, where the land – sometimes lunar, often bare and generally almost empty – meets the sea in dramatic fjords, while the cold surrounding waters teem with fish and many kinds of whale. Tourists love it; I did.

Icelanders have a reputation for being quirky – think Björk and her hauntingly odd singing. It might be tempting for people in Britain, America and other countries where cheap credit and financial alchemy also fuelled a huge property bubble to dismiss Iceland's plight as a bizarre special case. For a start, its population is so small. The whole country consists of as few people as a middling English town such as Coventry, or as Wichita, Kansas. In London terms, it's home to fewer people than Camden and Islington combined. That's not really a serious country, is it? (When its banks collapsed, the internet buzzed with jokes such as 'What's the capital of Iceland? Around $20.') As for the country's brash bankers and the incestuous political elite that got caught up in the frenzy, they may seem particularly naive. And Icelanders were surely greedier, crazier and more stupid than more sophisticated Britons or Americans. They're only *nouveau riche* fishermen, after all.

Tut, tut – silly little Iceland. But contrary to the way many foreign pundits have portrayed it, Iceland is not a freak show. Its people are highly educated – compare thoughtful Thorvaldur the carpenter with ghastly Joe the plumber. It generates cutting-edge software and biotechnology companies, such as Össur, a global leader in high-tech artificial limbs. At the 2008 Beijing Paralympic Games, the South African sprinter Oscar Pistorius won three gold medals wearing Össur's 'Cheetah' legs, running the 100 metres in 11.17 seconds. Any visitor to Reykjavik can also confirm that it is bubbling with culture – music, art, fashion; personally, I love GusGus's electro-house music. As for its bankers, they behaved scarcely more outrageously than, for instance, Dick Fuld of Lehman Brothers or the Royal Bank of Scotland's Fred Goodwin. Its politicians weren't obviously more credulous than, say, Gordon Brown during his time in charge of Britain's finances or George W. Bush. As for thinking that buying property was an effortless road to riches, surely nobody could ever believe such a crazy thing.

So we're left with size. Iceland's banks were too big, their losses too great, for such a small country to bear. But that is a difference of degree, not kind. So while Iceland is certainly an extreme example of what can go wrong when a financial bubble bursts, it is not a world away from what happened in Britain and other rich countries. (When Iceland collapsed, many thought Ireland would be next. 'What's the difference between Iceland and Ireland?' traders joked. 'One letter and six weeks.') Its fate should serve as a warning of what could happen elsewhere if global finance is not fixed. The country's banks grew so big that its government felt it could not allow them to collapse, but by taking on their debts it has dragged down the whole country with them. Deemed too big to fail, they have proved too big to save.

Britain is more like Iceland than people realise. At the end of 2008 UK-based banks had £7.9 trillion in assets. A £1.4 trillion economy hosted a banking system five and a half times as large.[3] RBS alone had assets equivalent to 166 per cent of Britain's GDP. When Gordon Brown stepped in to stop the banking system collapsing, he in effect pledged UK taxpayers' future incomes as collateral against banks' losses. Had the economy plunged into depression, as it threatened to, banks' losses could have lumbered British taxpayers with an Icelandic-sized bill. If international markets had decided that the losses would exceed what the government could reasonably expect to raise in future taxes, it would have been forced to turn to the IMF instead. Ireland, Switzerland, the Netherlands, Denmark, Sweden and others were similarly vulnerable. Ultimately, a government that has exhausted its capacity to borrow must either default on its debts or, if they are denominated in national currency, print money to inflate them away.

Since Britain's international banks were very active in foreign currencies, a collapse of the pound combined with huge foreign-currency losses could have caused an Iceland-style rout. Willem Buiter – a brilliant economist, then at the LSE's European Institute, with a caustic wit and a healthy irreverence for received wisdom – dubbed the City of London 'Reykjavik-on-Thames'.[4] 'The UK is much closer to Iceland than it is to the US,' he argues. 'I can now say these things in public without people rolling their eyes or giggling hysterically.'

Fortunately, the government's gamble paid off. The losses appear huge, but bearable. But next time, Britain and others might not be so 'lucky'. Since the crisis, big banks in America, Britain and the rest of Europe have got even bigger, while governments' capacity to borrow has shrunk, because growth prospects are worse and they have already taken on so much extra debt. Even in the US, whose capacity to borrow is huge, the vast costs of the crisis have opened up a black hole in the government's finances. Worse, by backstopping banks' losses, governments have given them licence to gamble at public expense – heads they win, tails taxpayers lose. By trying to make the banking system safer, they have made it more dangerous. The next crisis is already in the making.

Vulnerable beasts

Loathe them or hate them, banks are essential. They keep money flowing around the economy, making millions of payments each day from one person or entity to another more cheaply and conveniently than using cash. They also collect funds from savers and select which borrowers are worthy of credit. When they do their job properly, they help to allocate savings to more productive investments, boosting economic growth. But their most valuable function is that they transform short-term deposits into long-term loans. Banks offer savers a (usually) safe investment that pays a better return than cash and can be withdrawn as cash on demand – in bankers' jargon, their deposits are 'liquid'. At the same time, they provide borrowers with a secure, often cheaper and more convenient source of finance that can be used to make long-term 'illiquid' investments – such as buying a home or building a factory – because it cannot be called in at will. In effect, banks enable savers to fund long-term investments without tying their money down.

This confidence trick only works because few depositors are likely to want their money back at any time, and banks hold on to enough cash to meet their ordinary demands. But if too many depositors tried to take their money out at once, the bank could not pay out. Even a well-run bank whose loans are all likely to be paid back in due course is vulnerable to a bank run – a dash for cash that it cannot meet – because the loans it has made cannot all be called in at once. Whereas its liabilities to savers are liquid, its assets are 'illiquid'. Worse, if a bank tries to sell those assets quickly to meet depositors' demands, it may be unable to – or be forced to do so at fire-sale prices – and so end up unable to pay depositors back in full. Thus even a perfectly sound bank could end up insolvent as a result of a self-fulfilling panic. Worse, a collapsing bank can drag down other financial institutions from which it has borrowed. Bank runs are often contagious, with the failure of one bank generating a run on others. So while banks are very useful, even well-run ones can be dangerously unstable.

Bank runs were once common. But governments have changed that. By guaranteeing that small depositors will get their money back if a bank goes bust, they deter them from dashing for their cash whenever they hear a worrying rumour. They also agree to make emergency loans to banks that are believed to be solvent but that face liquidity problems – a shortage of cash – so that they do not collapse. Central banks – such as the US Federal Reserve, the European Central Bank (ECB) and the Bank of England – act as 'lender of last resort' on governments' behalf. Since central banks can print as much of their own currency as they like, they can supply unlimited liquidity to banks that face demands for cash in local currency. But they cannot print foreign currencies, so unless a country's authorities can obtain them on banks' behalf – either from the central bank's reserves or by borrowing them overseas – they cannot prevent a bank run by foreigners.

Consider an Icelandic bank that has taken in deposits in sterling from British savers, has borrowed on a short-term basis in dollars from an American bank and holds illiquid assets – such as loans to Icelandic companies – that it cannot sell quickly. Suppose Britons panic and want their money back, and the Americans decide not to extend their loans. Iceland's central bank can print only krónur, not pounds or euros. Once its foreign-currency reserves run out, it can borrow only as much as the Icelandic government could credibly raise in future taxes and transfer to foreign creditors. But in times of panic, foreigners may be unwilling to lend not just to Icelandic banks, but also to the Icelandic government. Thus banks that operate internationally are much more vulnerable to a self-fulfilling loss of confidence. Even if they are solvent, they may still suffer a bank run. That risk is much smaller if international banks are based in countries that use a currency that is widely accepted abroad. The US dollar and the euro are widely held as reserves by foreign central banks and are used to pay for international trade. It is thus much easier to persuade foreigners to lend to the authorities that issue them. That is one big reason why Irish banks (which are based in the eurozone) survived, but Icelandic ones didn't. Iceland's new government is now keen to join the EU in order to adopt the euro. Buiter argues that since the pound is no longer a major international reserve currency, Britain is more like Iceland than it realises.

As well as cash and illiquid long-term loans, banks tend to hold other assets that are usually liquid, such as corporate bonds (tradable loans to companies) or mortgage-backed securities (basically tradable packages of mortgages, as will be explained later in the chapter). These earn the bank interest and can usually quickly be sold for cash if need be. But during the financial crisis, the markets for these assets dried up – supposedly liquid assets became illiquid. A central bank can then perform another useful function. It can act as a 'market maker of last resort', lending cash to banks using these temporarily illiquid assets as collateral. (The risk, of course, is that these assets are not worth what banks say – or think – they are, so that the central bank is handing over good cash for bad assets.) By guaranteeing deposits and lending to banks that face a liquidity shortage, the authorities should be able to make the banking system much more stable.

Unfortunately, bankers have an uncanny knack for wreaking havoc. For sure, finance is an inherently risky business. No matter who makes lending decisions and how, mistakes will be made. We would all be much poorer if financiers weren't willing to take a punt on a budding Google or lend to someone who wants to learn new skills. The trick is to lend wisely, within reason, and to keep a watchful eye on market conditions and the wider economy. Yet bankers often make a mess of things. When times are good, they tend to lend too much to risky borrowers. When times are bad, they tend to cut back lending too much, denying credit even to sound ones. Worse, because bank credit plays such an important role in the economy, their mistakes tend to have much wider repercussions. They cause bubbles to inflate and burst, and they exacerbate the economic cycle of boom and bust. But the biggest problems occur when banks go bust. This can happen all too easily because they tend to lend huge sums with only a small amount of their own capital, so that a few costly mistakes can wipe shareholders out. When a big bank goes under, it can drag others down too – and if bank after bank collapses, savers fear for their money, everyone stops lending and making payments, and the economy grinds to a halt. That is the nightmare America and Europe faced in late 2008.

Why do bankers tend to make such bad mistakes? The simplistic answer is that they are too greedy. But that is unconvincing: surely greedy bankers want to make money, not lose it. A more plausible reason is that banks in general and individual bankers in particular do not pay the full price for their mistakes. When bankers' bets pay off, they earn a huge bonus; when they don't, they live to gamble another day; at worst, they walk away with nothing. When banks themselves fail, governments tend to bail them out, and the knowledge that taxpayers are likely to pick up the tab for their mistakes encourages them to gamble recklessly. All of that is true, but it is not the full answer. After all, banking crises struck with depressing regularity long before governments intervened – just look at the United States in the nineteenth century – so governments cannot shoulder all of the blame.

The fundamental reason is that the future is unknowable and bankers are human – like everyone else, they get caught up in the periodic waves of irrational exuberance that convince people to shell out outlandish sums for tulip bulbs, dotcom shares or bricks and mortar. But unlike everyone else, they can lend huge sums to validate their (and others') views, giving their mistakes a life of their own. As they compound their errors, they eventually overreach, making themselves and the economy vulnerable to even a slight reversal of fortune. Picture them as a magic circle of one-eyed giants growing bigger as they gorge themselves on cash. The rest of us are perched on them, feeding off the scraps. But these giants have a weakness. They each totter on a tiny stiletto of capital – and when a wrong move causes them to topple, everyone else can come crashing down with them.

Bubble trouble

Financial bubbles are nothing new. Shares in the South Sea Company, anyone? But worryingly, they have been getting bigger, broader and more frequent. In the late 1980s, Japan experienced an almighty bubble that saw property prices double in a decade.[5] The price of a square metre of prime real estate in Tokyo's Ginza shopping district – the Japanese capital's equivalent of London's Bond Street or New York's Fifth Avenue – came to exceed 100 million yen (around $1 million at the time).[6] The grounds of the Imperial Palace in Tokyo were more expensive than the whole of California.[7] Share prices also reached unprecedented heights: the Nikkei index peaked at nearly 39,000. After the bubble burst, prices slumped. Property prices fell by an average of more than 40 per cent. Some 'prime' property lost over 99 per cent of its value. In the twenty-first century, the Nikkei has never exceeded 19,000 and it was below 10,000 in November 2010.

During the dotcom bubble of the late 1990s, internet companies reached absurd valuations. Energised by evidence that information technology (IT) in general and the internet in particular were raising American productivity growth and caught up in the hype about all the new dotcom companies, US stock markets were bid up to new heights. By 2000, the frenzy had spilled over into normally sober society. The papers were full of stories of 'day traders' who had quit their jobs – and even grandmothers – who were making fortunes at home gambling on the stock market over the internet each day. People swapped share tips in the office or at the pub. The internet changed everything, it was said; sceptics just 'didn't get it'. Remember the AOL–Time Warner merger? With its inflated shares, America Online, a dial-up internet provider, bought Time Warner, the world's biggest media company, for $164 billion. 'For once the superlatives and the hype seem justified,' *The Economist* opined. In 2003 Time Warner dropped the AOL from its name and in 2009 AOL was spun off for $2.5 billion. Chemdex (later Ventro), a loss-making online marketplace for chemicals with scarcely any revenues, saw its market value swell to more than $4 billion in 2000; by 2001 its share price had plummeted from $239 to 37 cents.[8]

There was also boo.com, a British online fashion store, which burned through $180 million of investors' money and collapsed within six months of launching.[9] When the NASDAQ, the market of choice for US high-technology companies, peaked at 5,132 on 10 March 2000, it had more than doubled in a year. By late 2002, it had lost nearly 80 per cent of its value. Its composite index has never exceeded 3,000 since, and was just above 2,500 in November 2010.

The most recent madness is the global property bubble that inflated in the decade before the crisis. In the United States, house prices nearly trebled across ten big cities between January 1997 and their peak in June 2006, rising by 190 per cent.[10] People bought property that had not yet been built and sold it on without ever moving in. By April 2009, prices had fallen a third from their peak. In Britain, the price of the average house more than trebled from £54,656 in January 1997 to £186,044 at the peak in October 2007, a rise of 240 per cent.[11] Swapping more or less the same stock of houses for ever more inflated prices seemed like a failsafe way to get rich; you just had to get your foot on the 'property ladder'. By February 2009, the typical house was worth £147,746, a decline of over 20 per cent. In Spain, house prices trebled between 1997 and 2007.[12] This sparked a building boom, with residential construction soaring to 9 per cent of GDP in 2007. By October 2010, prices had fallen more than a fifth from their peak in April 2007 and were still declining.[13] Drive out of Madrid and you reach ghost towns with empty new houses and freshly paved streets where traffic lights rotate aimlessly. In Australia, where comparable figures started to be collected only in March 2002, the price of existing homes in eight capital cities rose by 76 per cent between then and January 2008, before dipping somewhat.[14] Prices have since rebounded; perhaps the bubble has yet to burst. The biggest bubble of all was in Ireland, where the value of all the houses in the country quadrupled in the ten years to June 2006.[15] The

price of a typical Dublin house shot up more than fivefold from
€82,411 in March 1996 to €429,754 at its peak in April 2007.[16]
Ireland was gripped by a collective frenzy. Construction swelled
to 12 per cent of GDP. Even its farmland became the priciest in
Europe. By the third quarter of 2010, Dublin house prices had
plunged by 44 per cent and were still on a downward trend.

This worldwide rise in house prices was the biggest bubble in
history, according to Pam Woodall, the then economics editor of
The Economist, who was among the earliest to warn of its dangers. In June 2005, a while before the bubble's peak, she wrote:

> According to estimates by *The Economist*, the total value of
> residential property in developed economies rose by more
> than $30 trillion over the past five years, to over $70 trillion,
> an increase equivalent to 100 per cent of those countries' com-
> bined GDPs. Not only does this dwarf any previous
> house-price boom, it is larger than the global stock-market
> bubble in the late 1990s (an increase over five years of 80 per
> cent of GDP) or America's stock-market bubble in the late
> 1920s (55 per cent of GDP). In other words, it looks like the
> biggest bubble in history.[17]

The McKinsey Global Institute reckons that the value of all
the residential property in America soared from $13.4 trillion in
1997 to $31.8 trillion in 2006, while in Western Europe it leaped
from $13.4 trillion to $38.6 trillion in 2007.[18] And as we shall
see, what began as a housing bubble eventually became a much
bigger financial bubble too.

Bubbles develop because financial markets are inherently
unstable. Why? Because they involve bets on an unknown and
unknowable future. Who knows what a house *ought* to be
worth today, let alone what it *might* be worth tomorrow? It
depends. It depends on a whole set of assumptions and guesses,
not only about what a financial asset might actually be worth,

but also on what you think other people think it might be worth, as well as on what they think you think they think it might be worth and so on.[19] Since everyone is making guesses about what other people are guessing, financial investors tend to move in herds. If many people think house prices are on the up, others follow to profit from the rise; if some start to doubt the story, others are quick to sell before prices tumble. Sometimes these bandwagons get out of hand and bubbles develop.

In his classic book *Manias, Panics and Crashes* Charles Kindleberger argued that bubbles follow a standard pattern.[20] First there is a displacement, an external event that kicks off the process and normally justifies an increase in asset prices. Then there is positive feedback, as investors spot there is easy money to be made and pile into the market, pushing prices up. This gives way to euphoria, when investors become manic and a large share of the population is sucked in, pushing prices still higher. Then comes the crash.[21] Often, the initial trigger for a bubble is an exciting new technology, like the internet. In other cases, it is simply a long period of economic prosperity and stability, as with the recent real-estate bubble. But what inflates them is not just investors' excessive optimism. It is generally a prolonged period of unduly low interest rates and lax lending by banks. In short, it is the mistakes of central banks and banks that give property investors the rope to hang themselves.

The serial bubble blower

The story begins in 1997, with the financial crisis that started in Asia. Even though America's economy was booming and the stock market was rocketing, Alan Greenspan, the chairman of the US Federal Reserve from 1987 to 2006, kept interest rates on hold. When the Asian crisis became a global panic in late 1998 and American share prices tanked, Greenspan cut US interest rates to calm nerves. That was reasonable, but his mistake was to keep interest rates low long after the panic had passed and with the economy still growing at full pelt. Soon, the stock market roared back with even greater gusto. Why? Because investors were now convinced that if share prices fell, Greenspan would step in with interest-rate cuts to prop the market up. Buying shares now seemed like a one-way bet.

When the dotcom bubble that he had helped inflate burst in 2000–1, Greenspan responded with massive interest-rate cuts. He slashed them to 1 per cent and kept them there until early summer 2004. During this period real interest rates were actually negative – the cost of borrowing was below the rate of inflation. Unsurprisingly, with borrowing so cheap for so long, this sparked a huge expansion of credit. Some of this wall of money ended up in the stock market, which took off again. But many investors who had had their fingers burned by the dotcom bust saw the property market as a safer bet. Lower interest rates not only encouraged greater borrowing, they also seemed to justify higher asset prices. (If you expect a share to pay a dividend of \$1.05 next year, that expected future dividend is worth \$1 today when interest rates are 5 per cent. But when interest rates fall to zero, the value of that expected future dividend rises to \$1.05. The same is true of anticipated rental income from property.) And they stimulated economic growth, fooling many people into confusing a temporary and unsustainable boom with a permanent improvement in long-term growth prospects. By the time Greenspan edged up interest rates in June 2004, house prices across ten big American cities had soared by two-thirds in four years. In effect, Greenspan inflated a new, even bigger bubble in order to rescue the American economy from his dotcom bomb. He then raised rates so slowly, in quarter-percentage-point steps, that by the time they reached 5.25 per cent two years later, house prices had risen by more than a quarter more. By keeping interest rates too low for too long, he caused the bubble to swell to gigantic proportions.

Other central banks were also too lax. The Bank of England started to raise rates earlier, from a higher base of 3.5 per cent, in July 2003. By then UK house prices had risen 70 per cent since the beginning of the decade. The Bank then nudged the base rate up to 4.75 per cent in August 2004, by which time prices had risen by a fifth more. The rate rises caused house-price inflation to grind to a halt. Had Britain's bubble deflated then, the pain would have been much less. But a year later, the Bank cut rates by a quarter point and the housing market took off again. It resumed raising interest rates only in August 2006, and house prices rose a further fifth until their peak in late 2007.

In Spain and Ireland, the housing boom was fuelled by the slashing of their interest rates when they swapped the peseta and the Irish pound for the euro. Official rates in Spain plunged from 4.75 per cent in April 1998 to 2 per cent at the euro's launch in January 1999, with an even steeper fall from 6.75 per cent in Ireland. Euro interest rates have remained (often much) below 4 per cent ever since, because growth in languid France, Germany and Italy was much slower than in bubbly Spain and Ireland. The ECB held real (inflation-adjusted) interest rates below 1 per cent for most of the period between mid-2001 and 2005. Since Spain and Ireland could not raise interest rates, their governments should have used other measures to limit mortgage lending.

Greenspan and his apologists argue that America had to keep interest rates low to accommodate a glut of savings from China and other countries. In their view, the crisis was made in China rather than in America. But this attempt to pass the buck won't wash. While surplus cash from abroad may have added to America's boom, it was just one factor that contributed to the crisis, as will be discussed later in the chapter. In any case, it does not excuse Greenspan's mistakes, still less banks' excesses.

Why did these unduly low interest rates inflate the prices of assets such as property and shares rather than consumer prices?

It is a good question. One reason is that cheaper imports and increased competition from China and other emerging markets kept a lid on inflation. Another is that improvements in technology pushed prices down – think how the price of rapidly improving computers and flat-screen televisions has collapsed. Productivity improvements throughout the economy from better use of computer and internet technologies played a big part. Such 'good deflation' makes us all richer, as it enables our money to stretch further.

Banking on a bubble

If central bankers – above all Alan Greenspan – are the villains of the piece, banks were their more than willing accomplices. They borrowed too much, lent far too easily and spawned devilish new financial products that sucked a torrent of cash into property speculation from short-sighted global investors in complex and opaque ways. In effect, they inflated a financial bubble. Just as investors got carried away by the promise of the internet in the dotcom era, they fell into the trap of believing that all this financial wizardry offered much higher returns with scarcely any additional risk. Policy-makers were bewitched by Wall Street's spell too. Even bankers believed their own hype.

Bankers like to think they are experts at making lending decisions, but they seem to make the same mistakes over and over again. The fundamental problem, as I mentioned earlier, is that nobody knows what the future holds. Who knows whether a borrower will make good on their promise to repay? Banks try to get a better idea by collecting lots of information about borrowers' past record and current financial status, but they still don't know how things will pan out in the future. One way to reduce the risk of default is to demand collateral – to require that borrowers pledge assets, such as property, that the bank can seize if they fail to pay back their loans. But that doesn't really solve the problem, because nobody knows what that property will be worth in the future. Worse, banks' own lending decisions have a big influence on what people are willing to pay for it – when banks are willing to extend big mortgages, people can pay more for houses; when they cut back, so must house-buyers. Because of this circularity, the security that collateral provides is often illusory. Far from reducing the risk of bank lending, it tends to encourage banks to make bigger and riskier bets.

The recent property bubble highlights this. Low interest rates and steady economic growth made people feel keener and better able to borrow more – and houses seemed like a safer investment than shares after the dotcom crash. Because times were good and people's mortgage payments seemed manageable, banks felt comfortable lending bigger sums, especially because they were secured against property. As banks lent more, property prices rose. At this point, you might think that higher prices would suggest that property was now expensive, and that this would deter prospective home-buyers from borrowing and banks from lending. But remember that nobody really knows what property will be worth tomorrow, and if people generally think it will be worth more, there is a good chance it will be. People who want to buy a place to live are joined by those who believe they can make a profit by selling on the property later (and, of course, many others buy for a variety of reasons). Banks are happy to lend more because the collateral against which they are lending appears more valuable and because the economy is booming and they are flush with cash.

What about contrarian investors? If they think prices are too high, why don't they speculate that prices will fall? One reason is because you can only sell property you own, not – as on the stock market – assets you don't. Another, as John Maynard Keynes warned, is that the market can stay irrational longer than you can stay solvent. So long as enough banks are willing to lend more, the weight of money is with the bullish buyers. Sceptical investors who stay on the sidelines have no impact on the market, while cautious bankers who are reluctant to lend lose business to more gung-ho ones. Over time, they may join the party or are likely to lose their jobs. Thus as property prices rise, demand for it tends to increase too. This is the positive-feedback stage that Kindleberger describes.

Next comes euphoria. People who have sold their houses at inflated prices have more cash to burn, while soaring prices attract more and more buyers into the market. Some think it is a quick way to get rich; others fear that if they don't buy now, they won't be able to afford to in future. Since housing appears to be a money-making machine, why not double up your bet – borrow more to buy a bigger and more expensive house? After all, it not only signals your elevated status in society, it also promises to make you even richer. You can't lose. In Britain, there was a huge increase in the 'buy-to-let' market that was predicated on prices soaring, since the returns to renting out property were poor. Even people who think prices have got out of hand have an incentive to buy provided they think there is a bigger fool behind them. The higher house prices rose, the more it seemed reasonable to lend – and the more banks lent, the higher property prices rocketed. This merry-go-round can – and did – go on for years.

Sometimes, asset-price bubbles are largely self-contained. Often, though, they spill over into the wider economy. Since housing is most people's main asset, the property bubble sparked a wider consumer boom. Why save? With the value of your house rising regularly, you could spend with gay abandon and still end up wealthier on paper. Better still, you could borrow in anticipation of future gains – why deny yourself anything now when you would be much richer tomorrow? People splash out on a new car, a fancy holiday, designer clothes, champagne, you name it. Banks are only too happy to oblige. As consumer spending soars, companies make bigger profits, see their share price rise, pay bigger dividends and shell out higher salaries. The boom cranks up another notch. The rich splurge on not-so-fine art, a market that is also bubble-prone – after all, who knows whether a painting by Damien Hirst will be worth £10 million, £100 million or 10 pence in ten years' time? It is an ideal time for crooks and charlatans to prosper, because people desperately want to believe that they too can get rich quick. Bernie Madoff – the man who made off with almost $65 billion before his imprisonment for fraud in 2009 – was made for his time.

The bubble years saw an unprecedented rise in household debt, for the most part secured against inflated house valuations. In the United States, it rose by 150 per cent between 1997 and 2007, from $5.5 trillion to $13.8 trillion.[22] Whereas in 1997 American families' debts amounted to 90 per cent of their annual after-tax incomes, a decade later they exceeded 132 per cent of their disposable income.[23] Their mortgage-related debt alone was $10.5 trillion – double what it was in 2000 and greater than their after-tax incomes. That didn't seem to matter so much while their home, shares and other assets were appreciating. Americans' net worth soared from $42.1 trillion in 2001 to $63.9 trillion in 2007. But by the first quarter of 2009, their wealth had plunged to $51.1 trillion. According to the McKinsey Global Institute, a think-tank, the crisis destroyed a bigger proportion of household wealth, in real terms, than was lost during the Depression.[24]

In Britain, the increase in debt was even greater. By the end of 2007, household borrowing had reached 185 per cent of disposable incomes, higher than the debt burden at the peak of Japan's bubble in 1990 – indeed, higher than in any other Group of Seven (G7) country ever. Mortgage debt had soared from around 50 per cent of GDP in 2000 to more than 80 per cent. Again, that seemed much less reasonable after house prices had fallen by a fifth and share prices by far more.

Rising debt ought to set alarm bells ringing. But during the bubble, new theories emerged to justify the madness. In the late 1990s, the internet was said to have created a 'new economy' where the old rules no longer applied. During the recent bubble, people bought into the claims that policy-makers had near-magical powers to keep growth and inflation on an even keel. Greenspan was hailed as a demi-god for apparently saving the American economy not once but twice. Gordon Brown boasted that he had conquered boom and bust. William White, then chief economist at the Bank for International Settlements (BIS), the central bankers' bank, was one of the few people who warned of the risks of impending disaster. But Greenspan and others dismissed his concerns. 'When you are inside the bubble, everybody feels fine,' White recalls. 'Nobody wants to believe that it can burst. Nobody is asking the right questions.'[25] In Britain, Brown brushed away similar concerns expressed by Vince Cable, the Liberal Democrat Treasury spokesperson. All this triumphalism was leavened by new-fangled financial alchemy that claimed to be able to turn dross into gold.

Black magic

It's not just the scale and the global spread of the recent property bubble that were unprecedented. It's the ingenious and reckless new ways that bankers found to speculate on rising house prices. After all, they reasoned, if even the dull saps who borrowed from banks could get rich quick from property, masters of the universe like them could do much better. They devised ways to draw in vast new pools of money for mortgage lending. They invented clever financial products that seemed to offer hefty returns with scarcely any risk, and others that promised a mul-tiple of the gains from actually owning bricks and mortar. They spiced things up further by lending huge sums to those who wished to buy these new financial products. In effect, they placed, and enabled others to place, bets on top of bets on top of bets – and at each turn, they earned a juicy commission. Crucially, this made the banks extremely vulnerable to a fall in house prices, not just because they owned lots of these new financial products themselves, but also because they had lent so much to those who had bought them. To make matters worse, many of the products were so devilishly complicated that banks had no idea what their potential losses might be. But why worry? House prices couldn't fall.

There is a limit to how much banks can lend using their sliver of capital – and they stretched it to breaking point. The more they borrowed and lent (or invested) with any given cushion of capital, the more profitable – and fragile – they became. In that respect banks are just like home-buyers. If you put down a £25,000 deposit to buy a £100,000 house and borrow the other £75,000, a 5 per cent increase in the value of your home earns you a 20 per cent return on your investment, since your capital of £25,000 has become £30,000. But if you buy a £100,000 house with a £5,000 deposit, a 5 per cent increase in the value of your home doubles your investment. That is the miracle of 'leverage' – the more you borrow to buy an asset, the bigger the returns on your capital. But while leverage allows you to multiply your gains when prices rise, it makes you acutely vulnerable when prices fall. A 5 per cent fall in house prices wipes out all your capital when you have borrowed 95 per cent of the value of your home, but only a fifth of it when you have borrowed 75 per cent. Thus while leverage can be lucrative, it can also be lethal. And like house-buyers, banks massively increased their leverage during the bubble years.

Highly leveraged banks convinced themselves and regulators that it was safe to lend more because of a big change in the way they doled out credit. Traditionally, banks would lend money to a property-buyer and then earn a profit as the mortgage was repaid. But this tied down capital that they could have been using to make other loans and exposed them to the risk of the borrower defaulting (and them not being able to recoup the amount outstanding by selling the property used as collateral). During the recent bubble, a different form of mortgage finance grew explosively. Banks packaged together a bundle of mortgages and then sold shares in them to outside investors. These 'mortgage-backed securities' allowed banks to shift mortgages off their books, earning a tidy commission, freeing up their capital for further lending and passing on the risk of default to others. While such securities have existed in the United States for decades, their use exploded during the recent bubble, while they also took off in Britain. This shift may look innocuous, but it was a revolution in finance. Bankers were no longer guardians of credit, their fortunes tied to borrowers for the duration of their loans; they were now distributors of credit, able to dole out loans to all and sundry with – in theory – scarcely an after-thought. Banking had once been about long-term relationships; it was now about short-term transactions. What was once a marriage had become a one-night stand – and the possibility of an unwanted pregnancy was ignored.

Outside investors snapped up the new securities. With interest rates so low, investing in safer assets, such as US government bonds, offered paltry returns. But mortgage-backed securities offered higher returns with seemingly little additional risk. After all, while the chances of any individual defaulting on a mortgage may be quite high, the chances of many doing so together seemed remote. So buying a share in a bundle of mortgages seemed pretty safe – provided house prices were rising. What's more, investors reasoned that they could sell the securities at the first sign of trouble. It seemed like a free lunch: higher returns for scarcely any additional risk. All sorts of investors who previously would not have gone anywhere near the US property market – German savings banks, British building societies,

Australian pension funds, Swiss insurance companies, local and even foreign governments – piled in.

But why just sell something once when you can flog it several times over? Bankers also bundled together packages of mortgage-backed securities and then sliced and diced their expected returns into so-called collateralised debt obligations (CDOs). The riskiest, highest-return securities would take the first hit in case of default; the safer, lower-return securities would pay out so long as most did not default. Ratings agencies, whose job is to vet the riskiness of securities, gave the apparently safer securities their seal of approval. It helped, of course, that they were paid by the banks to vouch that the new securities were as safe as government bonds. That was not the end of it. Banks also issued CDO^2s – CDOs backed by CDOs. Each time a loan was sold, packaged, securitised and resold, banks took their cut. Doubtless they would have gone cubed in due course.

Investors were so keen on a piece of the action that banks couldn't keep pace with demand. So they started issuing mortgages to all and sundry, reasoning that since they were passing on the risk of default to others, it didn't matter whom they lent to. Welcome to the wacky world of 'subprime' mortgages. Some were simply loans to riskier borrowers. But in the bubble's euphoric stage, truly egregious practices emerged. At the height of the dotcom bubble, investors poured money into internet start-ups with no revenues and no business plan let alone actual profits, because they thought they could quickly cash in by floating them on the stock market; now banks doled out so-called 'ninja' mortgages to people with no income, no job or assets. It looked like a winner for everyone. Mortgage brokers earned a fat commission. Banks got new mortgages to package and repackage for juicy fees. Poor people were delighted to become home-owners and get a foot on the housing ladder. Politicians looked on approvingly as the wonders of American capitalism democratised home ownership. And so long as house prices kept rising fast, poor people could just about keep up with the interest payments. As the price of their house rose, they could take out a bigger loan and use part of it to pay the interest on the mortgage.

In Britain, similar abuses emerged, albeit on a smaller scale. There was a boom in 'self-certification' mortgages – dubbed 'liar loans' – whereby borrowers could declare their own income and banks would not bother to check whether they could afford the repayments. Mortgage brokers even encouraged borrowers to lie. People on government benefits were granted mortgages with few questions asked. People nearing retirement took out twenty-five-year mortgages.[26] Banks also granted mortgages for more than the value of a property – as much as 125 per cent in some cases – allowing people with no capital and little income to borrow big sums in anticipation of future gains.

As the casino whirled, astronomical sums were bet. Issuance of US mortgage-backed securities not backed by federal agencies soared from $101.7 billion in 2000 to $917.4 billion in 2006, before dipping to $773.9 billion in 2007. By 2007, there was just shy of $3 trillion of non-agency mortgage-backed securities outstanding.[27] (Since the crisis, issuance has collapsed – to $24.2 billion in 2009.[28]) Global CDO issuance soared from $157.8 billion in 2004 to $651 billion in the twelve months to its peak in the second quarter of 2007, before collapsing to a measly $4.2 billion in 2009.[29] In Britain, issuance of mortgage-backed securities soared from virtually nothing in 2000 to some £90 billion in 2006, while CDO issuance reached £30 billion in 2007.[30] By 2007, 18 per cent of UK property loans were funded through mortgage-backed securities – a much lower proportion than in the US.[31] British banks funded an increasing share of their mortgage lending by borrowing from short-term money markets rather than from more stable deposits.

As banks made all these complex new bets with outside investors as well as with each other, they exposed themselves to a big new risk: that the contracts wouldn't pay out. So they decided to insure themselves through 'credit-default swaps'. But while some were issued to insure banks and investors against the risk of default on contracts they owned, many more were used to gamble on contracts that they didn't own defaulting. Because people were relaxed about the risks of default, vast amounts of insurance were sold at ridiculously low prices. What's more, because banks entered into a huge volume of these contracts with each other, they became acutely vulnerable to each other failing. The notional value of outstanding credit-default swaps exploded from almost nothing a decade earlier to – pinch yourself – $62 trillion at the end of 2007. As billionaire investor Warren Buffett noted in 2003, many of the new financial instruments were akin to 'financial weapons of mass destruction, carrying dangers that, while now latent, are potentially lethal'.

Flawed logic

There was a method of sorts behind all this madness. Most bankers – and the regulators who were meant to oversee them – assumed that financial markets were 'efficient'. By this, they meant that prices set by the market were 'right' since they were determined by rational investors acting on all available information and that mistakes were rapidly corrected by other profit-seeking investors. But in practice this isn't true. It's not just the long history of bubbles that disproves it. It's the fundamental point that the future is unknowable; that since nobody knows what prices ought to be, they take their cues from others; that human beings are emotional and fallible social animals who get caught up in collective delusions, while even rational types who disagree often have an incentive to follow the crowd; and that if enough people bet the same way, their bets can be self-validating for a (long) while. The notion that a whole society can get rich by swapping the same houses at ever more inflated prices is palpably nonsense, yet even now it has a vice-like grip on the British imagination.

Bankers and regulators also believed that packaging mortgages into tradable bonds and creating complex new contracts based on them benefited not just bankers and investors, but also the economy as a whole. Corporate bonds allow companies to borrow more cheaply from a wider range of investors rather than relying on bank loans. They also give investors an opportunity to diversify their portfolios by lending to a broad range of companies without tying down their money (since bonds can be sold on if need be). Similarly, bankers transformed mortgages from illiquid assets owned by local banks into liquid financial instruments that could be flogged around the world. This offered investors a wider range of investment opportunities. It allowed banks to economise on expensive capital – to lend more with less. And it made it cheaper and easier for borrowers to get credit, widening access to those who would previously have been denied it. While these new financial instruments were basically unregulated, they were sold only to professional investors who are meant to be financially savvy and able to take care of themselves. Regulators took bankers' word that all this financial innovation was beneficial. In theory, they were parcelling out risk across the financial system to those most willing and best able to bear it, enabling a huge expansion of credit without putting banks themselves at too much risk and making the financial system as a whole more stable. A British mortgage lender, for instance, would not be as vulnerable to a UK downturn because the risk of its mortgages going sour had been passed on and spread to others. As a result, bank failures were meant to be less likely (don't snigger, weep or gnash your teeth).

In theory, that might have been true. But in practice, increasingly, these assets were not simply sold on to outside investors. They were sold to other banks' trading desks. They were sold to investors but with banks still exposed to some of the risk through the use of credit-default swaps. They were repackaged into complex and opaque CDOs and CDO²s. And they were used as collateral to borrow from other banks. In short, banks were actually running ever bigger risks, especially since many of these complex new instruments were highly sensitive in unpredictable ways to small falls in house prices or slight swings in investor confidence. All of this created a complex web of relationships among banks, with each tottering on a wafer of capital, nobody quite sure what risks might topple them, and everyone vulnerable to being knocked over by each other's mistakes.

Not only did banks become more interconnected in complex and opaque ways, they also got bigger and more fragile. They borrowed and lent much more. They issued mountains of credit-default swaps. And they took on even bigger risks off their books through an unregulated shadow banking system of 'structured investment vehicles' and 'conduits'. These arm's-length vehicles were set up to get around regulators' caps on banks' risk-taking. But when these shadowy beasts began to collapse in 2007, banks felt obliged to take their losses back on to their books because allowing them to fail would shred their reputation. In practice, then, banks were locked in a tight embrace with these supposedly arm's-length vehicles.

Between 1997 and 2007 US financial-sector debt trebled. Banks and other financial institutions piled on nearly $11 trillion of borrowing, so that by 2007 they owed $16.2 trillion, equivalent to 115 per cent of GDP.[32] In Britain, financial-sector borrowing soared to more than 200 per cent of GDP.[33] Most of this borrowing was from other banks and financial institutions, reflecting the cat's cradle of connections described above.

Increasingly, banks seemed to believe that the old risks of banking no longer applied. They could rely on short-term borrowing because it would always be available and they could pile on long-term loans and investments because they could always be sold on if need be. But when banks lost confidence in each other, nobody was able to borrow any more – and when everyone tried to sell their assets at once, nobody could.

Bankers – and regulators – were also reassured by financial models that suggested that they were not taking on too much risk. Nobel laureates, no less, assured people that this new-fangled finance was sound. Few considered the possibility that the models might be wrong, or looked at the wider consequences of each individual bank's actions. Sceptics such as Nassim Nicholas Taleb, author of *The Black Swan*, who argued that bankers' models wrongly ignored the catastrophic risks of big unforeseen events – what Donald Rumsfeld had called 'unknown unknowns' – were ignored or ridiculed. In truth, recent experience is often a poor guide to future performance, and since the new financial instruments had no track record whatsoever, banks and ratings agencies' seemingly sophisticated evaluation of their riskiness was basically elaborate guesswork. But so long as growth was strong, inflation low and house prices kept rising, everything seemed fine.

City takeover

The longer the boom went on, the more it validated bankers' faith in their models, regulators' insouciance and an even greater extension of credit. Since the bankers were earning huge profits, the economy was booming and tax receipts were pouring in, the political pressure to leave the golden goose alone was overwhelming. In the United States, Greenspan was ideologically allergic to interfering with the market – except of course to prop it up when it faltered. Britain's New Labour government was fooled into thinking it could deliver a Scandinavian welfare state with American tax levels thanks to the seemingly endless bounties of the City of London.

Banks' huge political donations and lobbying also helped. Between 1998 and 2008, Wall Street paid an estimated $1.7 billion in political contributions and spent a further $3.4 billion on lobbyists, according to a report by Essential Information and the Consumer Education Foundation, two non-profit organisations. In 2007 the financial sector employed nearly three thousand lobbyists, or five for each member of the US Congress. Such purchasing of political influence is widely believed to have helped secure for Wall Street the repeal of the Glass-Steagall Act, which prohibited the merger of commercial and investment banks, the blocking by Bill Clinton's administration of a Commodity Futures Trading Commission initiative to regulate financial derivatives and a host of other helpful decisions.[34]

As former IMF chief economist Simon Johnson described in a brilliant article in the *Atlantic Monthly*, Wall Street's capture of America's policy-making establishment amounts to a 'quiet coup'.[35] More important than even its financial contributions is its cultural sway. 'Over the past decade, the attitude took hold that what was good for Wall Street was good for the country,' he says. It helped that Robert Rubin, who served as Clinton's Treasury secretary, and Hank Paulson, who served under George W. Bush, were both former chief executives of Goldman Sachs. 'A whole generation of policy-makers has been mesmerised by Wall Street, always and utterly convinced that whatever the banks said was true.' Britain's Labour government was also seduced by the bankers. On the eve of becoming prime minister, and only three months before Northern Rock collapsed, Chancellor Gordon Brown spoke in glowing terms of 'a new golden age for the City of London'.[36] What was good for the City was good for Britain: 'Let me say as I begin my new job, I want to continue to work with you in helping you do yours, listening to what you say, always recognising your international success is critical to that of Britain's overall.'

The financial sector milked its privileged position for all it was worth. It became enormous. In the US, it earned less than 16 per cent of domestic corporate profits between 1973 and 1985. This rose to between 21 per cent and 30 per cent in the 1990s and peaked at an astonishing 41 per cent in the present decade. Pay rocketed too. It had hovered around the US private-sector average from 1948 to 1982; by 2007, it had soared to 181 per cent.[37] The bigger the financial sector swelled, the more value to the rest of the economy it was deemed to provide.

But there is a contradiction here. A more efficient financial sector ought to cost less, not more. Remember high salaries are a cost of finance, not a benefit. The more bankers are paid, the bigger the benefits finance must provide in order to justify its existence. Granted, it is normal for demand for financial services to grow as people get richer and have more sophisticated needs. A more globalised economy also requires global banks to help companies manage their international finances and risks. But the main reasons why banks have grown so big is partly because they were making huge paper profits during an unsustainable bubble, but also, arguably, because they have been abusing their position as powerful and privileged middlemen to rip off investors. They mis-sell products to gullible investors, making a hefty commission. They take advantage of their superior information to manipulate markets to their profit. And they abuse the cheap credit provided by their previously implicit (and now explicit) government guarantee to gamble at public expense. As a result, finance has increasingly come to serve its own interests at the expense of the rest of the economy's.

Parallel universe

There is an alternative explanation for the crisis, which I alluded to earlier in the chapter. In the dying days of George W. Bush's administration, the White House issued the following statement:

The President highlighted a factor that economists agree on: that *the most significant* factor [my italics] leading to the housing crisis was cheap money flowing into the US from the rest of the world, so that there was no natural restraint on flush lenders to push loans on Americans in risky ways. This flow of funds into the US was unprecedented. And because it was unprecedented, the conditions it created presented unprecedented questions for policy-makers.

In other words, the crisis is all foreigners' fault.[38]

How convenient! America's housing bubble and financial excess – and the devastating crisis that followed – were made in China, not the US. Americans aren't to blame for gambling on rising house prices, running up huge debts and going on an unprecedented spree. Bankers aren't to blame for giving them the rope with which to hang themselves and tangling themselves up in speculative knots. Alan Greenspan, the man charged with keeping the US economy on an even keel, isn't to blame for leaving interest rates too low and letting the bubble get out of hand. Financial regulators aren't to blame for failing to sound the alarm. The Bush administration isn't to blame for ringing up huge deficits, cheering the bubble on and lionising Wall Street rather than taking some action – any action – to prevent a crisis. No – blame Beijing, not Washington.

You might think that such self-serving cant would have been jettisoned with the change of administration. Barack Obama would surely not stick with the story that 'It ain't America's fault.' He might find it convenient to absolve voters, but not the old guard of policy-makers. Yet the old line endures: American profligacy was fuelled by China's excess savings and US policy-makers were forced to accommodate the consequences of Beijing's undervalued currency by keeping American interest rates low. Obama reappointed Greenspan's successor, Ben Bernanke, the co-architect of this 'savings glut' argument, for a second term as chair of the US Federal Reserve in August 2009. But might the argument have some truth to it? Was the United States, an economic giant, really at the mercy of the policy decisions of much smaller economies such as China, Japan and Germany? Did the tail really wag the dog?

Hardly. America's string of bubbles inflated long before China started sending over its surplus savings. The housing bubble ballooned between 2000 and 2004 – the period when Greenspan kept interest rates at rock bottom – while China's surplus only surged from 2005 on. Pinning the blame on China's supposedly undervalued currency won't wash either: between 2005 and 2008, when China's surplus swelled massively, the renminbi appreciated by over a fifth against the dollar and by a sixth in real (inflation-adjusted) trade-weighted terms.[39] A study in 2007 concluded that 'There is little statistical evidence that the RMB [renminbi] is undervalued.'[40]

What's more, the US financial sector began raking in profits and gobbling up a big chunk of the economy long before Chinese cash arrived. And surely all those clever bankers were capable of recycling those foreign funds in productive, rather than destructive, ways – after all, that is what the financial sector is meant to do. Savings didn't have to be channelled into elaborate real-estate speculation. So yes, of course, foreign capital joined the festivities. But it didn't get the party rolling, it didn't keep on binging like there was no tomorrow, it didn't spike the drinks, it isn't to blame for the failure to take the punchbowl away and it was certainly not *the most significant* contributor to the hangover.

Don't just take my word for it. Listen to Stephen Roach, one of the world's most perceptive economists, the former chief economist of Morgan Stanley, an American bank, and now its chairman in Asia:

> The Chinese and the Germans were delighted to go along for
> the ride, selling goods and in some cases services to American

consumers that they could not afford. They set policies up that
were very much aimed at sourcing the US consumption
bubble. But the bottom line is that whether it was China's surplus savings, Japan's, Germany's or what have you, American
consumers went into debt beyond all conceivable norms of the
past. They levered [mortgaged to the hilt] their main asset,
they squandered their income-based saving, and took the US
economy to the brink that was no fault on any surplus economy . . . These were responsibilities that rest on the shoulders
of American consumers and the regulators and policymakers
charged with maintaining a more sane economic framework.
We let the system get away from us. For that I blame, more
than anybody else, the stewards of the US financial system,
especially the Fed. Ideology was more important in governing
monetary policy than common sense.[41]

Even if, as Greenspan and his apologists argue, China's surplus savings did push down long-term American interest rates,
the Fed could still have raised short-term ones to curb the
bubble. 'Interest rates are not one beast,' says Simon Johnson,
former chief economist at the IMF. This would have resulted in
slower growth in the short term, but saved us from a bigger
future bust. Nor was there anything stopping Greenspan from
clamping down on financial excess in other ways. The fact is,
'The financial sector liked money moving across borders,
because that it is how they made money,' says Johnson, who had
a ring-side seat at the IMF, which was charged with monitoring
the growing imbalances in the global economy. 'American
policymakers made ritualistic hand-wringing about imbalances,
but actually quite liked foreigners sending money over. They
saw it as valuable trade: the US was benefiting from selling
foreigners complicated financial instruments.' The bottom line
is: the inflows of foreign cash suited both the US financial sector
and the Bush administration.

The bubble bursts

The details of the financial bubble are extremely complex. But the underlying story is simple and familiar. Banks and investors gambled that US house prices couldn't fall. They were wrong.

A bubble at bursting point is an accident waiting to happen. It can pop in a number of ways. Rising property prices may prompt developers to build so many new houses that supply outpaces even bubbly demand and prices start to fall. The supply of bigger fools may be exhausted: once the last sceptic throws in the towel and buys into the market, the canniest investors will stampede for the exit before prices collapse, prompting that very collapse. This may happen earlier if enough speculators decide to cash in their profits and sell, prompting prices to fall. A piece of bad news may make people more pessimistic and lead them to pull in their horns. The riskiest borrowers may start defaulting, causing banks to rein in lending and leading to forced property sales that drive down prices. Often bubbles burst because the excessive credit that banks have created spills over into inflation, leading the central bank to raise interest rates. A higher cost of borrowing reduces the demand for new loans and causes some existing borrowers to default. Whatever the immediate trigger, the underlying reason why bubbles burst is that banks have lent too much and investors have bid up prices too high.

Subprime mortgages given to very risky borrowers proved to be the last straw for America's hyperextended housing bubble. By the summer of 2006, official interest rates had reached 5.25 per cent. While still low by historical standards, these drove up long-term mortgage rates and proved a pinch for American overextended home-buyers. House prices peaked that summer and then the unthinkable happened: they began to drift down-wards. By 2007, defaults on subprime mortgages began to rise as house prices continued their gentle decline. Cracks were appearing in the mortgage market, but so far the bubble was deflating relatively slowly. In the second quarter of 2007, house prices were less than 4 per cent below their peak twelve months earlier. Yet even such a small decline was enough to cause havoc in financial markets. The new financial instruments had multiplied the gains on the way up. Now they amplified the losses on the way down.

As house-price falls accelerated, and with them banks' appetite to extend new mortgage loans, the housing bubble went pop. By the first quarter of 2009 prices were nearly a third below their peak. Such a brutal collapse would have hit any economy hard. As prices fall and defaults mount, banks realise that the collateral against which they lent is less valuable than it seemed. As they rein in lending to try to cut their losses, they force companies and individual borrowers to cut back, causing prices to fall more, further eroding the value of banks' collateral and so on. The decline in lending affects spending in other areas too, causing companies to fire people and go bust. The bursting of a property bubble alone can cause a nasty recession, as Britain experienced in the early 1990s. Some people lose their jobs and their houses; others are trapped with a mountain of debt that exceeds the value of their property. What follows is a long and painful period when people struggle to pay back their debts. This 'deleveraging' requires them to save a big chunk of their income. An economy-wide increase in saving implies lower spending and hence slower growth, and often a recession.

But it was the combination of banks' excessive leverage, new-fangled financial wizardry and global connections that turned the bursting of America's property bubble into a global financial crisis. The opacity and complexity of the new financial contracts made them difficult to value and almost impossible to trade once the housing market turned. Since banks weren't sure what the securities they held were worth, let alone what securities other banks held and how big their losses might be, they stopped lending to each other out of fear that they wouldn't be repaid. Because banks had become so reliant on short-term borrowing to keep going, that loss of trust – like a bank run – became self-fulfilling. In modern jargon, it prompted a liquidity crisis. What's more, many banks accumulated such huge losses on their bad loans, toxic securities and credit-default swaps that these consumed the precious little capital they had, bankrupting them in all but name. In other words, this soon became a solvency crisis too.

These twin crises were largely made in America. But they were soon exported to the rest of the world because finance is now so international. Banks' foreign claims had grown from $11 trillion in 2000 to over $30 trillion by mid-2007.[42] Many foreign banks had foolishly bought American mortgage-backed securities. Many had also become too reliant on fickle short-term borrowing to fund their operations. Local subsidiaries of foreign banks (notably in Central and Eastern Europe, as well as in Latin America) drew in their horns when their Western parents' capital was eroded. And as banks notched up huge losses and could no longer borrow, they stopped lending to others, notably foreigners, transmitting the crisis from the financial realm to the real economy of companies and jobs.

Thus what began as a problem in an obscure part of the US financial system – the subprime market – became a global credit crunch that bit ever tighter from the summer of 2007 on. Among its first victims was Northern Rock, Britain's fifth-biggest mortgage lender. It had expanded too rapidly, through short-term borrowing in financial markets. This was cheaper and quicker than attracting more stable deposits from UK savers and Northern Rock assumed (incorrectly) that money would always be available on tap. But when the money markets dried up and banks stopped lending to each other, Northern Rock was starved of the cash it needed to function. In September 2007 it suffered the ignominy of a bank run, the first in the UK since 1866. The

Bank of England had to step in to rescue 'Northern Wreck' and in February 2008 it was nationalised.

This initial stage of the crisis culminated with the collapse in March 2008 of Bear Stearns, an American investment bank, and its government-orchestrated takeover by JPMorgan Chase. For a while this calmed nerves. But over the following months, as American house prices fell and those in Britain and elsewhere followed, banks' losses mounted and liquidity problems deepened. On 7 September, the US government took over Fannie Mae and Freddie Mac, two huge housing-finance agencies whose bonds had been widely purchased by foreigners, notably the Chinese government. Much worse was about to come.

The crisis entered a perilous new phase on 15 September, when Lehman Brothers, a larger American investment bank, went bankrupt. The Bush administration decided to let it fail, rather than rescuing it or nationalising it and winding down its assets in an orderly fashion. Lehman's chaotic collapse sent markets into a tailspin. Until then investors and creditors had assumed that major banks would not be allowed to go bust, so that any contracts with them would be honoured. Suddenly, they questioned that assumption. As trust evaporated, panic threatened to drag down the global financial system. Financial institutions started falling like ninepins. American International Group (AIG), the world's biggest insurer and a key player in the credit-swaps market; Washington Mutual, America's largest savings bank; HBOS, a British bank; Bradford & Bingley, a British mortgage lender; Fortis, a Dutch-Belgian bank and insurer; Hypo Real Estate, a German commercial property lender; Wachovia, a US bank; Dexia, a Belgian-French bank – all needed rescuing within two weeks of Lehman's collapse. It was the mother of all bank runs.

Think of the financial system as the plumbing of the economy. Just as modern living depends on a reliable flow of water, the economy depends on money flowing around it freely. If the pipes get clogged, all sorts of problems occur. From the summer of 2007 on, the pipes began to ice up. What was once a gushing torrent of cash became a trickle. Then Lehman went bust and the financial system froze.

For six weeks or so the global financial system teetered on the brink of collapse. Panicky investors sold off risky assets around the world and piled into cash and the relative security of US government bonds – known as Treasuries – instead. Stock markets tanked. Corporate-bond markets seized up. Oil prices plunged. Capital drained out of emerging markets. Only unprecedented interventions by governments and central banks eventually rescued the financial system from the abyss. Acting together for the first time, central banks slashed interest rates. America extended government deposit insurance to $3.4 trillion in money-market funds. Ireland guaranteed all bank deposits, forcing other European governments to follow suit. The 'short-selling' of financial shares – the sale of (usually borrowed) shares you do not own in the hope of buying them back at a lower price – was banned. The US government pledged to take up to $700 billion of toxic mortgage-related assets on to its books. Unfortunately, this initially fuelled the panic, because when Treasury Secretary Hank Paulson appeared before Congress to ask for a blank cheque for $700 billion, he seemed unable to explain how he planned to use the money. Congress first refused him, then finally relented. Gordon Brown helped to stem the panic in early October, notably by offering £50 billion to recapitalise British banks with government cash.

Between October 2008 and March 2009, governments cobbled together a hodgepodge of measures to rescue the banking system. To calm the liquidity crisis, central banks pledged to stump up unlimited funds to prop up the banks. Not only would they lend banks cash to fund their daily operations, they would accept mortgage-backed securities and other dodgy assets as collateral. To reassure the markets about banks' solvency,

governments pledged to absorb most of their losses and ultimately to rescue them if they failed. They guaranteed all bank
deposits and even all debts to unsecured creditors. All American
investment banks were either bought by commercial banks or
became banks themselves in order to secure better government
protection. The US government took stakes in all major
American banks, including 34 per cent of Citigroup, once the
world's largest. Germany's government acquired a quarter of
Commerzbank, the country's second-largest bank, and 90 per
cent of Hypo Real Estate, in addition to all the savings banks
already part-owned by regional governments. The Dutch government rescued ING; France's took stakes in the country's six
biggest banks.

The British government ended up owning 43 per cent of the
new Lloyds Group and 70 per cent of RBS. Traditionally conservative Lloyds TSB was laid low by hubris; the prospect of
dominating high-street banking led it to agree to take over
HBOS (the product of the merger between Halifax and Bank of
Scotland) whose huge losses then dragged it down. RBS (which
owns NatWest) was sunk by overpaying for ABN Amro, a
Dutch bank, in 2007, *after* the crisis was well on its way, as well
as by its holdings of toxic mortgage-backed securities. As an
RBS customer, I was cruelly reminded of its global aspirations
throughout my travels to research this book. Its advertising kept
popping up in airports – at Arlanda (in Stockholm), in Cape
Town and elsewhere – 'RBS – Make it happen.' What 'it' could
they be referring to? Crisis? Depression? Rage?

The banks' losses are huge. In October 2009, the IMF estimated that they would lose $2.8 trillion on their bad loans and
toxic securities by the end of 2010.[43] While banks had already
written down $1.3 trillion in expected losses by June 2009,
their capital would be hit by a further $1.5 trillion of losses by
the end of 2010. US banks are expected to lose $1 trillion, euro-
zone ones $800 billion, and those in the UK $600 billion –

equivalent to a whopping 26 per cent of GDP. Whereas toxic securities caused most of the earlier losses, two-thirds of the later ones are expected to come from loans – in areas such as credit cards, commercial property and corporate lending – that turn sour because of the recession. Banks face a capital shortfall of $670 billion, the IMF reckons, to reach a 4 per cent leverage (debt-to-capital) ratio. No wonder they aren't lending. In the first half of 2009, banks coined it, profiting from ultra-low interest rates, government guarantees and an absence of tougher regulation to make easy money. But even if that continues, they will still face a net drain of $310 billion by the end of 2010, the IMF reckons.

As banks collapsed, global finance became national again. International capital flows – foreign direct investment, purchases and sales of foreign shares and bonds, and cross-border lending and deposits – became a trickle, falling 82 per cent from $10.5 trillion in 2007 to $1.9 trillion in 2008, according to the McKinsey Global Institute.[44] Many went into reverse, as investors sold foreign assets and repatriated their money. Cross-border bank lending fell from $4.9 trillion in 2007 to *minus* $1.3 trillion in 2008 as banks cancelled or failed to renew more international loans than they made. Around 40 per cent of this decline was due to lending among banks drying up; the remainder reflects the withdrawal of loans to non-bank borrowers, notably in emerging economies. Britain was hit hardest. Whereas foreigners had poured $1.5 trillion into the UK in 2007, they withdrew $1.2 trillion in 2008.

As banks with global operations fell into the arms of national governments, politicians insisted that rescued banks keep the cash at home, exacerbating the collapse of cross-border lending. During the go-go years, the once-staid Union Bank of Switzerland had rebranded itself as UBS – slogan 'You and Us' – to advertise its ubiquity and unlimited aspirations. But when UBS threatened to collapse, it was the Swiss authorities that rescued it – and understandably required that it cater first to its Swiss customers. As Mervyn King, the governor of the Bank of England, has remarked, global banking institutions are global in life, but national in death.

Global recession

In the final three months of 2008 and the first three of 2009, the financial panic sent the global economy into freefall. In countries that had experienced a housing bubble, the bust made consumers slash their spending. Banks stopped lending, causing havoc with companies that relied on short-term bank financing. The downturn soon spread to economies that had been spared a housing bust or banking crisis through the withdrawal of foreign capital, tanking share prices, slumping trade and a general collapse of confidence exacerbated by the global media and the internet. From the start of 2008 to the spring of 2009, the crisis knocked $30 trillion off the value of global shares and $11 trillion off the value of homes, according to Goldman Sachs. At their worst, these losses amounted to around 75 per cent of world GDP.[45]

What was once a virtuous circle of rising trade and booming economic growth turned into a vicious spiral of plunging demand and collapsing commerce. As American consumers cut back on their spending and companies stopped investing, factories ground to a halt and imports plunged. This caused other countries' exports to collapse, in turn reducing their own demand for imports and so on. Countries that are particularly reliant on exports, such as Germany, Japan and South Korea, were hit especially hard. Trade finance dried up, making it impossible for many companies to send shipments. Slumping demand also caused the prices of commodities such as oil, metals and foodstuffs to dive, bringing relief for hard-pressed consumers but slashing the export revenues of many developing countries, such as the Gulf states, South Africa and Chile, as well as of rich ones, such as Australia. Export earnings from the world's forty-nine least-developed countries fell 48 per cent over the first six months of 2009 from the same period in 2008, according to the International Trade Centre, a think-tank sponsored by the WTO and the UN.[46]

The collapse was more brutal than during the Great Depression. Within ten months of its peak in April 2008, world industrial production fell by an eighth and stock markets halved in value.[47] In just three months, between November 2008 and February 2009, world trade plunged by a fifth.[48] Global foreign direct investment plunged from a high of $2 trillion in 2007 to $1.1 trillion in 2009, according to UNCTAD's *World Investment Report*.[49] But unlike in the 1930s, the authorities did their best to stave off a depression by slashing interest rates to almost zero, printing vast sums of money and propping up demand through tax cuts and increased government spending. The ECB was the most reluctant to cut interest rates, but compensated for this through huge emergency lending to banks against all sorts of dodgy collateral. The Bank of England's unconventional monetary policy was the most ambitious: by January 2010 it had bought £200 billion of UK government bonds – 30 per cent of the market – using freshly printed cash to try to drive down long-term interest rates. China's fiscal stimulus was first and boldest; America's was not approved until February 2009, and most of the spending will not come on line until 2010.

But by far the biggest intervention was the support extended to the banking system. According to the IMF, the governments and central banks of the US, the euro-zone and the UK pledged a total of $8,955 billion (£5,436 billion) to backstop the banks – $1,950 billion in liquidity support, $2,525 billion in asset purchases and $4,480 billion in guarantees.[50] In reality, the support was open-ended. In effect, as in Iceland, governments in America and Europe pledged taxpayers' future incomes as collateral to guarantee that the banks' debts would be paid in full. To the bankers the spoils, to mere mortals the losses.

Botched rescue

Eventually, confidence was restored. From March 2009, stock markets rallied. In May, the US government announced that its 'stress tests' had determined that America's big banks required just $75 billion in additional capital to cover future losses (far less than the IMF estimates). By the summer, some banks had started to repay the capital the government had injected into them. By the autumn, the casino – but not the economy – was in full swing again.

But stabilising the financial system has come at a huge price and has so far failed to restore bank lending. While governments were right to rescue the banking system – because its collapse would have dragged down the rest of the economy – they went about it the wrong way. They should have saved the banking system rather than existing banks. They should not have guaranteed banks' unsecured creditors – professional investors who funded the bubble by lending to the banks and ought to have paid for their mistakes. And they should have tackled the underlying problem of banks' dodgy loans and securities rather than simply pumping money into the system in the vain hope that zombie banks would continue lending. As the Bank for International Settlements points out, 'Past banking crises have taught us that early recognition of losses combined with quick, comprehensive intervention and restructuring is the key to a speedy recovery.'[51]

Increasingly, however, a different story is taking hold. The crucial mistake, many people argue, was not that existing banks were bailed out, it was that Lehman wasn't. Alan Blinder, a

former vice-chairman of the US Federal Reserve, has called the
decision to let Lehman fail 'a colossal error'. Christine Lagarde,
the French finance minister, denounced it as a 'horrendous' mistake. Financiers' forked tongues hiss that it was this decision that
caused the crisis, not bankers themselves. In their view, a deep
recession could have been avoided – or at least greatly miti-
gated – if Lehman had been bailed out. But they have it all
wrong. It was the chaotic manner of Lehman's collapse that was
calamitous; the principle that bust banks should be wound down
is sound. Even though, unforgivably, the US government had not
got around to enacting special insolvency procedures to wind
down banks in an orderly fashion by the time Lehman collapsed,
it could still have found a way to ring-fence Lehman's most systemically important operations.

More broadly, there was a far better way to deal with failed
banks than backstopping all their losses. The bad banks should
have been nationalised, since they were insolvent without their
government guarantees. Their shareholders would be wiped out,
as those of any insolvent company would be. Their bosses would
be turfed out. Creditors would lose their shirts, as lenders to
bankrupt companies should. Their bad assets and dodgy securities would be hived off into a bad bank and held until maturity
or sold off when possible. Once they were under state ownership, many of their loans and other obligations to each other
could have been cancelled out. The government could have
injected fresh capital into the nationalised banks, allowing them
to resume lending, unburdened by their past mistakes. Once
financial markets had stabilised, the banks could have been privatised again.

An alternative, in countries where nationalisation was not
deemed desirable or feasible, was to create new 'good' banks
instead. Rather than taking over existing bad banks, governments would create new good ones, initially owned and funded
by the state. The new good banks would acquire bad banks'

deposits and good assets, leaving the toxic stuff to stew with the old bad ones. The bad banks that were in effect insolvent would be stripped of their banking licences and allowed to collapse or wind down their portfolio of bad assets over time. If they collapsed, their creditors would be converted into shareholders. The new good banks could resume lending on commercial terms, with temporary government guarantees for their loans and investments until calm was restored to financial markets. In effect, the government would be guaranteeing new lending – which is vital to support the economy – rather than subsidising old mistakes, which is unfair, inefficient and encourages banks to gamble at public expense.

Either option – nationalisation or the creation of new good banks – would have been infinitely preferable to the current mess. It would have boosted the economy, because the freshly capitalised good banks, unburdened by the old bad loans and securities, could have quickly resumed their proper function of lending to sound companies. It would have deterred banks and their creditors from taking big, destabilising risks in future. It would have placed less of a strain on government finances. And it would have been much fairer, since banks and their creditors would have paid most of the price for their mistakes rather than taxpayers. By clearing the decks, the new banks could have started afresh, chastened.

Critics will say that such ideas are crazy. Yet as Simon Johnson, the former IMF chief economist, pointed out in early 2009, 'The challenges the United States faces are familiar territory to the people at the IMF. If you hid the name of the country and just showed them the numbers, there is no doubt what old IMF hands would say: nationalise troubled banks and break them up as necessary . . . as the US government itself has insisted to multiple emerging-market countries in the past.'[52] As for the good-bank proposal, similar suggestions were made by luminaries such as George Soros,[53] a billionaire speculator who knows a thing or two about finance, Willem Buiter[54] – a leading financial economist and former member of the Bank of England's monetary-policy committee whose Maverecon blog became required reading – and Nobel laureate Joseph Stiglitz, among others.

The reason why these proposals were rejected is not because they were barmy. It is because bankers' huge lobbying power and policy-makers' capture by financiers' self-serving ideas persuaded them that banks had to be bailed out for the common good. But it was the banking system – not the bankers who got us into this mess – which needed to be saved. We will pay a huge price for this mistake in higher taxes, slower growth and greater instability for years to come. And unless sweeping reforms are enacted soon, this botched rescue paves the way for an even more devastating future crisis.

2

Too Big to Fail?

How to curb bubbles and banks

The salient feature of the current financial crisis is that it was not caused by some external shock like OPEC raising the price of oil or a particular country or financial institution defaulting. The crisis was generated by the financial system itself.

George Soros, 2009

No bank should be allowed to become so big that it can blackmail governments.

Angela Merkel, German chancellor, 2009[1]

The banks must resume lending, but they must also adjust by becoming smaller, simpler and safer . . . even where they have been essential, the government rescue packages implemented so far appear to be hindering rather than aiding this needed adjustment.

Bank for International Settlements,
79th Annual Report, 2009

Capitalism progresses through trial and error – we've had the trial and endured the errors, so now it's time to change course. A safe and sustainable recovery depends above all on fixing the banking system and limiting future bubbles. Although the authorities – governments, central banks and regulators – claim to have learned their lessons from the crisis, they are in danger of repeating old mistakes and making new ones. Already, they have compounded their earlier errors – turning a blind eye to the bubble and the related financial excess – by rescuing existing banks and allowing them to continue gambling with a copper-bottomed government guarantee. Central bankers, led by the Fed's Ben Bernanke, look like repeating Greenspan's folly of inflating ever-larger bubbles to rescue the economy from the previous bust. Governments' proposed reforms appear to be ducking the central issue – that nobody, least of all institutions as dangerous as banks, should be too big to fail.

Financial reform is a devilishly complicated issue. But as people get bogged down in its intricate technicalities, they often overlook some simple but very important points. For a start, financial instability cannot be reformed away. Its underlying causes – greed, fear and uncertainty about the future – will always be with us. Bankers will make bad lending decisions. Investors and lenders will get carried away. Bubbles will inflate. But despite the flaws of financial markets, state-directed lending is generally worse. Nobody knows what tomorrow's successful companies will be; only trial and error will tell. Politicians are more likely to channel funds to powerful lobbies and to prop up declining industries that employ lots of voters than to fund upstarts with little clout that threaten established companies. You don't have to go to a communist country to witness that; just look at the appalling record of Germany's Landesbanks, regional savings banks that are controlled by provincial govern-ments. Just as politically run central banks used to cut interest rates before elections to curry favour with voters, politically driven banks would also be likely to relax mortgage-lending terms. Even if state banks could somehow be insulated from political interference, they aren't any good at picking winners and would be as vulnerable to fads as other lenders. So except when all else fails, governments should not get involved in allocating credit. They should focus instead on regulation.

Regulation is inherently imperfect too – as are regulators. Rules cannot anticipate every eventuality, still less prevent them. By trying to prevent the last crisis, they often sow the seeds of the next. The more complex they are, the easier they are to game and the likelier it is that they will have unintended negative consequences. Regulators are flawed human beings like the rest of us – they make mistakes, get caught up in bubbles and are prone to capture by powerful lobbies, not least in the financial industry. So, too, the politicians who oversee them and the journalists who scrutinise them. Watchdogs will always have fewer resources and less information than the financiers they are trying to oversee, so bankers can run rings around them if they want to. Thus while it may improve matters, regulation alone cannot prevent another crisis. Almost inevitably, in fact, regulation will create new risks by trying to mitigate others. For instance, if regulators force banks to hold more capital, limiting their profitability, banks are likely to find clever new ways to get around the regulations and take on even greater risks in order to restore their profits.

The surest way to prevent excessive risk-taking is to make people pay the price for their mistakes. If bank bosses had their assets seized when a bank went under, they would keep a tighter rein on risk-taking. If shareholders had unlimited liability for banks' losses, they would keep bankers on a tighter leash. If investment banks were partnerships where partners had everything to lose – as Goldman Sachs was until as recently as 1999 – they would be more prudent. If bankers' bonuses were paid entirely in shares that they could not sell until retirement, they would be more careful with their gambling. Above all, if governments didn't bail out failed banks, but rather let them die in an orderly fashion, their shareholders would keep closer tabs on what bank bosses were up to and their creditors would be more careful about lending to them. Capitalism works wonders by rewarding successful risk-takers, but without the discipline of failure it is a recipe for disaster.

Lean against the wind

All of this suggests some quite simple but profound reforms. For a start, the authorities need to take pre-emptive action to prevent bubbles getting out of hand. Until now, most central bankers have ignored signs that asset prices were getting bubbly. So long as consumer-price inflation remained under control, they were relaxed about soaring property and share prices. Worse, Greenspan repeatedly slashed US interest rates when share prices tanked, in 1998 and again in 2000, while the Bank of England trimmed interest rates in 2005 when property prices dipped. So while central bankers did nothing to stop asset prices rising, they tried to prop them up when they fell. This encouraged bubbly investors to think that share and property prices were a one-way bet. Bankers who know that the government will bail them out take ever bigger risks; likewise investors who think interest-rate cuts will save the day. This must change.

The crisis demolishes the complacent notion – championed by Greenspan – that bubbles are rare, almost impossible to identify, and should in any case be allowed to run their course, with central bankers limiting themselves to cleaning up the mess after they burst.[2] If Greenspan had raised interest rates earlier and taken other measures to prick America's property bubble, the world economy would not be in the mess it is now.

But wouldn't raising interest rates have caused a recession? 'It depends on how much the Fed raises interest rates,' says Stephen Roach, formerly chief economist at Morgan Stanley:

> The idea that it's black or white, that the US either has a boom or a bust is ludicrous. It's trying to make an argument by focusing on extremes. The Fed should have run a more responsible monetary policy. Interest rates should have been higher throughout this endless period of bubbles. We would have had slower growth. There would have been a sacrifice. Instead we had artificial growth that was engineered by a bubble-prone central bank. It's a cop-out – and I've heard this from Greenspan and others – that well, sure we could have burst the bubble but we would have had a recession. That's not a fair and accurate assessment of what the choices were. If we had had a Fed funds rate [official US interest rate] that was somewhat higher, as opposed to a lot higher, the bubble-driven recovery in the early part of this decade would have been more muted, but the imbalances and the excesses around the world would have been prevented. We would have had a far greater chance of avoiding the type of crisis and deep global recession that we're in right now.

From now on, central banks should be mandated to pursue financial as well as price stability. When asset prices are getting bubbly, they should raise interest rates even if consumer prices remain subdued. The ECB already takes account of credit growth in setting interest rates, while the Bank of Canada targets a consumer-price index that includes house prices. The BIS, which sounded the alarm during the bubble years, should be officially charged with monitoring global events and naming and shaming errant central banks.

Worryingly, though, the Fed – under Greenspan's successor, Ben Bernanke – looks like it is back to its old tricks. 'We're following the script that we did after the [dotcom] equity bubble, which is to flood the system with liquidity [cash] in the hopes that you'll limit the downside and then be prepared to clean up the mess if something happens again,' Roach says. 'That's exactly the procedure that got us into this horrible crisis.'

The problem is not just that each bubble is bigger than the last, making its bursting all the more painful. It's that the policy response to the bust causes the economy to become even more dangerously unbalanced. Low interest rates encourage people to borrow more – and now governments are incurring vast debts too. These debts worsen the subsequent bust and leave the authorities with less ammunition to fight future crises. When people feel they have too much debt, interest-rate cuts don't encourage them to spend. When governments have debts that are too big, their scope to stimulate the economy is constrained. If policy-makers inflate yet another bubble now, they will be almost powerless to save the economy when it bursts. As Roach remarks, 'When you have public debt moving up around the world to post-World War II records and you have policy [interest] rates at zero, what happens if you have another crisis? Greenspan and Bernanke say drop money from helicopters. Well, we're doing it. How will we get out of it?'

William White – the former BIS chief economist who also warned of the huge risks building up in the bubble years – argues that by slashing interest rates at the slightest hint of trouble, policy-makers cause even bigger trouble down the road:

> The policy reaction to each successive set of difficulties laid the foundations for the next one. Worse, the encouragement by lower interest rates of debt accumulation and spending imbalances was the equivalent of allowing undergrowth to accumulate in a forest. This undergrowth not only made subsequent downturns more dangerous; it also made the available policy instruments less reliable in response. Looking back over successive cycles, interest rates have had to be reduced with

ever more vigour to get the same (and sometimes reduced) response from spending. Most recently, new and untried policies such as quantitative and credit easing [printing money to buy bonds and drive down interest rates] have had to be introduced. Logically, the end point of such a dynamic process would seem to be the mother of all fires and few if any means of resistance.[3]

The collapse of global demand in late 2008 and 2009 was so severe that governments were right to reflate the economy with a big monetary and fiscal stimulus. But the fiscal packages should have been better targeted, as I shall explain in Chapter 4. Pumping vast sums of money into the economy without fixing the banking system was also a big mistake. Had banks been restructured in the way suggested in Chapter 1, they would now be in a better position to lend. The monetary stimulus could have been smaller and far more effective. Instead, the casino is rolling again, but zombie banks are sucking the life out of the economy as they try to repair their balance sheets. Oodles of money is gushing around the world but banks are not lending it to those with bright new business ideas, so it is bidding up asset prices instead. And as we try to inflate the next bubble to save us from the last, the lenders who made it possible know that they can throw the dice again, safe in the knowledge that governments will protect them if they lose.

Share prices have soared even while profit prospects remain grim. By October 2009, they were already massively overvalued by historical standards. Bond prices, which rarely rise in tandem with share prices, have soared too, buoyed up by central banks printing money to buy government bonds. Even Britain's overpriced housing market is perking up. Meanwhile, the misery endures for ordinary people. This is worse than the pre-crisis bubble – at least then growth was strong, unemployment low and wages were rising while financial speculation raged. The authorities' financial stardust is blinding us to the fact that this speculative recovery is a costly sham that paves the way for an even more devastating crash.

It is too late to fix past mistakes. But future ones can still be prevented. It is going to be exceptionally difficult to withdraw the exceptional stimulus that has been applied. Those with big debts will howl when interest rates start to rise, so policy-makers will be under huge pressure to keep them down. After all, if they raise them too early, and the economy sinks back, they will be pilloried. But if they keep the economy on steroids, the damage will only become apparent years down the line when they are safely ensconced in another lucrative job. Most likely, then, interest rates will remain too low for too long. Likewise, governments will be tempted to keep spending so long as consumers are paying down their debts. Again, if they tighten policy too soon, voters will scream. But if they pile on debts that are too big, the pain will be paid by governments and voters later on. Disaster is not inevitable. Bad habits can be broken. But the dangers are huge.

As the sober Bank for International Settlements puts it, 'The big and justifiable worry is that, before it can be reversed, the dramatic easing in monetary policy will translate into growth in the broader monetary and credit aggregates. That growth will, in turn, lead to inflation that feeds inflation expectations or it may fuel yet another asset-price bubble, sowing the seeds of the next financial boom-bust cycle.'[4]

Ultimately, the buck has to stop somewhere. Banks have passed on their huge debts to governments. Governments have nobody else to pass them on to. If they become unsustainably large, the only two options are to default or to inflate them away, which is a sneaky way of achieving the same thing. The end result would be a period of stagflation – a stagnant economy combined with rampant inflation.

Bring bankers to book

Changes to monetary and fiscal policy are vital. So too are reforms to the banking system. The problem is that banks' inherent riskiness has been compounded by government mistakes and a lack of effective competition. Banks need to be made safer, so that they are less likely to fail. Those that become insolvent must be wound down in an orderly fashion, not bailed out. No bank should be too big to fail. Removing the government's backstop will limit banks' risk-taking and cause the financial sector to shrink. Even so, the banks that have survived this crisis are bigger and more powerful than ever. They need to be cut down to size by competition watchdogs – just as America's trustbusters broke up J.P. Morgan's banking empire in 1933.

Bank lending in boom times should be more tightly controlled in a variety of ways. Banks should be forced to hold a much bigger cushion of better-quality capital. That would raise the cost of risky lending and provide them with a bigger buffer against losses. The capital that they are required to hold should rise automatically during booms, providing a further lever for restraining bubbles. Many countries – such as Australia, Brazil, China, India and Spain – already have countercyclical capital requirements.[5] Financial regulators should also have the discretion to raise these requirements further if other measures to restrain bubbles fail.

Bank lending should be restrained in the simplest and most transparent way possible. Giving complex (and arbitrary) risk weightings to different kinds of borrowing or, worse, trusting banks to use their own flawed risk-management models encourages them to take on risks that are either not properly regulated or not properly understood (or both). So as a backstop against regulators' and banks' mistakes, bank lending should be capped at a certain multiple of their capital. Such 'leverage ratio' requirements are already used in Switzerland and Canada.

During this crisis, banks incurred huge losses so quickly that their capital cushion vanished overnight. Raghuram Rajan of the University of Chicago has sensibly suggested that banks be obliged to issue 'contingent capital' – debt that converts into shares when the system is in crisis and a bank's capital ratio has become dangerously low. He also proposes that regulators ban bank dividends as soon as a crisis is brewing.[6] Banks' liquidity – their ability to meet sudden cash needs – should also be more closely monitored. These regulations should apply to all bank assets, whether they are on or off their books, and to all institutions that perform bank-like roles, whether they call themselves banks or not.

Despite these extra precautions, some banks will find ways to get around them, and mistakes will be made. It is essential, then, that banks be forced to draw up 'living wills' that allow their operations to be wound down as quickly and simply as possible without requiring a government bailout or causing a disastrous Lehman-style panic. Banks object that this is too costly. Tough. As Willem Buiter rightly points out, 'Much of the complexity and not a small part of the cross-border nature of many banks is part of a deliberate strategy to make the bank and its operations opaque and incomprehensible to regulators, supervisors, tax authorities, shareholders and competitors. Such regulatory arbitrage and tax arbitrage-driven complexity and internationalisation is socially inefficient.'

John Kay, a British economist, perceptively notes that while it is essential to keep the banking system going, this need not imply saving existing banks:

There are many services we cannot do without – the electricity grid and the water supply, the transport system and the telecommunications network. These activities are every bit as necessary to our personal and business lives as the banking sector and at least as interconnected. Even a brief hiatus in their supply is intolerable. But the need to keep the water flowing does not establish a need to keep the water company in business. In all industries where there is or might be a dominant position in the supply of essential public services, there needs to be a special resolution regime. The key requirement is that assets that are needed for the continued provision of these services can be quickly separated from the organisations engaged in their supply. The businesses involved must be required to operate in such a way that such a separation is possible. In some relevant industries such a scheme exists; in others it does not. In all cases, review and contingency planning is required.[7]

Buiter has outlined how this could be done in the banking sector. A special resolution regime should be created as an alternative to bankruptcy for banks otherwise deemed too significant to fail. This would require that banks' debts to unsecured creditors and other counterparties be forcibly and swiftly converted into shares until the banks are adequately capitalised. In effect, those who lent to a failed bank, rather than the government, would be forced to bail it out. No public money must go into a bank as capital or guarantees until all unsecured creditors and counterparties have been converted into shareholders. 'It must be possible to achieve such a mandatory recapitalisation by unsecured creditors and counterparties for any institution overnight, and without interrupting normal business,' Buiter argues, by requiring all systemically important financial institutions to draw up a regularly updated 'will'.[8]

This would have huge advantages. The threat of being wiped out would give banks' shareholders a better incentive to keep tabs on banks' management, while the prospect of forced conversion of their loans into equity would make bank creditors more careful about lending. The rapid and automatic recapitalisation of banks by private creditors would reduce the need to put public funds at risk and ensure that banks were able to lend again quickly. If all else fails, banks should be nationalised and restructured, not bailed out and allowed to live on after death.

Removing the government safety net that allows banks to borrow too cheaply and encourages them to take excessive risks would naturally cause the financial sector to become smaller and safer. Like any subsidised industry, the banking sector is bigger than it ought to be. Banks should also be made to pay the full cost of insuring small depositors against losses. Such measures would be infinitely superior to heavy-handed controls that tried to second-guess what size the financial sector ought to be.

Big and powerful banks also need to be cut down to size. On Britain's high street, competition has been vastly reduced, not just by Lloyds' takeover of HBOS, but also by Santander acquiring Bradford & Bingley and Alliance & Leicester in addition to Abbey. In investment banking, the collapse of Bear Stearns, Lehman Brothers and the takeover of Merrill Lynch by Bank of America has greatly reduced competition. Goldman Sachs, Morgan Stanley and JPMorgan Chase are now far too dominant. It's not just their size that is the problem. It is the scope of their activities and the many conflicts of interest that they involve. Competition watchdogs should investigate the best way to break up the big banks. It might be a good idea, for instance, to split commercial banking – banks that take deposits and lend them to companies and households – from investment banking. Commercial banks that are too big should also be broken up. Within investment banking, the manifest conflicts of interest between trading for banks' own account and advising and doing deals on behalf of clients need to be addressed.

All of this would reduce banks' excess profits, which derive from their government subsidies and market power. It would therefore also curb bankers' bonuses. If governments are still worried about excessive pay, they should raise taxes. Allowing banks to fail would also give shareholders and bank bosses a much stronger incentive to keep a lid on bankers' risky gambles. But clever (or rogue) bankers can still outwit them. So to deter them from betting the bank, bankers' bonuses should be paid almost entirely in stock that must be held for at least twenty years. Any shares sold before then would be punitively taxed. This would not prevent bankers borrowing against those shares if they wanted to use the funds for other purposes, but it would leave them exposed to big losses if the bank folded.

Other, more technical reforms are also desirable. One is to create a central clearing house for credit derivatives, to reduce the risks of a counterparty's failure causing havoc in the huge market for credit-default swaps. Another is to separate the payments and clearing system from banks' control and make it a tightly controlled utility, in the same way that other vital infrastructure networks are. Credit-rating agencies should be stripped of their role in vetting securities' riskiness; instead this should be done by independent, non-profit-making bodies.

A Europe-wide bank regulator, standard setter and supervisor is also needed. It would not only keep tabs on national watchdogs. It should be also charged with preventing repeats of the Icesave debacle, in particular by ensuring that governments have enough funds to guarantee the deposits of their banks' foreign subsidiaries. At a global level, the Financial Stability Board should monitor and coordinate national authorities' efforts. Financial markets are global. Banks operate across borders. Governments have to work together too.

Here's hoping

Don't meddle with the markets, financiers will shriek. Governments can only make matters worse. Nonsense. The financial system we have now is a monstrous government-backed racket; what we need is one where the normal rules of capitalism –

live and die by the market – apply. Finance is vital. It is the lifeblood of the economy. Savers, house-buyers, companies, new businesses, pension funds, insurance companies, big businesses, governments and the economy as a whole – all depend on a dynamic and efficient financial system. That's why the reforms proposed above aim to make the market work better, not stifle it.

Yes, pre-emptive action against bubbles will slow growth in the short term, but it will also avoid more painful busts. Yes, tighter banking regulation will raise the cost of borrowing, but so it should, because this has been unduly subsidised. Yes, breaking up the banks will be complicated, but it will foster greater competition, giving everyone who depends on the financial system a better deal.

Believers in free markets should support these reforms. They aim to make markets work better. So too should all those who want to see the influence of finance curbed. The millions of tax-payers who are paying for bankers' mistakes should also cheer. Business should support them too. Companies are among the biggest victims of the financial sector's abuses. Its profits come at their expense. Its failings damage the reputation of business as a whole. Its recklessness has caused a recession that is shredding corporate profits and bankrupting many otherwise sound businesses. Ultimately, cutting banks down to size will help to save capitalism, not kill it.

Unfortunately, governments and central bankers are being seduced by the siren songs of the bankers who led us into this mess. That is hardly surprising. The bubble inflated under Gordon Brown's stewardship of the British economy. Alan Greenspan's disciple Ben Bernanke is one of the architects of the bubble, while Obama's closest economic advisers, Timothy Geithner and Larry Summers, were tainted by the excesses of the Clinton era. And money talks. Between November 2008 and November 2009, Wall Street doled out $42 million to US legislators, mostly to members of the House and Senate banking committees and House and Senate leaders. In the first three quarters of 2009, the industry spent $344 million on lobbying.[9]

In America, the Dodd–Frank financial reform act is a step forward but does not address the too-big-to-fail issue convincingly. In Britain, Alastair Darling, the then Chancellor of the Exchequer, appointed 'Win' Bischoff, the former chairman of failed Citigroup, to co-chair the writing of a report on the future of UK international financial services. As Buiter (who has since become chief economist at Citigroup) remarked, 'That's rather like asking the Ayatollah Ali Khamenei to write a report on who won the Iranian presidential election. It really is the most ridiculous appointment since Caligula appointed his favourite horse a consul. You will not be surprised to hear that the report does not consider the size of UK banks to be excessive.'[10] (The Conservative–Liberal Democrat coalition government elected in May 2010 has appointed a commission on banking reform that is due to report by September 2011.) Politicians are under the spell of bankers. It must be broken.

Meanwhile the banks are back to their old tricks. In Britain, state-owned Northern Rock is offering 100 per cent mortgages again while Nationwide offers 125 per cent ones. Barclays Capital and Goldman Sachs are proposing new ways of skirting around capital requirements by reducing the amount of capital that has to be held against the assets that are being securitised.[11] Mostly nationalised RBS is offering two-year guaranteed bonuses to hire new talent. Banks are paying out huge bonuses again.

Governments missed the opportunity to reform the financial sector while it was on its knees. The longer they wait, the harder it will get. One has to hope that they are willing and able to do so. Simon Johnson, formerly chief economist at the IMF, is not optimistic. 'Before we fully tame finance we have to go through another crisis,' he says. For all our sakes, let's hope he is wrong.

3

Money Matters

*The global financial system
needs fixing too*

The outbreak of the current crisis and its spillover in the
world have confronted us with a long-existing but still
unanswered question – what kind of international reserve
currency do we need to secure global financial stability
and facilitate world economic growth, which was one of
the purposes for establishing the IMF?

Zhou Xiaochuan, governor of the People's Bank of
China, 2009

When global markets seized up in late 2008, it looked as if history was repeating itself. As in 1997–8, capital flew out of even well-managed emerging economies, forcing up the cost of borrowing and pushing down their currencies. Companies from Mexico to Brazil and South Korea suddenly went bankrupt.[1] Sovereign defaults and further drastic devaluations seemed likely. While people in the West were focused on the fragility of their own financial systems, it seemed as if – as usual – emerging economies would bear the brunt of the crisis.

Fortunately, China's huge stimulus package, announced in early November, helped restore confidence. Other emerging economies came up with their own, more modest measures. Many, notably South Korea, deployed their huge war chest of foreign-currency reserves to fight off attacks on their currencies. The Fed also stepped in with an unprecedented offer of dollars to Brazil, Mexico, Singapore and South Korea, the ECB with euros for Poland and Hungary. And while less healthy economies (including Hungary) had to be rescued by the IMF, the panic abated remarkably quickly. Even poorly run countries such as Hungary and Russia were soon able to bring their interest rates back down to cushion the downturn. But while many emerging economies have fared much better than feared, it was a close escape. They might not be so lucky next time. How many crises will it take before the flaws in the global financial system are finally fixed? (This chapter is a bit more technical than the others. If you are not particularly interested in the intricacies of the international financial system, you might want to skip to the final paragraph.)

As we have seen, financial markets are dangerously unstable, banks particularly so. That is true even in well-regulated domestic financial systems that have a lender of last resort and a national government to inject liquidity and tackle solvency problems. Yet the failings of domestic finance pale in comparison with those of the global system. One problem is that while financial markets and institutions are increasingly international, regulation and supervision remain largely national. That gives plenty of scope for banks and other financial institutions to play watchdogs off each other and escape proper oversight. In the absence of stronger international rules and supervision, closer cooperation among national authorities – notably through the Bank for International Settlements, the Financial Stability Board and the IMF – is therefore essential.

A second problem, especially for emerging economies with small, underdeveloped and poorly regulated financial systems, is that allowing in foreign capital risks swamping domestic markets, inflating asset-price bubbles and then causing a terrible bust. This problem is compounded by the fact that the global economy is divided into national currencies that often fluctuate wildly, creating additional instability. Currency volatility and misalignments cause problems even for large advanced economies, but even more so for smaller and emerging ones. When speculative capital floods into an emerging economy, its currency soars, choking off exports. When it drains out again and the currency plunges, it can wreak havoc, especially if local banks, companies and households – or the government – have borrowed in foreign currencies, as Icelanders have found to their cost.

Developing domestic capital markets and improving financial regulation and oversight is essential to limit the risks of asset-price bubbles. But governments can also reduce the risks of foreign-financed bubbles and currency instability by erecting firewalls to insulate economies from global capital markets. Among other things, they can try to control capital coming into a country and limit banks' and companies' borrowing in foreign currencies. 'I know capital controls leak. I know they lead to corruption,' says Willem Buiter. 'But the alternative is too awful, because the exchange rate and domestic financial markets can easily get swamped by international capital flows.' While such controls have become less common, many countries – including China, India and Chile – still maintain them.

Even with capital controls, crises can occur – and without them, they often do. What then? Unfortunately, a proper global lender of last resort does not exist to help out when countries run short of foreign cash.[2] That is not a problem for the US or the euro-zone, since their currencies are always in demand internationally; in the absence of a global currency, countries use the dollar and to a lesser extent the euro for international transactions. It is not usually a problem for other advanced economies either, since central banks generally – but not always, remember Iceland – lend each other cash in times of need. As I mentioned, that favour was also extended to Brazil, Mexico, Singapore, South Korea, Poland and Hungary during this crisis. But it is a huge problem for most emerging economies, which are generally left to fend for themselves. Only on occasion will an advanced economy step in to help, as when the United States rescued Mexico during the Tequila crisis of 1994–5. If all else fails, the truly desperate can seek emergency loans from the IMF with often unpalatable strings attached.

The recent crisis has forced many economies into the hands of the Fund: Iceland, a large part of Central and Eastern Europe (Romania, Ukraine, Hungary, Belarus, Latvia, Georgia, Armenia, Serbia) and Pakistan. But after their searing experience in 1997–8, most emerging economies – especially in Asia – have resolved never to fall into the IMF's clutches again. As I described at length in *Open World*, East Asian economies that had recently opened up to international capital suffered a devastating debt and currency crisis when foreigners (and locals) yanked their cash out and the asset-price bubbles that they had helped inflate burst. A brutal recession ensued, aggravated by the savage medicine that the IMF imposed on them as a condition for its emergency loans. Indonesia's economy, for instance, shrank by 13 per cent in 1998. In many countries, investment rates have not recovered since the crisis. They would benefit immensely from reforms that made it possible to tap foreign capital safely to finance greater investment, and thus grow faster. But in the absence of such reforms, policy-makers in Asia in particular but also in other emerging economies have decided that borrowing from abroad is too dangerous. Instead, they have accumulated foreign-currency reserves – mostly US Treasury bonds – to insure themselves against a future crisis. As a result, perversely, poorer countries actually lent richer ones $737 billion in 2007.[3]

Amassing reserves has many benefits. Since emerging economies are no longer net borrowers from foreigners, they are less likely to see a run on their currency (although many did during the global panic in late 2008). Because they have a stockpile of foreign currencies that can be sold to buy their own currency, they can prop it up if need be (as many did in late 2008). Perhaps most importantly, having a pot of foreign cash to dip into in times of need avoids ever having to borrow from the hated IMF again. In Britain, the humiliation of having to call in the IMF in 1976 is seared into the national consciousness, but it bears no comparison with the shame and loathing East Asians understandably feel.

Unfortunately, this self-insurance is hugely expensive. Funds that could have been used for productive domestic investments are instead piled (mostly) into US Treasury bonds that pay little interest and depreciate when the dollar weakens. Seven East Asian countries – Hong Kong, Malaysia, the Philippines, Singapore, South Korea, Taiwan and Thailand – have $1.2 trillion in reserves between them.[4] Japan, an advanced economy, has $1 trillion. Other big reserve holders are Russia ($400 billion), India ($250 billion) and Brazil ($200 billion). Those are vast sums – and the chances of incurring big losses are mounting as the US authorities print huge amounts of dollars and try to push the currency down to help America export its way out of recession. Yet the recent crisis has convinced many emerging economies that they ought to amass even more reserves to insure themselves against currency instability. 'They don't trust the IMF and they don't see any alternative,' says Simon Johnson, the former IMF chief economist.

China has accumulated the biggest currency reserves – a whopping $2.85 trillion by the end of 2010. Although its economy was largely unhurt by the crisis of 1997–8, the government also sought protection against a future one. But for the most part, China's accumulation of reserves has been accidental rather than deliberate. Emulating other successful East Asian economies, China has made exporting its economic lodestar. Producing lots of manufactured exports in ways that require lots of workers creates lots of jobs too. Since the Chinese government's priority is keeping unemployment down – not least because idle hands could lead to social unrest and perhaps even a challenge to the Communist Party's rule – exporting as much as possible to America in return for IOUs seemed like a good deal in the bubble years. But its huge reserves – which amount to $2,000 per Chinese person, equivalent to a third of the country's annual income – now leave it intensely vulnerable to a weaker dollar.

Accumulating reserves is not only costly for emerging economies. It is also a problem for the rest of the world, especially now that global demand is weak. To accumulate a dollar nest egg, countries must spend less than they earn. That was fine when America was spending beyond its means. But now that America and other debt-laden countries are trying to save more too, this depresses global demand. Everyone cannot save at once; someone must be willing to borrow. Otherwise the economy shrinks. So it is not just emerging economies that would benefit from reforms that enabled them to import capital safely, or at least to stop accumulating low-yielding and depreciating dollar reserves. America would also gain, because global demand would be stronger and the dollar weaker, both of which would boost US exports and growth. If emerging economies did not feel the need to save as much to protect themselves against crises, they could spend more. And if the rest of the world didn't need dollars to hold in reserve, settle trade and pay for oil and other commodities – or because their currencies were pegged to it – the dollar's exchange rate would be weaker. Nearly two-thirds (63 per cent) of allocated reserves are in dollars, a bit over a quarter

(27 per cent) in euros. (Sterling accounts for 4 per cent and the yen 3 per cent)[5]. A dangerous, dollar-dominated global financial system divided into volatile national currencies is increasingly damaging for the whole world.

How, then, might things be improved? One way to reduce the demand for dollar reserves is to make the global financial system safer. In the absence of global reforms, countries can strengthen domestic financial systems while protecting themselves through capital controls. Another is to improve other forms of crisis insurance, such as pooling countries' reserves or, more ambitiously, creating a proper global lender of last resort. A third is to bolster alternatives to the dollar as a global reserve currency.

Damage limitation is important. But an even bigger prize would be to enable emerging economies to import capital safely. Global capital markets ought to provide a safe and stable means of allocating capital from rich, mature economies to fast-growing adolescent ones. This would offer better returns to tomorrow's rich-country pensioners and a wider source of investment funds for today's emerging-economy businesses. In the very long term, a global currency is one solution. Expanding the use of regional currencies, such as the euro, and creating new ones would also help a great deal. But in the meantime, many improvements could be made.

Replacing reserves

Emerging economies with huge reserves could afford to become net importers of capital again, particularly if it took the form of foreign direct investment. When foreign companies invest in local factories and facilities – or buy local companies outright – the capital is not only tied down. It also provides good jobs, valuable foreign know-how and much-needed competition for local firms. But emerging economies should remain wary of inflows of short-term money that can inflate share and property bubbles. So it is prudent for governments to impose taxes or controls on volatile short-term capital inflows, as Chile does with some success. If countries can prevent too much hot money from flowing into a country, they may stave off a crisis before it starts. Governments should also curb companies' – and their own – borrowing in foreign currencies. As Martin Wolf, chief economics commentator of the *Financial Times*, rightly observes in *Fixing Global Finance*, 'Under adjustable exchange rates, the only safe way to borrow is in one's own currency. If that is impossible, borrowing must be limited.' Well-managed emerging economies with healthy government finances are starting to be able to borrow in their own currency. Some, such as South Africa and Brazil, have started to sell local-currency bonds to foreigners, as (more recently) has China.

Unfortunately, most emerging economies cannot borrow much in their own currency and far from running down their foreign-currency reserves a little, they are keen to amass more. One way to economise on their huge reserves would be to pool them. Under the Chiang Mai Initiative, launched in 2000, eight Asian economies have arranged a set of bilateral swap agreements.[6] This enables them to take out emergency loans without turning to the IMF. But when the crisis hit in late 2008, Asian governments turned to the US Federal Reserve for help rather than to the Chiang Mai arrangements. The Fed said yes to Singapore and South Korea but no to Indonesia. The problem, says Wing Thye Woo of the Brookings Institution, a think-tank in Washington DC, is that drawing down more than 10 per cent of a country's quota is subject to the same conditions as an IMF loan. 'What's the difference?' he remarks. 'None.' In May 2009 thirteen Asian governments agreed to expand the Chiang Mai Initiative to a $120 billion multilateral facility on which to draw in times of need. China and Japan contributed $38.4 billion each. Countries can now draw up to 20 per cent of their quota without conditionality. This is a big step forward. But for now, too little cash is available, with too many strings attached. The way forward, says Woo, is to offer pre-qualified loans to defend currencies against speculative attack. To prevent abuse, this requires careful monitoring that governments are pursuing sensible policies. Giovanni Capannelli of the Asian Development Bank reckons that the 20 per cent limit could be raised to 50 per cent or more once a new regional surveillance unit is established.

Another suggestion is for the Fed and the ECB to agree swap lines with the central banks of soundly managed emerging economies, as they did in late 2008. If such arrangements could be extended and formalised, they would offer emerging economies some of the security that advanced ones enjoy.

The best way to provide all emerging economies with help in a crisis would be to create a global lender of last resort. This would involve either the establishment of a new institution that emerging economies could trust or a comprehensive reform of the IMF. That would require a huge expansion of the IMF's lending resources, a shake-up of its 'quotas' and associated voting rights to give emerging economies more say, a loosening of the strings attached to its loans, and the expansion of pre-arranged borrowing lines that could be drawn down immediately and without conditions. It could then act as a true global lender of last resort, in the same way that central banks do domestically.

The good news is that the IMF is moving in the right direction. Although it would be better if the top job at the IMF were not reserved for a European in future, Dominique Strauss-Kahn has proved to be an inspired choice. The ebullient French Socialist has helped to 'humanise' the Fund, his leftish political background making him more sensitive than his predecessors to the social consequences of IMF actions, just as Mike Moore's Labour background served him well as director-general of the WTO. Strauss-Kahn is also aware of the need to win over emerging economies. 'The Fund cannot succeed in its efforts –

whether surveillance, financial support or technical assistance – unless all our members regard it as *their* institution, furthering *their* common interest and *their* strategic goals,' he says. 'Such legitimacy is essential for our surveillance to be considered even-handed and independent, and hence for it to be effective. It is also a critical prerequisite for the IMF to serve as a credible global lender of last resort.'[7]

The new importance of the G20 in global economic management is pushing the IMF towards reform. In April 2009 they agreed to triple the IMF's lending resources to $750 billion, with China chipping in. By September the IMF had already lent twice as much as it did during the 1997–8 crisis, and with fewer strings attached. The G20 also pledged to shift at least 5 per cent of IMF shares from over-represented economies to emerging ones by 2011. Astonishingly, Belgium and the Netherlands, whose combined population is a fiftieth of China's and whose combined GDP is less than a third of China's, have a bigger vote at the IMF than China does. The IMF has also introduced a flexible credit line, a pre-emptive insurance policy for well-managed economies. Mexico, Poland and Colombia have already tapped this facility. But these changes do not go far enough. Europe will remain over-represented, while the US will retain its veto, in effect, on lending decisions. If the IMF is to be trusted, it must no longer be dominated by Washington. And if it is to act as a true global lender of last resort, it needs a bigger pot of cash that is more readily available. More countries will need to qualify for its flexible credit line, while its normal lending needs to be disbursed faster and with fewer harmful conditions.

A reformed IMF acting as a global lender of last resort would make the global financial system much safer. An even bolder step would be to introduce a global reserve currency as an alternative – or replacement – to the dollar. This would separate the provision of global liquidity from the demands and constraints of American monetary policy – liberating for US policy-makers, reassuring for dollar-reserve holders. Such a currency already exists. The IMF issues special drawing rights (SDRs), which are based on a weighted average of the dollar, euro, pound and yen, but they account for less than 1 per cent of global reserves. This will rise to nearly 4 per cent after the G20 summit in London in 2009 decided that the IMF should issue a further $250 billion of SDRs. A United Nations panel chaired by Joseph Stiglitz, a Nobel-prize winning economist, suggested that SDRs' role be expanded. Zhou Xiaochuan, the governor of the People's Bank of China, the country's central bank, has made a similar proposal, which Brazil, India and Russia have backed.[8] 'China isn't pressing anything urgently,' says David Dodwell, who runs Strategic Access, a Hong Kong-based consultancy. 'But they've put a marker down and they won't drop it.'

In the short term, the supply of SDRs could be increased, the basket of currencies on which they are based broadened (notably to include the Chinese renminbi) and the scope of their use widened. Bonds denominated in SDRs could be issued to increase the currency's appeal.[9] SDRs could be backed by a broad pool of currency reserves, into which they would be convertible on demand. In effect, they would be an international reserve currency based on a composite of major currencies and managed by a reformed IMF. Over time, they might displace the dollar entirely, but in the meantime they would provide a much-needed alternative – and a boost to global growth and stability.

Regional currencies

Reforms to the global financial system are essential. But while more legitimate and effective measures to prevent and tackle crises would do a lot of good, they would not do away with the damaging instability of flexible currencies. Their wild swings and misalignments not only wreak havoc with economies, they also limit trade, investment and financial ties. One alternative would be a return to pegged exchange rates, or a system of targeted currency bands, along the lines of the EU's exchange-rate mechanism (ERM). But these have proved unsustainable for countries that allow capital to slosh around freely, since speculators can all too easily outgun governments' efforts to stabilise exchange rates. So why not follow the euro's lead and abolish national currencies altogether?

Supporters of flexible exchange rates claim that they help economies to adjust automatically to shocks. Yet consider Japan, which had a huge trade surplus in the pre-crisis years. Since the yen floats more or less freely, it ought to have appreciated, making Japanese exports more expensive and imports cheaper, shrinking the surplus. Instead, the yen fell. In January 2007, when Japan's trade surplus had become vast, the yen fell to a four-year low against the US dollar. Why? Because currencies are not just exchanged to pay for foreign trade, they are also traded on currency markets that dwarf the volume of international commerce. An astonishing $4 trillion is traded *each day* on currency markets, while world trade in 2008 was $16.7 trillion in a whole year. So currency traders, not those of goods and services, largely determine exchange rates. Currency markets are particularly bubble-prone. After all, who knows what a currency *ought* to be worth now, let alone what it *might* be worth tomorrow?

During the bubble years, investors borrowed huge sums in Japanese yen and other currencies with low interest rates and invested them in countries with much higher ones. This 'carry trade' pushed the yen down as borrowers sold it to buy up high-yielding currencies such as the Australian and New Zealand dollars, causing their trade deficits to swell. The carry trade unwound during the crisis as investors repatriated their cash, sending the yen soaring. But now that the financial system is recovering, it shows signs of taking off again.[10] Between March

2009 and November 2010 the high-yielding Brazilian real soared by 50 per cent against the US dollar, while the Australian dollar appreciated by nearly 60 per cent. Far from promoting a more stable and balanced pattern of global growth, then, the volatility and misalignments of floating exchange rates often spread instability and widen imbalances.

Sterling too got out of line during the bubble years. Since financial activity in London was booming and Britain had higher interest rates than the US, Japan or euro-zone, the UK sucked in vast amounts of foreign capital. Some was invested in relatively high-yielding government bonds. An even bigger chunk went into shares. To buy into all the foreign companies listed on the London Stock Exchange, international investors had to buy sterling, pushing it up to stellar heights. Britons buying houses in France felt rich, but manufacturers – and other exporters – were throttled. If the pound had played a balancing role, it would have fallen to help Britain's trade deficit to shrink. But on the contrary, it strengthened. In 2008, when Britain's financial bubble was bursting, sterling reached absurd heights of more than $2.10. Far from dampening the shock, it amplified it.

For sure, currency moves are sometimes helpful. The pound's collapse since the summer of 2008 has fortuitously given British exporters a big boost. Provided it remains low, it will help exports drive the recovery when global demand picks up. But its plunge came perilously close to a run on the pound. Had sterling continued to plummet, it could have deterred investors from buying UK government bonds, sabotaging the government's attempts to rescue the economy. What's more, the pound did not fall *because* the economy was unbalanced, still less *in order* to rebalance it. Nor did it fall because Britain's proudly independent policy-makers were willing it in the right direction. It plunged because currency traders' hunches about the future changed. The pound's next moves may be much less helpful.

Exchange-rate instability is a huge cost even for middling

economies such as Britain. 'To get the full benefits of financial integration, financial deepening and risk diversification you really need a common currency,' Buiter argues. 'As soon as you have multiple currencies, there's always a very nasty downside risk associated with unrestricted capital flows. We've seen that demonstrated again. That's why the euro-zone is such a good idea because it permits countries to have the benefit of full financial integration without the immense exchange-rate risk.' Ideally, a regional currency should encompass countries that trade a lot with each other, have flexible economies and allow people and capital to flow freely among them. The downside is that countries can no longer set their own interest rates and also lose the option of letting their currency slide to restore competitiveness. But as we have seen, floating currencies' moves tend to be determined by volatile financial markets, rather than by the need to restore external balance. And in small open economies, monetary autonomy is not all it's cracked up to be. A country such as Denmark that pegs its currency to the euro must accept the euro-zone's interest rates, plus a premium for the risk that the peg will slip. So why not go the whole hog and adopt the euro? A country such as Britain that targets domestic inflation is buffeted by the vagaries of currency markets, which in turn influence inflation and hence interest rates, while it too must pay a premium for the risk of currency volatility. Since in practice UK monetary policy is only partially 'independent', its 'loss' would not be a big blow. As a flexible, open economy, Britain could thrive within the euro-zone.

Regional currencies are only a partial solution to exchange-rate instability. The euro still swings up and down against the dollar, although as a bigger currency than sterling it takes bigger waves to move it. But unless the US and the EU were willing to make a credible commitment to dampen exchange-rate moves, this volatility is unavoidable. Even so, joining a bigger currency can provide huge benefits. Since its launch in 1999, the euro has allowed what were recently Europe's emerging economies to grow much faster by sucking in foreign capital without the risk of a currency crisis. Just look at how once-peripheral economies such as Spain and Ireland have caught up with – and in Ireland's case surpassed – the richer economies at Europe's core over the past decade. Certainly, part of this growth was bubble-driven and should have been moderated. But the positive dynamic is undeniable. When the crisis hit, those countries were spared a devastating run on their currency. Had the euro not existed, Ireland would almost certainly have suffered Iceland's fate. While it must now painfully cut wages and prices to regain competitiveness, its interest rates are near zero (while Iceland's are nearly 20 per cent) and its government can still borrow (whereas Iceland is in the hands of the IMF). Even Greece's hidebound and woefully mismanaged economy is better off with the euro. But unless it follows Ireland's example, it faces years of misery ahead. During the panic in late 2008 and early 2009, it is a fair bet that all national currencies would have been shaken, as they were during the ERM crisis of 1992–3. Countries outside the euro suffered as panicky investors sought refuge in safe havens such as the dollar and the euro. Many Central and East European economies with big current-account deficits came close to suffering an Asian-style currency and debt crisis (and may yet do); most had to seek an IMF bailout. Even Denmark – hardly an emerging economy – had to raise interest rates to protect its currency instead of cutting them to prop up demand. A big danger for Britain in the years ahead is a run on the pound if foreign investors lose confidence in the UK's public finances.

In due course, all the economies on Europe's periphery that send most of their trade there could join the euro. At the same time, the crisis has exposed flaws in the way the euro-zone is run. These need fixing. Euro-zone governments need to manage their finances prudently, while maintaining the fiscal flexibility to respond to economic shocks. Those that have borrowed too much need to be able to restructure their debts in an orderly way. And while there is nothing wrong with large financial flows from one euro-zone country to another – on the contrary, they are part of the rationale for the euro – governments need to be careful that these are funding productive investments rather than speculative bubbles. Above all, they need to tackle the banking crisis that is the underlying cause of the 'euro crisis' through an EU-wide solution that forces banks to recognise their losses and bondholders to recapitalise them if necessary.

Countries that trade primarily with the United States might do best to adopt the dollar, as some already have. But what about East Asia? Just as Europe's smaller currencies were once jostled by moves in the dollar–Deutschmark exchange rate, Asia's smaller moneys are caught between the dollar and the yen. Like Europe, they would gain a lot from a regional currency. The Japanese like to think that the yen could become Asia's currency of choice. But a far more plausible candidate is the Chinese renminbi. China is at the heart of East Asia's economy and in 2010 overtook Japan as the region's largest economy. Over the next decade, its influence can only grow. The problem is that its financial system is still state-led, its bond markets underdeveloped and its currency not freely traded. Sooner rather than later, that needs to change.

Set the renminbi free

Pegging the renminbi to the dollar – and the accompanying capital controls that limit the flow of cash in and out of the country mostly to trade-related transactions – has served China well. It escaped the crisis that swept through the rest of Asia in 1997–8. But as China's importance grows, its currency regime is becoming increasingly inappropriate. It became the world's second-biggest economy in 2010, yet its currency cannot be used outside China.

It is the world's biggest exporter, yet most of its foreign sales are priced in dollars. It is also the world's biggest creditor, yet it lends in dollars, the currency of the biggest debtor. Hitching the renminbi to Washington's wagon leaves it at the mercy of the Fed's monetary-policy mistakes – or simply their inappropriateness to China's needs. Pricing its trade in US currency makes the value of its exports depend on the vagaries of the dollar's ups and downs. This also means that it acquires vast amounts of dollars when it is running a big trade surplus. Lending in dollars exposes it to the risk that America will, in effect, default on its debts by debauching its currency, or simply that a declining dollar will erode them. As China's prime minister, Wen Jiabao, has remarked, 'Of course we are concerned about the safety of our assets. To be honest, I am a little bit worried. I request the US to maintain its good credit, to honour its promises and to guarantee the safety of China's assets.'[11]

These are all powerful reasons why, despite the risks that making the renminbi convertible entails, China and the rest of the world would be much better off if it became a freely traded currency – and one to which smaller Asian currencies might hitch themselves for stability. China recognises this. 'The Chinese are very serious about making the currency convertible,' says Victor Fung, the very well-connected chairman of the Li & Fung group of companies, 'but it will not be done overnight. It will be programmed and gradual, but the direction is very clear. If I were to hazard a guess, I would say it would take five years.'

As the first steps towards weaning itself off its unhealthy dollar dependence, China has to diversify its existing reserves and revalue the renminbi so as to stop accumulating more. But while it is starting to do the former, it has yet to do the latter. Two-thirds of Beijing's $2.4 trillion of foreign reserves are held in bonds issued by the US government and federal agencies. It needs to diversify this stockpile into a wider range of more productive investments – gradually, because if it sold off its dollar assets too quickly, the dollar would plunge. It could buy more euro-denominated assets. It could buy stakes in foreign companies around the world (although other governments may resist, as we shall see in Chapter 7). It could snap up other valuable resources, such as oilfields or iron-ore reserves. But all of this will do little good if it is still piling on more dollar reserves. That is why it is in China's interests to revalue the renminbi. Yes, that would reduce the value of existing reserves in renminbi terms. But the longer Beijing delays the inevitable, the more low-yielding dollar assets it will accumulate, and the bigger its eventual losses will be. Better to cut your losses than compound your errors. Revaluing the renminbi would also help China reduce its dependence on America's faltering consumers and bolster spending by its own consumers, as will be discussed in Chapter 4. China could revalue in small steps, as it did between 2005 and 2008. It might also want to peg the renminbi initially to a broader basket of the currencies of its major trading partners rather than hinging it solely on the dollar. But the ultimate aim should be to make it fully convertible.

For sure, China needs to proceed cautiously. If it threw open its markets to foreign capital, a torrent of cash could bid up the renminbi and Chinese assets to giddy heights. With global investors desperately looking for the next bubble to buy into, China would be an ideal candidate. The sales pitch writes itself: America's toast, China's the future – how could buying into China not be a good idea? Then the bubble would burst, money would pour out and the renminbi would collapse. Alternatively, the renminbi might actually weaken initially as Chinese companies and households rushed to diversify their assets by buying foreign ones. But China does not need to make the leap to full convertibility in one go. It could instead allow its currency to float while maintaining some capital controls, as Chile does. In the meantime, it needs to develop deep and well-regulated domestic financial markets – in particular, for government bonds – so that foreign investors' capital could be safely accommodated. As it loosened capital controls, it would need to keep tabs on credit growth and asset prices to prevent bubbles developing. And it would need to be particularly careful that banks didn't go on a wild borrowing spree. Eventually, it would need to scrap capital controls so that foreigners could invest in renminbi assets and freely repatriate their capital and income.

China is already making baby steps to internationalise the renminbi. It is beginning to settle some of its international trade in its own currency. Foreign banks will be able to buy or borrow renminbi from mainland lenders to finance such trade. 'If you want people to conduct trade in renminbi, you need to have some means for people to hedge [insure themselves against adverse currency moves],' Fung points out. 'And you need to make the supply of renminbi available to the external market.' In June 2009, Russia and China agreed to expand the use of their currencies in bilateral trade; Brazil and China are discussing a similar idea.[12] China is also entering into currency-swap agreements with other countries – Argentina, Belarus, Hong Kong, Indonesia, Malaysia and South Korea – whereby the People's Bank of China will make renminbi available to pay for imports from China if these countries are short of foreign exchange. Hong Kong banks are being allowed to issue renminbi-denominated bonds, a step towards building an international market for the renminbi. And China is providing loans denominated in renminbi to emerging-economy governments and regional development banks – a strategy employed by the Japanese when they were trying to internationalise the use of the yen. The renminbi is likely to be used much more widely in international trade and finance over the next decade as it becomes fully convertible and China's financial markets develop.

Eventually, a convertible renminbi could become an attractive reserve currency, initially for its Asian trading partners and then more widely. It could even form the basis for a pan-Asian currency that would allow East Asia to benefit from the enhanced currency stability and financial integration that the euro-zone enjoys. At the same time, this would, together with the euro, provide much-needed discipline on the dollar. Since foreigners would have a choice, American policy-makers could no longer assume that others had to hold dollars in reserve. They would also, paradoxically, gain greater freedom of action, since the dollar would no longer be the main source of global liquidity.

Reforming the world's monetary and financial arrangements will take time. It requires better national regulations and oversight, closer cooperation among national watchdogs and improved global rules. It also requires strengthened international institutions – in particular a global lender of last resort and ideally a global reserve currency too. It is a tall order. But in the meantime emerging economies can help themselves by developing well-regulated domestic financial systems, pooling their reserves and protecting themselves against the most dangerous forms of global capital. Enlarging the euro and internationalising the renminbi would also help. Ultimately, an improved global financial system is in every country's interests. It would make the world economy more stable. It would boost global demand. It would open up new opportunities for savers in advanced economies and companies in emerging ones. And it is a vital element of preventing the next crisis.

4

Where Next?

Reshaping the world economy

Many countries that relied heavily on exports as a growth strategy are now geared up to provide goods and services to heavily indebted countries that no longer have the will or the means to buy them.

William White, former chief economist of the
Bank for International Settlements, 2009

Tucked away in a nondescript office block on a small street in an uninspiring district of Stockholm is a hidden treasure. AU Holdings is a small Swedish company with big ambitions: to capture the Chinese market for dental alloys, the blend of precious metals used to make fillings. It is run by Darius Stenberg, a twenty-nine-year-old Japanese-speaker who quit university in 2003 to help out at the family firm, AllDental. He has transformed it, broadening its operations, securing a stock-market listing and launching it on the Chinese market. He can't be doing too badly, because he drives a black Ferrari 360 Modena.

China is the world's fastest-growing consumer market. It grew by 8 per cent a year in inflation-adjusted terms in the decade to 2009 – far faster than America's.[1] In the years ahead, as consumers in America, Britain and elsewhere are paying off their debts rather than shopping until they drop, it will become increasingly important. Relative to America's $10-trillion consumer market, China's is still small, at $1.6 trillion.[2] But since China's economy is growing so rapidly and consumption is exceptionally low by international standards, there is plenty of scope for it to grow extremely fast for the foreseeable future. With reforms to tilt China's growth towards higher consumption, the McKinsey Global Institute reckons Chinese consumer spending could top $7.6 trillion by 2025 – or even $9 trillion at a stretch (in 2008 dollars).[3] Even without reform, they think it could account for 18 per cent of global consumption growth over the next fifteen years – rising to more than a quarter with reform. Thus Chinese consumers could help rescue the world from the crisis caused by Americans' excesses. Together with consumers in other emerging economies, they could eventually become the new engine for the world economy. McKinsey reckons that, for instance, Indian consumers' spending could treble to $2.1 trillion by 2025.[4] That would be fantastic for people in emerging economies – and bring big benefits to people in advanced ones.

The Chinese market already offers huge opportunities for foreign businesses and everyone they employ. But the challenge, particularly for smaller companies, is how to break into it. Stenberg is undaunted. 'I'm not that risk-averse,' he says enthusiastically. 'And hard work can eliminate a lot of the risk. Here [in Sweden] you can trust everybody, you know everything works. There you have to check everything. But it's worth it. The opportunities are huge. China has 1.3 billion people. One hundred and fifteen million people a day read the *Beijing Evening News*. If I can place an ad there and capture just 1 per cent of that market, it's huge.'

Similar calculations based on China's huge population have long tempted Western businesspeople. 'As one nineteenth-century Englishman put it, if everyone in China lengthened their shirt tails by a foot, the textile mills of England would spin for a year,' Peter Mandelson recalled when he was the EU's trade commissioner. 'The twenty-first-century version would run: if everyone in China drove a Volkswagen. Or drank Bordeaux. Or had a Barclays bank account. Which they may yet.'[5] (I hope, for the Chinese's sake, that they are spared the horrors of banking with Barclays.)

Until recently, though, China was too poor and its market too closed for those dreams to be realised. That has changed. Over the past three decades, and especially since it joined the WTO in 2001, China has torn down the trade barriers that once surrounded its economy. According to Razeen Sally of the London School of Economics, it is 'the biggest opening of an economy the world has ever seen'.[6] This opening up has gone hand in hand with a spectacular rise in living standards. Average incomes in China rose tenfold between 1980 and 2008, doubling since the turn of the century alone. The ranks of the middle classes with greater disposable incomes have swollen even faster. The number of people in China living on between $2 and $13 a day (adjusted for differences in purchasing power) more than quadrupled from 174 million in 1990 to 806 million in 2005.[7]

As incomes are rising, so is spending. Luxury shopping malls where Louis Vuitton, Prada and Rolex jostle for attention are sprouting up across Shanghai; the world's biggest is in Beijing.[8] Chinese tourists – until recently a rarity – spent $43.7 billion abroad in 2009, a fifth more than the year before; soon, they are likely to be as ubiquitous as the Japanese became in the 1980s.[9] China now has more mobile-phone subscribers than any other country. In 2009, for the first time, the Chinese bought more cars and trucks than Americans did. In the late 1990s only five hundred Chinese residents knew how to ski; in 2008 5 million visited ski resorts.[10] Plenty of teeth need filling too.

China's market is not only expanding fast, it's evolving rapidly. That presents opportunities for fleet-footed start-ups that do not exist in the West's more settled markets. 'Here in Sweden the dental labs all have established suppliers and they don't want to change,' Stenberg says. 'There it's dynamic, people want the best deal, companies are growing and new labs are opening all the time.' He sells in China in two different ways. He exports alloys – which are like tiny metal bars that dentists melt to mould into fillings for individual teeth – from his premises in Stockholm; he also sells those made at his facilities in Beijing. Chinese import tariffs on dental alloys are low – less than 5 per cent, he says.

While he reckons that producing in China is around 20 per cent cheaper than in Sweden, its main attraction is that it enables him to bypass the complex rules governing the export of precious metals and medical products. But operating in China has its difficulties too. Security is a very big issue – Stenberg uses cameras and computerised monitoring systems to ensure that the alloys are not stolen – as is quality control. Whereas many foreign firms that produce in China have contracted out their operations to suppliers that they may be unable to monitor effectively, Stenberg keeps production in house. Perhaps the biggest struggle is coping with the vagaries of Chinese bureaucracy. 'It is a long, costly and uncertain process that creates uncertainty throughout the business,' he says. It helps that AllDental's Chinese operations are run by a Chinese manager who previously lived in Sweden for eleven years. 'He speaks Mandarin and Swedish, and understands how both the Chinese and the Swedes think and work.'

AllDental is already among the three biggest brands for dental alloys in China, which accounts for a third of the company's profits. Stenberg is leveraging his Chinese experience to start another venture in a seemingly unrelated field. Through a new company called Findads (as in 'find ads'), he has just launched in

China and other countries a new search engine called Wakazaka. With 230 million (and rising) registered users, China is already the world's biggest internet market. Findads will also own and develop webpages and outsource programming work to China.[11] A serial entrepreneur, Stenberg reasons that if he starts ten projects, seven will not succeed, two will do OK and one will work very well. Good luck to him!

Stenberg is not alone in profiting from the Chinese market. Spain's Inditex, which makes and retails fashionable clothing at low prices, notably under the Zara brand, is planning to open around half of its new stores in Asia 'with the emphasis on China', according to Pablo Isla, its chief executive. It has also signed a joint-venture with India's Tata group to roll out the Zara franchise there from 2010. Who would have thought that a European company could sell affordable clothes to China and India?

Another huge growth market is housing. China is planning to build four hundred million new homes over the next twenty years. Yes, that's twenty million homes a year for the foreseeable future. So it is not just a huge potential market for building materials, cement and so on, but also for household goods, furnishings and countless other products. If the Chinese embrace the joys of spending the weekend at IKEA and then battling to assemble their flat-packed furniture, it could be a bonanza for the Swedish company – and many others.

As it develops, China will become a vast market for consumer imports. But it is already having a massive impact on the global economy through the imports it needs to fuel its rapidly expanding production. It buys huge volumes of parts and components from East Asian economies, commodities and other raw materials from Australia, Africa, Latin America and elsewhere, and capital goods such as industrial machinery from Germany, combine harvesters from America, locomotives from Canada and engines from Britain. Foreign companies can also sell their expertise directly. 'Australia is one of the few countries in the world that has the capacity to take cars from concept to show-room,' explains Simon Crean, then Australia's trade minister. 'We have all the skills but a very small market. China knows it lacks all the skills but it has a very large market. And as it's developing beyond joint-venture operations to its own branded capability and its consolidation, it's looking for those skills.'

China's imports have rocketed over the past decade. Its pur-chases from developing countries in Asia soared from $12.3 billion in 1999 to $126.6 billion in 2008.[12] In its hunger for Africa's vast natural resources, it has become the continent's most important trading partner after America; its imports from Africa shot up from $2.3 billion in 1999 to $54.7 billion in 2008.[13] China leaped from being South Africa's fifth-biggest trading partner in 2008 to its largest in 2009.[14] Its imports from Latin America and the Caribbean surged from $2.9 billion in 1999 to $71.8 billion in 2008[15] – and in the first six months of 2009, it became Brazil's biggest export market for the first time. China's huge demand for imports is a big reason why developing economies have grown so fast in recent years, lifting millions out of poverty and giving millions more a better life.

Advanced economies are benefiting too. Britain's exports to China multiplied four and a half times between 1999 and 2008, America's five and a half times and Germany's nearly seven-fold.[16] That understates China's boost to advanced economies' exports, because they also sold more to countries such as Brazil that have grown richer by trading with China. Among the British businesspeople making a success of selling to China is Ian Lomax of Leeds-based ATB Morley. His company serves a niche market: it designs and manufactures electric motors for coal-cutting equipment. A company like that can only succeed by exporting, and China is its biggest market. 'Half of what we do ends up in China,' Lomax says. 'China is the biggest coal pro-ducer in the world but their domestic technology is one step behind ours.' In the 1980s, ATB Morley sold 98 per cent of its motors to the coal industry in Britain. But as the domestic industry shrivelled, the company sought salvation by selling abroad. 'Exporting to China rescued us when all our coal mines were being shut.' It now has a fifth of the Chinese market, the world's largest, and most of Australia's too. Its revenues have doubled, to £16 million, since 2002 and it provides good jobs for two hundred people. Thanks to the resilience of the Chinese economy (and the support it has provided to Australia's), ATB Morley is one part of British manufacturing that has been largely unscathed by the recession.

Westerners often wonder gloomily where tomorrow's jobs will come from. Increasingly, they will come from selling to China and other emerging economies. So instead of worrying that China is going to take everyone's jobs, people should be looking to the huge opportunities that its growth offers – and, like Darius Stenberg, go out and grab them. But while emerging economies' imports will almost certainly continue to grow fast in the years ahead, will they expand fast enough to fill the gap left by Americans and others tightening their belts? That is the trillion-dollar question on which the world economy's prospects for recovery rest. The answer depends in large part on whether politicians try to resist the necessary changes to the global economy or embrace them.

Lasting pain

Whatever happens next, advanced economies have already suffered their worst recession since the 1930s. In the twelve months to June 2009, Canada's economy shrank by 3.2 per cent, America's by 3.9 per cent, the euro-zone's by 4.7 per cent, Britain's by 5.5 per cent, Sweden's by 6 per cent, Japan's by 6.4 per cent and Ireland's by 7.4 per cent. Only Australia escaped a recession; despite a brief dip, the economy expanded by 0.6 per cent.

Some emerging economies have fared much worse. Russia's economy fell 10.9 per cent, Ukraine's 17.8 per cent, Latvia's 18.7 per cent, Lithuania's a terrifying 22.4 per cent. Schools are being shuttered, hospitals boarded up, social care slashed. In Latin America, Mexico was worst hit, in part owing to its proximity to the US, but also because of swine flu. Its economy was 10.3 per cent smaller. But Brazil's recession was short and shallow: its economy dipped 1.2 per cent in the year to June 2009, and rebounded sharply between March and June. South Africa's contracted by 2.8 per cent.

East Asia's export-led economies have rebounded like a bungee-jumper: they fell off a cliff in the last three months of 2008 and the first three of 2009, but bounced back in the second quarter of 2009. That left South Korea's economy only 2.5 per cent smaller than a year earlier, while Singapore's was down 3.5 per cent and Thailand's a heftier 4.9 per cent. Those falls are smaller than during the 1997–8 crisis.

Meanwhile, a handful of emerging economies have continued to grow fast. Indonesia is up 4 per cent, Vietnam 4.5 per cent, India 6.1 per cent and China 7.9 per cent. This resilience is partly due to the strength of their underlying growth, but also thanks to China's huge fiscal stimulus, which was launched in early November 2008, well before advanced economies introduced their own much-smaller moves. Beijing's quick reactions stabilised China's economy and gave a big boost to all the economies that export to it.

The blow to jobs is huge. In rich countries, 15 million jobs were lost between the end of 2007 and July 2009 according to the Organisation for Economic Co-operation and Development (OECD), a think-tank for rich-country governments.[17] From a twenty-five-year low of 5.6 per cent in 2007, the unemployment rate in the OECD surged to a post-war high of 8.8 per cent in

November 2009. Worst hit were the US, where joblessness more than doubled to 10 per cent in December 2009, Ireland where it trebled to 12.5 per cent and Spain where it doubled to an eye-watering 19.4 per cent (in November 2009). The rise has been more muted in Britain, where it reached 7.9 per cent (in the three months to October 2009). In emerging economies, the increase in unemployment has been much smaller, with the notable exception of Central and Eastern Europe.

The enduring burdens are the mountains of debt that consumers in many countries accumulated during the boom and that governments are piling up during the bust. Whereas in the bubble years growth in America, Britain, Ireland, Spain and elsewhere was supercharged by consumers borrowing to live beyond their means, in the years ahead it will be crimped by consumers saving more to pay down their debts – and, eventually, higher taxes. The longer economies remain in the doldrums and people on the dole, the more likely that their output and jobs will be lost for good. Skills are lost, companies collapse, plants and machinery are scrapped.

Previous financial crises left lasting scars. An IMF study of the consequences of eighty-eight banking crises in advanced, emerging and developing economies over the past forty years found that output per person tends to fall by around 10 per cent relative to its pre-crisis trend. The lost output is not recovered. Unemployment persists and crunched credit depresses investment. But a fiscal stimulus and reforms to help the economy adjust more rapidly can mitigate the losses. Growth does eventually tend to return to its pre-crisis pace.[18]

The aftershocks of this huge crisis are likely to be particularly severe. The problem is not just a lack of demand. It is a distorted pattern of supply.

The world economy remains geared towards resuming the old, unbalanced, unsustainable pattern of growth. Look around you. Britain's high streets are littered with banks, building societies, estate agents and other sharks that fed off the credit bubble. America is awash with empty houses, boarded-up shops and eerily quiet shopping malls. Wall Street and the City of London are crowded with bloated banks cranking up to generate often-unnecessary financial engineering. China's coastal regions are cluttered with factories primed to churn out consumer goods for American homes. Germany is full of idle car factories tooled up to make gas-guzzlers for which there is no longer enough demand. Japan has still not worked off the excesses of its own bubble two decades ago. For now, the focus is all on recovery, any recovery, at any cost. But unless the world economy shifts to a new, more balanced, more sustainable pattern of growth, the recovery is likely to be weak, lopsided and pave the way for another crisis.

The bad, old pattern of growth was driven by the seemingly insatiable debt-fuelled demands of American (and other) consumers. In crude terms, Americans borrowed and spent, while the Chinese produced and lent. But for now, America's anxious and overindebted consumers are no longer willing or able to continue spending like there is no tomorrow. Their incomes are stagnant (or falling), their house and shares are worth less, they are terrified of losing their job (and their health insurance) and in any case banks won't lend any more. Dawn has broken, and it feels more like dusk.

The big fall in American consumer spending is the main reason why global demand has collapsed. Left unchecked, this would have caused a depression: since one person's spending is another's income, if everyone tries to cut back at once, a vicious spiral ensues as falling production chases falling consumption downwards. So governments had to step in to try to fill the gap. In the G20 as a whole, budget deficits swung from 1.1 per cent of the group's GDP in 2007 to 8.1 per cent in 2009.[19] Britain's deficit ballooned from 2.6 per cent of GDP in 2007 to 11.6 per cent in 2009; America's from 2.8 per cent to 12.5 per cent.

Interest rates were also slashed to zero and buckets of money printed.

Governments have halted the freefall. But they have also made many mistakes. Some policies do little good; others will prolong the pain at huge expense. On the monetary side, interest-rate cuts were essential, but printing money without fixing the banking system is at best pointless and at worst reckless. If banks are broken, they won't lend. So either fix them or bypass them by lending directly to sound companies.

On the fiscal side, stimulus packages were also vital, but many governments tried to flog a dead horse rather than investing in a new one. An effective fiscal stimulus should be timely, targeted and temporary. Yet America's was late and Britain's particularly poorly targeted. In countries where consumers are overloaded with debt, bribing them to spend more is wrong-headed – on specific products, such as cars, doubly so. Britain's VAT cut was like trying to cure a drug addict by giving him another fix. America's cash-for-clunkers scheme was particularly bad: it subsidised overextended consumers to keep spending and an industry with huge overcapacity to keep producing. Germany's mistake was not that it encouraged consumers to spend; it was giving them handouts to buy cars in particular.

Everywhere the priorities should instead have been maintaining employment (but not specific jobs), protecting the vulnerable and investing in healthier patterns of future growth. Germany is subsidising the wages of employees who agree to work shorter hours – a measure copied by many other countries. By June 2009 more than 1.4 million Germans (many of them car workers) were on government-sponsored short time. But while such measures keep a lid on unemployment in the short term, they also stymie workers in yesterday's jobs from shifting to tomorrow's. Not only does this keep open some companies that ought to close, it deters workers from looking elsewhere. Why change jobs if you can earn 80 per cent of a full-time wage working only half of the time? Slashing payroll taxes (known as national-insurance contributions in Britain and social-security contributions in other countries) would boost disposable incomes and support overall employment, without trying to protect specific jobs at the expense of others. (This is such a good idea that it ought to be implemented permanently, as Chapter 11 argues.)

Cushioning the blow on the vulnerable is humane and also supports spending. In most of Europe, the incomes of the poor and the unemployed are automatically cushioned by the welfare state; in Britain, where support is less generous, exceptional extra payments could have been made. In America, where the safety net is threadbare, much greater emergency welfare spending should have been authorised.

The best way for governments to increase demand is through spending that encourages economic adjustment and boosts the potential for future growth. In all countries, governments could provide subsidies to workers – those still in jobs, as well as the unemployed – to retrain and acquire new skills, as Denmark does. In Britain and America, bringing forward and increasing investment in their crumbling infrastructure would put idle hands in construction to work, help shift the balance of the economy away from consumption towards investment and boost the economy's growth potential. Better transport networks, in particular, would boost exports. It is also a priority in emerging economies, where infrastructure struggles to keep pace with growing needs. But while China is investing 1.5 trillion yuan ($219 billion) of its 4-trillion-yuan stimulus package on transport – including $90 billion a year on railways for two years – America earmarked a paltry $8 billion for high-speed rail. (Britain is hoping for a high-speed rail link between London and Scotland by 2030.[20]) Japan, though, does not need more bridges to nowhere. In Germany and Japan, the priority should have been encouraging consumption – they, rather than Britain, ought to have cut VAT.

While subsidies to specific industries are generally a mistake, governments could have anticipated a global agreement to curb greenhouse-gas emissions by funnelling cash to promising clean-tech companies and to households investing in energy-efficiency and other eco-friendly measures. To its credit, the Obama administration is doing quite a bit of this. In Britain, where social housing is scarce and often shoddy, the government could have spent more to improve existing homes and build new ones. Conversely, in Spain, where there is a housing glut, providing funds to build low-cost housing was unhelpful. But what's done is done. Countries must live with their governments' recent mistakes. Unfortunately, they will make the challenge of reshaping the economy along healthier new lines trickier.

While global demand remains well short of global supply, governments must continue to fill some of the gap. This implies running up huge debts of their own. Government debt in advanced G20 economies is set to balloon from just 79 per cent of GDP in 2007 to 110 per cent in 2010, according to the IMF.[21] In America and Britain, the national debt is skyrocketing. These debts would be more manageable if governments had not been so lavish in bailing out the banks and their creditors. But tightening government belts prematurely is counterproductive. So long as companies are not keen to invest, government borrowing does not crowd out private endeavour. And if the recovery is not yet on a sustainable footing, pulling the rug from under it through tax hikes and spending cuts could cause it to relapse. Tightening too soon could swell government deficits rather than curbing them. Eventually, though, the deficits must shrink. In part this will happen automatically as the recovery boosts tax receipts and reduces welfare rolls. Governments must also prune their spending, pluck more taxes and reconsider what they should be doing and how, as is discussed in Chapter 11. The important point is that governments cannot – and should not try – to pile on debt for ever.

Until a more sustainable engine of growth emerges, advanced economies are likely to stutter along, as Japan's has done since its bubble popped in the early 1990s. They may have bursts of growth, but not a durable recovery. Eventually, growth will come from developing and investing in new ideas and businesses that enhance productivity. Thankfully, companies are not as overloaded with debts as households are. But since banks are not lending and companies lack the confidence to invest, this growth will take time. And if governments continue to borrow huge amounts when the economy picks up, they will drive up interest rates and starve growing companies of capital. In the meantime, the most obvious place to fill the shortfall demand is from abroad – from emerging economies where there is plenty of pent-up consumer demand and from mature ones, such as Germany and Japan, which consume much less than other advanced economies.

Out of kilter

In the decade between the crisis that began in Asia and the one that started in America, the world economy tilted dangerously off its axis. America's big bubbles and others' smaller ones distorted the entire global economy. Soaring oil prices added to the dangerous imbalances that developed, while emerging economies' understandable desire to pile up currency reserves to insure themselves against a repeat of the Asian crisis was also a factor. Americans and others lived increasingly beyond their means, while Asians and oil exporters saved a big chunk of their export earnings, amassing vast reserves, often in the form of US government bonds. The crisis has shrunk these imbalances, but there is a danger they will grow again as the economy recovers.

In 1997 America paid out $140 billion more to foreigners

than it received from them. This current-account deficit, equivalent to 1.7 per cent of GDP, swelled to $788 billion, or 5.9 per cent of GDP, in 2006.[22] The current account measures the balance between what a country is saving and what it is investing. A deficit implies that it is spending more than it is earning – and so is borrowing from foreigners (or selling off its foreign assets) in order to do so.

That is not necessarily a problem. Briefly borrowing big amounts is fine. Borrowing reasonable amounts for longer is fine too – provided the foreign funds are channelled into profitable investments whose returns exceed the cost of foreign borrowing, and so long as this external finance isn't suddenly withdrawn. But in America's case the borrowing was not just huge and prolonged, it also reflected a fall in savings rather than an increase in productive investment. In part this is because American consumers were on a bubble-fuelled spending spree that sucked in loads of imports. Consumer spending and residential investment soared from 71 per cent of American GDP in 1997 to more than 75 per cent in 2006. The US accounted for around a third of the increase in global consumption between 2000 and 2006.[23] The personal saving rate plunged from 4.6 per cent of disposable income in 1997 to a mere 1.2 per cent in the first quarter of 2008.

The US government also played its part. The Bush administration funded its huge tax cuts and the massive costs of the wars in Afghanistan and Iraq, as well as increased spending in other areas, through borrowing. From broad balance when Bill Clinton left office in 2001, the budget deficit swelled to 4.8 per cent of GDP in 2003. Even in 2006, at the height of the boom, when tax receipts were bulging and a prudent government ought to have been running a surplus, the deficit was 2.2 per cent of GDP. Thus it was a combination of private and public profligacy that caused America's foreign borrowing to rocket. Cumulatively, between 1997 and 2008 Americans borrowed

$6 trillion from abroad, equivalent to 42 per cent of their income in 2007.

From a global perspective, America's massive deficits mattered most. But from a national perspective, the deficits in Britain, Spain, Australia, Ireland and other countries were also worrying because they reflected a similarly unsustainable consumption boom. Britain's current-account deficit bulged from less than $2 billion in 1997 to a whopping $83 billion (3.4 per cent of GDP) in 2006. In total, Britons spent nearly $500 billion more than they earned between 1997 and 2008, equivalent to 18 per cent of their income in 2008. Again, the government is partly responsible. In Labour's second term Gordon Brown went on a borrowing-financed spending spree. A budget surplus in 2001 became a deficit of 3.3 per cent of GDP in 2005 that remained large in subsequent years. Spain's current account shifted from broad balance to an even bigger deficit of $145 billion (10.1 per cent of GDP) in 2007. Australia's deficit also rocketed, to $57 billion (6.3 per cent of GDP). Ireland's current account swung from balance in 2000 to a deficit of 5.4 per cent of GDP in 2007.

Since one country's borrowing is another's lending – clever financiers have not yet worked out how to ring up credit with outer space – these vast deficits were matched by equally large surpluses elsewhere. (At least in principle. In practice, such are the deficiencies of international statistics that they do not add up. In 2001 the world was officially running a current-account deficit of $161 billion. By 2007 this had become a surplus of $244 billion. Perhaps we are trading with aliens after all.)

From 1997 until 2001 America's swelling current-account deficit was largely matched by a swing from deficit to surplus in emerging economies, notably those devastated by the crisis of 1997–8. China's surplus shrank from $37 billion to $17 billion. But after 2001 the picture changed dramatically. As America's deficit continued to grow, huge surpluses developed, first in Japan and Germany, then in oil-exporting countries and later in China. By 2007 China had a surplus of $372 billion (11 per cent of GDP), Germany $250 billion (7.5 per cent of GDP) and Japan $211 billion (4.8 per cent of GDP), while Saudi Arabia's was $96 billion (25.9 per cent of GDP) and Russia's $76 billion (5.9 per cent of GDP).

Oil-exporting countries amassed the biggest surpluses. After 2002, when the oil price began to rise, their combined surplus surged from $85.5 billion in 2002 to $503.9 billion in 2006, the year in which the US deficit peaked.[24] By 2008 it had reached $672 billion. Between them, oil exporters rang up $2.8 trillion in surpluses between 2000 and 2008, compared with China's $1.4 trillion, Japan's $1.3 trillion and Germany's $1 trillion. Clearly, oil exporters' growing surplus partly reflected booming global demand. But the OPEC cartel's role in restricting supply to drive prices up cannot be ignored. The deficits in America and other countries would have been much smaller were it not for OPEC.

These global imbalances were clearly unsustainable. Countries cannot live beyond their means indefinitely. Eventually, foreigners are no longer willing to lend any more. Developing countries often exhaust their credit quickly and suddenly. But advanced economies enjoy greater capacity to borrow. Their people are richer, their governments more trusted, and they are generally able to borrow in their own currency – a huge advantage, as we saw in Chapter 3 – so their ability to repay is not threatened by a sudden loss of confidence in their currency. The United States enjoys an additional privilege: most global trade is denominated in dollars, so countries need its currency to conduct commerce with others; its financial markets are the world's largest, so foreigners have a huge appetite for dollars in order to invest in American shares and bonds, or to buy US companies outright; American government bonds are viewed as the lowest-risk – and most liquid – global investment; and most importantly, the dollar is the currency that foreign central banks prefer to hold in reserve for a rainy day.

The growing global imbalances had many economists worried. Restoring balance to the world economy was essential, policy-makers insisted with furrowed brows. G7 statements were penned, the IMF charged with monitoring the situation, countries coaxed to change their ways. Some, notably Nouriel Roubini of New York University – who was dubbed 'Dr Doom' – warned that investors could suddenly lose their appetite for American assets, prompting a dollar rout and a brutal readjustment of the world economy. But for years very little happened. The dollar drifted downwards and China allowed its currency to rise, but America's deficit and China's surplus continued to swell. With their economies growing strongly, neither the US nor China seriously thought it was in their interest to change course.

When the crisis eventually struck, it was not the one that Roubini and others had predicted. It was not a sudden stop of foreign financing that struck the US economy; it was the bursting of its property bubble and the ensuing banking crisis. Nor did the dollar plunge and US interest rates leap. On the contrary: as panic spread around the world in late 2008, investors sought refuge in the relative security of US Treasuries, strengthening the dollar and driving down American interest rates. The imbalances turned out to be more symptoms of the real problem – America's financial bubble – than the source of it. At most they were a contributory factor.

The crisis has roughly halved the world's gaping imbalances from their peak. America's current-account deficit declined to 2.7 per cent of GDP in 2009, Britain's to 1.1 per cent.[25] China's surplus was 6 per cent of GDP, Germany's 4.9 per cent, Japan's 2.8 per cent in 2009.[26] Oil exporters' surpluses have declined since oil prices plunged from their giddy heights of nearly $150 a barrel in late summer 2008. This adjustment has mostly occurred not through currency moves, but because collapsing demand in America has hit US imports – and thus others' exports – particularly hard.

Even so, the imbalances remain large – and the worry is that they will grow again as economies pick up. Soaring oil prices would swell oil exporters' surpluses and push up oil consumers' import bill. And unless the world economy reduces its dependence on American demand, growth will remain unbalanced. 'I'm still worried that the world is stuck in this unbalanced growth paradigm where it's desperate for another fix from the American consumer and Asian producers are unwilling to give way to their consumers in their economies,' says Stephen Roach. 'We desperately need a better balance in the global economy. If this is a recovery that ends up resurrecting the old imbalances, then I'm still going to be very concerned. It just means the next crisis will be worse than this one.' If the imbalances inflate again, the world may finally suffer the dollar crisis that many economists have long expected.

Dangers ahead

A sustainable recovery requires a thorough overhaul of the world economy to cater to new, more balanced and healthier patterns of growth. This involves a profound change in people's behaviour, a restructuring of the corporate landscape and a shake-up of government policies. Americans and Britons need to rediscover the virtues of living within their means, rather than wrongly viewing their homes as cash machines. Germans and Japanese need to give in more to the joys of consumption, rather than continually squirrelling away nuts for a rainy day – storms don't come much bigger than this. Economies dominated by housing and finance need to invest in more productive sectors. Those where exporters hold sway need to invest in sectors that service domestic consumers' needs. Everywhere governments should tackle the obstacles that prevent businesses and people from adjusting – gummed-up labour markets, entrenched producer interests, barriers to innovation and enterprise, misaligned currencies. Opening up further to international trade, investment and people flows would also help. At the same time, they must intervene where markets fail – shake up finance, encourage greener technologies, help people retrain and find new jobs, and make it safe for emerging economies to tap global capital markets.

The new opportunities are huge. But when people and countries are set in their ways, change can be difficult and slow. The bubble mentality is hard to break, as are deeply engrained saving habits. Dominant financial interests in the Anglo-Saxon world and export ones in Germany, Japan and Asia will fight reform tooth and nail. Governments may duck difficult reforms and pander to powerful lobbies. In any case, it takes time to pay down debts, retrain people and reinvest capital.

Four big dangers loom. The first is stagnation. Until the necessary adjustments and reforms are made and bear fruit, growth in advanced economies will remain weak. While low interest rates ought to encourage businesses to invest in future growth, they will not do so if potential markets – notably in emerging economies and cleaner technologies – remain stifled and sources of capital scarce. Sluggish growth would make debts harder to pay off, keep unemployment high and maintain government deficits large. Prolonged pain could provoke political extremism, protectionism and prejudice. Slow growth in advanced economies would also crimp emerging ones' expansion unless they fire up domestic demand. But while lower exports would slow their growth, it would doubtless still be much bouncier than in America and Europe because their underlying potential for productivity gains is so huge.

The second, related danger is beggar-thy-neighbour policies.

Instead of expanding the total pie, countries may try to grow by grabbing a bigger slice of the existing one. But since there is only so much pie to go around, they cannot all succeed. On the contrary, if countries tear each other to pieces for their share of the scraps, they will all end up worse off. Beggar-thy-neighbour policies can take many forms: higher import tariffs, anti-dumping duties, subsidies for domestic producers, protectionist standards and regulations, and 1930s-style competitive devaluations – pushing a currency down in order to price a country's exports into foreign markets. Such moves are provocative in boom times, and potentially explosive when economies are stagnant or shrinking. They could trigger a global trade war that ends up beggaring everyone.

The third big danger is soaring government debt. If private demand remains weak, the state may continue to fill the gap. While investors' limited appetite for many governments' debt will impose some belt-tightening as the economy stabilises America's capacity to borrow is far greater. The Congressional Budget Office projects that the cumulative deficit for 2010–19 will be $4.4 trillion, while other respected analysts think it could exceed $10 trillion.[27] While some of this could be funded by increasing personal saving, a lot would no doubt be financed by foreign borrowing. So long as the Chinese and other investors are willing to accumulate US Treasuries, this can go on for quite a while (although not indefinitely). In effect, the US government would be taking over where American consumers left off, running up huge debts to prop up American (and global) demand. America's current-account deficit would grow again, providing a red rag to protectionists. If investors eventually took fright at soaring debt levels, they would bid up interest rates, making it trickier for governments to balance the books – and ultimately threatening a debt and currency crisis. Greece's difficulties are a warning shot for other governments with unsustainable finances.

The fourth danger is that global growth will be relaunched by inflating new bubbles. Wouldn't it be so much easier for higher share and property prices to restore household wealth rather than having to go through the drag of scrimping and saving to pay down debts? Just print money and wish all your cares away. Consumers could quickly find their feet, financiers could go back to coining it, exporters could crank up their factories again. This time would, of course, be different. It wouldn't be a nasty old bubble, it would be a shiny new recovery. Already many asset prices are looking overinflated for these depressed times, while central bankers are primed to repeat their old mistakes. But this would pave the way towards an even more devastating bust.

The high spirits of the bubble years have evaporated. But while the music has stopped and the drinks are no longer flowing, the sore-headed partygoers are all dressed up with nowhere to go. They need to find better things to do. Instead they may just stand around, fight over the few remaining bottles of booze, raid their parents' drinks cabinet until it too runs dry, or find another way to get the party started again. To avert these four dangers, it is vital that policy-makers assist, rather than impede, the world economy's adjustment to a more balanced pattern of growth.

Economies adjust

One of markets' huge strengths is that they adjust. Price changes signal that resources could be more profitably used elsewhere and a million individual decisions make it happen. National economies – and the world economy even more so – are far too complex for anybody to divine what needs to change, let alone force billions of disparate individuals and companies to implement their plans. Left to their own devices, markets – people – will do lots of the heavy lifting necessary to reshape the global economy. For instance, many Americans don't need to be commanded to save more or have their spending controlled: prudence will lead them to do so. People in emerging economies will spend if given the opportunity. Most businesspeople don't need to be ordered to shutter loss-making factories: self-interest will make them do so. Give entrepreneurs free rein and they will build the industries of the future. The surest way to achieve a recovery is to accept that the world has moved on and to embrace change.

Flexible economies can adjust faster and more readily. That is one reason for optimism about America's prospects. Despite its many flaws, its exceptionally adaptable economy is capable of rapidly redeploying resources from bloated industries to burgeoning ones. Britain's flexible labour markets also put it in good stead. But many continental European economies – such as Germany and France – are much more inflexible. Industries that ought to shrink outstay their welcome, stunting the growth of emerging ones and needlessly raising unemployment. Many French people howl, take to the streets, kidnap their boss or even commit suicide at the first hint of factory closures. Small businesses are throttled by high taxes and regulations. Germany has the discipline to cut costs but not the suppleness to change course. Starting a business there is notoriously difficult. Since economies are forever changing – and a particularly significant shift is happening now – rigidity is a big weakness. Protecting yesterday's jobs at the expense of tomorrow's is not safe, social democratic or caring; it is the triumph of reactionary dogma over progressive pragmatism. As Denmark's example shows, and Chapter 11 argues, greater flexibility can go hand in hand with security for workers.

All countries should pursue reforms that boost competition and promote greater flexibility. Complete the WTO's Doha Round of world-trade talks. Throw open markets unilaterally. Welcome greater foreign investment. Loosen restrictions on foreign workers. Crack down on dominant companies. Tear up regulations that cosset incumbents and insiders. Allow loss-making factories to close. So that companies are more willing to hire, make it easier to fire. Help people learn new skills and find new jobs. Make it easier to start new businesses. Cut through red tape that holds small companies back. Foster links between universities, businesses and venture capitalists to emulate Silicon Valley's dynamism. Encourage openness to new ideas and fresh ways of doing things.

Allowing markets to adjust and helping them to work better will go a long way. But the world cannot rely on markets alone to make the necessary adjustment. Sometimes they send out the wrong signals. In other cases, their signals are obscured or blocked. Where markets send out misleading messages, governments can try to correct them. Inevitably, their efforts will be imperfect. Unavoidably, these will have other unfortunate side-effects. But when markets fail spectacularly, governments must step in – as judiciously as possible. Since markets fail to put a price on greenhouse-gas emissions, governments must. This will cause carbon-belching industries to shrink and stimulate the development of new cleaner technologies, as Chapter 10 argues. It could create a boom in clean-tech companies and green jobs – everything from wind farms to home insulation.

Future finance

Fixing the banks, along the lines suggested in Chapter 2, is a pre-condition for a healthy and sustainable recovery. Until lending to sound borrowers resumes, growth will be stunted. If existing banks won't lend, governments should create new banks that will. Nationalised banks could be commandeered to that end. At the same time, the financial sector needs to continue to shrink. But how can it lend more to healthy companies if it is slimming down? By instead slashing all the unproductive and often harmful lending among financial institutions that helped cause the crisis. If finance is allowed to supersize again as the economy recovers, it will crowd out other activities. It will suck in clever people who could be starting the next Google, finding a cure for cancer or coming up with new policies to help the poor. It will capture profits from more productive industries that could be gainfully reinvested instead of doled out as bonuses. And it will make another crisis all but inevitable.

Removing the government guarantees and other subsidies that artificially bloat banks will naturally cut them down to size. But where does that leave financial hubs such as New York and London – and indeed finance-heavy economies more broadly? 'In the overdeveloped world, the financial sector's going to contract everywhere,' Willem Buiter predicts. 'But London will contract more than most, partly because it was more overgrown than most, partly because the retrenchment and repatriation of cross-border banking will inevitably hit a global financial centre like London more than a primarily domestically focused one.'

Should a country like Britain try to attract as much international banking business as possible? Only if proper safeguards are in place. The danger is that financial centres will compete for business by offering recklessly lax regulations. That would be short-sighted, especially for a medium-sized economy such as Britain. The UK's top financial regulator, Adair Turner, was absolutely right to say that the Financial Services Authority (FSA) 'has to be very, very wary of seeing the competitiveness of London as a major aim'.[28] Just as Northern Rock was foolish to try to grab a bigger chunk of the mortgage market by offering 125 per cent mortgages to all and sundry, London would be mad to recklessly pursue market share. Compete on the basis of London's other merits, not by being a soft touch.

Buiter goes further. He argues that Britain needs to adopt the euro for London to remain a global financial centre. 'This crisis makes it clear that you can't be a global financial centre with a local currency,' he says. 'So I think London's position not just globally but also in Europe will be under threat if the UK sticks with sterling.' In any case, London and New York are likely to lose market share to Asia's financial centres – such as Hong Kong, Singapore and eventually Shanghai – as the centre of gravity of the world economy shifts east. Whereas finance is overdeveloped in most advanced economies, it remains underdeveloped in most emerging ones. They need to do more to nurture well-regulated domestic financial markets.

Manufacturing myths

Judicious reforms and market incentives will tilt the world economy towards a greener, more stable, less finance-driven future. But should governments also try to favour particular types of activity, notably manufacturing? As part of a backlash against the illusory profits of ethereal finance, politicians are increasingly keen to encourage the production of 'real' things that you can drop on your foot. 'The fight for American manufacturing is the fight for America's future,' says President Obama. 'We need less financial engineering and a lot more real engineering,' said Peter Mandelson, then Britain's business secretary and Gordon Brown's deputy in all but name. This is music to manufacturers' ears. So far, though, it is mostly rhetoric. But is a new industrial policy needed and could it be effective?

Where the market fails, governments can sometimes help. Among other things, they can fund basic research at universities, offer help to small businesses that banks neglect and provide information where gaps exist. Most importantly, they can help all businesses – and small ones in particular – by reducing red tape and burdensome taxes that hold them back. They should also encourage enterprise and widen opportunity. But should governments favour certain industries and businesses over others?

Many people argue that manufacturing is especially important. It once provided millions of relatively well-paid jobs in Britain and America – and still does in Germany and, to a lesser extent, Japan. It was 'the pillar on which we built the middle class', says Thea Lee, policy director for the American Federation of Labor and Congress of Industrial Organizations (AFL-CIO), the country's biggest trade-union federation, 'and it is hard to see how you rebuild the middle class without reviving manufacturing'.[29] It accounts for the lion's share of global exports, and thus helps pay for desirable imports. There is also something reassuringly 'real', solid and measurable about making things. Better still, productivity tends to grow much faster in manufacturing than in services – so wouldn't the economy be better off if there were more of it around?

Not so fast. It is precisely because productivity growth in manufacturing is so rapid that it tends to account for a reduced share of the economy over time – and an even smaller share of employment. Agriculture once employed nearly everyone, but even though people in rich countries eat much more than before, farmers are so much more productive now that we need only a few of them to feed us all. During Britain's Industrial Revolution in the eighteenth and nineteenth centuries, rising agricultural productivity released farmers from the land for more productive work in urban factories. More recently, that is what has driven most of China's growth over the past thirty years. Over time, factories have become far more efficient too. Car plants once employed throngs of people on assembly lines. Visit one now and you will see hardly anyone around: production is mostly automated and requires only a handful of workers to supervise it. So even if demand for cars remained buoyant, in time the numbers employed to make them would tend to shrink. In Germany, which specialises in industrial exports and cars in particular, manufacturing accounted for a bigger share of the economy in 2007 (23.9 per cent) than in 2000 (22.9 per cent).[30]

Over that period value added in manufacturing grew by a whopping 22 per cent. Yet employment in manufacturing fell by 7 per cent. Whereas in 2000 it accounted for 20.7 per cent of all jobs, in 2007 it made up only 19 per cent of them. Even in China, the workshop of the world, employment in manufacturing was lower in 2006 than a decade earlier (although it was rising after 2002).[31]

In rich countries, productivity gains in manufacturing have outpaced people's demand to accumulate ever more stuff. So workers have shifted to satisfying other needs, by providing a vast – and so far limitless – range of services. Service jobs are often dismissed as burger-flipping 'McJobs', but since people value the convenience of fast food, even McDonald's employees are providing a valuable service. Since they choose to work there, they presumably find it preferable to the alternatives. Besides, since its hamburgers are prepared on what resembles an industrial assembly line, perhaps their jobs should be reclassified as manufacturing ones. Conversely, many 'good' jobs in manufacturing are in fact service-related. Most people who work for car companies are now employed in service activities such as design, marketing and finance. Often the service component of a manufactured product is the most valuable part: for instance, designing and branding iPhones is more profitable than making them.

The prejudice in favour of manufacturing and against services is unwarranted. Is caring for the young, the old or the sick really less valuable than making cars? Is teaching less worthy than making televisions? Is being a plumber less important than making pipes? Is working for Google less useful than making computers? And while some people are happy to work in factories, others prefer clean, quiet, safe offices. Manufacturing – or farming for that matter – should not be dismissed, but nor should it be put on a pedestal. The belief that the rest of the economy is particularly dependent on manufacturing is misplaced: everything depends on everything else. Every producer is also a consumer – car workers need food to eat and doctors to look after them, and so on. And many goods are only valuable thanks to the services that come with them. Fancy a computer with no software? How about a television without programmes?

The important thing is not what people do, but whether it adds value – in the broadest sense. In advanced economies, it may be making great cheese or superb wine – or cheap plonk for those on tight budgets. It may be high-tech manufacturing, such as pharmaceuticals and aerospace, and even low-tech stuff, such as food processing, that needs to be done locally. Mostly, though, the value added is in services. Jobs that cannot be mechanised or outsourced – everything from childcare and cleaning to retail and restaurant work – as well as ones in high-tech services such as telecoms, software and media. Last but not least, do not neglect jobs that create benefits that market prices do not capture. Mothers (or fathers) looking after their children, charity work, blogging.

All that said, manufacturing may have shrunk too far and too fast in countries such as Britain and America where housing and finance squeezed out other activities. During the boom years, the bubbly pound made many manufacturing companies uncompetitive. Now that sterling has slumped, manufacturing is likely to enjoy something of a revival provided the pound doesn't bounce back. A weaker dollar would also help what remains of American industry; the delicate issue of China's exchange rate will be dealt with later in the chapter. More importantly, strong growth in emerging economies – where demand for all the material things that Westerners take for granted is taking off – could provide a lucrative new market for high-end American and European manufacturers. So the future for manufacturing isn't as bleak as it seems.

But let producers' efforts and consumers' choices dictate what companies make. In general, governments shouldn't try to second-guess what countries are good at, which companies are best and what people want to spend their money on. They simply don't know. Remember: these are the same fad-prone, lobbyist-led, vote-chasing politicians who thought that a bigger financial sector could only be better too. Even if they were cold, rational, clear-sighted, incorruptibly selfless creatures – or delegated the decisions to independent bureaucrats – they wouldn't stand a chance. They don't have the information to make such judgements. Nobody can predict how technology will develop, what its best applications are and what people will want. Google's success could not be planned.

In practice, the new industrial policy sounds depressingly like the old, failed one. 'We've committed three-quarters of a billion pounds to new manufacturing innovation in Britain,' Peter Mandelson said in his bravura performance at the Labour Party conference in September 2009. 'Investing in low-carbon cars and aircraft. New digital platforms. Plastic electronics. Life sciences. Industrial biotechnology. Wind-turbine development and wave power. This isn't us picking winners as happened too often in the 1970s, when more often the losers were picking us. This is us giving public support to new technologies without which they may never get off the drawing board.' Fine – now go to YouTube and rewind a little:

Recovery remains fragile and uncertain, especially in manufacturing and one of its cornerstones, the car industry. Our car scrappage scheme has been so successful the money is running out. The industry has asked that the scheme be topped up . . . So today I am extending [it] . . . this government will stand behind Vauxhall workers in Ellesmere Port and Luton where the workforce themselves have been the main driver of change. And the same goes for Jaguar Land Rover too.[32]

Hang on a minute. Should we be taxing overindebted

consumers to subsidise other debt-laden consumers to buy new cars? When public finances are tight, are car workers' jobs more deserving of subsidy than others – say, nurses'? Are Vauxhall/Opel/GM cars that people don't want to buy an industry of the future? As for Jaguar Land Rover, the UK subsidiary of India's Tata Motors that makes carbon-belching luxury cars and SUVs for the rich, it is hard to think of a company less deserving of poorer taxpayers' money. Peter Mandelson is a brilliantly intelligent man, but even he should not be trying to pick winners. Nor should Obama or Merkel – especially since, as Mandelson himself wisely warned, such protectionist actions could spark a subsidies war. Industry should not get special favours from governments. British manufacturers should rely on the market, not Mandelson.

Amid all the hue and cry about manufacturing, Britain and America should be quietly thankful that they are so reliant on services. Yes, they are suffering because finance grew especially big, but demand for many other services has proved far more resilient than manufacturing during the crisis. Services account for three-eighths of Britain's exports ($283 billion in 2008), notching up a trade surplus of $85 billion.[33] They make up more than a quarter of America's ($522 billion in 2008), providing a surplus of $158 billion against the backdrop of a gaping trade deficit. And while America's goods exports collapsed during the crisis – and service sectors such as finance, transport and tourism also slumped – its exports in a range of business, professional and technical services actually rose.[34]

An excessive reliance on manufacturing exports is a weakness, not a strength. Because of it, Germany and Japan suffered deeper recessions than America. So while Britons and Americans ought to become more like the Germans in some respects – more frugal, less financially frenzied – in others the Germans should become more Anglo-Saxon: more free-spending, less fixated on factory exports.

In praise of consumption

It is deeply unfashionable – almost blasphemous – to say so now the Era of Excess is over and we live in a new Age of Austerity, but consumption is wonderful. It's what makes the world economy whirr round. Without consumption there is no production, no income and no jobs. While some people have spent too much and have no immediate desire for more, there are plenty of people in the world with unmet needs. Germany and Japan pat themselves on the back for being prudent – of squirrelling away surplus savings while others spent – yet now that their customers in English-speaking (and many Mediterranean) countries are no longer spending, their production has slumped. Now is their time to be profligate. The world (and your own) economy need you. If you've got it, spend it. Emerging economies are also bursting with people who would love to go on a spending spree. Now policy-makers have to make it possible. But for countries such as Germany, Japan and China that have long focused on exporting, it may be trickier than it seems to stimulate domestic spending and restructure their economies to cater more to home-grown consumers.

The problem starts with the fact that households get a much smaller share of the economic pie than in America or Britain. They then save a bigger chunk of it. As a result, whereas consumption accounted for 71 per cent of the US economy in 2008 and 67 per cent of Britain's, it was only 55 per cent in Japan, 54 per cent in Germany and a mere 37 per cent in China.[35] Consumption in Britain and America is arguably too high. But if Japan and Germany raised theirs to Canadian rates – 60 per cent of GDP – it would give a big boost to domestic as well as global demand. Had Germans spent like Canadians in 2008, consumption would have been $220 billion higher. Had the Japanese done likewise, it would have added $246 billion. If China emulated Hong Kong's rate – 53 per cent of GDP –

consumer spending would have been $692 billion higher in 2008. This would have filled the shortfall left by a slump in American demand of nearly 5 per cent of GDP. Together with higher spending in Japan and Germany, it would be equivalent to nearly 2 per cent of global GDP. Of course, this cannot happen overnight – and it would require a currency appreciation (or a burst of inflation) to displace exports and encourage imports. But it could happen faster than people think, not least because China's economy is growing like gangbusters. Even without much reform, China's household consumption is growing by nearly 10 per cent a year.

Before looking at China in greater depth, consider Germany and Japan. One way to boost their consumption would be wage increases. Employee pay has fallen dramatically as a share of national income in both Germany and Japan since 2000. Companies have trousered workers' productivity gains as fatter profits instead of paying them out as higher wages. But since unemployment is high and fatter wages would cost jobs, why not spread the benefits more widely by cutting taxes instead? A big cut in payroll taxes – especially in Germany, where they are painfully high – would boost wages, employment and consumption. Governments could make up the income in other ways, as Chapter 11 explains. If Chancellor Angela Merkel was feeling really daring, she could also reverse the increase in VAT from 16 to 19 per cent that she introduced in 2007.

In both countries an ageing population that is allergic to allowing in young immigrants is part of the reason why saving rates are unusually high. German households' high savings rates may also reflect a cultural predisposition towards prudence – but economics also plays a big part. Japanese households used to be famously big savers too, less so in the two decades since their own bubble burst. In both countries the underlying problem is that they prioritise business interests over consumer ones. This reduces the share of the pie available for personal consumption – and because their domestic economies are so sluggish and inflexible, their firms naturally prioritise foreign markets instead. It's easier to sell Porsches or Lexuses to Wall Street traders than to set up a cleaning company employing Polish or Filipino workers to service domestic consumers' needs. It's also less difficult to cut costs by clamping down on wages than to shake up the economy through real reform.

Germany and Japan should view the crisis as an opportunity for reform – not to embrace American-style casino capitalism, but to cater more to their own people's needs. Merkel is adamant that prioritising exports is the road to recovery. Certainly, China's huge infrastructure spending will create lots of demand for German machinery and capital goods. But while Germany is right to be proud of its exporting prowess, it should also recognise that the purpose of selling products to foreigners is to make Germans better off. A bonfire of regulations would allow thousands of new service companies to spring up – offering everything from affordable Polish plumbers to nifty price-comparison sites. It is much easier to start a business in Albania or Sierra Leone than it is in Germany, according to the World Bank's respected Doing Business rankings for 2010.[36] Strikingly, considering Germany prides itself on its corporate competitiveness, investment accounted for a smaller share of the economy in 2007 than in consumer-crazy America.[37] Why are German entrepreneurs in Silicon Valley rather than the Ruhr? What is so wrong with allowing in foreigners to provide good care for elderly Germans? Were Germans really better served by stashing their savings in Landesbanks that bought American toxic assets? Even allowing for the financial bubble's inflation of American and British growth, Germany has performed dismally over the past decade. Now that demand for its exports has collapsed, perhaps it should try its hand at something else too.

The Japanese have taken a bit more to consumption in recent years; their problem is that big exporters cream off too much of the profits from their employees' hard work while small domestic companies are too inefficient to pay better wages. You can't spend more if you aren't earning more – especially if you're averse to borrowing. Like the rest of the world, Japan is pinning its hopes on rising exports to China, but like Germany, it ought to shake up its service sector to boost growth and consumption. Opening up to foreign competition – and foreigners – would help.

Don't hold your breath. While the new Japanese government is a breath of fresh air after a half-century of rule by the Liberal Democratic Party (LDP), it does not seem keen on liberalisation. But on the plus side, in September 2009 the then finance minister, Hirohisa Fujii, said that Japan 'needs to think more about domestic demand'.[38] The government seems keen to boost household spending with tax cuts and reforms to the country's welfare and pensions systems.

A stronger euro and yen might yet tilt the German and Japanese economies towards domestic needs, but previous experience suggests that this will encourage further wage restraint in order to offset the currency appreciation. If the English speakers and Mediterraneans remain sickly and Germany and Japan do not do enough to boost demand, the future of the world economy rests on the shoulders of emerging economies – and of China in particular.

Markets of the future

How did the world economy avoid a depression? The authorities in America and Europe tend to hog all the credit – Gordon Brown saved the banks (and the world), Ben Bernanke dropped buckets of cash from helicopters, even Germany finally launched a fiscal stimulus. Yet emerging economies deserve a big share of the thanks. Domestic demand in the BEEs – China, India and Brazil – has proved far more resilient than in the As. Even as exports slumped, consumption continued to grow. Governments provided a further boost by cutting interest rates and increasing spending. Whereas in previous recessions Brazil was obliged to hike interest rates and slash government spending, exacerbating the downturn, this time it has slashed rates and hiked spending by 1–1.5 per cent of GDP – a bigger boost, proportionately, than Britain managed. Above all, China's quick reactions – a 4-trillion yuan ($585-billion) fiscal stimulus, equivalent to 13 per cent of GDP, announced in early November 2008 – saved the day. This huge spending boost helped halt the devastating collapse in confidence. China can afford it – it was running a budget surplus in 2007 and even after the stimulus its national debt is likely to be only around 20 per cent of GDP.

Most of China's stimulus has come in the form of investment – notably in infrastructure – that could be spent quickly. This in turn has boosted imports. All the new railways require German machinery, Australian iron ore and British coal-mining equipment to build. Improved infrastructure will also help spread prosperity – and spending – from China's coastal regions to its inland ones. But much of the extra investment has taken the form of loans to Chinese industries. State-owned banks pumped out an astonishing 7.3 trillion yuan ($1.1 trillion) in loans in the first half of 2009.[39] One worry is that much of the money will be wasted, leaving banks with lots of bad debts down the line. There is even a danger, argues Yiping Huang of Peking University, that the People's Bank of China will repeat the Fed's mistake and inflate a Chinese bubble. Another fear is that by propping up investment demand in the short term, China's stimulus will exacerbate excess supply in export industries in the medium term. If China is suffering a glut in its export sector, it will be tempted to keep the renminbi as cheap as possible so as to find a bigger market for its goods overseas. But this is a recipe for confrontation for other countries – not least America – that are also trying to export their way out of recession. It is time for Chinese consumers to come into their own.

Joanne Chen was born in 1976, just before China embarked on its market-based reforms. 'In my parents' time, they didn't have food,' she told me. 'They ate from the trees and didn't have rice. They were very, very poor. When I was a child I remember I didn't have much food one year. Now things are much better.' She earns 1,200 yuan (a bit over £100) a month selling electric cables for a lighting company called Bingsheng Lighting in Haiyan City, in Zhejiang province, two hours' drive from Shanghai. She also earns a commission on all sales. 'Anything a client asked for I would search for because China is the world's factory,' she is keen to point out. When we met, she was thirty-three and I thirty-five. 'I'm a dragon and you are an ox,' she giggles.

It is a hazy day in Haiyan. It feels light years away from the glitz of Shanghai, but it still looks remarkably prosperous. Its spanking-new four-lane highway is lined with modern buildings and houses. Joanne's life is improving quickly too. 'Before everything stayed the same. Now things change very fast. After five years they are not the same. Most change is good,' she says. 'Before we couldn't buy a car, we just had bikes. Now we have a motorbike. My son loves it.' She says she cannot afford to buy many European or American products, but she has a Nokia mobile phone that was made in China. Naturally, she aspires to even better things. 'In five years I want to change to a bigger house and buy a car. I want to let my parents travel around China. And I want my son to grow up healthy and have a smiling face to everything.' She would like to travel outside China when her seven-year-old son, who calls himself Jerry after the cartoon mouse, has grown up. 'Now most people can travel freely as life is rich. The government gave us more holidays.

Before, I just had one day a week holiday, now I have two.'
She'd also love a German car.

China's remarkable economic growth is built on the hard work
of hundreds of millions of people like Joanne, and they have benefited handsomely from three decades of liberalisation. Growth has
been so rapid that their wages and consumer spending have
soared. But Chinese workers have not gained as much as they
might have done because companies and the government have
grabbed a big share of the proceeds from growth. Wages and other
household income fell from 72 per cent of GDP in 1992 to 55 per
cent of (a much bigger) GDP in 2007. And since Chinese households also save a big share of their income, consumption is
particularly low. While Chinese incomes are two and a half times
Indian ones, consumer spending is only two-thirds greater. It has
long been desirable for producer interests to give way to ordinary
people's – but now it is essential. China's prime minister recognises
this. 'We should focus on restructuring the economy, and make
greater effort to enhance the role of domestic demand, especially
final consumption, in spurring growth,' Wen Jiabao says.

The key to boosting household income, argues Fan Gang,
director of the National Economic Research Institute in Beijing,
is to create more jobs. A third of the Chinese still work in agriculture; China needs to create two hundred million more jobs in
cities to complete the shift from rural poverty to urban jobs that
pay at least twice as much. Since manufacturing can only absorb
so many people, the government needs to tear down the barriers
that stifle the service sector. Millions of small service-sector businesses that employ lots of people could provide a new engine for
China's economy – and a bigger outlet for domestic consumption.

The basic problem, says Yiping Huang, is that China's
reforms are still incomplete. While the economy has opened up
to the world and many domestic markets have also been freed
up, other markets remain rigged or under government control.

The big capital-intensive companies that dominate many industries benefit from cheap energy, capital and land. Electricity is subsidised, while banks pump out cheap loans by paying savers paltry interest rates. Local governments underprice land in order to attract factories to locate there. All of this artificially boosts corporate profits. And because companies scarcely pay any dividends, their earnings are mostly reinvested. So the main reason why China saves so much is that its big companies hog such a big chunk of national income.

Eliminating these corporate subsidies and injecting greater competition into cosseted sectors would reduce companies' excess profits, while getting them to pay out bigger dividends would spread the wealth more widely, says Fan Gang. At the same time, the small labour-intensive exporters that provide most of the jobs cannot rely on credit from banks, so they too are forced to save a lot in order to fund their investment. Liberalising the financial sector so that it lends more to small companies, entrepreneurs and the service sector is vital. But that will be difficult for the Chinese state, because it involves loosening its grip over the economy.

Households not only get too small a share of the pie; they also save a lot of it. A big reason for this is because – irony of ironies in a nominally communist state – China no longer has much of a welfare state. Its coverage is patchy and its benefits poor. So Chinese workers save a big chunk of their income to pay for their children's further education, provide for their retirement and in case they fall sick or lose their job. They have to put aside even more because Chinese banks pay such pitiful interest rates and it is difficult to get credit to buy a house or a car, or pay for education.

Joanne's parents are fortunate: they now get a state pension. 'They get 1,200 yuan each a month. It is more than they used to earn when they worked.' But the family still faces many other expenses. Joanne says that college tuition fees now cost perhaps

10,000 yuan a year – two-thirds of her annual salary. 'When I was studying, it was only 300 yuan,' she points out. She also has to pay for her family's healthcare (only 10 per cent of the cost in the case of expenses covered by a government health card). She spends all of her salary, but her husband, who earns 1,600 yuan a month, gives her 1,100 to put in the bank each month. Thus her household saves two-fifths of their monthly income (excluding Joanne's annual bonus).

The government could help boost consumption in several ways. In the absence of free trade unions, it should at least look more kindly on workers' wage demands. (Joanne has no complaints, though. 'My boss is my classmate. He helped me. At the start, when I didn't make any sales, he said, "Don't give up. You can do it." He trusted in me. So I think I will work for him for my whole life. My boss is a rich man, but he works hard every day, he doesn't have a holiday.') Tax cuts would put more money in people's pockets. Shaking up the banking system would ensure that they earned better returns on their savings. Improving the availability and quality of consumer goods in poorer parts of China would help, as would making it easier for consumers to borrow to pay for big-ticket items. But the most important reform would be to provide a proper welfare state that boosts spending on pensions and healthcare and reduces the need to save. In *Reforming Pensions*, Nicholas Barr of the London School of Economics suggests that China could immediately widen the coverage and increase the generosity of its pay-as-you-go pensions scheme, putting money in pensioners' pockets, while reforming and continuing to foster the development of private pensions saving.[40] Creating a publicly funded healthcare system would remove one of the biggest reasons for precautionary saving. Developing a social safety net that protects the poor and the unemployed would also help, as would providing more social housing, in particular for the hundreds of millions of migrant workers. A welfare state would benefit all Chinese people. It would reduce the need for households to save. And it could give the Chinese government a new source of legitimacy.

The government is starting to do all these things. It doubled spending on healthcare, education and social security between 2005 and 2008.[41] It has increased pensions coverage and payments to low-income households. It has pledged to provide basic healthcare for 90 per cent of the population by 2011. But while it needs to go further, all of this takes time. Even in China, a welfare system cannot be established overnight. Once it exists, people's savings habits will take time to change. For instance, they will want to be sure from personal experience that they can count on the healthcare system before they stop saving for a medical emergency.

Reorienting China's economy towards satisfying consumer needs would benefit the Chinese. By making consumer goods more available and credit easier, providing a proper welfare state, reforming the financial sector and shifting investment towards efficient service-sector industries that employ lots of people, the McKinsey Global Institute reckons China could boost the share of consumption in the economy from 37 per cent in 2008 to 45–50 per cent by 2025, creating jobs and boosting GDP by 15 per cent.[42] This shift is also essential for the global economy's future growth. During the bubble years, China was not to blame for producing goods that Americans wanted to buy. But it would suffer – as would the rest of the world – if it now persists in trying to flog products that Americans are no longer purchasing. Growth would be slower and the risk of a global trade war greater. It would be far better to fire up domestic demand.

But as China redirects resources from selling to foreigners to catering to the Chinese, its real exchange rate must rise – preferably through a revaluation of the renminbi rather than a burst of domestic inflation. That would cause a cascade of desirable changes. It would lift consumers' purchasing power, sucking in more imports. It would spur companies to invest more of their energies in servicing domestic needs rather than foreign ones. It would encourage exporters to move upmarket, leaving space for lower-cost producers in Vietnam or Bangladesh to capture a bigger slice of low-end manufacturing such as clothing and footwear. It would help head off protectionist pressures in America and Europe. And it would reduce China's current-account surplus, so that it was no longer spending less than it earns and investing its surplus savings in shaky dollar assets.

Only a decade ago, China's economy was a pygmy. Now it is an emerging giant. As Napoleon predicted two centuries ago, its growth – and that of other emerging economies – is 'shaking the world', as we shall see in the next chapter.

5

Awakening

*Emerging economies'
rise and rise*

The Chinese miracle is best summed up by observing that
in 1978 Deng [Xiaoping] said that China could not do
without global capitalism. Three decades later it is clear
that global capitalism cannot do without China!

Rajiv Kumar, Indian economist, 2009

The tallest building is now in Taipei, and it will soon be
overtaken by one being built in Dubai. The world's
richest man is Mexican, and its largest publicly traded
corporation is Chinese. The world's biggest plane is built
in Russia and Ukraine, its leading refinery is under
construction in India, and its largest factories are all in
China . . . The United Arab Emirates is home to the most
richly endowed investment fund. The world's largest
Ferris wheel is in Singapore. Its number one casino is not
in Las Vegas but in Macao, which has also overtaken

Vegas in annual gambling revenues. The world's biggest movie industry, in terms of both movies made and tickets sold, is Bollywood, not Hollywood.

Fareed Zakaria, *The Post-American World*, 2008[1]

People used to call globalisation Americanisation. In the future, you can call it 'Easternisation'.

Baba Kalyani, founder of Bharat Forge, 2009

When you arrive in Shanghai, the buzz is exhilarating. It starts on the maglev train into town, which accelerates to 431 kilometres per hour (268 miles per hour) in just four minutes. Propelled by powerful magnets that lift the train up and hurtle it forward, you literally fly towards the city centre, rocketing past a blur of houses and cars. In a flash, you have arrived.

Impressed? You should be. While maglev trains were pioneered in Britain – at Birmingham airport, of all places[2] – and the technology on display in Shanghai is German, it is in China, until recently one of the world's poorest countries, where they are now most prominently showcased. Compare that, for instance, with landing in the shabbiness of Gatwick and trundling towards London on the so-called Gatwick Express, which travels at a third of the average speed and costs over three times as much.

The maglev drops you off in Pudong, the business district in eastern Shanghai that has sprouted on what was marshland twenty years ago to become China's commercial and financial centre. If you continue your journey by taxi, only the cheapness of the ride reminds you that this is still a relatively poor place: you can cross this vast city for only a few pounds. (Opt for the Metro, with its hyper-modern Tokyo-style subway trains featuring video screens blaring ads at you, and it will set you back a mere 3 yuan, around 30 pence.)

You can cross the Huangpu River, which bisects modern Shanghai from north to south, via five tunnels and four major bridges. The most recent, Lupu Bridge, is the world's longest arch bridge. To picture it, think of the iconic beauty of Sydney Harbour Bridge. It rises so high above the river that as you drive across it, you again feel like you are flying, *Blade Runner*-style, through a cityscape punctuated by massive skyscrapers.

Lupu Bridge's vaulting arch – whose 550-metre span has knocked New River Gorge Bridge in Fayetteville, West Virginia, off its pedestal in the record books – connects the two halves of the vast Shanghai Expo site. Just as the first World's Fair, the Great Exhibition of 1851, served to show off Victorian London's industrial and cultural prowess, the Shanghai Expo, which ran from May to October 2010, was the city's chance to impress on the world stage.

It grabbed it. Undaunted by the financial crisis and the global recession, Shanghai went on a spending spree to remake itself. This city of 19 million people shelled out $45 billion – more than the outlay for the 2008 Beijing Olympics, and indeed more than the British government's recession-fighting fiscal-stimulus package in 2008–10 – to upgrade its infrastructure, build new transport links and spruce itself up for what organisers promise will be the biggest and most extravagant Expo ever.[3] It built two new airport terminals, eight new subway lines and extensions that expanded the Metro network to nearly the size of New York's, new parks, roads and bridges, as well as a $270-million stadium and performing-arts centre shaped like a flying saucer. Across the city, Haibao, the Expo's smiling blue mascot with a cheeky quiff, waves exuberantly at you, its other arm posed almost cockily on its hip. Emblematic of the Expo's slogan – 'Better City, Better Life' – a $700-million promenade was built on the Bund, the city's historic riverfront, with traffic driven into tunnels underneath it. 'Every city has its own historical moment to transform and develop itself, and now it is Shanghai's moment,' says Tu Qiyu, a professor of urban studies at the Shanghai Academy of Social Sciences.

Hubris? Perhaps. But Shanghai is already well on its way to becoming a world-class city and soon a leading (if not yet a global) financial centre – again. Stroll along the Bund, as millions of tourists do each year, and the grand colonial buildings that once housed banks and trading companies remind you of the city's importance in an earlier era of globalisation. At number 12 is the HSBC Building, built in 1923 as the Shanghai headquarters of the Hongkong and Shanghai Banking Corporation and described at the time as 'the most luxurious building between the Suez Canal and the Bering Strait'. In the mid-nineteenth century the British took advantage of an enfeebled Chinese state to wrest control of its customs operations. Tens of thousands of Europeans and Americans flocked to Shanghai to strike it rich. But that era came to end as the Japanese invasion, the Second World War and the Communist revolution of 1949 cut off Shanghai from the global economy. The city began to open up again thirty years ago, when China's leaders embraced market reforms. Over the past twenty it has re-emerged with a fanfare.

To get a feel of Shanghai's revival, take a lift to one of the top-floor terrace bars along the Bund. The busy traffic on the Huangpu River reminds you of the city's importance as a cargo port – since 2006 the world's busiest. Across the river, a succession of skyscrapers jostle for attention: the Oriental Pearl Tower, a bulbous pink space rocket; the even taller Jin Mao Tower, a modern take on a traditional Chinese tiered pagoda; the Shanghai World Financial Center, the world's third tallest building, which twists upwards to what looks like a giant bottle-opener. It will soon be dwarfed by the 632-metre-high Shanghai Tower, which locals have dubbed 'the Dragon'. As night falls, the buildings light up: one even plays videos on a vast screen on its side.

Now, like a century ago, Shanghai has an increasingly cosmopolitan feel. Its bright lights and brash, anything-goes

'I have opportunities to go abroad to America or Europe. It's part of globalisation – not just foreign things coming to China, also Chinese people going to see the rest of the world,' Victor gushes with an infectious enthusiasm. 'I've been to the US for business and pleasure. I've also been to Japan, Thailand and Indonesia. I may be going to Europe later this year.' Also, his partner is American. 'I like communicating with foreigners. There are no opportunities in my home town to find a foreigner to talk to and fall in love with.'

Since he graduated from college in 1998, Victor, who is thirty-six, has worked for three multinational companies. He started off in Beijing working for a US company that made LCDs (liquid-crystal displays). Then he moved to Shanghai to work in procurement for another American company. Since 2007 he has worked for Haldex, which makes automotive parts, mainly braking systems. Its customers include big names such as Volvo, General Motors, Hyundai and Caterpillar. 'We have been very badly affected by the crisis,' he told me when we met in March 2009. 'Sales have fallen by more than half. They have laid off 40 per cent of the employees. We are cutting costs and looking for new customers, especially in emerging markets and China. It's a game of survival.

'I'm worried about my job,' he says. Haldex are thinking of relocating the Shanghai office to Suzhou, where the manufacturing facility is. That would be a big disruption. 'My life, my relationship are all here.' His face brightens. 'But I'm doing well. I contribute a lot to the company. I saved it 12 million Swedish kronas last year. I've been promoted. I got a bonus. There's still lots to do to improve logistics and the supply chain.' He is also studying for an executive MBA with Rutgers University. Despite the crisis, Victor is optimistic. 'I believe there is always an opportunity in a challenge. When I speak with my co-workers and friends we all think that despite this crisis, there will be solutions to all these problems and the future will be brighter.' It is that

spirit of can-do optimism that is perhaps the Chinese people's
greatest strength. Europeans – and even Americans – could learn
from it.

Victor is a poster-child for the new China. Thoughtful, open-
minded, globally aware – he is both grateful for the opportunities
of the new globalised China and aware of its limitations. I asked
him how he felt about the growing feeling in the West that China
was taking away jobs from Americans and Europeans. 'I disagree that China's growth poses a threat to America and Europe,'
he insists. 'China's development does not depress employment
opportunities in America and Europe. Globalisation is the spirit
of the free-market economy. It is Adam Smith. It is natural to
purchase and source from low-cost countries.' He pauses. 'Before
the crisis, we in China also used to blame globalisation sometimes. We would say that America and Europe are exploiting
China by transferring labour-intensive and low-tech manufacturing to China. We earn a few cents' profit and Wal-Mart sells it
for $10. Is the US exploiting China? There are always several
ways of looking at a situation. It's more expensive to do things in
the US. People don't want to do certain jobs.'

While the crisis has altered his appreciation of America, he
remains a fan of the market system. 'Ten years ago, I dreamed
of emigrating to the US and living an American life,' he
explains. 'I don't any more. There is a major flaw in the US
economy – Americans' consumption behaviour. Americans use
their credit card to buy everything. Chinese people spend 20–30
per cent of what we are sure we can get tomorrow. We save a
lot in case we lose our job. We save to buy a car and home.'
Does he believe in free markets? 'It depends on the definition. I
believe in free markets with appropriate government regulation. Through this crisis, the Chinese Communist Party has
enhanced its image and reputation. The Chinese economy is
not as badly affected as America and Europe. We used to think
the Chinese government interfered too much but now we realise

it helps us, it's necessary.' Across Asia many people said similar things. They had lost faith in America, but not in globalisation. They were in favour of markets, with appropriate government safeguards. And despite the crisis, they felt the future was bright. It certainly looks it.

Emerging powers

Shanghai's rise and Victor's life story illustrate a remarkable transformation of the world economy in recent years. In 1998 Britain's economy was fractionally larger, in dollar terms, than China's and India's combined – astonishingly, considering the UK's population was less than 60 million at the time, whereas that of China and India combined was approaching 2.3 billion. Twelve years later China's economy alone was two-and-a-half times bigger than Britain's; combined with India's, it was over three times as big as the UK's.[4] Yet measuring China's and India's economies in dollar terms understates their true size, because a dollar goes much further there than it does in the United States. Allowing for these differences in purchasing power, China's economy has swelled from 6.7 per cent of the world total in 1998 to an estimated 13.3 per cent in 2010. India's has grown from 3.5 per cent of the world economy to an estimated 5.3 per cent over the same period. In effect, China's weight in the world economy has doubled in twelve years, while India's has risen by half. Add them together and you find that China and India together account for nearly a fifth of the world economy (18.6 per cent), almost as much as the United States, which accounts for a fifth (20.2 per cent).[5]

Perhaps even more remarkably, whereas as recently as 1998 advanced economies accounted for three-fifths of the world economy, by 2010 they accounted for a bit less than half (49 per cent).[6] Emerging and developing economies – poorer countries – now account for over half of the world economy for the first time since the Industrial Revolution.

This has profound implications in all sorts of areas – world trade, global energy use, global business and the way global institutions are run, to name but four. Start with trade. In 2000 advanced economies accounted for two-thirds of world exports, emerging ones for one third. By 2010 advanced economies' share had slumped to an estimated 54.7 per cent, and emerging ones surged to 45.3 per cent. Soon emerging economies are likely to account for over half of world exports too. Their share of world imports has risen sharply as well, albeit from 31.7 per cent to 43.7 per cent.[7]

In 1978, when China embarked on its market-opening reforms, its goods exports were a mere $10 billion (at current prices). Twenty years later they were $184 billion – a bit over a quarter of America's and two-thirds of Britain's. By 2008 they had reached $1,428 billion, overtaking America's and three times larger than Britain's.[8] China exports four times more each day than it did in all of 1978. In the first half of 2009, its exports also inched ahead of Germany's.[9] In ten years, China's share of world goods exports has nearly trebled, from 3.3 per cent to 8.9 per cent. When I wrote Open World, China was still a bit player in world trade; now it is a force to be reckoned with.

China's impact on the world economy is viewed mainly through the prism of its soaring exports. 'Everything's made in China these days. My [adopted] daughter's made in China too. There's nothing wrong with it,' jokes Tim Harcourt, author of The Airport Economist[10] and chief economist of the Australian Trade Commission. But contrary to public perception, China's imports have soared too. Between 1998 and 2008 they rose eightfold in dollar terms, to $1,133 billion – 6.9 per cent of the world total. Although America's imports, at $2,166 billion, were still nearly twice as large, China's have grown much faster (by an average of over 23 per cent a year) than America's, which rose by less than 9 per cent a year. India is still a pygmy in world trade, although its share of world goods exports doubled from 0.6 per cent in 1998 to 1.1 per cent in 2008. Brazil's importance has also increased. Its exports more than trebled between 2002 and 2008, from $60.4 billion to $197.1 billion, boosting its share of global exports from a paltry 0.76 per cent to 1 per cent within six years.[11]

World trade in commercial services – which includes everything from tourism and transport to business and financial services – is around a fifth of trade in goods. Despite all the hoopla about India's prowess in IT services, its total service exports, at $103 billion in 2008, were smaller than China's ($146 billion) and both were dwarfed by Britain ($285 billion) and the United States ($518 billion).

The entry of China into the global economy has been a momentous event not just for America, Europe and other advanced economies but even more so for other emerging economies that earned a living exporting the kind of low-end manufactured products that China could produce more cheaply. Most affected have been countries such as Mexico and Turkey, which previously relied on their relatively low costs and proximity to major markets to specialise in lower-end manufacturing. Yet to their surprise, they have also benefited from soaring exports to China. The prospect of Chinese competition also caused terror among poorer East Asian economies: they were convinced the panda would eat their lunch. For a time, it looked like it might. But then it turned out that if they couldn't beat the panda, they could join it.

As the trade figures cited earlier highlighted, China has since the turn of the century become the world's factory – the place where most high-volume manufactured goods such as toys, televisions, mobile phones, clothes and many other things are made. But to be more precise, it is mostly the world's assembly plant – the place where bits and pieces made elsewhere, primarily in the rest of East

Asia, are put together into finished products. As trade barriers have fallen and technology has made it easier to coordinate supply chains that stretch across many different companies in many different countries, the way in which many products are made has been revolutionised. No longer are they made in a single place; instead their manufacture has been broken up into little bits and scattered among a network of suppliers that often specialise in a tiny part of the process. An Apple iPod assembled in China is made up of a display from Japan, a multimedia processor from Singapore, a central processor from Taiwan and memory from South Korea.[12] The design and branding are American. East Asia's economy has become a dense network of production links, centred on China.

Expensive oil

Look next at global energy use. Emerging economies' energy consumption overtook that of advanced ones in 2005.[13] In 2009 China surpassed the US as the world's biggest energy consumer. The International Energy Agency (IEA) forecasts that China and India will account for a bit over half of the increase in primary energy consumption between 2006 and 2030 – and emerging economies as a whole for 87 per cent. (Such long-term forecasts should be taken with a big pinch of salt, but they provide an idea of what might happen if current trends persist.) Over that period annual global energy consumption is forecast to rise by nearly half.

The world is not going to run out of energy – or even oil and gas – any time soon. Coal supplies are vast, while remaining proven reserves of oil have nearly doubled since 1980. They are enough to supply the world with oil for more than forty years at current rates of consumption. Add in petroleum reserves that geologists think exist, plus oil recoverable from oil sands in

Canada or convertible from coal and there is enough of the black stuff to keep the world humming for hundreds of years. But increased demand from emerging economies is likely to push up oil prices. The world got a foretaste of this in the summer of 2008, when prices spiked to nearly $150 a barrel. As the world economy slumped, prices fell by three-quarters, but by October 2009 they had hit $80 a barrel again.

High oil and gas prices are painful for consumers, but they are necessary. They stimulate greater investment in discovering and developing new oil supplies, which is essential to meet rising demand. They encourage companies and consumers to use an expensive resource more efficiently. But perhaps most importantly, they provide a huge incentive to develop alternative, low-carbon energy sources and technologies. When petrol is prohibitively expensive, electric cars are much more attractive. High oil and gas prices can help kickstart the development of all sorts of technologies, from bioplastics to solar power. So even if governments fail to agree and implement big cuts in global carbon emissions, market forces will encourage greater efficiency and the development of low-carbon alternatives. And if governments do adopt sensible measures to stimulate the development of clean technologies, advanced economies' continuing energy use and emerging economies' rising energy consumption need not be a problem, as Chapter 10 explains.

But might higher oil prices put an end to globalisation? The huge increase in world trade over the past two centuries, which has accelerated in recent decades, has been largely driven by the falling cost of cross-border commerce. Governments have slashed the tariffs and other trade restrictions that artificially raise the cost of imports. Meanwhile improvements in technology have driven down the cost (and increased the speed) of transporting goods over long distances. But the huge container ships that ply the world's oceans, the cargo planes that zip from continent to continent and the lorries that transport goods to their final destinations all require oil. Until alternatives, such as biofuels, are commercialised, only trains can be powered with anything except oil (or liquid gas).

Until cheaper alternatives are widely available, higher oil prices could certainly have a big impact on the world economy. Least affected would be high-value services where transport costs are relatively unimportant, such as finance, IT and business services – although business travellers might switch to cheaper flights and hotels, while videoconferencing could replace more long-haul business trips. Worse hit could be long-haul tourism, although rising incomes, notably in emerging economies, will provide a big boost to demand. For many people, seeing the world is a priority as soon as they can afford it. Still, if flights were more expensive, people might opt for trips to neighbouring countries rather than distant ones. In the case of goods trade, bulky, low-value items and commodities would be affected far more than lighter, higher-value ones. So trade in steel might be hit hard but that in electrical components or flowers might still flourish. Again, though, higher transport costs would tend to favour regional trade over global commerce. Thus higher oil prices might dampen some trade as well as diverting it from distant places to nearer ones. According to Jeff Rubin and Benjamin Tal of CIBC, a Canadian bank, world trade scarcely grew as a share of global output during the era of high oil prices between 1974 and 1986.[14] When the cost of shipping freight across the Atlantic and Pacific oceans soared after the 1973 oil-price shock, the US sourced much more of its imports (excluding oil) from Latin America and the Caribbean and much less from Europe and Asia.

Over time, the pattern of production would be reorganised. Heavy industry might cluster together, just as steel mills were once located near coal mines and supplies of iron ore. But factories making mass-market footwear or furniture are unlikely to reappear in the US or richer parts of Europe. Instead cheap manufactures destined for North America might move back from China to Mexico. Rubin and Tal calculate that when oil cost $20 a barrel in 2000, it cost 90 per cent more to ship a standard forty-foot container to the east coast of the United States from East Asia than from Mexico. It was still much cheaper to import many things from Asia, though, because wages there were so much lower. But if oil cost $200 a barrel, shipping goods from East Asia would cost three times more than from Mexico. That is equivalent to slapping an extra 15 per cent tax on Asian goods, on average.

In the EU's case, production might be diverted from Asia to Eastern Europe, Turkey and North Africa. Latin America might again be supplied from Brazil rather than from China. In East Asia's case, goods might be made, rather than just assembled, in China, or shift to even lower-cost locations such as Vietnam. To some extent, then, a world with expensive oil might tilt towards more concentrated, regional production.

That is not a million miles away from the world we live in now. In 2007 world trade was equivalent to just over three-tenths of global output.[15] It seems pretty globalised, until you realise that nearly half (46 per cent) of that trade takes place within three big regions – East Asia, North America and the European Union. Half of East Asia's trade takes place within the region,[16] as does half of North America's,[17] while two-thirds of the EU's does.[18] Those three regions are much more self-contained than is commonly assumed: North America's exports to the rest of the world account for only around 5 per cent of GDP, the EU's for 10 per cent, and East Asia's for a bit less than 15 per cent. Since together these three regions account for four-fifths of the world economy, the bulk of global economic activity is already regional.

How can that be true? Aren't Coca-Cola, Toyota cars and Dell computers ubiquitous? They are indeed, but that is deceptive. For a start, most economic activity is local. Think about what you spend your wages on. A big chunk goes on taxes, which are spent on local services such as healthcare or education or redistributed to local people such as pensioners or the unemployed. Another big bit goes on your rent or mortgage, which is again entirely local. Then there are all the other nearby services you may use, such as restaurants, bars, gyms, beauty parlours, therapists and counsellors, builders, plumbers, cleaners and so on. Only a small share of people's spending goes on tradable goods, such as televisions or clothes. While these are increasingly shipped in from far away, many foreign-branded products are in fact made domestically or regionally. Coca-Cola syrup is distributed globally, but the bottling takes place locally. Toyota cars are assembled in America, Australia, Brazil, Britain, China and many other countries besides Japan. Dell computers are assembled in the United States, Brazil, China and Malaysia. Europe has been served from Ireland, but the plant is shifting to Poland in 2010.

In a world with much more expensive oil, global trade in weightless services and light, high-value products would no doubt continue to grow. But manufacturing production, particularly of heavier and cheaper goods, would doubtless become more concentrated regionally. Global companies would still be important. They would just tend to look more like Toyota, which produces cars everywhere, than Sony, which makes most of its electronic products in Japan. So globalisation would change shape, not come to an end. It would operate more through foreign investment and less through foreign trade.

This has some profound implications. If production of a particular product was increasingly concentrated in a single place in a region, rather than scattered across it, competition for foreign investment among countries within a region would sharpen. That would give a big advantage to the economy with the largest domestic market, especially in regions where trade is not entirely free. Foreign companies would tend to want to locate their factories near major consumer markets and would also want to avoid the risk that their products could be kept out. In East

Asia, which has yet to create a pan-regional free-trade area, let alone a European-style single market, this would place China at a huge advantage. Even the hint that China could keep out, say, Thai-made televisions might persuade many companies to locate there.

In North America, where the North American Free Trade Agreement (NAFTA) is riddled with loopholes, Mexico would be the obvious location for lower-end manufacturing, but Canada would be very vulnerable to American protectionism. Indeed it already is. Just as many products stamped 'made in China' are actually assembled there from parts made across Asia (and the world), many of those 'made in the USA' include parts and components made in Canada, and vice versa. The Obama administration's 'Buy American' provisions are proving a headache for companies that manufacture construction equipment and water-filtration systems, for instance, which contain parts from both countries that are shipped back and forth across the border as they are being made.[19] If instead of being shipped back and forth repeatedly, they were made in a single place, the prospect of, say, costly delays owing to customs inspections at the US border – for homeland security, of course, nothing to do with protectionism – would be a strong incentive to concentrate production in America. 'If we don't fix the border with the US, Canada has a very serious problem,' says David Emerson, a former Canadian trade (and foreign) minister, who has thought a lot about the implications of higher oil prices for globalisation. 'It's not well enough understood how serious the risk is to us.' Many of the car assembly plants in Ontario, for instance, might relocate across the border.

The EU is fortunate to have a single market. So long as national governments respected it, small economies would be at much less of a disadvantage. Trade flows freely within the EU, and EU rules prevent governments from handing out subsidies to attract foreign investment. But high-cost locations on the periphery of Europe, such as Finland, northern Sweden or Scotland, would be at a big disadvantage. Governments would need to invest in efficient rail links to try to offset this. In any case, distance would matter much more.

A more Toyota-like model of globalisation would also make the world more vulnerable to protectionism. Governments are far freer to restrict foreign investment than trade. World trade is governed by WTO rules, which apply equally to all, with the option of impartial arbitration and legally sanctioned retaliation when disputes occur. These multilateral rules raise the cost of restricting trade, particularly for big and powerful countries. But efforts to agree a Multilateral Agreement on Investment at the OECD were killed off in 1998. Moves to include investment rules in the still-unfinished Doha Round of negotiations at the WTO were blocked in Cancún, Mexico, in 2003. Investment is instead regulated by a plethora of bilateral investment agreements, which are far more malleable. Great, say critics, governments should be free to keep out foreign multinationals. At the time, they assumed that the multinationals would be Western and the governments from developing countries. But that is less and less true. Investment now flows increasingly from south to north and south to south, as emerging economies invest in both advanced and less-developed ones.

Indians take over Germany

Baba Kalyani does not look like a revolutionary. When we meet at his office on a Saturday afternoon, he is dressed in a button-down Bharat Forge monogrammed shirt and black loafers. He comes across as understated, sometimes even unassuming, yet his deep voice and measured tone convey authority. In any case, his achievements speak for themselves. If you are driving a Western car, chances are an Indian company called Bharat Forge helped make the chassis and the engine. Within a few years this nimble upstart has become the world's second-largest forging company, behind Germany's Thyssen Krupp. It supplies the world's top five car and commercial vehicle manufacturers. One of a rapidly growing breed of emerging-market multinationals, it has expanded overseas by buying up and bettering Western businesses. After hundreds of years during which Western firms, starting with the East India Company, have put their stamp on the rest of the world, trail-blazers such as Baba Kalyani are suddenly turning the tables.

Kalyani comes from a very humble background. He was born in a small village about a hundred miles from Pune, a leafy city in the Indian province of Maharashtra. His father was a farmer with no formal education. But he was very entrepreneurial, a trait his son has inherited. Back in 1963, when the Indian economy was tied up in knots by growth-sapping rules and regulations, he moved to Pune to try to set up a manufacturing business. By 1966 he had a small business making components for agricultural equipment.

Kalyani started off at a local Maharati school, where teaching was in the local language of Maharashtra. When his father could afford it, he was packed off to an English-speaking boarding school, the King George Royal Indian Military College, one of four established by the British army when India was part of the British Empire. From there he went to engineering college and then to the Massachusetts Institute of Technology (MIT) in the United States to do his master's degree. When he returned to India in 1972, he started working for his father. Within less than a year his father handed over the reins. At that time, the company was small, with sales of less than $1 million a year.

Kalyani explains:

That was the beginning. We kept on growing largely fuelled by the ambition to be the best in our business in India. In the early 1970s, early 1980s there was no thought in anybody's mind, including mine, that we were ever going to be in the global marketplace. We were overawed by what was happening in the West. India in those days was a highly controlled and regulated economy. Everything required a licence, everything required permissions. Most of the time, it took months if not years to make things happen. Those were the days when if you wanted to be a CEO [chief executive] the number-one quality you needed was how to manage the environment, not how to manage your business.

In the mid-1980s Kalyani started trying to export, because companies with overseas sales had a higher status than wholly domestic ones. But everything changed in 1991 with the government's sweeping economic reforms. 'Overnight, substantial controls on industry were removed,' he recalls. 'Licensing disappeared. Capacity restrictions disappeared. Import controls went away. The capital markets were liberalised. It was a big change.'

This was a turning point, for India as a whole and for Bharat Forge in particular. Kalyani quickly realised that contrary to the conventional wisdom about manufacturing in India, his company couldn't succeed on the basis of cheap labour. 'We were probably one of the first companies in India to realise this and do something about it,' he says. 'The basic reasoning was that you had cheap labour, capital was expensive, so you used very little capital, a lot of people and very little technology. The thinking was that you paid five hundred rupees a person per month and you would get a big advantage by doing that. But nothing was further away from the truth.' Kalyani defied the conventional wisdom and chose a different strategy. 'We realised in the late 1980s that the business model we needed to adopt was high-technology, very capital-intensive and a highly skilled workforce, not cheap labour, but highly automated,' he says. 'It was the complete reverse of the traditional Indian business model. Some people still follow it today but I don't think they're very successful.'

It was a big gamble. 'We took a leap of faith by making some huge investments in setting up a very modern facility,' he explains. 'The investments were larger than our annual sales. It was completely new to India. We were criticised very heavily by the media because they saw this as completely out of sync with what was happening in the country.' Because interest rates were very high, the company had to innovate to keep investment costs down – in effect, they had to do more with less, boosting the productivity with which their capital was employed. More broadly, manufacturing was being written off as India's service industries, first call centres then more complex IT services, took off. All the attention was on companies such as Infosys and Wipro, whose modern facilities in Bangalore I visited for *Open World* in 2001.

'We had some difficult times. But within two, three years we made a success of it. All of a sudden our business started growing at a very dramatic pace, largely from customers overseas. It almost became a case study for Indian industry of how to gain sustainable competitive advantage,' Kalyani tells me with justifiable pride. They began exporting first to the United States, then Europe, China and the rest of Asia. 'Very soon we were significant players in our business across the world.' His tastefully decorated office proudly displays the many awards he has won – businessman of the year, entrepreneur of the year, regional top exporter.

Kalyani then realised that to be a global leader, Bharat Forge needed a presence near their customers in the major markets where they operated. 'If you go to Daimler, Mercedes, BMW or Audi, they've got their suppliers in their backyard, they drink beer together in the pubs, and we're four thousand miles away, don't even speak the language – those are handicaps you can't overcome by being far away. That's the good part of globalisation, that these things started getting possible.'

They tested the water by buying a small company in Leeds, in northern England. 'It was such a fantastically successful experience for us and then we went to Germany, which is *the* place for this kind of industry.' In 2004 Bharat Forge bought a much bigger German company, Carl Dan Peddinghaus, that had just gone into receivership but had great technology and supplied all the major car companies in Europe. 'We worked very hard to buy this company. It took us a year, with the court receiver, the unions, the existing management and convincing the customers that we were the right owners for that business.'

Kalyani faced huge resistance, a blend of protectionism and prejudice. Germany is a country where a leading politician objected to allowing in skilled Indian IT professionals on the basis that it should want *'Kinder statt Inder'*, children not Indians. He recalls:

The first obstacle was that a large part of German industry in this business started talking about us in a very derogatory manner. The first thing they said was that 'These Indians have got money from the government. They will buy a company here and take everything back to India, take all the technology, take all the jobs away.' The second part was, 'These guys, how will they manage the business in Germany, what do they know about manufacturing?' We had to go through these issues because they affected the seven hundred people who were employed at this company in Germany. Unless and until you can get people to accept you as an owner, it becomes extremely difficult to manage. You're all the time in an unseen conflict situation.

But, with a keen attention to detail and good people management, 'we were able to turn the business around in three months' time'.

Their customers were impressed. Soon they got lots of other proposals and bought six companies in Europe. 'Each one of them we made a success. We turned them around, we started growing them, we invested, so employees were happy that we were not stripping these companies down and taking their jobs away. In fact, until the end of last year [2008] we were growing.' Within six years Bharat Forge became the largest forging company in Europe and the second largest in the world. It also bought a company in China and another in the US. It went from being a $100-million, largely domestic company in 2000 to a $1.2-billion global company in 2007–8 with three-quarters of its business outside India. In 2000 it employed three thousand people, all in India; by 2007–8 that had doubled to six thousand, half of them outside India and sixteen hundred in Europe alone.

Buying spree

Within less than a decade Bharat Forge has taken a global industry by storm. While its achievements are particularly impressive, it is by no means the only Indian company that is going global. The first big foreign acquisition by an Indian company came in 2000, when Tata Tea bought Tetley Tea, a British business with a global brand, for $435 million. It was a delicious role reversal. When Britain colonised India, it cornered the market for tea. For centuries tea was an Indian resource commercialised by Britons. Now a leading British brand was in Indian hands. Since then Tata Steel, the world's lowest-cost producer, has acquired Corus, which was once British Steel. Tata Motors, another arm of the huge Indian business empire, has taken over Jaguar cars and Land Rover from America's Ford. In 2007 United Breweries, based in Bangalore, bought Whyte & Mackay, a Scottish whisky distiller. Indians are now selling Scotch.

Other entrepreneurial Indian companies have also gone on a buying spree. Mittal Steel, a global company created by Indian billionaire Lakshmi Mittal, overcame European protectionism and prejudice to acquire Arcelor, the product of a merger between firms from Spain, France and Luxembourg, and form the world's largest steel company. The Reliance Group, Indian's largest company and the world's biggest maker of polyester fibre and yarn, has investments around the world. Wipro has bought technology companies in Portugal, Finland and California. Ranbaxy, which makes generic drugs, has bought Ethimed of Belgium and Mundogen, the Spanish generics arm of GlaxoSmithKline.[20] In 2007 Indian companies spent more on foreign mergers and acquisitions (M&A) than firms from any other emerging economy. Indian investment in Britain in 2006 and 2007 was larger than British investment in India.[21]

Companies from other emerging economies have also expanded abroad rapidly. In 2006 Brazil's Vale bought Inco, Canada's second-biggest mining company, for $18.9 billion – the largest foreign purchase by a Brazilian company – to become the world's second-biggest mining company and the largest producer of iron ore. Another Brazilian company, Embraer, has overtaken Canada's Bombardier to become the world's largest maker of regional jets. Brasil Foods, the planned product of the merger between Sadia, Luiz Fernando Furlan's company, and Perdigão, another Brazilian food giant, will be a global force. Quintessentially American Budweiser beer is now brewed by a Brazilian-managed company, InBev, which bought Anheuser Busch for $52 billion in 2008. Datatec and Dimension Data, two South African IT companies each with revenues of around $4 billion a year, have snapped up companies in Britain, the US and many other countries.[22] Factories in China owned and managed by Taiwanese companies such as Hon Hai, Quanta and Asustek assemble most of the world's laptop and desktop computers.[23] Taiwan's Acer, which made the laptop on which this book was written, has overtaken America's Dell, which made the one on which I wrote *Open World*, as the world's second-largest seller of personal computers.[24]

Chinese companies' global ambitions have run into the most resistance, as we shall see in Chapter 7. Even so, Lenovo has snapped up IBM's personal computer business. Haier, which makes household appliances, is also becoming a global brand. It has overtaken America's Whirlpool as the world's biggest refrigerator maker, and has operations around the world. TCL, a consumer-electronics company, broke into Europe by buying the French Thomson TV brand. BYD, which will feature in Chapter 10, is the world's largest maker of nickel-cadmium batteries. Chery, China's biggest car exporter, has factories in Iran, Russia, Indonesia, Malaysia, Egypt and Argentina.[25] Geely, China's biggest privately owned car maker, has bought Volvo off Ford. Huawei, a supplier of networking and telecoms equipment that was rebuffed when it tried to buy America's 3Com, has displaced Philips as the most prolific applicant for international patents.

Pankaj Ghemawat of IESE Business School in Barcelona points out that lesser-known, narrowly focused companies – such as CIMC in shipping containers, Wanxiang in auto parts and Pearl River Piano – have built on their success in exporting from China by acquiring and reviving foreign companies, using materials, design and know-how gained at home. Wanxiang has combined some small troubled auto-parts makers based in the US Midwest and rationalised production among them. It now owns stakes in more than thirty companies worldwide. CIMC turned around a maker of truck trailers in Indiana. Pearl River purchased a faded, upmarket German piano brand and retooled it.

The global picture confirms all this anecdotal evidence. In 1993 none of the world's top one hundred non-financial multi-nationals (ranked by foreign assets) were from emerging economies; by 2008 eight were, according to UNCTAD's *World Investment Report*, the leading reference on such matters.[26] ArcelorMittal was the biggest, followed by Hong Kong's Hutchison Whampoa – which owns 3, a mobile-phone provider, among many other things. Next are CITIC, a Chinese conglomerate, and Cemex, a Mexican cement producer, whose purchase of Britain's RMC in 2004 was the biggest-ever foreign acquisition by a Mexican company. Close behind are Samsung, a Korean electronics company and the world's biggest, Petronas, a Malaysian oil giant, Hyundai, a Korean car maker, and the China Ocean Shipping Company.

Together, the top one hundred non-financial multinationals from emerging economies (by foreign assets) had $907 billion in foreign assets in 2008 and $997 billion in foreign sales. They also employed more than 2.6 million people overseas.[27] Sixteen were from Hong Kong, thirteen each from China and Taiwan, eight each from Russia and South Africa, seven from Singapore, six from Malaysia, five each from India and South Korea, four from Mexico, three each from Brazil and Kuwait, two from Turkey, and one each from Argentina, Egypt, the Philippines, Qatar, Thailand, the United Arab Emirates and Venezuela.

In 1990 emerging economies owned a mere $145 billion of assets abroad (8 per cent of the global stock of foreign-owned assets). Their spending on factories, offices and other operations abroad as well as on cross-border M&A – known collectively as foreign direct investment (FDI) – accounted for just 5 per cent of the global flow.[28] But by 2008 their spending had soared to $296 billion, 15.4 per cent of the global total – and in 2009 they accounted for a fifth of global flows. This gave them a 14.2 per cent share (worth $2.7 trillion) of the stock of global FDI.[29]

Emerging economies' share of global cross-border M&A has also surged. In 2007 emerging-economy companies spent $140 billion (13.5 per cent of the global total) on more than a thousand cross-border deals. Even in 2008, when the financial crisis hit home, they spent nearly $100 billion (14.8 per cent of the global total) on 962 deals.[30] Pull all this together and it is the beginning of an astonishing transformation. Until recently global capitalism was all but synonymous with Western (and Japanese) companies; now, for the first time, it is becoming genuinely global.

Power shift

The crisis looks set to accelerate the big shift in the world economy from advanced economies (the As), notably America and Europe, towards emerging ones, notably the BEEs – China, India and Brazil. The BEEs were hit much less hard by the global crisis, in part because their banks were in much better shape. They are also bouncing back faster and stronger, because they are not weighed down with huge debts and because they are continuing to reap huge productivity gains. The upshot is that the BEEs' weight in the world economy is set to rise quickly. Indeed they are likely to account for the lion's share of growth in the world economy over the next decade.

Of course, the BEEs' development is unlikely to proceed in a straight line. They will have to overcome many challenges. In Brazil's case, Luiz Fernando Furlan cites infrastructure, bureaucracy, the tax system and education. In India's case, Shankar Acharya, formerly chief economic adviser to the Indian government, mentions rigid labour laws, terrible infrastructure, anti-business regulations and outstanding protectionism. We looked at some of China's challenges in the previous chapter. But as Bill Emmott, the former editor of *The Economist*, points out, such a daunting list of challenges can also be seen as an indication of emerging economies' potential. 'The process of economic growth is in part one of removing obstacles, rather as the dredging of boulders from a river will permit the water to flow more smoothly,' he says.[31]

Inevitably, the BEEs will have their share of bumps and perhaps even the odd crash along the way. But now that people's energies have been unleashed and are being channelled more productively, it would take a disaster or truly appalling mismanagement to arrest their development. The underlying dynamic is as follows. Rising agricultural productivity is releasing people from the land. As people move *en masse* from farm to factory – and increasingly into service jobs too – productivity grows in leaps and bounds. Capital is accumulated as firms plough their profits, often earned from exports, into higher investment. So long as the funds are invested wisely in combination with better technologies, an economy can develop fast by upgrading its industrial efficiency and shifting towards higher value-added products and services. Foreign competition stimulates continual productivity improvements – often based on foreign know-how – while culling inefficient companies. Because emerging economies were so inefficient to start off with, there is huge scope for them to catch up quickly. And now that capital and new technologies move around the world easily and people from emerging economies can learn from studying and working in advanced ones, economies can progress on several tracks at once. Development is no longer happening in neat stages; some parts of the BEEs are stuck in the eighteenth century while others are at the cutting edge of the twenty-first.

Here's a simple way of thinking about the world economy. In 2008 the total output produced in the world was worth a bit over $60 trillion.[32] At market prices, advanced economies accounted for a bit over two-thirds of it, emerging economies for a bit under a third. (Allowing for differences in purchasing power, namely that a dollar goes further in emerging economies, emerging economies already account for half of the world economy.) Now assume that advanced economies grow at an average of 2 per cent a year between 2008 and 2020 – no mean feat considering that period includes a deep and prolonged recession and then years of struggling with huge debts – and that emerging economies grow at 6 per cent a year (in dollar terms), with China and India growing at 8 per cent a year. (It is not a forecast, just a rough-and-ready calculation.) In that case, by 2020 the output of advanced economies will have grown from $41.4 trillion to $52.5 trillion (at 2008 prices), while emerging economies will have grown from $19.3 trillion to $41.7 trillion. Not only will emerging economies then be rapidly approaching half (44 per cent) of the world economy at market prices. They will also have accounted for two-thirds of the growth of the world economy over that period – with China alone accounting for a fifth of it, India over 5 per cent, the rest of Asia a further 10 per cent and Brazil nearly 5 per cent. Together, the BEEs would account for a fractionally bigger share of world growth over that period than the EU, US and Japan combined. Even if emerging economies fare less well, they are still likely to account for over half of world growth over the next decade or so, especially if their currencies appreciate, boosting the size of their economies in dollar terms. The bottom line is simple: the world will increasingly look east (and south).[33]

The world will be transformed. For the first time since the Industrial Revolution, poorer, non-Western economies will be the locomotives of the world economy. The decisions taken in Beijing, Delhi and Brasilia will have an increasing impact not just on their neighbours but globally. The institutions that provide a semblance of governance for the world economy – notably the International Monetary Fund, the World Trade Organization and the G7 – will have to reflect this, or become increasingly irrelevant and illegitimate.

Luiz Fernando Furlan recalls attending G8 meetings with Brazil's president, who was invited as an onlooker, not an active participant. 'I went with President Lula to several G8 meetings. The presidents and prime ministers invited by the G8 were normally in a side room with a screen and earphones. It was like

being in a sports stadium where you are watching but not playing. But now that has changed a lot. Brazil's standing has risen
thanks to its democracy, stability, credibility and Lula's leadership.' Lula's lobbying even outdid Obama's when he helped
secure the 2016 Olympics for Rio de Janeiro. Brazil is also host-
ing football's World Cup in 2014.

The crisis has already shaken up the way the world economy
is run. The new importance given to the G20, which includes
emerging economies as well as advanced ones, is a big step in the
right direction. Its pledge in September 2009 to shift at least 5
per cent of the shares in the IMF to emerging economies from
over-represented countries, and transfer at least 3 per cent of the
vote share in the World Bank, was a welcome start.[34] The G20
should play a much bigger role from now on. As Robert
Zoellick, president of the World Bank, says, 'The G20 should
operate as a Steering Group across a network of countries and
international institutions.'

Ceding power in global institutions might bruise national egos,
but it does not threaten the global economic system. By and large,
the BEEs support free trade, the WTO and closer cooperation in
other areas of international economic policy because it provides
huge opportunities for them to grow and catch up with Western
living standards. 'China and India don't want to disrupt the current world order,' says Kishore Mahbubani, a former Singaporean
diplomat. Naturally, they will want some things to change – but as
China's accession to the WTO in 2001 highlighted, the BEEs do
not want to upset the apple cart.

Doing Doha

The biggest worry is not that the BEEs will be too assertive, but
that they will not take on enough global responsibilities. Granted,
emerging economies have already made a big contribution to

bolstering open markets. While the US Congress seems unable even to approve one-sided deals with small countries such as Panama, they have opened up to trade and foreign investment unilaterally. China, in particular, is 'in many ways, today what Britain was in the second half of the nineteenth century – the unilateral engine of freer trade', according to Razeen Sally, author of *New Frontiers in Free Trade*. By opening up over the past two decades, before and after joining the WTO, it has also encouraged other East Asian economies – and even India – to liberalise further for fear of losing trade and FDI to China. Beijing has also exercised global leadership through its prompt stimulus package, which has been central to limiting the fallout from the crisis and relaunching global economic growth. But the BEEs need to play a more constructive role at the WTO if the much-delayed Doha Round is ever to be completed.

Among other things, the Doha Round aims to free up farm trade somewhat and reduce the scope for countries to raise their tariffs on industrial imports. Launched in November 2001 in the aftermath of 9/11, it quickly lost momentum, juddering from one stalemate to another. At the ministerial meeting in Cancún in 2003, emerging economies signalled that America and Europe could no longer stitch up a deal and present it to them as a *fait accompli*. Their voices had to be heard; they could – and would – say no.

But since then only Brazil has moved from a negative agenda – we can block this – to a positive one: trying to build a broad deal that advances their interests and global free trade. Celso Amorim, the country's foreign (and previously trade) minister, has exercised genuine leadership. Luiz Fernando Furlan, his successor as trade minister, became frustrated with other countries' obstructionism:

Before I took office I thought that the WTO and the Doha Round would be a solution for many issues in international trade and related to globalisation. But after I took office, I was so disappointed as nothing would move. Many times I thought of not even going to Hong Kong [a big ministerial meeting in 2005 that achieved little]. It seems that some countries that launched globalisation are now afraid of it because competition is increasing and emerging economies are growing faster than advanced ones.

Brazil's positive attitude is laudable. India, in contrast, has prided itself on being Dr No. Particularly under the stewardship of the obstreperous Kamil Nath, the country's commerce minister from 2004 to 2009, India has consistently been a deal-blocker. This is despite the huge advantages that its economy has gained from opening up to international trade and could hope to gain from further global liberalisation. Nath's replacement in 2009, Anand Sharma, will hopefully be more constructive.

In China's case, the problem is not that Beijing opposes freer trade. On the contrary, it has thrown open its economy to an unprecedented extent for a large emerging economy. The issue is, rather, that China has largely been a bystander in the Doha Round. In part this is understandable, since it has been busy implementing its WTO accession agreement. But it has also left a big hole in the talks, because the huge market that America, Europe and the rest of the world are most interested in has not sought to leverage that interest to demand that others open up their markets to foreigners, not least the Chinese themselves.

The WTO desperately needs Chinese leadership. The United States is no longer willing to exercise leadership in global trade, while the EU has always been a reluctant liberaliser. China, which could gain huge prestige and economic benefits by filling this vacuum, has yet to step into the breach. As a result, ambitions for the Doha Round have shrivelled so as not to offend protectionist interests in America, Europe and India too much. But this is a vicious circle. As Doha has become a midget, interest in its economic payoff has waned. Reaching agreement has become more a matter of political symbolism – showing that the system is not broken – than an economic imperative. Only bold leadership from China – and a little Indian goodwill – can revive the Doha Round and the WTO's longer-term future as a forum for global trade liberalisation.

Of course, there are other obstacles. Negotiations among 153 member countries where everyone has a veto are inherently unwieldy. Attitudes towards free trade in America and Europe are lukewarm at best. Trade negotiations are no longer technical matters for experts meeting behind closed doors: they are a deeply politicised jamboree that touches on sensitive matters of domestic regulation, such as health and safety and the environment, involves a wide cast of new players, notably NGOs, and is played out in front of the television cameras. But notwithstanding all of this, everyone wants to sell more to China – and China has most to gain, relatively, from freer global trade. So China is the key to breaking the deadlock, especially now that the crisis has dented confidence and consumer spending in the West.

It's not just in global trade that the BEEs are vital. China, India and Brazil are also crucial to global climate-change negotiations, as is discussed in Chapter 10. And they have a central role to play in shifting the world economy towards healthier patterns of growth.

From cars to windmills

Bharat Forge is already leading the way. 'In 2007 our business was 25 per cent India and 75 per cent the rest of the world,' Baba Kalyani recalls. 'It was a good story for us – till the global meltdown destroyed the automotive industry.' He crosses his arms. By November 2008 they had halved production at their US and European plants.

Even before the crisis, the automotive industry suffered from huge overcapacity. Kalyani doesn't expect car sales in North

America and Europe to return to pre-crisis levels for a long time
once government incentives to trade in old cars for new are
phased out. Only emerging markets such as China, India and
Latin America are likely to see rapid growth. The market for
commercial vehicles – vans, lorries and the like – has suffered an
even bigger collapse. The impact on suppliers like Bharat Forge
has been particularly severe because vehicle makers have also
been running down their stocks. 'We are running at 10–15 per
cent of capacity,' he says.

Kalyani is reorienting his business towards India. 'In
2011–12, hopefully the downturn will have run its course, [and]
at that time we see the business as maybe 40 per cent India and
60 per cent outside, but growing. Clearly, the opportunities in an
emerging economy like India or China are much greater than in
North America or Western Europe.' In future he sees his business as being split half-half between advanced economies and
emerging ones. 'The shift is clearly to the east,' he says.

Kalyani is also shifting his company's strategy away from grabbing market share in existing businesses to creating new
businesses through innovation:

> We are investing pretty heavily in research and development
> and innovation both in India and in Europe. I'll give you one
> example of this. Three years ago, we started work on a
> renewable business, from scratch. So we created a company
> in Germany – because technical resources in Germany in this
> sector are better than any other place in the world, it's
> expensive but it's still probably one of the best – and we
> started with one guy and now we have a hundred-strong
> engineering team in Münster and we have developed a full-
> fledged wind-energy business. We are selling wind turbines
> which are designed and developed by us. We see renewables
> and green energy as an attractive opportunity for us.

Bharat Forge's growth and transformation epitomises emerging economies' amazing development over the past twenty years. They are much bigger, richer and more important than before. Now, China and India are at the forefront of the big shift towards clean technology and renewable energy. In all sorts of areas, the BEEs can help develop new solutions and apply them globally – so long as world markets remain open. But will they?

6

Facing the Dragon

The protectionist menace

As you head north out of Chicago on the Metra, a sporadic suburban rail service that trundles along tracks frequented by seemingly unending heavy-goods trains, the view shifts from decaying industrial sprawl towards neat lawns, large wooden box-houses and picturesque lakes. Even in the midsummer heat, it's all very green – and seemingly serene. As you pull into the apparently prosperous 'village' of Round Lake Beach, you might think it was a picture of suburban bliss.

Appearances are deceptive. Unemployment in Round Lake Beach is 17 per cent and rising. This town of fewer than thirty thousand people is feeling the full blast of two big shocks: the sudden collapse in demand provoked by America's housing and financial bust, and a gradual (but cumulatively large) increase in foreign competition, mostly from China. The Great Recession has amplified and accelerated the Big Shift East: cash-poor and credit-starved American companies have been hit particularly hard by a general fall in orders as cost-cutting businesses and value-conscious consumers opt instead for cheaper Chinese products.

That's tough if you work for a company like Midwest Printed Circuit Services. Unlike Bethlehem Steel, the rusting (and now bankrupt) behemoth I visited in *Open World*, Midwest is not an industrial dinosaur. It is a small and nimble company founded in 1984 that specialises in the higher-value and higher-tech end of the market for printed circuit boards, the ubiquitous silicon and copper building blocks of most electronic devices. Its boards are in NASA's space shuttles, most American fighter jets and missiles and a host of industrial controls and instruments, such as Honeywell thermostat switches. And until a decade ago it was growing fast.

If even a company like that now struggles to compete with China, what ails America may be deadly serious – a fully blown 'American disease'. Or perhaps the root of the problem lies abroad: maybe China's artificially low currency, repressed wages and other government subsidies give producers based there (including, of course, many Western multinationals and their contractors) an 'unfair' and irresistible advantage. Whether America's loss of competitiveness derives from domestic deficiencies or foreign fiendishness, perhaps part of the solution is (or should be) measures to tilt the playing field back towards US-based producers. Some would call that protecting American jobs, others protectionism. Whatever you call it, it can seem mightily appealing when the unemployment rate is in double digits.

'China is an economic invader,' says Joe Fehsenfeld, Midwest's fifty-four-year-old founder and owner, over lunch at the local Applebee diner. 'And while economic invasions may happen gradually and under the radar screen, they are invasions all the same.' Not surprisingly he takes it personally, since nearly all of his life savings are tied up in the company. He believes that America must respond to the Chinese threat, but has lost faith in the ability and willingness of his country's leadership to do so. Courteous and softly spoken, he has an affable manner that belies his tough words. With his thin-wired glasses, grey polo shirt, easy-iron trousers and receding grey hair he looks more like an ageing computer repairman than a fire-breathing protectionist. Developing the metaphor, he adds, 'I sometimes wonder – is the US Rome?' (Throughout our discussions he refers to America and Europe as 'Western civilised nations'; presumably that makes the Chinese the barbarians at the gates.)

'Governments are there to protect our borders,' he declares. 'Unless we preserve our own economies, we no longer have the ability to provide the jobs that are necessary to keep our standard of living going and ultimately you will decline. The United States needs to make jobs a major priority, putting Americans back to work, like the Chinese are doing. We are on the verge of losing some of our high-tech areas of manufacturing. Should we do so, there may be no point of return.'

Like so many Americans in these difficult times, Fehsenfeld seems torn between his country's quasi-religious duty to be optimistic and the sinking fear that America is in decline. At times he veers from lamenting his company's fate to proclaiming his belief in a brighter future. Describing himself as a conservative, he is a firm believer in free markets, self-reliance and individual choice. He is a caustic critic of the US government bailouts of General Motors and Chrysler. 'I favour opportunity, not government intervention. When the government intervenes and takes on socialistic tendencies, the individual becomes lost.' He is also against government intervention in healthcare. Even though healthcare costs are an 'extreme burden' for his company that 'limits our ability to compete', he opposes a 'national takeover'. Yet this allergy to government meddling jars with his insistence that it must intervene 'to preserve American jobs' (and his company). And while he 'deeply objects' to unions – Midwest is not unionised: 'people can leave if they choose; most choose to stay' –

he works with unions to lobby government for help. You might say he is a free-marketeer who has been mugged by reality.

He tries to justify this inconsistency by claiming that tougher trade laws would benefit all of the American economy, not just a privileged part of it. But that isn't true – consumers and companies that benefit from access to cheaper imports would lose out, and over the longer term growth, innovation and enterprise would be slower. Perhaps his defining characteristic, though, is that he is a nationalist. 'I try to buy American things. I believe we need to support one another. Nationalism is not uncommon. The Chinese embrace it.' Chicago-born, he says he hasn't travelled much – 'I've never been to Asia.' But Asia has certainly come to him.

It all started, he says, with the Asian financial crisis of 1997–8. The collapse in Asian currencies encouraged a big wave of offshoring – a shift in production from America to lower-cost locations in Asia – with email and the internet making it easier to organise production across different continents. Soon after, in March 2000, the dotcom bubble burst and orders from American telecoms and IT companies dropped off a cliff. Within five years sales halved. His company barely had time to scramble to its feet before the financial meltdown and the Great Recession hit in mid-2008. Within a few months revenues halved again. And all along, competition from Asia – first Taiwan and South Korea, and now China – has eroded sales.

Midwest has never been a big company – 'I've always believed that you didn't have to be the biggest in order to be the best,' Fehsenfeld says. It has ninety employees, around 350 clients a year (ranging from Fortune 500 companies to much smaller ones) and sales of $8.5 million (a bit over £5 million) in 2008. By all accounts he is a good employer. 'We create opportunities for our employees,' he says, with justified pride. 'The jobs are technical positions, highly specialised, highly trained. The average tenure here is fifteen years.' A typical worker earns $30,000 to $50,000 a year – decent pay for people who have not had the benefit of a university education. 'We don't require college degrees; we provide technical training internally,' he explains. Corporate excess disgusts him – 'It damages the image of business in general, the ethics and morals we try to uphold.' Managers have taken a 20 per cent pay cut to see the company through these difficult times and so that as many shift workers as possible can continue working forty-hour weeks at $12 an hour. Fehsenfeld himself is not taking any pay.

That may help explain why he is among the last men standing. While global sales of printed circuit boards have risen considerably over the past decade, America's industry has shrunk by two-thirds, to some $4 billion in sales in 2008. It is the latest stage of a broader decline in American manufacturing, which has shrivelled from 25 per cent of the economy in 1967 to 17 per cent in 1987, 15.4 per cent in 1997 and 11.7 per cent on the eve of the crisis in 2007.[1] Now, every other day seems to bring news of another American maker of printed circuit boards folding. In March 2009 Bartlett Manufacturing collapsed into Fehsenfeld's arms, allowing the merged company to rehire some of the workers Midwest had been forced to lay off in late 2008. None had found jobs in the interim.

One of the lucky ones to be rehired was Jonathan Polit. 'I was very worried when I lost my job,' he says. 'There weren't any other jobs going. Companies weren't even accepting applications.' Unemployment benefit was a paltry $250 every two weeks; thankfully, his wife earns a living doing hair and nails. 'I was very worried when I lost my healthcare, especially for my wife.' Wearing a brown cap backwards over his red hair, he strokes his beard thoughtfully. 'I'm twenty-nine and because I never completed college I've relegated myself to going for jobs that are available. I did well. I'm married, I've bought a house. Up to a few years ago I've been very lucky, making decent money without a college education. Now those chickens have come home to roost. I'm regretting it now. Maybe if I'd been a doctor or a lawyer, things would be better now. I'm up to my eyeballs in debt and I should have been more careful with my money.'

Despite his precarious position, his views on trade with China are more pragmatic than Fehsenfeld's. A keen musician, he says he can buy a foreign-made guitar of comparable quality for half the price of an American one. 'Obviously, I'm going to buy the one that's less expensive. Of course, I'm better off as a result. I don't regret it for a second. I don't even consider myself unpatriotic. It's practical.' He doesn't think trading with China is a bad thing. 'Could the terms be better? Certainly. But avoiding business with China wouldn't be productive. And we're tied into China because they own $700 billion of Treasuries [US government bonds].' Not surprisingly, though, he is worried about his job. 'What could I do about it? I could find a different job in a different industry and that would solve it for me.' Perhaps most importantly, he has a healthy sense of perspective about what's at stake globally: 'I have to worry about not living well; others have to worry about not living.'

'I have no ill will towards anybody who wants to better themselves,' says Fehsenfeld. 'Everybody deserves an opportunity.' He pauses. 'But not at the expense of others. Not to say that I'm protectionist, but our government has not protected our industries. It hasn't enforced our own trade laws, which were set up to protect American industries against unfair practices. It's too late now: the barn door is open.' Asked if he feels hard done by, he replies, 'Not by globalisation, more so by our administration. The manufacturing industry used to get legislators' attention; now we struggle to.' This has implications for national security, he argues, since dependence on foreign electronics 'limits our ability to defend ourselves'.

Currency manipulation, subsidised materials and supplies, environmental standards, human-rights issues – Fehsenfeld rattles off the charge sheet against his Chinese competitors. He claims that China's currency could be undervalued by as much as 40 per cent, making it impossible for companies like his to compete. 'There should be in globalisation some minimum acceptable standard of environmental rules and regulations that everyone must comply with,' he insists. 'We have quality standards throughout the world, ISO or otherwise; why shouldn't there be some minimum environmental standards?' In the same vein, 'Perhaps there should be a minimum standard of human-rights observations too. Culturally, that's the biggest issue – how we view human life and how they do is entirely different. We measure it by the individual – the soul that's there – and they measure it by the millions.' Ahem. 'Everyone's always trying to do things cheaper. But is cheaper the answer? At what moral cost? It would be cheaper if all children were made to work. Where do you draw the line?'

'There is a race to the bottom mentality in corporate America,' he says. 'Multinational corporations have lost allegiance to any nation. They are aligned only to themselves. They use their resources to minimise their taxes, maximise their bottom line and exploit the lower-cost centres of the world without consideration of American workers.' Yet he admits that in 2005 he started sourcing the building blocks of his printed circuit boards abroad, in Taiwan, China and South Korea. 'It gives us a cost advantage,' he says. 'It helps us be competitive.' Thus his company benefits from freer trade as well as being threatened by it. But he insists he has little choice. Few American suppliers remain. Even so, he concedes that he probably could source US supplies if he was determined to.

Fehsenfeld even outsourced some of Midwest's production to Taiwan and South Korea after 1998. He stopped doing so in 2005 not for ideological or moral reasons but because of problems with 'quality, service, delivery and communication'. Surely, though, if Asian production is of inferior quality, American firms with higher costs such as Midwest could occupy the top end of the market? Fehsenfeld responds that the US industry has shrunk so much that it no longer has a critical mass to be competitive. Research and development (R&D), for instance, has shrivelled; since the recession hit, he has stopped such spending altogether. 'Now we are a second-class producer, as opposed to leading edge,' he says. Is it too late? 'It may be.'

Bob Denbo, his head of business development, is more optimistic. He says that while Midwest cannot compete with China on high-volume, routine tasks, it can succeed as a niche, high-end manufacturer. It can compete for smaller, more complex orders. It can win contracts that require a fast turnaround. It can build long-term relationships with companies and gain useful inside knowledge of their needs and wants. 'We often find mistakes in the drawings and designs companies send us. We can spot them more easily because we know what they are looking for. So we can save them the time and expense of producing a faultily designed product.' And, of course, the people at Midwest speak English. 'The language barrier is still a big problem with many Chinese companies,' he says. So perhaps Midwest may have a future after all – and I hope it does. A straw in the wind: while his daughter has become a lawyer, Fehsenfeld's youngest son, aged twenty-four, decided to join the company six weeks before our interview.

While Midwest may yet pull through on its own, Fehsenfeld wants the US government to take action against China. But bringing a trade case is prohibitively expensive – he says it costs upwards of $1 million – and only big industries can afford to lobby the government effectively. 'Your automotive industry is heard, your financial sector is heard, your healthcare sector is heard. The favouritism is towards big business and the smaller businesses are second-class citizens. We have no real ability to have an impact.' He doesn't anticipate any government help.

But salvation might yet come from all of American manufacturing ganging together to press for action against what industrialists and unions see as China's currency manipulation. He thinks the US should threaten China with trade sanctions if it refuses to let its currency float (upwards). That could bring about a devastating trade war, with much wider repercussions. China is financing a big chunk of America's budget deficit. As Bob Denbo says, the US should respond 'delicately'. The Chinese 'could ruin the US economy. Our fates are intertwined. We are mutually dependent.'

The China price

Midwest's pain is undeniable. But as its employee Jonathan Polit points out, trade with China brings huge benefits to American consumers. Consider that Wal-Mart – America's (and the world's) biggest retailer, which owns Asda supermarkets in Britain – was responsible for $27 billion in US imports from China in 2006.[2] Its low prices help people's money stretch further – in effect, making them richer. That is a particular boon for those on low (or fixed) incomes – such as the poor, the old and the unemployed – not to mention those who have taken a pay cut in order to keep their jobs. Because poorer people are more likely to shop at Wal-Mart and tend to spend a bigger chunk of their income on goods, such as clothing, that have got much cheaper thanks to Chinese imports, they benefit more than most. Research by Christian Broda and John Romalis, both of the University of Chicago, suggests that the cost of the typical basket of goods consumed by the poorest tenth of American households rose 7.3 per cent less than the basket consumed by the richest tenth between 1994 and 2005, thanks largely to China and Wal-Mart.[3] Thus imports from China narrowed the widening income gap between rich and poor in America. By boosting the poor's purchasing power, they offset half of the increase in income inequality over that period. So, despite fears that trade with China is increasing inequality, it is actually reducing it. As Robert Lawrence of Harvard University points out, low-skilled workers lost out in the 1980s, long before trade with China surged.[4] Nobel laureate Paul Krugman has found no evidence that trade with China harms American wages.[5] Most of the recent rise in inequality in America is due to the soaring incomes of the very rich, not trade with China. Blame finance, not foreigners.

Nor do Chinese imports harm employment. Before the crisis, when the United States was already importing huge amounts from China and running a big trade deficit with it, unemployment was at its lowest for decades. So while trade with China may threaten the jobs at Midwest, it is not destroying American jobs overall. That is true more broadly: studies find that unemployment rates are no higher in countries that are more open to trade.[6] As Joe Fehsenfeld is the first to admit, the biggest blow to his company in recent years has come from the credit crisis and the ensuing recession. China is not responsible for most of the job losses, bankruptcies and economic dislocation since 2007.

Even so, the crisis has sharpened fears among many companies that China is going to gobble up their business, while many workers in America, Europe and elsewhere are increasingly worried that most of the jobs are about to disappear east. After all, if 1.3 billion Chinese people are willing to work for much lower wages than those in advanced economies, surely either wages in America and Europe will be driven down to Chinese levels or all the jobs will disappear to China. If the Chinese can make *everything* cheaper, how can Americans, Europeans (and Mexicans) possibly compete?

The big flaw in this logic is the assumption that because Chinese wages are lower, Western workers cannot compete with them. The average manufacturing worker in China earned $1.36 an hour in 2008, according to estimates by the US Bureau of Labor Statistics.[7] That is sharply up from $0.54 an hour in

2002, but still much lower than the $32.26 in the United States, $35.81 in Britain and the whopping $48.22 in Germany.[8] Yet which country has the world's biggest manufacturing sector in terms of value added? America. In 2007 the US accounted for 20 per cent of global manufacturing, to China's 12 per cent.[9] (China's manufacturing sector seems larger than it really is because most things labelled 'made in China' are in fact only assembled in China from parts and components made elsewhere. Using value added as a measure of the size of the manufacturing sector eliminates the double-counting involved in attributing to China everything that is assembled there.) Which country was the world's biggest exporter of manufactures in 2008? Germany. How so? Because German workers are much more productive than Chinese ones (and German companies make products that foreigners want). Workers in advanced economies generally have higher skills and lots more capital equipment to work with, employ more advanced technologies and often benefit from better management and organisation.

In any case, labour costs are not the only factor that determines where an industry locates. While most of Europe's textile business has disappeared, Inditex thrives making affordable clothes in Spain by quickly designing, producing and delivering to its Zara stores garments that capture the latest fashions. And while producing in China is cheap, it is often risky. One issue is quality control. Mattel, the US toy maker, has come under fire for selling dangerous toys. Another is security. Companies have to be careful that their proprietary ideas, technologies and products are not ripped off. A third is bureaucracy and corruption. Companies may get tangled up in a web of complex rules and regulations that the greasing of palms can cut through.

Suppose, though, that the Chinese could make everything cheaper (and better). How, then, would Americans and Europeans pay for what China produces? Their dollars and euros would be worthless because there would be nothing to buy in America or Europe that the Chinese could not produce cheaper themselves. They couldn't even be used to buy oil and other natural resources, because other countries would have no use for dollars and euros if they could buy everything for less from the Chinese. More to the point, why would China hand over its valuable products in exchange for worthless bits of paper? If your trading partners have nothing valuable to offer in exchange, there is nothing to gain from trade. So if China could make everything cheaper, America and Europe would have to be self-sufficient. China wouldn't want to sell them anything, and nor would anybody else.

Clearly, such fears are absurd. As China's exports rose, the value of the dollar and the euro would eventually fall. This would make Chinese products relatively more expensive and American and European ones relatively cheaper. Long before China made everything cheaper, exchange rates would adjust and prevent this being so. But couldn't China intervene to hold the renminbi down against the dollar and the euro? Yes, it could – and indeed does – buy up the dollars and euros that its exporters earn with renminbi, keeping its exports cheaper. But while it might want to accumulate dollars and euros for now, there is no point in doing so unless they can be spent on something valuable at some point. Eventually, then, it would stop doing so and exchange rates would adjust.

Protectionist perils

In the meantime, couldn't America and Europe try to offset China's increased competitiveness, whether acquired by fair means or foul, by slapping taxes on Chinese imports? One option would be to put a tariff on selected imports, such as printed circuit boards, with which domestic producers are struggling to compete. Another would be a blanket tax on all Chinese imports – say a 40 per cent tariff to offset the alleged undervaluation of its currency.

Consider the selective tariff first, and say it is 40 per cent. This would raise the costs of every company in America that continued to buy Chinese printed circuit boards. Since their profits would be squeezed, they would try to cut costs elsewhere (by trimming wages or jobs, for instance) or to pass on the cost to their customers. But if they raise their prices, they are likely to lose business; if those sales were overseas, American exports would be lower – and if their sales fall, they are likely to have to cut back further on wages and jobs. Customers who are willing to pay the higher price would be worse off, and would have less to spend on other things. Clearly, some companies that used to buy Chinese circuit boards would stop doing so. They would tend to buy the next-cheapest acceptable alternative instead, which may be, say, Indonesian, rather than American. And if Indonesian printed circuit boards are, say, 20 per cent more expensive than the Chinese ones were before the tariff was imposed, US-based companies would again face all the consequences of the higher costs that I described above. So far, then, it's all pain and no gain for America.

Midwest might then start lobbying for taxes on Indonesian printed circuit boards – in fact why not on all foreign competition, just to be sure? Since nobody accuses Indonesia of manipulating its currency, that might seem desperately unfair – and it would be – but needs must. Eventually, a combination of tariffs could be found that guaranteed American makers of printed circuit boards a domestic market. Profits would rise, jobs would be secured and investment would flow into the industry. But the net result would be that America had diverted spending, capital and jobs from productive parts of the economy – notably exporters – towards uncompetitive ones. Consumers would be worse off too, because they would have to pay higher prices. America as a whole would lose, because it would have shifted its energies towards less productive activities and because higher taxes would reduce economic activity. In short, a tax on imports is a tax on exports, jobs and consumers. By trying to hobble foreigners, we end up shooting ourselves in the foot. But the costs of protectionism don't stop there. China and other exporters are likely to retaliate. Other American exporters will then suffer, as will the people who work for them. As Mahatma Gandhi once remarked, 'An eye for an eye, and soon the whole world is blind' – and lame.

Some people argue that by temporarily sheltering an industry from international competition, governments could give it breathing space to become more competitive. America's printed-circuit-board industry might plough the extra profits it makes under government protection into R&D and new equipment that raise its productivity and lower its costs. Eventually, it might be able to compete with China without government crutches. Perhaps it could. But then you have to weigh all the costs (detailed above) of the temporary protection now against the potential benefits of having a world-beating industry in future.

Look at it this way. If it were profitable to invest more, why aren't companies such as Midwest – which know the market better than the government does – doing it anyway? Perhaps they can't get the finance. That is a big concern in these credit-crunched times. But it wasn't a few years ago, when credit was flowing freely. So the fact that companies didn't invest more before the crisis suggests that protecting them might not be such a good investment by the government after all. And if the industry's real problem now is that it is starved of financing, the right way for the government to help is to get banks lending again on normal commercial terms. That would allow the industry to up its game without burdening everyone else with the costs of protectionism.

There is a bigger reason why protectionism is unlikely to

turn a failing industry into a flourishing one. It does not provide the right incentives for businesses to adapt. Without China breathing down its neck, America's printed-circuit-board industry would have little reason to try to become more competitive. More likely, it would milk its captive domestic market for all its worth. It would devote its energies to finding new reasons to maintain its 'temporary' protection rather than to upping its game. And it would channel its profits to lobbying politicians to that end rather than to productive investment.

Cynical? Hardly. Logic and bitter experience tell us that protectionism doesn't work. Just look at Europe's Common Agricultural Policy (CAP), which was originally designed after the Second World War to prevent Europeans starving. Fifty years later, European farmers still have their snouts in the subsidy trough and the CAP's rationale has mutated with the times. Now, apparently, hedgerow-slashing and pesticide-mad farmers have become environmental stewards. Please!

Or consider America's car industry. Decades of government protection have hardly turned General Motors into a world-beater. It has excelled at lavishing munificence on its top executives, providing expensive healthcare to its employees and keeping its former ones in clover, not at developing cars that people want to buy. It has proved a master at passing the begging bowl around in Washington DC – it received $50 billion in government handouts in 2008 and 2009 – rather than at fixing things in Detroit. As Bob Denbo says, 'They say we have to protect these eighty thousand union jobs. But what's so special about GM's employees? The government bailout isn't supporting the small businesses that create the most jobs.' Governments tend to help the politically powerful, not the potentially efficient. And as Joe Fehsenfeld, who drives a GM van, says, 'What's Ford going to do?' Quite. Special favours for clapped-out companies are handicaps for healthier ones.

Tackling the renminbi

What about an across-the-board tax on Chinese imports? If China is, in effect, subsidising its exports by holding its currency down, surely other countries ought to level the playing field. But hang on a minute. Who is losing out here? China is selling us its goods on the cheap; some might call that a great bargain. Yet far from rejoicing at this sale of the century, we want to punish them for it. Does that make any sense?

Not really. For a start, an inconvenient truth that protectionist lobbies gloss over is that it is almost impossible to know what the 'correct' value of a currency is. Since nobody knows for sure what the Chinese renminbi 'ought' to be worth, let alone what it *would* be worth if it floated freely, how can one possibly set an appropriate tariff on Chinese imports to compensate for its supposed undervaluation? A study in 2005 by two IMF economists, Steven Dunaway and Xiangming Li, found that estimates of the renminbi's supposed undervaluation ranged from zero to almost 50 per cent, depending on the methods and assumptions used.[10] This is not is an academic quibble, it is a fundamentally important point. Nobody accuses Britain or America of intervening in currency markets to push the sterling–dollar exchange rate up or down. Yet within the space of thirteen months the pound plummeted from over $2 on 15 July 2008 to $1.35 on 23 January 2009 and then bounced back to over $1.70 on 5 August 2009. When the pound was worth more than $2, some analysts thought it should be worth more; when it was worth a mere $1.35, some thought it should be worth less. So how many dollars *should* a pound buy? Nobody knows. If America and Britain tried to slap taxes on each other's exports because of what they thought their currency ought to be worth, the only certainty is that tempers would flare and trade would flop.

Many people – and economic models – jump to the conclusion that China's currency is undervalued because it is running a large current-account surplus. But that doesn't prove anything: it may simply reflect countries' different savings and investment rates. As we have seen, Chinese businesses and households are big savers, whereas Americans and now their government spend beyond their means. If so, a stronger renminbi (and correspondingly weaker dollar) would have little impact unless it changed savings behaviour in the two countries. Strikingly, the renminbi appreciated by over a fifth against the dollar, from 12.1 cents to 14.6 cents, between 2005 and 2008, the period when China's surplus ballooned, so China can hardly be accused of letting its currency slide to secure a competitive advantage. From July 2005 to February 2009 the renminbi rose by 28 per cent in real (inflation-adjusted) trade-weighted terms, according to the Bank for International Settlements. *The Economist* calculates that the renminbi strengthened by almost 50 per cent against the dollar in real terms between 2005 and November 2011.[11]

The growth of China's trade surplus with America tells us even less. In large part it reflects Asia's changing supply chain. Much of what America buys from China today – including printing circuit boards, Fehsenfeld confirms – once came from Japan, South Korea and Taiwan. China now imports components from these countries, assembles them and exports the finished goods to America. Knock these out and America's bilateral deficit with China shrinks by more than half.[12] Those, such as Fehsenfeld, who urge China to let its currency float (up) should be careful what they wish for. If China set its currency loose, it might conceivably fall, as Chinese savers and businesses with all their funds tied up in China rush to diversify their investments.

All that said, there is a strong case for revaluing the renminbi as part of its adjustment towards a more consumer-oriented economy, as I argued in Chapter 4. But if China delays doing so, would America gain by forcing its hand and imposing a tariff of, say, 40 per cent on all Chinese imports? No. Prices in Wal-Mart would rise. American companies that buy Chinese printed circuit boards would face higher costs. That would have similar knock-on effects to a selective tariff, but on a much larger scale. While some US producers would gain, America would mainly import more from countries with slightly higher costs than China's, and over time, production destined for America would shift from China to, say, Indonesia and Vietnam. Often the China-based exporters that would be harmed by the tariff are American-owned. In short, such a tariff would be a tax on American consumers and companies that would mainly encourage them to buy more expensive imports from China's competitors. A lot of pain for very little gain.

Worse, China would most likely hit back. It could restrict American imports and investment. It could make life difficult for American companies that have operations in China. Most importantly, it could stop buying – or sell off – US government bonds. China has long provided cheap and stable finance for the US government's deficits. Since these are now huge, higher borrowing costs would be catastrophically expensive. America is thus extremely vulnerable to pressure from its creditors, the largest of which is China. In July 2009 China was reckoned to own $800 billion (and rising) of US Treasuries and a further $500 billion of bonds issued by US agencies (such as Fannie Mae and Freddie Mac, which play a crucial role in the US housing market) that have a government guarantee.[13] According to Brad Setser, then at the Council of Foreign Relations, now working for the Obama administration, 'On current trends – and, to be sure, a lot could change . . . China's holdings of Treasuries should top $1 trillion in about a year.'[14] That would be around the summer of 2010. If China chose to dump Treasuries for, say, German and other euro-denominated government bonds, this would send the US government's borrowing costs up and the dollar down, a perilous combination. Rising interest rates could strangle America's recovery. Even if China simply bought fewer US Treasuries, this would drive up American interest rates.

Worse, the US government might have to borrow in euros – or even renminbi – just as the Carter administration was forced to borrow in Deutschmarks when America was suffering from stagflation.

Now a precipitate sell-off of US Treasuries would not seem to be in China's immediate interests. But if the US and China stumble into a mutually destructive trade war, all bets are off. In the heat of an argument, countries have a tendency to shoot themselves in the foot – which is how trade wars start in the first place. Even the hint of a Chinese sell-off could cause other investors to dump US Treasuries. And since China has a strong interest in diversifying its foreign reserves towards a wider range of assets with higher returns, it could view a more measured (but still significant) shift away from Treasuries as a way of killing two birds with one stone.

Paradoxically, the huge pain that China could inflict on America is a reason for hope that a trade war can be avoided. The Obama administration is well aware of America's vulnerability, as are many ordinary Americans, as my interviews with Bob Denbo and Jonathan Polit illustrated. So it is unlikely to press the issue of China's currency too forcefully. Tim Geithner, Obama's Treasury secretary (finance minister), has stepped back from officially branding China a currency manipulator, a move which under US law would compel the administration to enter formal negotiations with China to end the manipulation. But Congress may force the president's hand. American legislators periodically propose bills that would require the US to slap trade sanctions on Chinese imports if it refuses to revalue its currency. The latest, the Currency Reform for Fair Trade Act, was reintroduced in May 2009 with Democratic and Republican support, along with the backing of industrial lobbies and the AFL-CIO, America's biggest trade-union federation. The House of Representatives passed it in September 2010, but it does not yet have the approval of the Senate. If America's trade deficit with China remains large, the economy weak and unemployment painfully high, protectionist business lobbies and unions could eventually get their way, confronting President Obama with the dilemma of whether to defy Congress and veto it. Fingers crossed that he would.

The Chinese are not our enemies. But treating them as such could spark an anti-Western reaction. 'The government-controlled media could portray America and Europe as not friendly,' says Victor Ren, whom we met in Chapter 5. 'They could say that the West exploited China for cheap labour, created the crisis and now is blaming China for the crisis and raising barriers. But on the other hand, China knows this would make the situation worse. So I hope we would work very hard to convince America and Europe not to take a protectionist route, that we would buy more US debt and open our markets more to America and Europe.' As he wisely points out, 'Protectionism is a double-edged sword. Globalisation has reached a point where China is integrated to the world. So China needs the rest of the world, and the rest of the world also needs us. America and Europe need China's market and financial support to help themselves out of the crisis.'

What about human rights?

Currency issues aside, many Westerners have qualms about trading with China because of its record on human rights. Certainly, it is a convenient pretext for those who have a protectionist agenda. But it is also a worry for many people with genuine ethical concerns. The question is: what is the best way to address the issue?

In some cases, Western countries have imposed trade sanctions on countries whose human-rights record they particularly disapprove of. Those imposed on South Africa during the apartheid era are generally believed to have accelerated the demise of white rule. But in most cases, sanctions hurt ordinary people without improving their government's treatment of them. Sanctions on Burma have done little good, while the United States's embargo of Cuba has helped sustain the Castro regime. In short, sanctions rarely work.

Sharan Burrow, the head of the Australian Council of Trade Unions (ACTU) and president of the International Trade Union Confederation (ITUC), the world's biggest union group, points out that the situation in China cannot be compared to that in Burma. 'Are there pockets of human-rights abuse?' she says. 'Absolutely. Do we abhor them? Yes, we do. Do we raise them with our Chinese counterparts and the Chinese government? Yes indeed. But the Chinese labour law, apart from freedom of association, was better than the Australian laws under John Howard.' All of the ordinary Chinese people whom I inter- viewed for this book felt that human rights and trade should not be linked. They felt that the economic growth that trade brings is making them freer as well as richer. They objected to foreign- ers interfering in what they felt were Chinese affairs. And they were sceptical of the motives of those who wished to use China's human-rights record to restrict trade.

David Fung, a Chinese-Canadian businessman, takes a typi- cally pragmatic view. He says the Chinese see human rights as earned privileges, which Westerners redefined as human rights once they were rich enough. Human rights, he says, are of little significance when people are struggling to survive – and Westerners who try to impose their values on others are engaged in a kind of new liberal imperialism. Taking a broad historical perspective, he argues that China is still at the stage of Magna Carta, the thirteenth-century agreement that transferred power from the English king to the nobility, with the 17 million mem- bers of the Communist Party playing the role of the landowners. 'It took until the second French revolution, in 1848, for power to be ceded to the people,' he says. 'Real democracy can only come about once the necessary institutions have been established.' Fung is no patsy. On the contrary, he is a bit of a rebel: as a student leader in 1965 he brought Hong Kong to a standstill to campaign for Chinese to become an official language alongside English. In 1967 he succeeded. 'My youthful ideals haven't changed,' he says.

Restricting trade with China would not just harm the people it purports to help. It could easily prove counterproductive. As Burrow rightly puts it, 'Will we have disputes, union ones and national ones? Yes. We'll see clashes over labour and human rights, our commitment to democracy, Tibet. We'll have disputes about a whole bunch of stuff, but Chinese people have a right to development and they will eventually find their own way to democracy.'

India calling

Controversies about globalisation often seem to revolve around China. Increasingly, it is the lens through which globalisation is viewed – and unfortunately, the focus is often negative. But in one area at least, fears are targeted elsewhere. In the fevered debate about offshoring, they centre on India.

The worries about trade in services should sound familiar because they echo the debate about trade in manufacturing. First it was low-skilled clerical jobs, such as those in call centres, that shifted to India, the refrain goes. Now, it seems, even higher-skilled jobs in IT and other services are heading out the door to India and other emerging economies. Is there no end to the kinds of jobs that can be shipped overseas? Help! At this rate, we'll all end up unemployed.

Many commentators claim that trade in services is particularly threatening, principally, it seems, because it affects middle-class professionals like themselves. Some even claim that the conventional finding that free trade is beneficial does not apply to higher-skilled service jobs. More likely, they are particularly adept at special pleading. The main difference is that imported goods arrive through a port and offshored services through a fibre-optic cable.

A much-hyped forecast by Forrester Research, an American market-research company, suggested that 3.3 million service jobs in the United States and 1.2 million in Europe would be offshored between 2005 and 2015.[15] That sounds huge, until you realise that this implies 55,000 job losses in America every three months out of the 7 million jobs typically lost each quarter as a result of ongoing economic change.[16] In the EU, this represents a mere 2 per cent of service-sector jobs.

Other studies have tried to identify the total number of jobs that *could* be at risk. The McKinsey Global Institute concluded that 160 million jobs worldwide, 11 per cent of the global workforce, were at risk of being offshored.[17] The study found that whereas only 3 per cent of jobs in retail and 8 per cent of those in healthcare might be offshored, half of those in software and IT could. Another study came to an even more alarming (or alarmist) conclusion: that nearly one in five jobs in advanced economies – the US, the then fifteen rich EU members, Canada and Australia – were at risk.[18] These are jobs that use IT intensively, can be traded or transmitted using IT, involve codifiable information and do not require face-to-face contact. Many of these jobs are in accounting, consultancy, finance and R&D. The simpler the tasks, the easier they are to offshore.[19] Not to be outdone, Alan Blinder of Princeton University reckons that roughly 25 per cent of US jobs are offshorable.[20]

But despite the scare stories, remarkably few service jobs have shifted overseas. According to an analysis of US Department of Labor statistics on mass layoffs, only 1.6 per cent of job losses in 2004 and the first half of 2005 were attributed to relocations overseas.[21] More recent data from the European Restructuring Monitor, which counts losses of more than a hundred jobs or at least a tenth of the workforce in establishments with more than 250 employees, found that in the third quarter of 2010, offshoring and delocalisation cost 1400 jobs, a mere 1.1 per cent of the job losses in Europe over that period.[22]

In some areas, the offshoring of service jobs to other countries is likely to accelerate in coming years. One area of growth is likely to come from the public sector, says Mark Kobayashi-Hillary, a British outsourcing expert and author of *Who Moved My Job?*[23] With public finances under strain in many rich countries, governments will be looking to cut costs wherever they can. If public sensitivities can be overcome, shifting big IT projects overseas is an obvious source of savings. Already Steria is delivering finance and accounting work for Britain's National Health Service from India. In these tough times, many companies will also be looking to cut costs and reorganise their operations to become more competitive. One huge potential growth area involves small and medium-sized companies, which have so far outsourced little of their work. Kobayashi-Hillary also spies a growing trend towards 'nearshoring' to locations that are closer and can be visited more often – Americans to Mexico and Latin America, Western Europeans to Eastern Europe, the French to Morocco. At the same time, Brazil's IT service sector is growing quickly, while African countries that have installed good broadband networks, such as South Africa and Kenya, are getting in on the act too.

But winds are also blowing in the opposite direction. Big wage rises in India have shrunk the potential gains from offshoring, as has the pound's devaluation in Britain's case. While unemployment remains high in advanced economies, hiring staff locally is cheaper than usual. The recession is also amplifying a consumer backlash against offshoring. Gripes about the poor quality of service provided by Indian call centres are combining with public anger at companies that are cutting local jobs in favour of foreign ones. Many banks and insurers in Britain, such as NatWest, Nationwide, Halifax and First Direct, use the fact that they don't offshore as a marketing tool. Add to that worries about data security and other concerns, and many firms are reviewing the risks involved with offshoring, Kobayashi-Hillary told me over a coffee in a sunny courtyard near the British Museum in London.

The accounting scandal at Indian technology giant Satyam in 2009 didn't help, although it wasn't as disastrous for the reputation of the whole Indian industry as it might have been. Outsourcing more complex tasks has also often proved more problematic than expected, causing some firms to bring them back in-house. It requires trust that is often lacking, while managing arm's-length relationships can be tricky. And some of the keenest users of offshoring – banks and insurance companies that need armies of back-office staff to process claims and take calls from customers – have been flattened by the financial crisis. These issues are discussed at greater length in his most recent book, *Talking Outsourcing*.[24]

In any case, the potential job losses from offshoring need to be seen in context. Just because a job *could* be offshored does not mean it will be. All manufacturing jobs *could* be moved overseas, yet as we saw earlier in the chapter, they haven't been. Even if a large number of service tasks are eventually performed in India rather than Indiana, the shift will not happen at once, so economies will have plenty of time to adjust.

For now, the numbers are small. They are also dwarfed by the job losses from new technologies. Computers, the internet and IT in general are continually replacing millions of jobs that were once done manually. Email displaces secretaries and postal workers, Expedia replaces travel agents, internet banking does away with bank-branch and call-centre jobs. 'Cloud computing' is likely to lead to a cull of IT support jobs; companies will be able to do without the guy who comes round to sort out your computer problems when all the heavy-lifting occurs on servers elsewhere. Yet neo-Luddites who want to smash up computers are fortunately few and far between. As a result of all these wonderful technologies, new jobs have been created elsewhere – high-skilled service jobs that rely on IT as well as service jobs of all skill levels that cannot readily be mechanised or offshored: lawyers, psychotherapists, personal trainers, chefs and waiters, cleaners, childcare and so on. Remember: unemployment was at record lows in many countries before the crisis struck.

In effect, offshoring is just like technological change: it replaces old jobs with cheaper and better ways of doing things, making space for new and more productive jobs. It creates new jobs in companies that export to India and other emerging economies, whose living standards have risen thanks to globalisation. Indian IT service companies, such as Wipro, Infosys and Tata Consultancy, also employ increasing numbers of people in Europe and America. It also safeguards countless jobs by making companies more competitive and thus better able to support the jobs that they retain in-house. Studies of companies in Britain, Ireland and Sweden find that those that offshore tend to be more productive and pay higher wages; often they are foreign-owned.[25] A study of two thousand Irish firms finds that offshoring also boosts innovation – far from hollowing out production, it helps to upgrade it.[26] Where it is done well, offshoring enables consumers to enjoy lower-cost and often better-quality services.

Overall, offshoring benefits both advanced economies and emerging ones. The McKinsey Global Institute calculated that every dollar invested by American companies in offshoring customer services to India benefited the US by $1.12–1.14.[27] Each dollar produced 58 cents in cost savings, plus 9 cents in extra exports to India and profits repatriated by Indian-based US providers. A further 45–47 cents came from the re-employment of US workers who lost their jobs in the process. The Indian economy benefited by some 33 cents for every dollar of investment. Globally, then, the gains came to $1.45–1.47 per dollar of investment. Similar calculations for European countries came up with smaller gains, in large part because German companies tend to offshore to Eastern Europe, where wages are higher than in India and hence the savings smaller. Also, Germany's economy is less flexible, so workers are less readily redeployed to more productive uses. All of this means that the benefits of offshoring are only 80 cents per dollar spent. The figures are similar for France (86 cents).

In one respect the popular debate about offshoring is correct. India is indeed the world's biggest exporter of IT services. But in second place is not China, although it does export more IT services than France. It is Ireland, while Britain is third. Both actually export more IT services than they import.[28] The US is just behind in fourth place – and while America's overall trade deficit is vast, its exports of IT services are almost as big as its imports. As a study about the impact of offshoring on American workers by Runjuan Liu of the University of Alberta and Dan Trefler of the University of Toronto concluded, it is so far 'much ado about nothing'.[29]

Protectionism doesn't work

A sure-fire way of helping domestic companies that compete with imports would be an across-the-board tax on all imports, not just Chinese or Indian ones. Pitch it high enough and soon domestic companies would be raking it in, while industries that have all but disappeared in America and Europe, such as toys, clothes and televisions, would get a new lease of life. Hurrah! America and Europe would be making things again. But they would also be much poorer. Prices would be much higher. Productivity would be much lower, because people and other resources would be redirected from high-productivity sectors, such as IT, towards low-productivity ones, such as making shoes. Competitive exporters would be hardest hit. Since productivity would be lower, so would average wages. Growth would also be much slower, because without foreign competition, there would be less pressure to innovate and improve productivity. And all that's assuming the rest of the world doesn't retaliate. If it did, as it most likely would, a rerun of the Great Depression of the 1930s would be on the cards. Then, America's Smoot–Hawley Tariff Act of 1930 – and the tit-for-tat protectionism that other countries responded with – pushed world trade off a cliff, and with it the global economy.[30] So those, notably Ha-Joon Chang of Cambridge University, who propose that governments introduce 'limited protectionism' to ease the pain of the global recession need their heads examined.[31]

Franklin D. Roosevelt famously said that the only thing we have to fear is fear itself. The crisis has undermined America's and Europe's self-confidence. The danger is that in trying to resist what they see as a darker future, Americans and Europeans neglect their strengths and bring about what they are trying to avoid. The dragon to fear is not China (or India), it's protectionism.

When pessimism shapes public policy, when fear of the future becomes a refusal to change, the huge potential of globalisation may be thrown away. By trying to impede China's development, we would be dealing a grievous blow to the biggest export market of the future. Instead of trying to restrict trade, governments should be focusing on opening up world markets. China is keen to conclude the Doha Round, says Tony Miller, who used to represent Hong Kong at the WTO. 'China is likely to make pragmatic concessions at the last minute, but it wants to see a commitment from America and Europe that they still believe in the Round.' Businesses also need to learn from the experience of Darius Stenberg, whom we met in Chapter 4, and other successful exporters.

The economy that has had the most success in selling to China is probably Australia. Its exports to China swelled tenfold between 1999 and 2008.[32] So long as their economic ties were based primarily on trade, the Australian koala was happy to cuddle up to the Chinese panda. But now that Chinese companies are keen on buying up and investing in Australian ones, Aussies are feeling less comfortable with this tight embrace, as we shall find out in the next chapter.

7

Panda Panic

*The backlash against
investment from China*

> The ability to purchase and control foreign assets could
> soon become the most potent symbol yet of the shift of
> economic and political power to Asia – if they are
> allowed to occur.
>
> Bill Emmott, *Rivals,* 2008[1]

Bob Hawke has always been ahead of the game. He was a mod-
ernising centre-left politician and slayer of sacred cows long
before Bill Clinton or Tony Blair. As Labor prime minister of
Australia from 1983 to 1991, he freed up the country's hidebound economy and opened it out to the world, building the
platform for its incredible success since. He led the way in
embracing Australians' cultural diversity, casting off the noxious
legacy of its racist White Australia policy. And having first visited China in 1978, as president of the Australian Council of
Trade Unions (ACTU), he was among the first to realise China's

economic potential as it emerged from decades of Communist isolation and misery.

'In my first press conference as prime minister to the international press corps and the Australian foreign correspondents I said that more than anything else Australia's future wellbeing would depend on the extent of its enmeshment with Asia in general and China in particular,' he recalls. 'There was a lot of scepticism from our intelligent journalists who pooh-poohed the idea, but they don't now.' Back then, trade was a much smaller share of Australia's economy, and it was directed mainly at Europe and North America. Commerce with China was negligible. Now, more than half of Australia's trade is with East Asia, and China has nudged ahead of Japan as its largest trading partner.[2] Exports to China grew by over a third in 2008, trebling since 2003, and now account for over 3 per cent of national income.[3]

Unlike many other countries' trade with China, Australia's is balanced. The value of the minerals, fuels, metals, wool and wheat it sells to China, along with the college education it provides to burgeoning numbers of Chinese students, is equivalent to that of the clothes, mobile phones, computers, toys and other products it buys from China. Thanks to the resilience of China's economy and its demand for Australian exports, Australia's economy barely skipped a beat during the global financial crisis. The government's coffers were bulging when the crisis hit, giving it plenty of scope to pump up the economy with fiscal stimulants. As China's stimulus-led recovery has gathered pace, with its focus on investment in infrastructure that requires lots of raw materials, Australia is bouncing back too. Australia has always been a lucky country, some might say, but in this case it has also made its own luck.

So long as Australia's economic ties to China were mainly through trade, most Australians were relaxed about them. 'The clichéd view of China until 2007 was that China is busy making us rich,' says Mark Thirlwell, the genial Brit who runs the international economics programme at the Lowy Institute, a Sydney-based think-tank. 'As quick as we can dig stuff out of the ground, the Chinese will buy it.' (The Lowy Institute was set up by Frank Lowy, Australia's richest man, who arrived in the country penniless in the 1950s, made his fortune by founding the Westfield Group, the world's biggest developer and operator of shopping centres, and would most likely not have been admitted to the country under its current immigration rules.) China's booming demand for commodities, such as iron ore, to fuel its economic growth has benefited Australia twice over. It has provided a rapidly growing market for Australian commodity exports and also driven up the global price of all the commodities Australia sells. By making Australia's exports more valuable, China has boosted Australia's economy by 2–3 per cent, Thirlwell estimates.

Worries that Australia may be becoming unhealthily dependent on trade with China are wide of the mark. Exports to China have supplemented, not replaced, those to traditional markets, such as Japan. Other exports continue to grow at a rapid clip, albeit not as fast as those to China. 'We've diversified our exports,' points out Mitch Hooke of the Minerals Council of Australia. Australia's mineral exports to China, moreover, are often used to fuel the assembly of manufactured goods for export to America, Europe – and Australia. 'We're selling them what we do well, and we're buying back cheaper what they do well,' Hooke says. Australia is not just a large, reliable nearby supplier of the resources that China's economy needs and a provider of university education for Chinese students, it is a 'window on the West' and a 'useful interlocutor' with Europe and America, says Alan Dupont of the University of Sydney.

Imports from China have mainly displaced more expensive manufactures from elsewhere rather than domestic production, so Australians benefit from lower prices without worrying about lost jobs. 'If you decided to design an economy that would work really well next door to China's, you'd come up with one that didn't look too dissimilar to Australia's,' Thirlwell observes, rattling off remarks over coffee at a breakneck pace. 'So if people thought about China, they didn't think about it stealing jobs and creating unemployment, they thought about electricians, engineers, people with skills being able to migrate to Western Australia and double their salaries.' Perth and other places in Western Australia, where there are huge mining operations, are boom towns thanks to trade with China. The country's top union leader, ACTU president Sharan Burrow, agrees that trade with China has benefited Australian workers.

As Australia's trade with China has boomed, boosting people's living standards, their cultural connections have got closer too. Open an Australian newspaper these days and the first few pages are chock-full of stories about China, far more so than in Europe or the United States. 'More and more Australians are eager to learn about China,' says Henry Pan of the Chinese Australian Services Society (CASS), 'and there are many more Chinese-speaking people around so people are also more likely to bump into them.' Among Australia's population of just over 20 million, a quarter were born abroad, 280,000 of them in China or Hong Kong.[4] In the 2006 Census, 670,000 Australians identified themselves as having Chinese ancestry – some as far back as the mid-nineteenth century, when the Chinese flocked to Australia during the gold rush.[5] The door was slammed shut during the White Australia period, but since then a new wave of ethnic Chinese migrants have arrived. After the Tiananmen crackdown in 1989, Hawke allowed forty thousand Chinese students to stay in Australia.

Since the turn of the century Australia has attracted growing numbers of skilled workers from mainland China. The Chinese are also the biggest group of foreign students in the country, while Australian universities are increasingly setting up campuses in China and across Asia. In 2007 Malaysian-born Penny Wong, then the country's climate change minister, became the first federal minister of ethnic Chinese origin. As prime minister from December 2007 to June 2010, Kevin Rudd, a former diplomat in Beijing and fluent Mandarin speaker, pledged to increase spending on Asian-language tuition to encourage more young Australians to learn Chinese.

Australia has probably gone further than any other Western country in embracing China. From the mid-1990s until recently Australians saw China's development, and their closer ties with it, in an almost entirely positive light. Their trading relationship shows the benefits of seeing China's economic growth as an opportunity rather than a threat. But recent developments also highlight the potential challenges of adjusting to China's rise.

The koala and the panda are no longer bosom buddies. Australians are increasingly ambivalent about the implications of their country's more intimate relations with China. A 2008 poll by the Lowy Institute for International Policy showed that while 62 per cent of Australians agreed that 'China's growth has been good for Australia', 60 per cent thought that 'China's aim is to dominate Asia'. Of those saying China would become the leading power in Asia, 59 per cent were 'somewhat uncomfortable' (42 per cent) or 'very uncomfortable' (17 per cent) with this.[6]

One flashpoint has been increasing Chinese investment in Australia. Before 2007 the total stock of Chinese investment in Australia came to a measly A\$6 billion (£3 billion). But between 2007 and early 2009 the Australian government approved a further A\$34 billion in Chinese investment in the country. (This is still a drop in the ocean compared with investment from Britain and America, which in each case exceeds A\$400 billion.[7]) In early 2009 a big fuss was kicked up at the prospect of Chinalco, a Chinese state-owned aluminium company, increasing its stake in Rio Tinto, a mining company (ironically British) with large operations in Australia. This $19.5-billion acquisition would have been China's largest-ever investment abroad.

'Keep Australia Australian,' cried Barnaby Joyce, the leader in the Australian Senate of the National Party, the second-biggest opposition party, at the prospect of Chinalco increasing its stake in Rio Tinto from 9 per cent to 18 per cent. 'The Australian government would never be allowed to buy a mine in China. So why would we allow the Chinese government to buy and control a strategic asset in our country? Stop the Rudd government from selling Australia.'[8]

Joyce tapped into a deep populist vein. Australians are notoriously prickly about foreign investment in the country – and the prospect of the Chinese government investing in Australian mining operations stoked up nationalist fears of a foreign land grab.[9] Malcolm Turnbull, the then leader of the Liberal Party, the main opposition party, felt compelled to come out against the deal too. The government said the opposition was trying to whip up racist fears of a 'yellow peril', but delayed the deal long enough for it to fall through. It had approved previous (much smaller) Chinese investments, but with strings attached.[10]

The government then inflamed matters by drafting a white paper in April 2009 suggesting that the country needed to bolster its defences against an eventual military threat from China. To make matters worse, in July China arrested Stern Hu, a Chinese-Australian executive of Rio Tinto, on charges of spying, later reduced to commercial espionage and bribe-taking, causing alarm among international companies with investments and employees in China. Australians increasingly realise, according to Alan Dupont, that China is 'a complex country, not a cuddly panda bear'.

Kevin Rudd had made a virtue of his Chinese connections during his victorious 2007 general-election campaign. But the opposition turned this against him, accusing him of being a Chinese stooge – 'The Manchurian Candidate', as in the 1962 and

2004 films. A potentially huge asset for Australia – its prime minister's exceptionally good understanding of its main economic partner, and thus an opportunity to develop a privileged relationship with the world's rising power – was turned into a liability. Perhaps because he was wary of being portrayed as being too close to China, Rudd became increasingly lukewarm towards China.

Hawke thinks this is a mistake:

> It needs to be made clear that we welcome Chinese investment in this country. Like China itself, we will always take into account the national interest, but we welcome it [Chinese investment] and we see our future as very much entwined with China and China's growth. I think we need to say those things. That we don't see China as a threat and that we believe it's appropriate, as Rudd has earlier said, that China should assume a role in the financial and political global structures commensurate with its economic importance.

A sprightly seventy-nine-year-old – he will be eighty by the time this book is published – Hawke has not lost his way with words. His handshake is firm, his eyes twinkle and his sentences come out perfectly formed. Straight off the golf course when I interviewed him, he still managed to look quite dapper in a white tracksuit, while the big quiff in his hair has lost none of its lustre. He visits China regularly, five to six times a year, he tells me, and has been eighty-one times in total.

A protectionist drift

Australia is not alone in having qualms about foreign investment in general and Chinese investment in particular. While most emerging economies are continuing to open up to foreign direct investment (FDI), many advanced ones are restricting it. In a study for the Council on Foreign Relations, an American think-tank, David Marchick of the Carlyle Group and Matthew Slaughter of Dartmouth College found that between 2006 and 2008 at least eleven big economies, which together received 40 per cent of all FDI inflows in 2006, approved or were seriously considering new laws that would restrict certain types of foreign investment or expand government oversight.[11] Under the cover of protecting national security or safeguarding supposedly 'strategic' industries, Marchick and Slaughter argue, a 'protectionist drift' is under way. That is worrying, not least because no global agreement exists to keep investment protectionism in check.

Sometimes this protectionism targets other advanced economies. France told America's PepsiCo to keep its hands off Danone, which makes strategically important yoghurt. In 2008 Japan blocked the Children's Investment Fund, a UK investment group, from increasing its stake in electricity wholesaler J-Power because it would 'disturb the maintenance of public order'. In 2010 Canada blocked a bid by BHP Bilton, an Anglo-Australian mining company, for the Potash Corporation of Saskatchewan and then announced it would tighten its foreign investment rules. But mostly such protectionism targets emerging economies. In 2006 the US Congress cited security concerns to block the acquisition of some American port operations by Dubai Ports World, which is owned by the government of the United Arab Emirates, an ally of the United States. Senator Frank Lautenberg, a leading opponent of the transaction, fulminated, 'Don't let them tell you this is just the transfer of title. Baloney. We wouldn't transfer title to the Devil; we're not going to transfer title to Dubai.'[12]

Hardest hit is China. In 2005 the US Congress stymied an $18.5-billion offer by China National Offshore Oil Corporation (CNOOC) to buy Unocal, an American oil company, citing dubious concerns about national security. (In 2008, however,

CNOOC was allowed to buy Awilco, a Norwegian oil-services company.) In 2008 an attempt by Huawei, a private Chinese company, to buy 3Com, an American technology firm, fell foul of US fears about technology transfer. 3Com makes routers, switches and other computer-networking-related products which would no doubt be terribly dangerous if they fell into the wrong hands. This anti-Chinese reaction is reminiscent of the anti-Japanese backlash of the late 1980s when Sony's purchase of Columbia Pictures in Hollywood and Mitsubishi's acquisition of the Rockefeller Center in New York were demonised as a Japanese takeover of America.

In large part the resistance to Chinese investment is motivated by old-fashioned protectionism. No doubt it also springs partly from racial prejudice. But mixed in with those misguided objections are seemingly more legitimate concerns about whether state-owned Chinese companies are investing for commercial reasons or political ones and the risks of becoming too dependent on companies that belong to China's authoritarian government. Overhanging all of this are political fears about China's rise and its perceived greater assertiveness.

Investment protectionism is likely to become a huge issue in the years ahead. As we saw in Chapter 5, companies from emerging economies are increasingly trying to acquire Western ones. As Baba Kalyani explained, they often encounter fierce resistance. This investment is even more controversial when the buyers are state-owned, as many Chinese companies still are. And traditional state-owned companies are increasingly being joined by other government buyers – sovereign-wealth funds (SWFs), which invest in a wide range of assets on governments' behalf. As we saw in Chapter 3, emerging-economy governments increasingly want to diversify their huge foreign-exchange reserves away from US Treasury bonds and they are increasingly looking to buy stakes in Western companies through SWFs.

While SWFs aren't new, their number and size has multiplied

in recent years. Of the forty known ones in existence, sixteen were created since 2001.[13] Between them they were reckoned to have $3.2 trillion in assets under management at the end of 2008, according to the McKinsey Global Institute.[14] That is not pocket change, but it is still only a fraction of what global pension funds ($25 trillion), mutual funds ($18.8 trillion) and insurance companies ($16.2 trillion) manage. Many oil exporters and Asian countries have particularly large sovereign-wealth funds. In 2007 the Chinese government established China Investment Corp (CIC), with $200 billion of the country's foreign-currency reserves, mostly to make purchases abroad. But as Guonan Ma of the Bank for International Settlements cheekily points out, the world's biggest SWF is arguably America's part-nationalised Citigroup.

China has reacted to the backlash by directing more of its energies to investments in places such as Africa and Latin America, where its capital is more gratefully received. In 2007 Industrial and Commercial Bank of China (ICBC) announced it would buy 20 per cent of South Africa's Standard Bank, the continent's largest, for $5.6 billion.[15] Most of its other investments have been in mining and oil.

The Chinalco case has also rekindled Chinese interest in investing in Canada. In 2005 Noranda, then Canada's biggest mining company, had rebuffed a $4.7-billion takeover bid from China's Minmetals. But in June 2009 Sinopec, China's biggest oil company, bought Canada's Addax Petroleum for $7.2 billion. In July CIC, China's sovereign-wealth fund, bought a $1.5-billion stake in Teck Resources, a Vancouver-based mining company. But here too politics intrudes.

Jack Austin is a retired Liberal politician who was part of his country's first trade mission to China in 1971, when Pierre Trudeau was prime minister. 'The road from Beijing Capital airport to the Beijing Hotel was a narrow two-lane road filled with tens of thousands of bicycles, often blocked by donkey cars or these one-cylinder put-puts that we called lawnmowers,' he recalls. 'The journey took two and a half hours.' He says Canada had built a special relationship with China that in 2005 was evolving into a 'strategic partnership'. But since 2006 Canada's Conservative government has squandered that good-will. Critics say prime minister Stephen Harper, an evangelical Christian with populist leanings, has placed his personal moral values above the national interest. David Emerson, who was trade and foreign minister in the Harper government, says reli-gious lobbies hold undue sway in the ruling party. 'They [the Harper government] think the Chinese are anti-Christian and are of a lesser moral quality than they see themselves to be,' Austin says. As a result, 'Chinese firms would think twice about making major investments in Canada,' says Wei Shao, a Vancouver-based corporate lawyer who facilitates such bids.

China has also snapped up much smaller, and therefore less controversial, stakes in Western companies, notably financial firms. With awful timing, CIC invested in Blackstone, an American private-equity group, just before the financial crisis. CITIC, China's largest securities firm, took a stake in the American investment bank Bear Stearns only months before its collapse. Another Chinese company bought into Fortis, a Belgian bank that went bust in 2008. China Development Bank also took a small stake in Britain's Barclays.

But while China may think twice about investing in Western banks after getting its fingers burned, the issue of Chinese investment is going to loom large in Western countries over the next decade as China's economy grows, its companies seek to expand internationally to gain better access to foreign tech-nologies, raw materials, skills and markets, and it tries to diversify its mountain of $2.85 trillion in foreign-currency reserves. Australia's anguished debate is thus of much wider significance.

Hands off

While global capital markets can be dangerously volatile, foreign direct investment is generally a good thing. Unlike more flighty forms of foreign finance, when international companies build a factory, open a new mine, buy a company (presumably because they think they can manage it better) or inject capital into a business by buying a stake in it, that investment tends to stick around. This extra capital tends to boost growth, employment and living standards.

Foreign capital is particularly important for a country like Australia that is not awash with domestic savings. It has lots of land and resources, but relatively few people and a small capital stock. Throughout history it has needed to import people and capital from overseas. Foreign investment often brings with it better management practices and new technologies, which rub off on local firms too, lifting productivity. It is reckoned to have added A\$25 billion to Australia's national income between 1996 and 2006.[16] Because extra capital makes employees more productive, it tends to boost wages too. So keeping out foreign investment is generally a mistake. Just as trade barriers curb imports and drive up their cost, investment barriers crimp foreign investment and raise the cost of capital.

Unfortunately, Australia's foreign-investment rules are notoriously protectionist. The OECD, a think-tank for advanced-economy governments, rates them as among the most restrictive in advanced economies.[17] Foreign investment is stringently vetted and must pass an opaque 'national-interest' test that is open to abuse. Yet the government claims that in practice Australia is open to foreign investment: 99 per cent of deals are approved, according to then trade minister Simon Crean.

It has to be welcoming, Thirlwell argues, because it needs foreign capital to balance the books. If Australia scared away too many foreign investors, markets would take fright and the

Australian dollar would plummet. He argues that the vetting process is a useful defence against protectionist sentiment, because it allows the government to claim that deals it approves have been carefully scrutinised and shown to be in the national interest. 'It's not a bad insurance policy for keeping people reasonably happy.' While the formal approval process is not transparent, controversial deals do spark a big public debate and intensive media scrutiny.

These are all mitigating factors. But Australia's investment rules do still have a big cost – and whatever the merits of the country's investment rules in general, the Chinalco debacle casts serious doubt over whether the country is open to Chinese investment in particular. A director of the country's Foreign Investment Review Board (FIRB) told an Australia–China investment forum that it preferred foreign investments in large companies to be kept below 15 per cent and that investments in greenfield projects should be below 50 per cent.[18] Even when deals are approved, the delays imposed by the vetting process cost A\$4.5 billion a year, according to consultants at ITS Global.[19] And Australia *does* reject some important deals. Shell, the Anglo-Dutch oil giant, had a \$10-billion bid for Woodside Petroleum turned down in 2001. Other deals are withdrawn. Many, like the Rio Tinto case, fall through because of the vetting process. Alan Oxley, a Melbourne-based trade expert, says the rules are biased against China, with the national-interest test providing political cover for anti-Chinese decisions. For instance, when one company wished to attract Chinese investment, the first question FIRB members asked was 'Can't you get the money from someone else?'

Perhaps most importantly, the rules deter many foreign companies from even trying to invest. The OECD estimates that Australia could raise its stock of foreign investment by around 45 per cent if its investment rules were as liberal as Britain's, which are the least restrictive among advanced economies.[20] Since the total stock of foreign investment in Australia was valued at $312 billion in 2007, the OECD's research implies that Australia is missing out on a whopping $140 billion of foreign investment.[21] Think how many good new jobs that could create.

While many American and European companies are starved of credit and clinging to their cash for survival, Chinese ones have buckets of capital to invest and are keen to expand internationally. Australia is a prime place to do so. But it doesn't seem to want Chinese money. Simon Crean insists that Australia welcomes further Chinese investment in the resource sector, but distinguishes between investment in new capacity (good) and buying existing assets. 'How does that advance our national interest?' he asks. Answer: it provides additional foreign capital.

In 2008 Oz Minerals, a Melbourne-based producer of copper and other minerals, ran into trouble refinancing its debts. 'We were anxious,' says Darryl Gerrity, the mayor of West Coast council in Tasmania, whose area includes two mines that belonged to Oz Minerals. But now that China's Minmetals has been allowed to acquire them – albeit subject to the condition that it maintain a primarily Australian management team – it is expanding exploration in the area. While one of the mines – a nickel project called Avebury – remains closed, Minmetals says it hopes to reopen it eventually. Gerrity says China's deep pockets and need for resources could make it a better owner than Western companies in the long run. Chinese companies 'won't be at the whims and fluctuations of the world market', he says, adding that 'we're not as vulnerable as we were' when local mines were owned by Western conglomerates.[22]

Answering the objections

Opponents of Chinese investment in Australia object on several grounds. They assert that since China is not open to Australian investment, Australia should turn away China's. They believe that investment in the natural-resources sector is particularly sensitive. They claim that it would give Chinese buyers access to price and supply information that would allow them to drive a harder bargain. And they argue that Chinese state-owned companies are the long arm of a Chinese state bent on global domination rather than normal commercial entities out to make a profit.

The argument that Australia should turn away foreign investment if others do is deeply flawed. Why shoot yourself in the foot just because others do? When Bob Hawke and his finance minister Paul Keating opened up the Australian economy to foreign trade, they did so unilaterally. They didn't do it to benefit outsiders, they did it to help Australians. The same is true for foreign investment. Even if China did prevent foreigners investing there, it would not be a good reason to stop China investing overseas – although, of course, China and the rest of the world would gain if it opened up more to foreign investment, notably in the services sector. But in any case, the total stock of foreign investment in China is over three times greater than Chinese investment overseas, and the inflow of foreign money dwarfed the outflow of Chinese money by a similar factor in 2007.[23] At $96 billion, China's overseas investment around the world is dwarfed by that of the US ($2.8 trillion), the EU ($8 trillion), Japan ($542 billion) and Australia ($278 billion).

Yet there is something about oil, minerals and other natural resources that often provokes a nationalist response. People seem particularly keen to shout 'hands off, it's ours' over things that have landed in their lap by chance rather than by their own efforts. Yet the industry itself welcomes foreign money. 'We have no problem with it [Chinese investment],' says Mitch Hooke of the Minerals Council of Australia, a bluff, larger-than-life figure with a colourful turn of phrase. 'Those who want to make some political mileage out of this issue have always been against what they call "selling off the farm". I'm more inclined to growing the farm. You can't actually shift the farm. It's still in Australia.'

Chinese capital could help Australia develop its natural resources, to their mutual benefit. When foreigners are buying into Australian companies, rather than simply lending to them, 'they're bringing expertise, they're bringing commitment, and you don't have anywhere near the risks of the flight of capital, which precipitated the Asian crisis'. Hooke is absolutely right. The Australian government retains ultimate control of the resources that lie beneath Australian soil. Businesses are granted the right to exploit resources on condition they pay taxes, support the local community, protect the environment and abide by national laws. Whether the companies are Australian-, British- or Chinese-owned, their licences can be revoked. Contrary to what Barnaby Joyce claims, the government cannot 'sell Australia' – but it can help develop it.

In the Chinalco case, a more sophisticated objection was that the Chinese company would have gained access to sensitive pricing and supply information about Rio Tinto that it could have used to its advantage (and presumably to Australia's detriment). That's possible, but in another (smaller) case a Chinese company was allowed to buy into Fortescue Metals subject to conditions about information sharing. Presumably, similar conditions could have been applied in the Chinalco case. The bigger point is that there is nothing unusual about companies further up the supply chain buying into ones lower down. It happens in all sorts of industries, for all sorts of reasons. It is only a problem for public policy if it unduly restricts competition. Yet it is hard to see how Chinalco's investment in Rio Tinto would have given it a big influence on aluminium prices – and if it had turned out to be a problem, the matter could have been investigated by Australia's competition watchdog.

What about the fear that Chinese state-owned companies have sinister aims? Perhaps – but so what? Many people think

profit-seeking is sinister, but companies do not have to be benevolent do-gooders for others to benefit from their activities. When
they compete within the framework of the law they tend to produce things consumers want more cheaply. So irrespective of
corporate motives – whether they seek to advance the power and
glory of the Chinese Communist Party or that of their chief
executive – there isn't a problem so long as markets remain competitive and companies operate within the law. That is the
yardstick by which any foreign investment should be judged.

In the 1980s Japanese investors who were influenced by their
government were also said to be bent on global domination,
and were involved as shareholders in both the production and
consumption of products. Yet their investments in Australia have
not proved problematic.

In a similar debate over investments in European gas companies by Russia's Gazprom, the country's quasi-monopolist gas
producer, the issue is not whether Gazprom is an arm of the
Kremlin – it clearly is – but whether its investments will give it a
dangerous stranglehold over European gas supplies. The worry
is that it will. So the solution is to inject greater competition into
European gas markets, develop alternatives sources of supply
and until then be very careful about allowing Gazprom to
increase its dominance over European gas supplies.

It would surely be better, then, to assess all investment decisions on the basis of transparent competition rules that apply
equally to all companies, foreign and domestic. That would give
greater certainty to investors and allow Western countries to
benefit from a wider supply of cheaper investment, while also
protecting Westerners against the emergence of harmful monopolies, whoever their owners might be. At the same time, agreeing
a multilateral agreement to constrain investment protectionism –
at the OECD, WTO or elsewhere – should be an urgent priority.
Only in very rare instances is national security a genuine issue,
rather than a protectionist figleaf. As Marchick and Slaughter,

the authors of the Council on Foreign Relations study, observe, 'No one has pointed to a SWF investment that compromised national security in any country in the last five decades.'[24]

The perils of prejudice

Australia's backlash against Chinese investment is not only damaging its economy and its previously close relations with China. It is also harming attitudes towards Chinese Australians.

Henry Pan was awarded the Order of Australia in 1997. He has served on many government and judicial boards. 'There is no doubt of my loyalty and commitment to this country,' he says. Born in Singapore of Chinese parents, he came to Australia in the early 1970s to study mechanical engineering and returned later that decade to settle after the White Australia policy was jettisoned. In 1981 he founded the Chinese Australian Services Society (CASS), which provides a cradle-to-grave programme of services and activities to Chinese Australians. It helps around five thousand people a year. Pan has also contributed to the Australian economy, working for Pacific Power, New South Wales's state-owned electricity provider, handling its international business. 'I never imagined that I'd need to use my Chinese language skills to earn a living,' he remarks. Tragically, he had to stop working in 2000 after being blinded in a brutal (non-racist) assault.

Pan says Australians' attitudes towards Chinese immigrants have greatly improved since the 1970s but that he's still 'branded differently'. 'CASS provides a very good service to the Chinese community and we would like to extend this provision to other Australians,' he explains:

So we formed a subsidiary, CASS Care Ltd. It's a brand name. You don't need to know what it stands for, just like people don't know that Qantas's name comes from Queensland and Northern Territory Air Services. Yet people ask. 'Why are you so keen on helping other people? You are Chinese.' 'No,' I say, 'we are Australians.' Like Anglicare, the service arm of the Anglican Church, which helps all Australians, we are an Australian organisation, we are registered in Australia, we are Australians running this organisation, why can't we have CASS Care providing services to everyone?

Pan was not surprised by the Chinalco affair. 'There is a very deep bias against the Chinese and it takes a long time to change.' Even so, it 'made me feel that I'm not being taken as an Australian'. And it has had a negative impact on the way Chinese Australians are treated. 'We have taken a step back,' he says. But he remains positive: 'First we have to counter the negative impact, and then continue taking two steps forward.'

What's so worrying about interdependence?

'When it comes to the rise of China, you have to be a realist that when push comes to shove, their push is bigger than our shove,' says Barnaby Joyce.[25] But what is often overlooked amid all the knee-jerk worries about greater dependence on China is that China needs the rest of the world as much as we need it. It remains a poor country that relies on foreign technologies and resources. Even as it gets richer and more technologically advanced, it will still need imports as well as export markets, foreign investment into the country as well as outlets for its own outward investment. Growing interdependence ought to be less unsettling – and can certainly be mutually enriching.

While China's rise clearly has major political and strategic implications for the rest of the world, and there will sometimes be disagreements and even conflict, it should not preclude closer economic ties. Whatever the worries you may have about the Chinese regime, we surely ought to welcome all the new opportunities for the long-suffering Chinese people (and ourselves). Even if (conceivably) the Chinese government does aspire to dominate the world eventually, it will not do so for the foreseeable future – and by then the country will have changed out of all recognition. But in the meantime, treating China as a threat could foster needless antagonism, doing ourselves as much harm as it. And the closer China's economy is intertwined with the world, the greater the incentive on both sides for friendly relations.

8

Don't Stop

A newly mobile world

Gary Speed loves living life to the full – and now his city of choice is no longer London, it's Shanghai. 'There are very few cities in the world that have Shanghai's energy and freshness,' he chirps. 'I first visited Shanghai in 1998 and it's amazing how much it has changed. It was totally undeveloped and unsophisticated then. I never thought I would want to live there. Now it's like London for eating out, drinking and shopping.' He moved to Shanghai in 2005. 'An opportunity came up to start a business in the line of work I was doing in London – commodities trading. I remember that when Russia and Ukraine opened up in the early 1990s I was too young and inexperienced to take advantage of the opportunities. What was happening in China was similar and by then I had the necessary experience. It felt like the opportunity of a lifetime from a business point of view.

'When I arrived it felt like it was at the frontier, that I was riding the crest of a wave,' he raves. 'And you could live like a king. You would need to earn three to four times more in

London or New York to have a similar lifestyle.' The buzz and the lifestyle were irresistible. 'But now it's getting much more expensive. Rents are on a par with London, eating out can be too. Transport is still much cheaper, though. The pollution is horrible, although I think that will change. They're introducing clean buses for the Expo in 2010. And being a foreigner is much less of a novelty. As China is getting richer, you become less special here.' He doesn't plan to stay for ever. 'I'm scared of getting stuck here.' But he doubts he will return to London immediately. 'It's no longer the place to be, like it was ten years ago. I might downshift and move to Spain.' He's thirty-seven.

If Gary was Chinese and worked in Britain, he'd be called an immigrant. But because he is British and works in China, he's thought of as an expat. We are so conditioned into thinking of immigration as a movement *to* places such as Britain, America or Australia that we use a different word to describe people who move in the opposite direction. But increasingly, migrants are heading east as well as west, south as well as north, a trend that is likely to accelerate as emerging economies such as China, India and Brazil continue to develop.

The crisis has heightened the appeal of working in China, which is still booming. Sun Hande, who oversees the registration of foreign workers in Shanghai, says that his office receives some three to four hundred work-permit applications a day. 'The economy is bad in general. But I am lucky to be on the right side of the world,' says Marisa Espanyol, a thirty-five-year-old property lawyer working in Shanghai who moved to China after spending nineteen years in Canada. 'It's my best move so far.'[1] According to Jim Rogers, an American billionaire investor who co-founded the Quantum Fund with George Soros, 'If you're in London, you're in the wrong place at the wrong time . . . You have to move east.'[2] People seem to be following his advice. Jason Tan, who specialises in placing people in financial jobs in China for Robert Walters Talent Consulting, says in early 2008 he used to handle one candidate a week at most. A year later it was two or three a day, returning Chinese as well as fully fledged foreigners.

'Shanghai hasn't been affected too much by the global recession,' Gary says. 'Lots of foreigners are still attracted to it. Young people are increasingly coming here. They've read and heard about China, they believe it's the future and that they can get good jobs here.' Not all the newcomers come to take up high-level jobs. 'I was at a local Sichuan restaurant the other day and I was amazed to see a Frenchman waiting tables,' he explains. 'You're starting to see foreigners doing Chinese people's jobs. And they're competing with Filipinos who speak fluent English. There are also lots of foreigners living and working here illegally, including Americans and Europeans.' Westerners illegal immigrants? Whatever next?

More than a hundred thousand foreigners officially live and work in Shanghai, according to Chinese government statistics for 2009.[3] That total has risen thirteenfold in thirteen years. They include Japanese, Americans, Europeans and many others. While Shanghai attracts more foreigners than other Chinese cities, they are increasingly going to work in other parts of the country too. As foreign investment has poured into Chengdu, the capital of Sichuan province, whose cuisine is known for its fiery hot peppers, it has attracted nearly twenty thousand foreigners from 125 countries and regions.[4]

Africans are also flocking to the country to live the 'Chinese Dream'. In Guangzhou, the area around Hongqiao has been dubbed 'Chocolate City' by local taxi drivers. Every afternoon tens of thousands of Africans carrying large black plastic bags or backpacks emerge in small groups to look through the market stalls. The stalls are filled with 'tail goods' – jeans, unbranded television sets, hand-assembled mobile phones and other goods from thousands of small factories throughout Guangdong that did not meet quality standards. As many as a hundred thousand

Africans may now live in Guangzhou, according to *Guangzhou Daily*. Official statistics record that the number of Africans has grown by some 30–40 per cent a year since 2003. They come mainly from Nigeria, Guinea, Cameroon, Liberia and Mali. Many are small traders; some hope that by struggling for a few years they will be able to open a trade company or service centre, and get rich from servicing the rapidly growing trade between China and Africa. More than twenty thousand Africans are reckoned to be resident in Guangzhou for more than six months.[5] Already there are more than six hundred thousand foreigners in China – and the big move east has only just begun.

Two steps forward, one step back

After the oil crisis in 1973 many foreign workers who might previously have gone to Europe went to the newly rich Gulf States instead. A prolonged period of stagnation in America and Europe would doubtless also redirect migration patterns. For now, fewer Mexicans are risking their lives crossing the border to the United States, where low-end jobs are no longer plentiful, and some migrants are going back. Fewer Africans are risking death trying to reach Spain in flimsy boats, while some Moroccans are heading home.[6] Poles are deserting Britain, while many Brits are coming back from Spain. After a decade of record-breaking immigration, more people are leaving Ireland than arriving.[7] Iceland's foreign recruits are abandoning its frozen economy. Across the world, some unemployed migrants are going home, while others are staying on illegally for fear of not being granted a visa to return if they leave. Migrants are also sending less money home, causing hardship for people and places that depend on these remittances. Across sub-Saharan Africa, the region most dependent on migrant money – household incomes in Somaliland are doubled each year by money sent home by migrants – remittances are reported to have fallen by 4.4 per cent in the first six months of 2009.[8] The World Bank estimates that remittances to developing countries fell to $316 billion in 2009 from their record high of $336 billion in 2008.[9] But at a time when governments are cutting their aid budgets and private capital flows have drained out of many developing countries, remittances are still proving much more resilient than other capital flows.

People's future migration decisions are hard to predict – especially when the world economy is in such flux. But whatever new patterns emerge as the global economy recovers and changes, the crisis has highlighted several important trends that are often overlooked in the feverish debate about what is narrowly and misleadingly known as 'immigration'. The first is that mobility is not a one-way street: people are increasingly moving across the world in all directions. As Angola's oil-rich economy booms, up to a hundred thousand Portuguese people have gone to work there in the past five years.[10] It's not just Chinese people moving to Australia, North America and Europe; it's also foreigners moving to China. The United States is no longer the only land of opportunity; there is a Chinese Dream as well as an American one.

Second, migration is less permanent than it once was. People who move once often move on again, back home or somewhere else. Travel is much cheaper than before, people are more aware of job opportunities elsewhere, not least thanks to the internet, and there is a bigger choice of attractive places to go to. Some Chinese people move to Canada, then America and then back to China or on to other countries. Others move to and fro repeatedly, like international commuters. Academics use terms like 'return migration', 'circular migration', 'on-migration' and 'secondary migration' to describe these phenomena, but such terms fail to capture the richness of what is going on. These newly mobile people are a bit like bees that fly around from flower to flower, cross-pollinating them. So perhaps it's time we jettisoned the loaded and inaccurate term 'immigration' and started talking instead about a kaleidoscope of mobility.

This new mobility represents the stirrings of a global labour market which could generate huge gains for the world economy. It promises a new world of opportunities for people, a wider and more flexible pool of talent for companies to draw on and greater competition, as well as the increased creation and spreading of new ideas and businesses both within individual economies and across global migrant networks. All of that generates faster economic growth. So far it is the privilege of a few – the rich, the highly skilled, university graduates, businesspeople, investors and a few others – and the fortunate: those whose family connections give them access to tightly restricted labour markets and the greater freedom of movement that goes with citizenship of a Western country.

Except in the EU. There a remarkable experiment is creating a Europe-wide labour market of twenty-seven countries and five hundred million people, in which most (and soon all) can move freely. Who would have guessed twenty or even fifteen years ago that East Europeans would soon be free to live and work throughout most of Western Europe? Who would have dared think that open borders from Lisbon to Lithuania would so quickly be perceived as 'normal'? This dynamic and flexible new market highlights the huge potential benefits from greater global mobility and dispels many of the scare stories about it.

But while the crisis has underscored this new mobility, it has also prompted a backlash and led governments to restrict it further. Economic gloom and high unemployment are sharpening fears that foreign-born people take jobs and drain straitened public finances, while fanning latent racism and xenophobia. Immigration rules are being tightened and foreign workers urged to leave. As a condition of their government bailout, American banks have been forced to rescind job offers to foreigners graduating from US universities. Immigration reform that would allow illegal migrants to regularise their status in the United States and make it easier to hire foreigners on temporary visas has fallen down the agenda in Washington DC.

Britain was hit by strikes and unrest against foreign workers, who as European Union citizens have a right to work there freely. The previous Labour government tightened the criteria and restricted the number of visas available for skilled workers from outside the EU to some 45,000, down from 69,000 before the introduction of its points system for vetting prospective migrants; less-skilled ones are not allowed in at all. The Conservative–Liberal Democrat coalition that ousted Labour in 2010 is introducing an immigration cap that aims to slash net migration to 'tens of thousands' a year, starting with a limit of 21,700 visas for skilled workers from outside the EU in 2011. Italy has reduced its quota for foreign workers and criminalised irregular migrants, while prime minister Silvio Berlusconi has declared himself hostile to the idea of a 'multi-ethnic' Italy. It is also sending boatloads of African migrants back without bothering to check whether their asylum claims are valid. Spain has all but stopped recruiting workers overseas and is offering to pay foreigners to leave so long as they don't return for at least three years. Germany, the only big EU country that still prevents East Europeans from the new EU member states from working there freely, is granting fewer work permits to foreigners.

Australia has cut the number of work visas it offers to skilled foreigners by a fifth and restricted the skill categories to health, engineering and IT.[11] Old fears about 'boat people' arriving from Indonesia have also flared up again. A spate of attacks on Indian students is another worrying development. The Gulf States have expelled thousands of foreign workers, most of them South Asians. Malaysia has thrown out many (mostly Indonesian) foreign workers and stopped issuing most work permits in January 2009. Along with Singapore, it is encouraging employers to fire migrant workers first and to replace them with unemployed nationals. South Korea stopped issuing new visas to temporary migrant workers in February 2009. Thailand has announced that it will not issue new work permits or renew those of around half a million foreign workers. Japan is bribing Brazilians of Japanese origin whom it lured over a few years ago to go back to Brazil for good. Wellington Shibuya has decided to take the 300,000 yen (around $3,000) and return to Brazil. 'They told us, "Come, come, welcome to Japan,"' he says in halting Japanese. '"We'll give you a job, a place to live. Welcome, welcome." Now they don't have a job for us, they're saying, "We'll give you a little money, but don't come back. Bye bye."'[12]

A few countries have bucked this protectionist trend. In December 2008, as the crisis was engulfing the global economy, the Swedish government threw open the country's labour market to workers of the world of all skill levels. Thanks to the reforms, Swedish companies can hire whomever they want on two-year renewable work permits so long as they have advertised the position within the EU. Not only can they now compete more easily to attract Asian graduates from American universities, they could also hire, say, a Russian lorry driver with lots of contacts in Eastern Europe and thus expand their business there, says Stefan Fölster, chief economist of the Confederation of Swedish Enterprise. New Zealand is also maintaining its large annual intake of (mainly skilled) foreigners.

China is also making it easier and more attractive for talented foreigners to come and work there. For instance, in July 2009 it offered extended residency permits to, among others, foreign businesspeople, investors, professionals, scientists and university professors. Myrthe Beulens, a Dutch woman in her thirties who moved to Shanghai in 2007 with her husband, a manager at a foreign company in Shanghai, is among those who have been granted an extended three-year residency permit. She said the new rule was 'very convenient' as they no longer have to renew them every year. 'I enjoy living in China and especially in

Shanghai, to work here and to develop our careers, so we are very happy with this opportunity [to stay longer],' she said. 'It's nice to think that the government here wants us to stay longer.'[13]

China is also urging those who have previously left the country, or have Chinese ancestry, to 'Go East'. Kong Weipeng, who was born in Shandong province in eastern China, moved to the US after graduating from Beijing University in 1997. He got an advanced degree in financial studies at Pennsylvania State University and landed a job as a trader at Bear Stearns in 2004. When it collapsed in 2008 and was taken over by JPMorgan Chase, he says he had the option of staying, but decided to go back home. 'I think the capital market in China is just rising,' he says. He found a job at an investment fund in China and left New York in late 2008. 'It's hard for Chinese to fit into the local community entirely' in the US, he says, and besides, 'my parents are still in China'.[14]

Han Zhang Zheng returned to China after earning his master's degree in engineering from Britain's Nottingham University and immediately began work for a stem-cell-research firm. 'Right now, no nation is changing as swiftly as China,' he said. 'There are so many opportunities for people in my generation.'[15] The returnees bring with them knowledge of Western practices, business acumen and communication skills. Some have started new businesses. Robin Li, a graduate of New York State University, co-founded China's largest internet search engine, Baidu. Indeed so many Asians are now choosing to head east that America may be suffering its first ever brain drain, according to Vivek Wadhwa of Harvard Law School.

Adiós, or hasta la vista?

The internet revolution started in America, but was often led by foreigners. More than half of the start-ups in Silicon Valley over the past decade have a migrant as a chief executive or lead tech-nologist.[16] Google, Yahoo!, eBay, YouTube, PayPal – all were co-founded by people born outside the US. Immigrant inventors contributed a quarter of global patent applications from America in 2006. Migrants are also at the centre of the clean-tech revolution that is our best hope of limiting climate change. But now, 'Some of the most highly skilled workers in American corporations are returning to the lands where they were born and foreign students who would normally be the next generation of US science and engineering workers are buying one-way tick-ets home,' Wadhwa says, on the basis of research with hundreds of company executives, surveys of more than a thousand foreign students and more than a thousand returnees, and multiple trips to India and China.[17]

The average Asian returnee is in their thirties, has a master's or doctoral degree and is trained in science, technology, engineering and mathematics – precisely the type of people the US needs to fuel its economic recovery. 'Among the strongest factors cited by these ex-immigrants as a reason for coming to the United States were professional and educational development opportunities,' Wadhwa says. 'Ironically, this was the same reason they returned home. And they had advanced their careers in the process.' They were also lured by social factors such as closeness to friends and the ability to care for ageing parents. Interestingly, three out of four indicated that visa or residency-permit considerations had not influenced their decision to return home. In fact, 27 per cent of Indian respondents and 34 per cent of Chinese held permanent resident status or were US citizens.

Foreign students at US universities are also keener to go home than before. In the 2004–5 academic year, roughly 60 per cent of engineering doctoral students and 40 per cent of master's-degree students were foreigners. Previously, most remained in America to work after graduation. Among Chinese holding PhDs, 92 per cent were still in the US five years later, as were 85 per cent of

Indians – and most ended up staying permanently. But now, most students surveyed wanted to stay in the US, but only for short periods. Some 55 per cent of Indians, 40 per cent of Chinese and 30 per cent of European students wanted to return home within five years. More than three-quarters expressed concern about obtaining work visas, and nearly as many worry that they will not be able to find US jobs in their field. The US Congress has capped the number of H-1B temporary work visas available for highly skilled migrants at a mere 65,000 a year. That is far fewer than are admitted to Australia, whose population is a fourteenth of America's.

The survey found that only 7 per cent of Chinese students, 9 per cent of Europeans and 25 per cent of Indians believe that the best days of the US economy lie ahead. Conversely, 74 per cent of Chinese students and 86 per cent of Indians believe that the best days for their home country's economy lie ahead. 'The anti-immigrant groups will no doubt celebrate the departure of foreigners,' Wadhwa says. 'But the impact of a reverse brain drain could potentially be profound and long-lasting for the United States. The country is effectively exporting its economic stimulus.' He estimates that as many as two hundred thousand skilled workers from India and China will go home over the next five years, compared with roughly a hundred thousand over the past twenty years.

From an Asian perspective, this influx of talented people with American education and experience is an unalloyed boon. 'The returnees are a lot more innovative and entrepreneurial than the locals are,' Wadhwa says. 'So you're already seeing huge benefits to India and China from people who came back.'[18] From a European perspective, it is worrying that far fewer European than Asian students want to go home, underscoring fears about Europe's relative decline. But from an American perspective, the prognosis may not be as bleak as Wadhwa makes out. Some of the outflow may be cyclical: foreigners may be keener to stay on in the US when the economy recovers. Those who have left may not be gone for good. Those who are US citizens or permanent residents – and thus have a right to come and work in the US whenever they please – are particularly likely to return at some point in their career. Even those who have left for ever can still benefit America by using the contacts and experience they gained there to forge new trading links. From a global perspective, this new mobility is helping to create and transfer new ideas, technologies and entrepreneurial sparks faster and wider than ever, boosting economic growth, innovation and trade.

Shifting students

The biggest category of mobile people is not international business executives, it is students. Increasingly, people are going to university abroad and most countries are eager to welcome them. More than three million people studied abroad in 2007, up from 1.9 million in 2000.[19] Most of them (2.5 million) were studying in the advanced economies of the OECD. Education is an increasingly large export earner for rich countries, and can also be a way of attracting talented foreigners to stay on and work.

In 2007, the latest year for which comparable figures are available, the 211,000 international students that Australia attracted accounted for nearly a fifth of the country's student population. Britain ranks second in terms of enrolment numbers (351,000) and as a share of the student population (14.9 per cent). Switzerland, New Zealand, France and Germany also have relatively big foreign-student populations. In terms of sheer numbers, the United States attracts most (595,000), although they are only 3.4 per cent of the student population.

But perhaps surprisingly, relatively few foreign graduates stay on to work in the country where they studied. The OECD reckons that Australia has the highest stay rate: perhaps a third of foreign graduates eventually work there. In Britain, only around a quarter of foreign students are working in the country six months after graduation. In Canada, a mere 15–20 per cent are eventually employed there. In the United States, stay rates vary a lot according to students' country of origin. Previously, over 80 per cent of Chinese and Indian doctoral completers stayed on in America, whereas less than a quarter of those from Brazil did. But now, the Chinese and Indians are increasingly moving on too.[20] Until recently non-EU graduates of German universities, who were therefore highly skilled and well versed in German language and life, were not allowed to stay on and work in the country. Absurdly, Britain's coalition government wants to make it harder for foreign graduates to stay on and work. Clearly, countries need to do more if they want to hang on to talented foreign graduates.

Bye bye Britain

Many Britons seem convinced that the whole world wants to live in the UK. It's true that lots of foreigners flocked to work in the UK during its unprecedented economic boom, especially after 2004 when it opened up to citizens of eight new EU member states, notably Poland, collectively known as the A8 countries. But few planned to stay permanently, and now that boom has turned to bust, they are leaving in droves. They are joining many others who have been leaving Britain for decades. Contrary to the belief that migration to Britain is a one-way street, there is a churn of people in both directions as well as more permanent departures.

Few countries are as diligent at counting people who leave as they are at totting up those who come in. Some don't bother to count them at all. If governments only measure immigration, no wonder many people ignore the scale and nature of emigration.

Fortunately, the Institute for Public Policy Research (IPPR), Britain's top think-tank for migration research, has done a sterling job of trying to fill in the gaps for the UK.

Britain is a country of emigrants as well as immigrants: it experienced a net loss of 2.7 million British nationals between 1996 and 2006, including Gary Speed's move to Shanghai.[21] There are more Brits abroad than foreigners in Britain; Brits in Spain outnumber Poles in Britain. While 6.2 million foreigners entered the country between 1975 and 2007, 3.2 million left over that period.[22] At least 61,000 foreigners left Britain each year, rising to a peak of 194,000 in 2006 – a population the size of Portsmouth. Most spent less than four years in Britain. Of the migrants who arrived in 1998, only a quarter were still in the country a decade later. That to and fro has accelerated in recent years. Among the East European migrants from the A8 countries who arrived after 2004, half had already left again by 2008.[23] Many of these A8 workers move back and forth regularly. In effect, they are international commuters. Britain's open door has thus proved to be a revolving one.

The crisis has highlighted the increasingly transitory nature of many people flows. In the year to September 2008, just before the British economy fell off a cliff, the number of foreigners leaving the country rose by nearly 30 per cent, according to the Office of National Statistics.[24] Among A8 citizens, emigration doubled. Whereas in the year to September 2007, 227,000 East Europeans had registered to work in Britain, the inflow more than halved to 106,000 in the twelve months to September 2009 and has since stabilised. Among those registering to work in the year to March 2009 (the most recent period for which data is available), 62 per cent said that they intended to stay less than three months (up from 55 per cent among those arriving in the year to March 2007). Only 7 per cent planned to stay longer than two years, down from 9 per cent (22 per cent didn't know).[25]

Unsurprisingly, mobility is greatest among those who can

move from country to country relatively freely. Highly skilled foreigners who increasingly have a choice about where they want to work are particularly footloose. So too are A8 citizens of all kinds who are free to work legally wherever they please in the EU (with the notable exception of Germany). But even among less-skilled migrants from developing countries, mobility is increasing, as improving prospects in emerging economies (and worsening ones in Britain) tempt many to move on. Many people move to Britain with a fixed aim in mind – to study, learn English, do a particular job, save up some money – and move on once that has been achieved. The homeward tug of friends can also be strong. Paradoxically, though, the tightening of immigration restrictions encourages many people to stay longer, for fear they could not return at a later date if they wanted to. Yet the easier it is to come and go from Britain, the more likely it is people will leave – and come back.

Arrivederci Australia

Even in countries such as Australia and New Zealand, whose societies are largely based on permanent settlement by immigrants, people increasingly come and go. I briefly became an immigrant to New Zealand in May 2009 when I had to obtain a temporary work permit after the Office of Ethnic Affairs invited me to spend two and a half weeks touring the country speaking about the economic benefits of diversity. Temporary migrants to New Zealand are increasingly common, although most stay longer than I did. The number of foreigners granted a temporary work permit exceeded 130,000 in 2007–8, roughly five times more than a decade earlier. One in six was British, one in nine Chinese. They outnumbered those who arrived on a permanent and long-term basis by more than two to one. Such temporary migrants, some of whom go on to become permanent settlers, accounted for more than 2 per cent of New Zealand's population in 2006.[26]

At the same time, many supposedly permanent foreign settlers leave each year, as do many New Zealand citizens. While 85,200 people arrived in the country on a long-term basis in 2007–8, 80,500 left. Those arriving included 23,000 Kiwis who had previously left the country. Those departing included 58,300 New Zealand citizens and 22,200 foreigners who had previously arrived on a long-term basis.[27] Over time, more than a quarter of supposedly permanent foreign settlers end up leaving again.[28] Increasingly, then, New Zealand is a staging post, rather than a final destination.

Australia too is caught up in this whirlwind of global mobility. Henry Pan of Sydney-based CASS, whom we met in Chapter 7, says that it is very common for Chinese immigrants not to stay in Australia for a long time, but rather to split their time between the two countries. Some look after their elderly parents in China or have a home there. Many are involved in trade with China – including many of those who were allowed to stay after the Tiananmen crackdown and have since become Australian citizens.

We can get a particularly good picture of what is going on because Australian officials meticulously document everyone who comes and goes – one of the merits of its otherwise overly bureaucratic immigration system. At the end of 2008 264,700 foreigners were resident in the country on temporary work visas; they include foreign engineers in mines in Western Australia and British backpackers working their way around the country for a year, as well as apprentices and other trainees.[29] A further 289,800 foreigners were studying in the country.[30] New Zealanders are counted separately: 525,000 were there as permanent or temporary residents, students or visitors.[31] In total, then, perhaps a million foreigners were temporarily resident in Australia at the end of 2008.

At the same time, many supposedly permanent migrants do not stay for ever, while some Australians move on too. While 205,900 foreigners settled in the country 'permanently' in 2007–8, 76,900 people left 'permanently'. Of those leaving, half were born in Australia and the other half were people born abroad who had previously settled 'permanently'.[32] Nearly a third of those who left said they intended to move to East Asia; the proportion was one in four among those born in Australia and three in eight among those born abroad.[33] Among the foreign-born, China and Hong Kong were the second most popular destinations after New Zealand.

Ciao Canada

Like Australia and New Zealand, Canada is a former British colony that now welcomes permanent settlers from around the world. But it is also home to increasing numbers of temporary residents. In 1998 Canada counted 488,000 temporary stayers; by 2008 this had risen to 880,000.[34] The number of temporary workers more than doubled to 363,000, while the foreign student roll doubled to 243,000. Some go on to become permanent residents, many leave, others move back and forth. Canada does not keep tabs on people who leave, but researchers estimate that around a third of business immigrants or skilled workers leave within five years.[35]

Some 2.7 million Canadians live overseas, according to research by the Asia Pacific Foundation of Canada, a Vancouver-based think-tank. They account for around 9 per cent of the country's population, a bigger share than the equivalent figure for the United States, India or Australia. Many are recent migrants to Canada who have moved back to their home country or on to another. Yuen Pau Woo, the Asia Pacific Foundation's president, estimates that there could be six hundred thousand Canadians in Asia alone, most of whom are foreign-born. Half of them are likely to be in Hong Kong. Canadian authorities often perceive such people as 'failed immigrants who couldn't hack it in Canada', Woo says, when they are nothing of the sort. His research shows that those who leave are in fact generally outperformers, above-average earners with more dynamic credentials. 'The common perception of return migrants as failures is not just wrong,' he argues, 'it's damaging to Canadian interests.' Quite. Talented people move around, because they are ambitious and their skills are in demand. The connections they create can be very valuable to all the places they have ties to. They need to be nurtured, not neglected or dismissed.

On the move

Keeping track of how many people are moving around, let alone why, is frustratingly difficult. Unlike goods, people aren't (yet) tagged when they cross international borders. Within the EU's Schengen zone, people can move from country to country without even showing their passport. As we have seen, the bureaucratic categories that immigration systems apply to people are misleading, and countries count people differently.

Despite all these difficulties, the OECD tries to compile comparable figures, albeit only for its rich-country members. It finds that 2.5 million people went to work abroad on a temporary basis in 2006, three times as many as did so on a more permanent basis. This understates the increasingly temporary nature of most migration, because bizarrely the OECD counts people who move about freely within the EU as permanent migrants, when clearly most are not. The French bankers and Polish builders who until recently congregated in London were anything but permanent settlers.

Still, the OECD figures help fill in a bit more of the picture that this chapter has sketched out. Germany and Japan, both of which are loath to allow in permanent immigrants who might further sully their ethnic purity, allow in quite a few foreigners temporarily. Germany admitted 379,000 mostly seasonal workers in 2006, while Japan let in 164,000 apprentices and other foreign workers. The United States allowed in 678,000 foreigners on temporary work visas legally, while many more entered or stayed on illegally.[36]

Around 1.7 million citizens of a rich OECD country moved to another OECD country in 2006. Some 110,000 Germans became immigrants – sorry, expatriates – in 2006 by moving to another OECD country. And 1.4 million foreigners left OECD countries. Again, this figure is an underestimate because the United States, Italy, Spain and Greece do not count people leaving.[37] A Dutch study found that among those coming to work in the Netherlands between 1995 and 2003, more than half had left within five years.[38] Likewise, nearly half of those who came to work in Norway in 2001 were gone five years later.[39]

Using data from the 2000 Census and the 2005 American Community Survey, OECD researchers calculate that at least 19 per cent of migrants who arrived in the United States in 1999 had left again by 2005.[40] More than half of Europeans had left, as had nearly half of Canadians, while only a quarter of South Americans and less than a fifth of Mexicans had departed.[41] More recently, the population of South Americans in the United States has declined by as much as four hundred thousand from a peak of about three million in 2006, according to Jeffrey Passel, a demographer at the Pew Hispanic Center in Washington DC. Much of the decline is among high-skilled workers from Colombia, where the security situation has improved, and Brazil, whose economy has seen huge growth in recent years.[42]

As all this data highlights, the notion that migration is a one-way movement of permanent settlement is increasingly outdated. Most is now temporary, especially within the EU but also even in

English-speaking settler countries. Isn't it time the public debate about 'immigration' recognised this reality?

Going home

People move on, or go home, for all sorts of reasons. A new job beckons. They fancy a change. They have saved up enough. Or they lose their job. Their visas expire. The stress of playing hide-and-seek with the authorities becomes unbearable. They miss their family. In some cases, the decision to leave can be as difficult as migrating in the first place was.

In *Immigrants: Your Country Needs Them*, we met Inmer Oscar Rivera, a Honduran who had risked his life making his way up through Mexico to Ciudad Juárez and was planning to take his chances trying to cross the border to work in the United States. Now meet Oscar, a Honduran who made it across that dangerous line in the desert seven years ago and has now decided – with a heavy heart – to go back. 'America is a great nation,' he says. 'It's a beautiful country. Thanks to this country I have been able to achieve a comfortable life and get an education. I don't want to leave, but I have to.'

It is very difficult to get a measure of how many undocumented migrants in the US might be going home. Those who didn't clock in when they arrived are hardly likely to clock out when they leave. The Pew Hispanic Center reckons that the total number living in America has dipped slightly, to 11.9 million.[43] The Mexican government estimates that slightly more people (139,000) returned to Mexico from the US in the first three months of 2009 than left (137,000).[44] According to official statistics, the number of people apprehended trying to enter the US illegally fell to 724,000 in 2008, the lowest since 1973.The Department of Homeland Security says this decline is related to tougher border-protection efforts. But Wayne Cornelius of the

University of California in San Diego says the slumping US economy is the most important factor. 'The principal reason for this
change in propensity to migrate is the lack of job opportunities
in the US, rather than tougher border enforcement,' he says.
'With such uncertainty . . . it is less rational for would-be
migrants to invest thousands of dollars hiring a "coyote" and
risking their lives in the desert to migrate illegally.'[45]

Anecdotal evidence also suggests that quite a few Mexicans
are leaving. Annette Taddeo, a Colombian-American business-
woman and Democratic politician whose office is near the
Mexican consulate in Miami, says there has been a big fall in the
number of people coming to the consulate and to local restaurants. According to the Mexican consul, many Mexicans have
left, mostly men who have lost their jobs in the battered construction industry. Women, apparently, are still coming to the
US, as service jobs are easier to come by.

Carlos Pereira, who runs the Centro de Orientación Del
Inmigrante (CODI), an organisation that helps migrants in
Miami and campaigns for immigration reform, confirms that
lots of people are leaving. 'People come here every day. They say
they are tired and want to go. They say they'll save a little money
and leave. Our advice is that they should wait to see how the
economy and the political situation develop. But it's more dig-
nified to go home. They say, "I prefer to live free in my home
than in a golden cage here."' That will be music to the ears of all
those who wish the United States were rid of all the foreign
workers who do the menial work Americans no longer want to
do. But at a personal level, it can be a tragedy.

Even today, Oscar's voice trembles as he recounts how he
made it to the United States in 2002. 'I crossed the border on my
own,' he says. 'It was tough, but I made it. I spent a year in Los
Angeles. It was very difficult; I didn't know anyone. I spent a
month sleeping in a warehouse.' For many irregular migrants,
California is a stopover before they fan out across America to

where the jobs are. 'After a year, I came to Miami,' he continues. 'I had to start afresh again. I didn't know anyone. It was very tough. I was getting up for work every day at four a.m. and working all day.' Eventually, though, things got better. 'Now I'm living in South Beach, I work in a bar and I have a place with my own shower.'

Oscar works seventeen hours a day, six days a week. 'I get home at six in the morning, wake up at eleven and get to work at one p.m. It's modern slavery.' He earns $3.85 an hour, but he can make up to $100 a night in tips. He sends home $400 a month to his family in Honduras. His wife and three children live in the city of San Pedro Sula, where they have opened a small store with the money he sends back. It pays for his kids' education and helps support his ageing mother. Oscar is thirty and hasn't seen any of them for the past seven years. Because he is in the United States illegally, he cannot easily travel back and forth. 'The loneliness is difficult,' he says, 'but you get used to it. Loneliness becomes your best company.' Sometimes his kids break his heart. 'I don't know if I love you,' one said. 'You're not here.'

Life is tough in the United States. 'Not having documents is suffocating,' Oscar says. 'Businesses exploit you. You are always hiding. We need immigration reform. I sent an email to our president.' Your president? 'Yes, he's my president. I live here. It's my country. I consider myself an American citizen. I love this country. If I could, I would give this country more. I would study. I would help this country to get back on its feet.' Oscar seems like just the kind of guy America ought to want to hang on to. 'I'm afraid of being deported so my money is hidden,' he continues. 'Otherwise I could put it in the bank to invest. I think Obama has good intentions. Immigration reform might not happen this year [2009], but maybe next.'

Why, then, is Oscar planning to leave? 'I want to see my mother. She is in her seventies and she said to me, "I'm going to die without seeing you." I feel powerless. There is no more hope. My mother is getting ill. It's awful. I say to her, "Wait for me. Don't die now." Imagine if she died before I saw her.' Oscar holds back tears. 'I came in through the back door. I will leave through the front door. I would like to come back through the front door too.' If only he could.

Making the most of mobility

The benefits of the new mobility are clearest where people can move as freely as possible. Globally, highly skilled people and employees of multinational companies are in this fortunate position. As I mentioned earlier, Sweden now allows its companies to recruit workers of all types from any country. Within the EU, most EU citizens can live, study, work, retire and indeed move for whatever reason they choose within the EU's twenty-seven member states. (Germany and Austria are meant to lift their controls on A8 citizens by May 2011. Bulgarians and Romanians, who joined in 2007, should be able to work throughout Europe without restrictions by 2014.) Australians and New Zealanders can also move freely between their two countries.

For individuals, greater mobility offers a wider range of job opportunities and thus a better chance to get ahead. By moving to a different country, people can often earn a multiple of what they did previously. They also have an opportunity to learn a new language, experience a different culture and meet new people. They can acquire useful new skills, contacts and experience that may be valuable elsewhere.

Increasingly, people can split their lives between several countries: doing business in one (or more) and living in another; spending part of the year in one country and part elsewhere; or shuttling back and forth between countries over several years. People who work for big global companies are often posted from country to country; international bankers split their time between London, New York and Tokyo; Britons live in France and commute to work in Britain; seasonal workers pick grapes in New Zealand or strawberries in Spain and then go home; Polish builders do up British people's houses during the winter and erect their own back home over the summer. *Newsnight*, the BBC's flagship news programme, featured the case of a Polish doctor who spends alternate weekends in Scotland providing the out-of-hours care that British GPs (general practitioners) neglect. This allows him to care for his Polish patients during the week, tend to Scottish ones on weekends, top up his Polish salary with much higher British wages and spend most of his time with his family in Poland.

In a global economy where companies are increasingly foot-loose, people who are not tied to a single location have more options, and thus greater bargaining power. Mobility is particularly valuable when some national or regional economies are suffering while others are booming: people who lose their jobs can seek work elsewhere rather than languishing unemployed. With New Zealand's economy stagnant while Australia's is growing again, Kiwis can seek work on the other side of the Tasman Sea. While their economy is in the doldrums, Americans can try their luck in China. If prospects in Britain remain dim, more Britons may go to work on the Continent, as many did when unemployment was high in the 1980s.

Colm Maghee studied IT in Galway before moving from Ireland to Britain to study music. In London he worked in IT support jobs for three years. 'By then I'd had enough of London,' he says, 'so I decided to come home.' The twenty-seven-year-old got a job through a telephone interview on his way to Heathrow with his rucksack on his back and his guitar in his arms. Four months later, in December 2008, he lost his €30,000-a-year job for Fulltiltpoker, an American online poker company, when the global economy tanked. 'I was told on

Friday, "You don't have a job on Monday."' When I spoke to him in June 2009, he hadn't had any luck finding work. 'Agencies are advertising jobs in IT support in the Czech Republic. The pay's not great: €18,000 to 20,000. I'm kinda tempted, though,' he says. 'I'd just be going for the job. If you're unemployed for too long, you become unemployable.' I asked him if he'd thought of going back to Britain. 'I would consider it, but there aren't many jobs going there either.' Colm is not alone. 'A lot of well-educated people in Ireland who have lost their jobs are trying to emigrate,' says Michael Hennigan of FinFacts, the country's top business website.

A mobile workforce enables businesses to employ the right people in the right place at the right time. Companies that operate across several countries need to be able to redeploy their staff quickly as circumstances change. Smaller ones can seize opportunities that they would otherwise miss out on – for instance, a small machine-tools business that has just received a big order from China but cannot find the requisite employees locally or an organic farmer who cannot meet surging demand without foreign labour. Firms often cannot win foreign contracts unless their employees can move too. For instance, Indian IT consultancies may need to post staff for a while in the countries where their clients are based.

Employers of every size benefit from being able to tap the widest pool of talent possible. In many cases, job requirements are more specialised than before. An employer may be looking for someone who speaks Mandarin, has knowledge of the Chinese market, has mastered a particular IT system and has good interpersonal skills. Even in a big country, such people may be rare, so being able to look further afield is vital.

Increasingly, they will come from emerging economies. China already generates more university graduates a year than all of Europe, and India is catching up fast. Companies based in countries that restrict access to foreign talent are at a disadvantage to those located in more open places. This may cause them to lose business or to relocate. British football clubs, for instance, would not be as successful if they had to rely on local players. More broadly, global competition for people with skills that are in short supply will intensify as the global economy picks up – just as big-spending Manchester City is trying to poach top players from its local rival Manchester United.

In countries where labour laws make it difficult to hire and fire permanent employees, temporary workers give companies much-needed flexibility. Sectors whose employment needs vary a lot seasonally (such as agriculture), year to year (such as public services, where budgets and priorities change) or according to the economic cycle of boom and bust (such as construction) can adapt more readily thanks to foreign labour.

For economies as a whole, greater mobility can bring huge benefits. It ensures workers are better matched to job opportunities and makes it easier for economies to adapt to change, helping them to grow faster. In our globalising world, where the economy is forever changing and opportunities no longer stop at national borders, it is increasingly important for people to be able to move as freely as capital and products do. Free trade encourages countries to specialise in what they do best, but in order to do so they often need to import capital and people from overseas. This enables countries to reap the benefits of economies of scale, foster dynamic clusters and improve the variety, quality and cost of local products and services. London would be a local financial centre, not a global one, if it could not attract foreign banks and international bankers. Bangalore would be a less successful IT hub without talent schooled at US universities and foreign venture capital.

Australia could not have met China's booming demand for its resources had it not imported lots of outside capital and foreign technicians on temporary '457' visas, and would otherwise have notched up slower growth. Not enough Australians have the requisite skills in metallurgy, earth sciences or environmental management. 'Australians know we've got capacity constraints,' says Mitch Hooke of the Minerals Council of Australia. 'We can't get skills, we can't get labour, we can't get tyres, we can't get fuel, we can't get trucks.'

The economic gains from mobility are greatest when everyone can move freely. Within the EU, nearly everyone can do so. Other obstacles to working abroad are also being lifted. For instance, EU rules increasingly require member states to recognise each other's qualifications and to make it easier for workers to keep their pensions entitlements when they move around. Other changes make it easier to establish and restructure businesses that cut across national borders – and thus to move people around between them.

The free movement of labour in the EU is often portrayed as opening the floodgates to immigration. In fact, it is creating a dynamic and flexible Europe-wide labour market of five hundred million people. This is extending the gains from the EU's single market in goods, capital and (patchily) services, and encouraging the allocation of labour to its most efficient use. Just as Britons benefit from being able to go to France for surgery (which is classified as trade), they benefit when a French surgeon comes to operate on them in Britain (which is classified as migration). Free migration is a form of free trade.

Increased mobility also makes the economy more flexible, allowing it to adapt more readily to change and thus boosting growth and stability. Ongoing economic change requires a continual reallocation of labour from declining companies, industries and regions to emerging ones. Sometimes these changes are transitory – such as London's increased need for construction workers ahead of the 2012 Olympics or the demand for extra workers in booming economies; in other cases, they are more permanent, such as the shift from rural and rust-belt industrial areas to service-focused cities. Just as it is a good thing for people to move from Liverpool to London if their labour is in demand there, so too if people move from Lisbon or Lithuania. Job shortages can quickly be met by migrant workers, who tend to be more willing, once arrived, to move to where the jobs are, and to change jobs as conditions change.

The benefits of increased mobility are greatest at a local level. The smaller an economic unit is, the more it has to gain from accessing a wider pool of labour. But they are also significant at an economy-wide, macro level. Greater flexibility enables the economy to grow faster for longer without running into inflationary bottlenecks. That enables people to enjoy higher living standards, lower unemployment and lower interest rates than otherwise.

Increased mobility is as beneficial in a downturn as it is in an upswing. By heading elsewhere as an economy weakens, migrant workers help smooth its adjustment. Unemployment rises less than otherwise, making the recession shorter and shallower and putting less of a strain on public finances. Labour mobility is a particularly important safety valve for economies in the eurozone, which cannot devalue their currencies or alter their interest rates independently of those set by the European Central Bank in Frankfurt. In the case of a small country like Ireland, migrants leaving can cushion the blow of the recession and speed up the economy's adjustment.

Enlightened unions agree. Britain's Trade Union Congress wholeheartedly supports the free movement of labour within Europe. The TUC reasons that it is better for workers to be able to come and work in Britain legally, and thus with full employment rights and the opportunity to join a union, than for them to come illegally and so be vulnerable to exploitation. Thorkild Jensen, the head of Dansk Metal, the Danish metalworkers' union, is also in favour, so long as foreign workers are hired under local wage agreements. 'We believe it is important that employees can move to where the work is,' he says. 'When we had high unemployment, lots of our members went to Norway to work on offshore oil and gas facilities.' Anna Ekström, president of the Swedish Confederation of Professional Associations (Saco), says, 'The problem was not that Sweden was invaded by people from the Baltic States, the problem is that most of them went to London.' When Polish dentists set up shop in Stockholm, her response was, 'We welcome Polish colleagues as long as they provide professional care.'

A study for the European Commission puts the benefits of opening up Western Europe's labour markets to East Europeans at nearly €50 billion a year.[46] These annual gains could double by 2020, the report by the European Integration Consortium reckons, as the remaining restrictions are lifted. The influx of workers from the east has scarcely harmed West Europeans' wages and employment, and few claim welfare benefits. Clearly, the picture is positive. Yet this study, like most that look at the economic impact of migration, greatly understates its true benefits. It assumes that economies are machines that shift from one static equilibrium to another and that economic growth comes out of a black box called productivity growth. But in fact economies are dynamic organisms that are in constant flux, where growth comes from the competitive spur to innovate and imitate and flexibility is at a premium. Increased mobility stimulates economic growth by bringing together diverse people to come up with new ideas and start up new businesses, and by smoothing the ongoing transfer of resources from less productive uses to more productive ones. In short, it sparks growth and facilitates it.

Scare stories

Europe's amazing experiment has dispelled many of the myths about the free movement of people. Open the doors, critics say, and we'd be swamped: everyone would come and society would collapse. It is a deep-rooted fear, as if immigrants were the barbarians at the gates. But in fact most people don't want to leave home at all, let alone for ever. Do you? Those who do move don't all want to go to the same place. Since *Immigrants: Your Country Needs Them* was published in 2007, I have spoken about migration around the world. In nearly every country, many people seem convinced that everyone wants to come live there. They can't all be right.

Consider Britain's recent experience. Of the seventy-five million East Europeans who could have moved there since 2004, only one million have, and most have already left again. Most only want to work abroad for a short while to learn English, experience another country and earn enough to buy a house or set up a business back home. Surveys show that people from outside the EU have similar aspirations. But perversely, tighter immigration controls encourage those who do get into the EU to stay on, for fear that if they left they could not come back if they needed to. One of the main reasons why four million 'guest workers' ended up staying in West Germany is precisely because the country closed its borders in 1973; before then, most tended to go home. And has society collapsed since Britain allowed in East Europeans? Hardly. On the contrary, the newcomers have filled jobs that not enough locals can or want to do – caring for the sick in the National Health Service and the elderly in care homes, renovating council flats for the poor, waiting tables, pulling pints, picking strawberries and many other things besides. Contrary to fears that they would be a drain on public finances, they have paid their way.

Christian Dustmann and his team at University College London found that A8 migrants who had been in Britain for at least a year – and who were therefore eligible to claim government assistance – are 60 per cent less likely than natives to receive state benefits or tax credits, and 58 per cent less likely to live in social housing.[47] On the basis of the four years of data available since 2004, they showed that the newcomers 'contribute significantly more to the tax and benefit system than they receive'. The A8 workers are younger, likely to have fewer children and better educated on average than the native population, with more than a third having stayed in full-time education until they were at least twenty-one. Their average hourly wage, certainly when they first arrive, is lower than that of native Britons. But their employment rates are high – 90 per cent for men of working age and 74 per cent for women, compared with 78 and 71 per cent for natives. As their English and their understanding of the labour market improve, their wages tend to rise fast.

In 2008–9 A8 workers paid 37 per cent more in direct and indirect taxes than they received in benefits and from public services such as education, the NHS or social housing, the study calculates. Since the British government was running a budget deficit over that period, and thus overall spending exceeded what was raised in taxes, UK-born individuals contributed 20 per cent less than they received. Even using conservative assumptions, this wave of immigrants has 'made a substantial net contribution to the UK fiscal system', say Dustmann and his colleagues. 'From the fiscal point of view, this immigration has not been at all a burden on the welfare system – rather, it has contributed to strengthen the fiscal position.'

Despite its huge benefits, this new mobility is unsettling for politicians and many voters. Their mindsets are stuck in a bygone era where people generally stayed put, those who moved did so for good and ossified state bureaucracies relied on the world standing still. Our attitudes and institutions need to adapt. European governments – and to a lesser extent those elsewhere – need to learn to cope with having a large, transitory foreign population around. This is a task the private sector, which accommodates lots of foreign visitors each year – 30 million in Britain's case – manages just fine. Likewise, healthcare, schools and other local services need to become more responsive to local people's changing needs – whether it is for Polish interpreters or patients' desire to choose who treats them, when and where. Since foreigners more than pay their way, the issue is flexibility not finance.

British jobs for British workers

The new mobility has brought big benefits to Europe in general and Britain in particular. But it has also sparked a backlash that has gathered momentum as the crisis has pushed up unemployment. Britain has experienced protests and wildcat strikes against foreign workers. Protesters march under the banner 'British jobs for British workers', the unfortunate phrase used by prime minister Gordon Brown in 2007 that echoes a slogan from the 1970s of the racist National Front. So far the protests have mainly focused on power stations and oil refineries. But Owen Morris of the UNITE trade union has set his sights on a more high-profile target – preparations for the 2012 Olympics in London.

London's plans may not be a patch on Beijing's remodelling for the 2008 Olympics, but they are ambitious all the same. Huge swathes of the city's dilapidated and deprived East End are being redeveloped; an Olympic stadium, aquatics centre, velodrome, Olympic village, media centre and a host of smaller projects built; London's rickety transport systems upgraded. A desolate landscape of derelict warehouses and industrial decay is being transformed into a gleaming Olympic Park. With a budget of £9.3 billion, it is one of the largest construction and engineering projects in Europe – and it couldn't be finished on time and at a reasonable cost without the help of foreign workers.

But Owen Morris isn't happy. 'This is not meant in a xenophobic way,' he says, 'but there are not enough British workers there. They're only using cheaper European alternatives. We just want a fair crack of the whip.' He accuses Olympic contractors of hiring foreign (mainly East European) agency workers on worse pay and conditions than required by national trade-union agreements with employers. The Olympic Delivery Authority, the body charged with managing the Olympic project, denies this. It says it has been advertising jobs first in local job centres. 'We are providing jobs and training at a difficult time for the economy, exceeding our targets on the employment of local people,' a spokesperson said.[48]

In May 2009 Morris organised for several hundred construction workers from around the country to congregate outside the Olympic Park in an unofficial protest to demand more jobs for British workers. He says preference should be given to local people and that 'they should be bringing those [foreign] lads up to our level'. The protesters later went on to lobby members of parliament. While Morris is a shop steward for UNITE, the protest was organised independently. 'The trade unions weren't happy about the Olympic protest,' he explains. 'They tried to knock it on the head. [Gordon] Brown said keep away, it's our showpiece.' That's why it was the ideal way to get the media and politicians' attention, he smirks.

Owen and I chatted over a pint in a pub at London's Liverpool Street station. Dressed in a blue Umbro shirt, jeans and white trainers, he looks like quite a bruiser with his mop of brown hair, boxer's nose and a big tattoo of flames on his left arm. By trade he is a steel erector, one of the strong men who put together the huge steel structures that form the frame of big buildings, sports stadiums and other large construction projects. He explains that he is blacklisted from most construction sites for being a trade-union agitator, but is working at Wapping Tube station. 'I'm earning £500 a week,' he says. 'It's better than the dole, but I would normally earn £750 a week working at a power station.'

Morris is certainly media-savvy. But if you take him at his word, his political judgement is less sound. He claims that the protesters used the slogan 'British jobs for British workers' to 'get the media's attention and make Gordon Brown sit up and eat his own words. For the first few weeks the slogan served its purpose. It put what we were talking about in the papers. But those bigoted idiots at the BNP [British National Party] stole what we were fighting for.' That is hardly unexpected. If the real issue they wanted to highlight was trade-union rights, they ought to have framed it as such. Unfortunately, the protesters have not disavowed the slogan, as they ought to do if its use was simply an ill-judged public-relations stunt.

Morris himself is a man of the hard left, not the extreme right. Born in Barnsley but living in Surrey, he stood as a candidate in the South East region for the 'No2EU – Yes to Democracy' alliance assembled by Bob Crow of the National Union of Rail, Maritime and Transport Workers (RMT) in the 2009 European elections. 'I have no problem with the free movement of labour across Europe as long as it's not the free movement of exploited labour,' he says, coughing from the Benson & Hedges cigarettes that he breaks off periodically to smoke. But he opposes Britain's membership of the EU, which made this mobility possible.

Now thirty-eight, Morris has worked in six countries across Europe over the past twenty years, illegally in pubs and clubs in the Spanish resort of Benidorm in 1989–91 and as a steel erector in various countries on a cash-in-hand basis. When he was working in Belgium in the mid-1990s, 'people were pissed off at UK workers,' he says. 'We didn't speak to anyone and kept out of everyone's way.' The difference, he explains, is that he was paid *more* than local workers. 'It's a double-edged sword,' he says. 'There are more Brits working in Europe than foreigners in the UK. And they are screaming out for Brits [on construction projects] in the Middle East.' Protests against foreign workers are deeply regrettable. But fortunately, so long as Britain does not leave the EU, the new mobility looks here to stay.

Immigrant entrepreneurs

The biggest benefits of mobility can be witnessed in an enterprise cluster such as Silicon Valley or a cosmopolitan city such as London, New York and, increasingly, Shanghai. Mobile people are a self-selected minority who tend to be young, hard-working and enterprising. Like starting a new business, migrating is a risky enterprise and a lot of effort is needed to make it pay off. An influx of young, industrious types not only boosts the productivity of the economy directly; it also tends to stimulate greater productivity gains from native workers. Polish builders may spur their British counterparts to up their game, for instance, as well as transferring new skills to them. More broadly, foreigners' diversity and dynamism boost competition, innovation, enterprise and trade, raising long-term productivity growth and living standards.

Miami has long been seen as a gateway to the Americas. But despite its geographical proximity to Latin America, Miami did not become a trading hub until the 1960s, when Cubans and other Latino immigrants began to arrive. Over the past fifty years Miami has been transformed from a quiet resort town into a dynamic metropolis that connects North America to Latin America and the Caribbean. A combination of massive immigration – over half (51 per cent) of Miami's population is foreign-born, the only city in the US where this is true – and the opening up of Latin America to international trade and finance have placed it centre stage. 'Hispanic immigrants knew how to do business in Latin America, they knew the culture, they knew the language,' says Thomas Boswell of the University of Miami. 'Only then did Miami make the most of its enormous geographic advantage.' Ninety per cent of Latinos in Miami used to be Cuban. Now less than half are. The Latino population in Miami is increasingly diverse – not just Cuban and Mexican, but also Argentinian, Brazilian, Colombian and Honduran.

'Bolivar's dream has come true in Miami,' says Carlos Saladrigas, a successful entrepreneur, referring to the South American independence fighter who wanted to unite the Americas. 'It's the one place we can all meet and be brothers. It's true pan-Americanism.' The city's diversity attracts some and repels others. 'Miami feels pretty threatening to people in Peoria,' says Saladrigas. 'Most corporate headquarters don't like to come here. But it is very attractive to Europeans who are more used to cultural diversity. For Latin Americans, it's like having the best of both worlds: a lifestyle that looks and feels like living in Latin America and yet if you have a heart attack, rescue is going to be there in three minutes.'

Doesn't Miami risk becoming so Latino that it is no longer American? Saladrigas disagrees:

> To be American is to adhere to a set of values, freedom, commitment to individual initiative, hard work, the so-called American Dream. If you buy into that, it doesn't matter if you're Hispanic, Polish, Protestant or Catholic. That's the cohesiveness, not the language you speak or your race. That will allow America to grow in a very diverse way. The whole issue about language is hogwash. If there is a language that is absolutely predatory, it's English. Why would you worry about Spanish? Give me a break. Every immigrant will learn English if not in the first generation, in the second. It is prevailing in the world, never mind in the United States.

Saladrigas arrived in the United States as a child refugee. Aged twelve, and without his parents, he was among twenty thousand Cuban children whisked out of the country soon after Fidel Castro took power. He spent time with an aunt in Miami, then with a cousin whose husband was abusive. After a while they threw him out and he was taken in by friends of his parents, who eventually made it to Miami a year later. 'I was lucky compared to many of the others who left, many of whom never saw their parents again,' he says.

His parents arrived penniless. His father, a lawyer in Cuba, washed dishes in a hospital. His mother, an entrepreneur who had a high-end clothing store, picked tomatoes on a farm. When she developed cancer, Saladrigas dropped out of high school to look after her. Aged seventeen he met his wife and soon after they were married. 'I was selling encyclopaedias and shoes at the time. I met her at church and I tried to sell her some, without much success, so I ended up marrying her instead.' He completed high school doing night classes and then enrolled in college at night, because he was working full-time as an office boy during the day. 'I barely slept. Every time I had a test, I didn't sleep at all.' He graduated in accounting among the top 2 per cent in his class. With his boss's help and encouragement, he applied to do an MBA at Harvard Business School. He got a scholarship and worked at night to support his wife and two children, and also got food stamps. When he returned to Miami, he soon joined PepsiCo and was rapidly promoted.

'Immigration is a process of natural selection,' Saladrigas says. 'Immigrants are more risk-takers, and in a society like America that rewards risk-taking, this is great. It provides a whole new source of new ideas and people.' In October 1984 he started his own business with a colleague, with $34,000 in savings. His idea was to lease out employees to small businesses, reducing their administrative burden and using their collective bargaining power to save on health insurance, pensions and other costs. 'It was very hard at the beginning. It took us nine months to get our first client. People liked the concept, but nobody wanted to be the guinea pig. By November 1985 all I had left in my bank account was enough to pay that month's mortgage. Eventually we got a few clients and began to build mass. By 1996 we took the company public and in 2000 we sold it to a payroll processor. Soon after I retired.' Out of nothing, he built a billion-dollar business. Now, he has set up a group of businesspeople to help encourage the development of micro-businesses in Cuba using the remittances sent home from Cubans abroad. 'The Cuban people are highly educated. If we can empower them, we're going to see a lot of business development and growth,' he enthuses.

What is the secret of his success? 'We always had hope that next year would be better,' he says. 'Optimism is a big driver.' But times have changed. 'America is less a country of opportunity today than it was then. Education is not as widely available and financed as it was then. It's much more expensive and there are fewer loans and scholarships available. And it's much harder to live on one income today. But business opportunities still exist if you find a niche.'

It's not just in America that newcomers are more entrepreneurial than most. In Britain too, foreign-born people are much more likely to start a new business than UK-born ones. Jonathan Levie of the University of Strathclyde finds that immigrants' propensity to start a new business is nearly twice as great as that of lifelong residents.[49] His analysis of surveys of more than twenty thousand people in 2003 and 2004 for the Global Entrepreneurship Monitor (GEM) shows that whereas 4.3 per cent of UK-born people were either actively trying to start a business or had been running their own business for more than three months but less than three and a half years, 8.4 per cent of foreign-born people were. Recent arrivals who have been in Britain less than five years have a higher propensity to start a business (8.4 per cent) than people who have been in the country five years or more (5.7 per cent). Contrary to the belief that only some immigrant cultures are entrepreneurial, data from the GEM surveys from 2002 to 2008 show that all categories of immigrant are more entrepreneurial than white UK-born people. Whereas 5.4 per cent of white UK-born people have started, or are trying to start, a new business, the figure is 6.8 per cent among Asian immigrants, 7.8 per cent among white immigrants, 8.5 per cent among black immigrants and 9.8 per cent among mixed immigrants. Interestingly, though, the highest enterprise rates are found among UK-born blacks (11.3 per cent).[50]

Many Italians take a dim view of immigration. Migrants are often viewed as criminals, or as simply a source of cheap labour. But they are also increasingly entrepreneurs. Foreigners have started some 165,000 businesses in Italy – and the number has tripled since 2003. Moroccans, Romanians and Chinese are the most active, representing almost 45 per cent of all foreign entrepreneurs. A prize ceremony in 2009 for entrepreneurial migrants, hosted by MoneyGram, a US-based money-transfer company, featured among its finalists Marius Tiberius, a Romanian running a wholesale food company; Dava Gjoka, an Albanian heading a social cooperative for foreigners; and fashion designer Margarita Perea Sanchez from Colombia.

'Immigrant entrepreneurs have an edge over Italians, who see the crisis as an insurmountable obstacle,' says Massimo Canovi, a MoneyGram director. 'They have a different mentality and approach. They fight for the future, while we [Italians] are anchored to the past and stuck in traditional schemes.' The 2009 winner of the MoneyGram award was Khawatmi Radwan, who founded Hirux International, an electric appliance exporter. From Aleppo in Syria, Radwan has been in Italy since the age of seventeen and his Milan-based company has an annual turnover of €60 million. 'Foreign-owned companies always need to be a step ahead, they are subject to more inspections than Italian ones and must invest in innovation,' he says.[51]

Unleashing the power of diversity

Cosmopolitan cities, regions and countries – such as London, British Columbia and New Zealand – have a huge resource that they do not make the most of: the diversity of their people. So too do companies with a diverse workforce. They could reap huge gains by tapping into the dynamic energies of a diverse workforce.

New ideas do not just spring from individual ingenuity; more often they emerge from group interaction. If there are ten people in a room trying to come up with the solution to a problem and they all think alike, then no matter how talented they are, their ten heads are no better than one. But if they all think differently, then by bouncing ideas off each other, they can come up with solutions to problems faster and better, as a growing volume of research shows.[52] Take HIV research. For years American researchers struggled to find an effective anti-HIV medication. They came up with all sorts of drugs that worked more or less well, but none that was effective for long. Then a team led by a Taiwanese American, David Ho, had a bright new idea: why not try a cocktail of drugs? And it worked. Think how many lives that has saved worldwide. Or consider that nearly half of America's business start-ups funded by venture capital were co-founded by immigrants. If even a huge economy like the US relies so heavily on diversity to fuel the industries of the future, just think how important it is for much smaller ones.

The extra creativity that diversity creates can benefit all kinds of organisations that need to innovate and solve problems – a government searching for vote-winning new policies, civil servants seeking more effective ways to implement policy objectives, an NGO trying to put its message across better, a small business looking to market its products better or a larger one that wants to become greener.

Diverse societies not only tend to create more new ideas, they are also generally more receptive to them. Exposure to different cultures tends to broaden people's horizons and make them more accustomed to difference. Psychological research shows that this is especially true of people from a mixed cultural background and those who speak two or more languages. This mental flexibility helps both managers and employees to think 'outside the box', to be more open to change and to adapt more readily to it, not least because diverse workforces have a wider variety of skills at their disposal. Diverse societies that are more open to change also tend to generate more potential entrepreneurs and a more receptive audience for new business ideas. As we have seen, immigrants and people from minority backgrounds, in particular, tend to be more enterprising.

Diversity offers huge benefits – increased creativity and innovation, added adaptability, more enterprise, increased trade, a magnet for talent and greater variety – which together make us richer. Yet those benefits are not automatic. How, then, can diverse places do more to unleash their dynamic potential? Go back to those ten people in a room trying to come up with the solution to a problem. If they all think differently, they may not only be more creative, they are also like to disagree more. They may fail to understand each other or talk at cross purposes. They may end up arguing or even come to blows.

Clearly, unless it is properly managed, diversity can generate more heat than light. That's why diverse societies need robust democratic institutions and laws underpinned by liberal values so that people can live together peacefully and productively and settle their issues through political negotiation. They also benefit from having a common language. Helping newcomers and indeed everyone in society to be fluent in the local language, without neglecting the other languages they may speak, is a vital investment. People also need to be aware of the potential for conflict and misunderstanding, and try to avoid them.

While the power of diversity may be wasted if it is not properly channelled, it can also be lost if it is not actively cultivated. For a start, those diverse people actually have to be in the same room together, since many of the benefits of diversity come from different people interacting with each other. Once they are there, they also have to be encouraged to speak their minds. They have to feel that their diversity is valued or they may do their best to suppress it – or simply go and work elsewhere. People have to listen to their ideas, be open to what they have to say and follow through, or else they may give up trying. So to unleash the power of diversity, you have to bring people together, believe in them, value them and match words with actions.

In practical terms, it means encouraging different people to mix at school, at work, in the street and socially. Doing more than just paying lip service to the benefits of diversity and instead truly valuing it. Actively seeking to attract different employees and migrants. Making newcomers feel welcome. Allowing people to be different and still feel that they belong. It means businesses and organisations treating people as an asset, rather than as a cost. Helping everyone to fulfil their potential – investing in education and training, removing the barriers to employment and enterprise, especially for minorities and immigrants, vigorously enforcing anti-discrimination laws and encouraging social mobility more generally. Last but not least, government, businesses and organisations all need to be geared towards promoting innovation and enterprise, and to invest in new ideas.

In *Immigrants: Your Country Needs Them*, I looked in depth at how foreign-born entrepreneurs in Silicon Valley were starting up new businesses that were powering America's internet revolution and fostering trade with Asia and other parts of the world. As we will see in Chapter 10, migrants are also at the centre of Silicon Valley's clean-tech revolution. Meanwhile other vibrant cities, such as Vancouver, are also starting to harness the connections between mobility, enterprise and trade.

Vibrant Vancouver

While Shanghai is a Chinese city that is becoming increasingly cosmopolitan (again), Vancouver is a Canadian city that is becoming increasingly Chinese – and aspires to be North America's gateway to Asia. It came to life as a Pacific gateway after the Canada Pacific Railway first connected the west coast to the rest of Canada in the late nineteenth century. The aim was to make it easier to ship Asian goods – mainly tea and silks from Japan – across the continent and on to London, explains Yuen Pau Woo of the Asia Pacific Foundation of Canada. But whereas previously it was just a trading post, now it is much more than a well-connected port: it has become a North American city with distinctly Asian characteristics. Thanks to successive waves of immigration two in five people in the city are of Asian origin. 'I like to call Vancouver North America's Asian capital,' Woo says. This greater diversity promises much richer and more varied connections than before.

The biggest wave of Chinese immigrants came between the mid-1980s and late 1990s, primarily from Taiwan and Hong Kong. Now they increasingly come from mainland China – business-people, skilled workers and students, and those with family in Canada. 'It's not difficult to fit in here,' says Wei Shao, a lawyer who advises on business between Canada and China. 'Vancouver is a multicultural city. People here are more than just tolerant, they are quite receptive to newcomers. So you don't see the tension you might see elsewhere.' Children mix well at school and there is increasing demand among non-Chinese people, particularly busi-nesspeople, to learn Mandarin. 'Increasingly, immigrants' children don't see themselves as boxed in,' says David Fung, a Hong Kong-born businessman who arrived in Canada in 1966. 'They live all over the city, although there are ghettoes for those who choose not to leave them. Canadians' attitude of acceptance is slowly moving towards invisibility [colour blindness].'

Shao – who was born in Xian, where the famous terracotta warriors were unearthed – moved to Vancouver in 1994 after graduating from a Canadian university. 'It wasn't known as a gateway to Asia then,' he says, 'but in my mind it was already a bridgehead.' As mainland China has developed, Chinese connections and knowledge about the country and its business culture are increasingly valued in Vancouver. It is now home to lots of 'astronauts' – wealthy Chinese businesspeople who still have active business interests in China and split their time between the two countries. Notoriously, they include the family of Huang Guangyu, who became China's richest man by building up the country's largest consumer electronics retailer, Gome, but was arrested by the Chinese authorities on suspicion of fraud in 2008.

The city and the provincial government of British Columbia are doing their best to promote Vancouver's role as a gateway city. 'We're Canada's best asset on Asia Pacific,' says Jack Austin, a retired senior politician. But the Conservative federal government's hostility to China sours things and Vancouver is not yet a centre of commerce between North America and Asia. 'We're not making the most of our human assets, the Chinese diaspora,' says David Emerson, a former trade and foreign minister, and architect of the Pacific gateway strategy. The city's economy is still dominated by a handful of forestry and mining companies that prioritise trade with the huge and familiar American market next door, to which Canada sends four-fifths of its exports. But that is beginning to change. Alongside mainstream business activity, Chinese Canadians are developing new trade and investment links with China. For instance, in July 2009 a local company run by a Chinese Canadian invested C$800 million in a coal-to-methane plant in China's Xinjiang province.

David Fung says the complacency of traditional Canadian businesses leaves plenty of openings for newcomers to develop business opportunities with China. 'If all the Canadians were that diligent, we'd have a hard time,' he chuckles. 'Immigrants provide renewal constantly. When my children become complacent, the next set of immigrants who come in are hungry. They keep on pushing forward.' Life was very tough when

Fung was growing up in Hong Kong. 'When my father became sick, I came home from school and there was one plate of vegetables between the six of us,' he recalls. 'The next day I was working. By the time I finished high school I had six jobs. I learned to sleep not in bed, but on buses.' Now, through his own company, ACDEG International, he has investment partnerships in a range of industries – chemicals, forest products, biomass energy, electricity generation, original-equipment-parts manufacturing and packaging-waste recycling – that connect China and Canada.

Toby Chu, who was also born in Hong Kong, has established CIBT, a company that runs a global network of business, vocational and language schools. It is the largest private-college operator in western Canada and one of the largest foreign ones in China, which is the biggest education market in the world, with over 258 million students of all ages. CIBT provides Western courses in Chinese colleges and brings over Chinese students to study in Canadian ones. China Education Resources, founded by Chengfeng Zhou, a former lecturer at Beijing United University, creates textbooks, curricula and online education resources for China's kindergarten and school children. These aim to help shift the country's education system from memory-based learning to creative thinking.

Across Canada, the Asia Pacific Foundation has identified more than 140 Asian ethnic business associations that facilitate trade and investment among Canadian firms and Asian partners. Woo, who was born in Malaysia and grew up in Singapore, envisions Vancouver becoming 'a place where the ideas, the contacts, the networks, the buzz can take place, a place where connections are made rather than simply as a place where you park yourself as a base. It's not just about business connections and networks, it's about being a centre of ideas of, and for, the Asia Pacific region.'

Other places are also tapping into the trade and investment

links migrants can generate. One study found that if New Zealand receives 10 per cent more migrants from a particular country, its exports to that country tend to grow by 0.6 per cent – with a particularly big rise in tourism.[53] Or take Spain, which is not renowned for its links with Eastern Europe, but which has seen a huge rise in migration over the past decade as its economy boomed and opened up. Between 1999 and 2008 the inflow of East Europeans rose tenfold, while the share of Spain's trade going to the region rose by 170 per cent. According to a study by Giovanni Peri, of the University of California at Davis, and Francisco Requena of the University of Valencia, migration from Eastern Europe explains half of Spain's increase in exports to the region over that period.[54] Their intuition is that migrants' networks and knowledge of their home markets allowed Spanish firms to boost their exports. Trade creation was particularly strong in Spanish provinces where a critical mass of migrants developed, notably after 2002. Whether this trade will dip now that East Europeans are leaving remains to be seen.

Making the most of the new mobility is a huge challenge for flat-footed governments that are still organised on the basis that people belong in a single place. In some cases, they need to do more to encourage mobile workers to stay on longer, just as a good employer might encourage a valued employee to remain with the company. But they should not regard someone's departure as a failure, let alone a permanent loss. On the contrary, it is important to try to retain links with footloose migrants and to tap into their new networks. Just as people stay in touch with former colleagues and business partners because they might put work their way or do business with them again in future, so cities and countries need to nurture the contacts they have established with mobile people.

While the debate about immigration often boils down to raw emotions and simplistic, ever-more outdated notions of its economic impact, the new kaleidoscope of mobility is challenging old prejudices and confounding erroneous beliefs. Now, more than ever, we need to take off our blinkers to appreciate the rich diversity of connections that people on the move are creating.

9

Food Fight

Eat local?

'It's difficult to live on 325 rand [£25] a week,' says Kitty de Kock. 'I have to support five people – myself and my four children. Last week was a rainy week and we don't get paid when it rains. I made only 12 rand [90 pence]. My children were suffering. They were hungry and crying. All they got to eat was a bit of porridge. I'm sad to tell everybody that they're going hungry.'

Kitty works on a fruit farm near Cape Town that supplies Tesco, Britain's largest supermarket chain and the world's biggest buyer of South African fruit. Her job is to cut back the plum trees so that the fruit grow bigger. She toils nine hours a day, five days a week for fractionally more than South Africa's minimum wage of 291 rand a week. The working conditions are 'sometimes good, sometimes bad', she says. 'In the orchard, the grass is long. I have to work with wet shoes.' She gets ill a lot. 'One time I breathed in some of the pesticides,' she recalls. 'I went to see the doctor. My face was red and swollen. He didn't treat me as he said I was OK. He just gave me some cream. I had to pay for the medicines and the doctor. It cost me 210 rand.'

These tales of woe take place against a backdrop of breath-taking natural beauty. A valley of lush, rolling greenery and fertile red earth nestles between craggy mountains crowned by billowy clouds. Foreign tourists come here to sample local wineries, blissfully unaware of how farm workers like Kitty live. Unlike the rest of sub-Saharan Africa, Cape Province has a temperate, Mediterranean climate that is ideal for growing grapes and other fruit.

Now thirty-eight, Kitty has been a farm worker since she was seventeen. She used to work on another farm in neighbouring Paarl. 'The circumstances were very bad,' she recalls. 'My husband was fired and I was having a baby. We were evicted. The farmers weren't allowed to evict us but we didn't know our rights.' Wearing jeans, a mauve fleece and a pink cap that says 'Jesus is Lord', she speaks softly, almost placidly, smiling frequently and radiating a motherly warmth. A hot-under-the-collar militant she is not. She is recently divorced but still lives with her husband, as well as her four children, aged nineteen, fifteen, ten and five. The eldest is looking for a job – 'any kind of job'.

You reach her home by driving off the asphalted main road on to a long, muddy track. When you enter the farm, the path is lined with well-kept trees. As you turn a corner, the farmhouse looms in front of you, a big white building with a satellite dish. Kitty's quarters are more modest. 'Our house has one room. Water runs in through cracks in the walls. We only have cold water. It's not clean. Sometimes we get ill from worms in the water. We have a bath, a toilet and a TV too.' As we chat, Kitty plays with her mobile phone compulsively.

'I've been working on the farm for five years. Around sixty people work here. Twenty men, forty women,' she explains. 'Women are strongest.' Most are members of a women-led trade union, Sikhula Sonke, which means 'we grow together' in

Xhosa, a language famous for its many click sounds. 'Every farm has its own supervisor, always white,' Kitty says in Afrikaans, the language of the farmers of Dutch origin who dominated South Africa in the apartheid era. She speaks only a little English. 'We have a very good understanding because I am the shop steward on the farm. The supervisor takes 10 per cent deductions from our pay for various costs. That is OK. Before they used to take 150 rand.'

In May 2009 the *Guardian* interviewed Kitty and other South African farm workers in collaboration with Sikhula Sonke, which works in partnership with British campaign groups War on Want and ActionAid. Its focus was that Tesco was earning £3 billion a year in profit while farm workers like Kitty scrape by on a pittance.[1] I contacted Sikhula Sonke in order to investigate a bit further and met with the farm workers interviewed by the *Guardian* in early July 2009.

'I asked to talk to the boer [farmer] to make living conditions better,' Kitty says. 'Our children are suffering. But the boer didn't listen to us. The supervisor listens but doesn't deliver. It's only empty promises.' But she thinks Tesco will make a difference. 'Tesco came to see us at the end of May,' she says. 'I really think they are honest and genuine. I'm thankful because for me I know things will change.'

Kitty hopes for a better future. 'I dream about a bigger house with a swimming pool and a car – a very warm house with proper living conditions. That my children go to college, everything going well, that my children don't go hungry. I would be on top of the world.' I ask her if she thinks her dream will come true. 'I hope so, not just for me, for my children. I don't want them to suffer any more.'

Dianna Hlati is luckier than Kitty in one respect. After an eight-year wait she has received a government-provided house, in which I interviewed her and the other women. 'The roof leaks, but it's better than living on the farm,' she says. But it doesn't come cheap: it costs her 385 rand a month. Whereas Kitty is bubbly, she is subdued and anxious. She too earns only 325 rand a week, but as a seasonal worker she doesn't work from March to June each year. When I interviewed her she hadn't worked since March and was worried about whether the farm would take her back. She supports three children: a daughter aged eighteen and two boys aged eleven and four. The bills are piling up. She must pay school fees of 250 rand a year, transport of 140 rand a month and electricity of 150 rand a month. 'It's very hard. I have very little for food and clothes. My older son is a good football player. He is a goalkeeper but I can't afford to buy him gloves. They cost 200 to 300 rand.'

Work is tough. 'It's very hard. It's tiring and painful. But I try to do my best.' Her arm has been painful since she fell (not at work) and had to have an operation. 'I told Tesco about the working conditions and about how they fined some workers 150 rand for taking some grapes. Before we used to get given grapes but after we joined Sikhula Sonke they took that away. I asked Tesco to talk to the farm owners about the way they are treating workers. Tesco seemed honest and genuine. They seemed to care about us.' I asked her whether it would be a good idea for people in Britain to stop buying South African fruit from Tesco. 'It's not a good idea because there would be no jobs,' she replies. Kitty agrees. 'If Tesco stopped buying fruit [from our farm] it would be terrible. Retrenchment would follow.'

Sanna Louw is a supervisor on a farm that grows table grapes. You may have seen her face: ActionAid displayed it on a leaflet urging Peter Mandelson, then Britain's business minister, to bring the country's supermarkets to heel (although they spelled her name wrong). Aged forty-three, she oversees three hundred seasonal workers. 'Picking grapes is very difficult as you're always reaching up with your arms in the air,' she says. She too earns 325 rand a week, with which she supports her husband, four children and a grandson. Worse, the farmer recently tried to get rid of her. 'He told me there was no work for my husband and son any more.'

Thankfully, Tesco came to the rescue. 'Tesco came to see us in early June and took some pictures. I told them it was difficult to support my whole family on my own,' Sanna explains. 'Tesco said that if the owner told me to leave the farm, I should get in touch and they would help me. The owner was furious with Tesco for taking the pictures. Tesco said they would protect me and come back to find out how I was doing. The farmer treats us badly but Tesco cares. Things got better after Tesco came. They put warm water in the house and fixed the wall after five years.'

Wendy Pekeur, the general secretary of Sikhula Sonke, used to be a farm worker herself. Sitting in her office in Stellenbosch, the town at the heart of South Africa's most famous wine-producing region, she explains that the union was initially an NGO called the 'Women on Farms' project. Now it has four thousand members, eight permanent staff and a budget of three million rand a year, funded in part by Britain's Comic Relief as well as by the Africa Group of Sweden. 'We registered as a trade union in order to have access to the farms,' Wendy explains. 'Farmers have to recognise us.'

'Farm workers are the lowest workers in South Africa,' she says. 'They earn 1,251 rand a month. That's not enough to meet basic needs. They spend over 70 per cent of their wages on food, and transport is expensive in isolated rural areas.' Things have got better, though. 'In 2003 people were still paid 40 rand a week. Some were still paid in wine. Wages have got better. Unions are now recognised. But working conditions are the same or worse.' Wendy thinks a fair wage is 5,000 rand a month. (Kitty thinks it should be 1,000 rand a week, Sanna 600, Dianna 500.) They also want better working conditions. 'Farm workers need job security,' Wendy says. 'Labour brokers should stop using outsourced labour. Farm workers need security of tenure. There is no protection for workers. If they lose their job, they lose their home and their whole livelihood.'

Wendy's main gripe is with the South African government. 'I'm disappointed at the economic progress since the end of apartheid. Too many politicians are only working for their own interests.' Sikhula Sonke called on its members not to vote in the 2009 election that saw Jacob Zuma elected president. 'We spoiled our ballots and demanded better conditions.'

'The labour laws are there but implementation is poor,' Wendy says. 'There are only six hundred labour inspectors in the whole country.' South Africa has a population of 48 million. 'Quite a few Sikhula Sonke members are harassed. Shop stewards are dismissed' – although when they go to arbitration, they usually win. The slow pace of land reform is another problem. Only 4 per cent of land was redistributed in 1996; the government's target is 30 per cent by 2014. Ninety-nine per cent of farmers are still white. 'The government doesn't do very much,' Wendy says. Kitty agrees. So does Sanna: 'The government doesn't care about us. They do nothing for farm workers.'

Sceptics might wonder if Kitty, Dianna and the other workers are naive about Tesco's good intentions. Yet Wendy, who is more worldly-wise, also thinks Tesco is a force for good. 'Tesco are genuine about trying to make things better,' she says. 'That's the impression. They told us to contact them directly if we have any concerns. If we have a dispute with the farmers, we tell them that if we don't resolve it, we'll let Tesco do it. So the name Tesco has become a very powerful tool.' Boycotting Tesco would not be wise, she says. 'Workers would suffer and lose their homes.' Her message to British consumers is: 'Continue eating South African fruit. Ensure ethical standards are met and workers are not exploited.'

By buying fruit from Tesco, British people can help improve the lives of Kitty, Dianna, Sanna and others like them. But old-fashioned protectionism is combining with new-fangled localism to deny people in poorer countries the opportunity of a better life. Although South Africa has signed a 'free trade agreement' with the EU, its exports to Europe still face high tariffs. Under the Byzantine rules of its protectionist Common Agricultural Policy, the EU slaps import duties of as much as 17.6 per cent on the table grapes which Dianna and Sanna pick, as well as stipulating an 'entry price' that sets a floor below the import price. In the case of plums, which Kitty helps to pick, the duties are up to 12 per cent, plus a more stringent entry price. Since most of the world's poor work on farms, anyone who cares about poverty and injustice should be campaigning to scrap the CAP and other countries' agricultural protectionism. When the interests of rich European farmers deny opportunities to poor African ones, is it any wonder that they try to come and work in Europe instead?

Unfortunately, Europe is moving in the opposite direction. Michel Barnier, France's agriculture minister from 2007 to 2009, has called for the EU to erect new tariffs at its borders to encourage European self-sufficiency in food.[2] Germany has urged Europe to demand higher environmental and health standards from countries such as India, China and the US that seek to export to Europe. Cosseted Western farmers have also acquired powerful new allies: 'localists' who favour strict limits on foreign entanglements in general and on food trade in particular.

Food follies

Open the comment pages of a British newspaper these days and you will find pundits fretting and fuming about all sorts of things. The cost of living is exorbitant, food prices are sky-high and housing remains unaffordable even after the bubble has burst. The country is overcrowded and cannot comfortably accommodate any more immigrants. The local environment is under strain from intensive farming, while flying in foreign produce is frying the planet. One food scare follows another. Animals are mistreated. Big supermarket chains, notably Tesco, are responsible for all manner of evils – monopolising people's shopping, screwing small farmers and generally getting too big for their boots. Pull all these threads together and some people conclude that Britain (and other countries) should reject 'corporate globalisation' and return to a local, indigenous economy of small shops and farmers, with fewer (foreign) people around.

Few people are that extreme. But many more espouse a watered-down version of such views. They try to buy local (or British). They grumble about immigration. They think profiteering supermarkets should be cut down to size (while still doing their weekly shop there). Such views cut across the political spectrum. They are held by a disparate group of conservatives, nationalists, left-wingers and environmentalists with a shared distaste for globalised modernity, while the farmers and small-business owners whose narrow interests such an agenda serves are happy to go along for the ride. They highlight how the new dividing line in politics is between those who believe in openness and progress and those who are sceptical or hostile to it.

Many of these fears came to a head in 2007–8 when global food prices spiked. Look, critics cried, foreigners cannot be relied on to feed us – we need 'food security' instead. Newspapers were full of suggestions about how to grow your own vegetables in your window box – and why not keep a cow in your living room too? Taken to its logical conclusion, this implies a return to subsistence farming, which was hardly secure (or pleasant), as any small Indian farmer can tell you.

Food is an emotive issue – especially if you think you might run short. But while soaring food prices did cause misery for the poor in developing countries, there was never any prospect of people in rich countries starving. So the real issue in Europe was price, not quantities – food-price inflation, not food security. Thus the very term 'food security' is a protectionist canard, designed to evoke memories of wartime deprivation in Britain and tap into broader insecurities elsewhere.

What, though, caused food prices to soar? Some blamed faceless 'global markets', conveniently ignoring that since governments meddle so much in agriculture such markets are anything but free. Others put a face on their scapegoating. It was those dastardly Asians again – how dare they eat more meat instead of rice as they get richer! The typical Chinese person ate a mere 50 grams of meat a day in 1985; now they eat more than 135 grams.[3] Disgusting – that's a bit more than a quarter-pounder a day. But in fact, the Chinese eating a bit more beef each year and the Indians a little more lamb cannot be responsible for food prices shooting up so rapidly.

The main reason why grain prices rocketed is not that live-stock destined for Asian dinner tables needed more feed. It's that the US government massively expanded its subsidies for ethanol made from domestic maize in 2005. American farmers rushed to take advantage of this latest boondoggle by tearing up other crops, such as wheat and soya beans, and planting more maize, while diverting maize that they previously exported to the US government instead. In 2007 the demands of America's ethanol programme alone accounted for over half the world's unmet need for cereals.[4] Without that programme, food prices would have risen much less.

Obscenely, American ethanol subsidies cause poor people in developing countries to starve. According to the World Bank, the grain needed to generate enough ethanol to fill up an SUV would feed a person for a year.[5] Not to be outdone, the EU is imple-menting its own biofuel targets. Meanwhile other governments – such as Argentina, India, Russia and Ukraine – made matters worse by restricting their exports, pushing prices up further. Thus it was global protectionism, not global markets, that caused most of the recent food-price spike.

Protectionism was not only responsible for the price hikes in

2007 and 2008. It is also to blame for the high prices that Europeans endure every day. The sprawling morass of tariffs, subsidies, quotas, tariff-quotas, rebates, price-support payments and other devilishly complicated handouts known as the CAP costs European consumers an extra €33.7 billion in higher prices in 2008, according to the OECD.[6] Converted at the average exchange rate for 2008, this is equivalent to £26.8 billion.[7] Britons and other Europeans are also stung with higher taxes to pay for all the subsidies – €77.6 billion (£61.7 billion) in 2008. In total, Europeans hand over a total of €110.5 billion (£87.8 billion) a year, or 0.9 per cent of GDP, to farmers each year. That works out at £750 (€943) for a family of four.[8] So scrapping the CAP would lead to lower food prices and lower taxes, boosting Europeans' spending power. America's farmers also have their snouts in the subsidy trough. They received handouts totalling $96.4 billion, or 0.67 per cent of GDP, in 2008.[9] South Koreans fork out a whopping 2.4 per cent of their national income to their pampered farmers each year.[10]

All farmers – including small ones – benefit from the CAP. But since subsidies increase roughly in line with farm size, the biggest handouts go to rich large landowners, many of whom inherited their land through the accident of their aristocratic birth. This is the most reactionary subsidy scheme one could imagine – millions of middle- and working-class taxpayers keeping the lords of the manor in clover on the pretence of helping the peasants. The EU keeps the recipients of taxpayers' money shrouded in mystery, but figures uncovered by Oxfam, a campaign group, showed that an elite 3 per cent of landowners gobble up a fifth of total CAP payments to the UK.[11] Of more than a hundred thousand organisations that received payments in England in 2004, 2,269 received more than £100,000, 304 more than £250,000 and fifty-three more than £500,000. Among them were the Duke of Westminster, who received £448,000, and the Duke of Marlborough, who got his hands on £511,000, and many other aristocrats.[12] Around the EU, 1.8 per cent of recipients received more than €500,000 each.[13] Other big beneficiaries are food-processing companies such as Ireland's Kerry Foods, Britain's Tate & Lyle and France's Béghin-Say.

Small isn't always beautiful

Even though the CAP inflates the price of food and puts money directly in farmers' pockets, many small farmers struggle to survive. At this point, localists bring in their second bogeyman – big supermarket chains. The reason why small farms are struggling, they claim, is because supermarkets abuse their power to screw down farm prices and drive your friendly local shops out of business. Since supermarkets all but monopolise the marketplace, consumers have little option but to shop there, allowing them to rake in huge profits at small farmers' and shoppers' expense. Cut supermarkets down to size, localists argue, and everyone would be better off.

But that's nonsense. Nobody is forced to shop in supermarkets. Most people do so because it is cheaper and more convenient. Many people in the part of London where I live were delighted at the opening of a mid-sized Tesco Metro. It offered a wider choice of better-value products than the small stores in the immediate vicinity and provided much-needed competition for the more expensive, large supermarket a bit further away. Far from bemoaning Tesco's arrival, many people wish it would open a larger superstore.

It's hard to argue that Tesco is abusing its position as market leader when it is generally so much cheaper than its competitors. It is cheap because it is big and efficient – and it is big because it is popular. Far from foisting its own preferences on people, Tesco prospers by giving people what they want. Organic? No problem. Local? Fine. Fairtrade? Here you go. Strawberries in winter? Sure. Discount brands in a recession? Of course. Better working conditions for South African fruit pickers? We'll do our best. It rings up hefty profits by expanding the volume and range of what it sells, not by inflating its margins, which averaged 6.1 per cent in its June 2009 results.[14] Despite repeated investigations by Britain's competition authorities, supermarkets have repeatedly been cleared of harming consumer interests. (Where they are found to be overly dominant, their market power should of course be curbed.)

Nor is the romantic notion that small traders and shopkeepers are 'nice' while supermarkets are nasty profit-seeking brutes accurate. The butcher and the baker are not in business to be benevolent, they are out to earn a profit like other businesspeople. My personal experience is that while some are pleasant, others are not. (Tesco staff, on the other hand, are almost always friendly.) Like any high-cost business, small shops can only prosper if they offer customers something special that makes them willing to pay higher prices – such as proximity, later opening hours, products not available elsewhere or particularly good-quality food and service. People can shop in small local stores if they want to. That they often choose not to suggests that they do not value small shops as much as localists wish they would.

Like small shops, small farms tend to have higher costs than larger and more efficient enterprises. Whereas large farms can reap economies of scale which lower their production costs, smaller ones are much less productive. So if supermarkets use their bargaining power to get a better deal from suppliers for their customers, the highest-cost ones will inevitably struggle unless they have a particular advantage that allows them to charge higher prices. So if consumers value produce from small – or local – farms, brand it as such and charge a mark-up. Small dairy farmers might also want to stop selling a commodity (milk) and try to make a prize-winning cheese instead. But it is one thing to buy a few pricey products from small farms, quite another to expect everyone to buy all their food from them. Our weekly shop would be exorbitantly expensive if we all had to rely exclusively on small local farms to feed us.

Expensive land

The underlying reason why so much of the farming sector in Britain is uncompetitive has nothing to do with the supermarkets. It is that land and labour costs are more expensive than elsewhere. Even when they earn the UK minimum wage, strawberry pickers in Britain are much better paid than those in Mexico or Morocco. Since strawberry picking is not particularly pleasant, few people want to do it. Those who do are often foreigners for whom the wages on offer are more attractive than those back home. If Britain kept out foreign workers, strawberries would most likely go unpicked, because the much higher wages needed to tempt British people to pick them would make them prohibitively expensive. Often, then, foreign workers are helping to keep British farms going.

Why is agricultural land so expensive? One reason, ironically, is the CAP. Because agricultural land entitles farmers to a guaranteed income from the EU, it is a more valuable asset than otherwise. A study for the European Commission estimates that the price of agricultural land would be 30 per cent lower without the CAP. Where large landowners have a local monopoly on farm land, as the Duke of Buccleuch does in large parts of Scotland, they can get their hands on the EU subsidies by charging much higher rents to their tenant farmers. By one calculation, the Duke of Buccleuch may thus extract as much as €31.3 million a year from his 277,077 acres.[15] But the main reason why agricultural land is expensive by international standards is that Britain is a rich country where land is relatively scarce.

You see – it's those nasty immigrants again. Except actually it's not. Planning regulations stipulate which uses land can be put to. Housing for Polish migrants (or anyone else) cannot be built on agricultural land. So while a large influx of foreigners might conceivably drive up property prices in cities, it does not affect the price of farm land.

But are immigrants even to blame for the high cost of housing? During the bubble years, anti-immigration campaigners blamed rising house prices on the influx of recent migrants. Never mind that such house-price inflation also occurred in Britain in the 1980s, when the country was losing people. Ignore the fact that the total influx was relatively small – perhaps 1 million temporary migrants between 2004 and 2008 and more permanent annual additions of fewer than two hundred thousand people in a country of 60 million – while house prices were registering double-digit gains most years. Gloss over the fact that house prices have since plunged even though the population has continued to rise. Still, you can be sure that the argument will be trotted out again when the housing market recovers.

Environmentalists and anti-immigration campaigners often argue that Britain is full up. That's what the *Daily Mail* said in the 1930s as an argument not to allow in German Jews. Yet Britain's population has risen by over 10 million since then. Even now, if Britain's land area was equally distributed among its residents, there would be enough for an acre – the size of a football pitch – each. The real reason why Britain may feel cramped is that the distribution of land is so unequal. Some seven hundred thousand people live in rural areas, with 58.5 acres each, while 53.4 million people live in urban ones, with 0.07 acres of living space each. Rich landowners, subsidised by the vast majority of landless and land-poor taxpayers, still own most of the country, while most people are penned into small urban reservations. Nine in ten people in Britain live on a mere 7 per cent of the land.[16]

Contrary to the belief that England will soon be concreted

over as cities encroach on green space – within thirty years, the
Council for the Protection of Rural England warned in 2005 – at
the current rate of development rural England would not
disappear until 3950! So the way to make housing more affordable is not to throw out hard-working immigrants who
contribute to the economy and tend to use up very little housing
space, it is to clamp down on property speculation, relax planning restrictions and tax away rich landowners' unearned and
undeserved gains to pay for the infrastructure and other developments that this would require.

Now look again at the consequences of Britain's relatively
expensive agricultural land. Because land is pricey, farmers have
an incentive to economise on it. They try to squeeze as many animals as possible into as small a space as possible. They spray
vast amounts of fertiliser and pesticides on their land to boost
agricultural yields. They cut down hedgerows and try to make
use of every available inch of space. If they didn't, British food
would be astronomically expensive. So if you are worried about
intensive farming, animal welfare and environmental degrada-
tion, it would be far better to be importing food from countries
with vast open spaces, where land is cheap. Countries such as
New Zealand, South Africa, Thailand, Argentina, Australia and
many others. In fact, most of Britain's food needs could be supplied from one country – Brazil.

Good value and green

Brazil ought to be the world's breadbasket. Nature has made its
poor north-east an open-air greenhouse: the sun always shines,
the soil is fertile and the low humidity acts as a natural barrier to
disease. Grapes mature in 120 days, instead of 180 days elsewhere, allowing two harvests a year. Asparagus can be cut twice
as often as in temperate climes. The state of São Paulo in the

south-east produces the world's cheapest sugar and orange juice. The endless savannahs of the centre-west are ideal for growing soya, by far Brazil's biggest agricultural commodity. Brazil is the world's largest exporter of beef, coffee, orange juice and sugar, and it is closing fast on the leaders in soya, poultry and pork. Its agricultural productivity is soaring as traditional farmers embrace modern methods, invest in better seeds, fertiliser, livestock breeding and equipment – such as high-tech harvesters fitted with GPS systems to reduce crop losses – and make use of the internet to keep up to date with global commodity prices. Funds are also being poured into better agricultural infrastructure, improved and more conveniently located slaughterhouses and processing facilities, and research and development. 'A large part of the agriculture of the rich world is dependent on subsidies,' says Luiz Fernando Furlan. 'Here it's the opposite. But despite a lack of infrastructure, high taxes and very high interest rates, we are still competitive.'

Unlike its competitors, Brazil is not running out of land. Agriculture occupies 60 million hectares now; it could stretch out to another 90 million hectares without touching the Amazon rainforest, says Silvio Crestana, director of Embrapa, the main agricultural research institute.[17] Despite these huge natural advantages, Brazil's food exporters are still dwarfed by those from subsidised European and American farmers. Tariffs and subsidies are not the only obstacles they face. They also include spurious technical regulations and sanitary standards that act as covert protectionism. Furlan fumes that he cannot sell any chicken in America, even though it is deemed perfectly safe to eat in Europe and Japan, which are hardly known for their lax food standards. If rich countries abolished their trade barriers and subsidies, Brazil could realise its full potential. The real value of its agricultural and food output would soar by 34 per cent and real net farm income by 46 per cent, according to calculations by the World Bank.

But wouldn't importing more food from far-off places such as Brazil be bad for the environment? It's true that flying in food generates greenhouse-gas emissions, although shipping it in much less so. But according to Britain's Department for the Environment (Defra), most (85 per cent) of the environmental cost of food transport is incurred within the UK, not least when lorries are stuck in traffic on congested roads. What's more, whereas in colder places such as Britain or the Netherlands, live-stock have to be kept in heated barns over the winter, while tomatoes and other produce are grown in heated greenhouses, such measures are not needed in warm places such as Brazil. Overall, growing food in Brazil and importing it would generate less carbon dioxide – while the best way to curb emissions would be to improve food distribution in the UK, not least through road pricing to reduce congestion.

Researchers at Lincoln University in New Zealand found that lamb raised on the country's clover-choked pastures and shipped 11,000 miles by boat to Britain produced 700 kilograms of carbon-dioxide emissions per tonne while British lamb produced 2,900 kilograms of carbon dioxide per tonne, in part because poorer British pastures force farmers to use feed. In other words, it is four times better for the planet for Londoners to buy lamb imported from the other side of the world than to buy it from a producer in their backyard. Similar figures were found for dairy products and fruit.[18]

Green beans air-freighted from Kenya allow consumers to eat fresh beans when British varieties are out of season. Each packet has a little sticker with the image of a plane on it to indicate that carbon dioxide from aviation fuel was emitted in bringing them to the UK. Yet beans in Kenya are produced in a highly environmentally friendly manner. 'Beans there are grown using manual labour – nothing is mechanised,' says Professor Gareth Edwards-Jones of Bangor University, an expert on African agri-culture. 'They don't use tractors, they use cow muck as fertiliser;

and they have low-tech irrigation systems. They also provide employment to many people in the developing world.'[19] Allowing for these differences, one finds that beans air-freighted from Kenya cause fewer carbon emissions than British ones grown in fields on which oil-based fertilisers have been sprayed and which are ploughed by tractors that burn diesel. As Britain's trade and development minister, Gareth Thomas, remarked, 'Driving six and a half miles to buy your shopping emits more carbon than flying a pack of Kenyan green beans to the UK.'[20]

To sum up, if people feel like eating local produce, they are free to do so. But that is a personal choice, not a sensible prescription for how everyone ought to eat. People who eat foreign food have nothing to feel guilty about; on the contrary, they can help improve the lives of people like Kitty de Kock. The arguments for new-fangled localism are as unconvincing as those for old-fashioned protectionism. Freeing farm trade would save consumers and taxpayers money, benefit people in poorer countries, provide safe and healthy food, and be good for the environment. That is an appetising prospect by any measure.

10

Clean is Cool

How to tackle climate change

Justin Rowlatt, BBC *Newsnight*'s self-styled 'ethical man', spent a year trying to live as 'greenly' as possible. He gave up the family car, stopped eating meat, switched the lights off, collected rainwater, made compost and performed a variety of unsavoury stunts for the television cameras. At the end of this excruciatingly unsustainable experiment with giving up the carbon-producing trappings of modern life, his new 'carbon footprint' was measured. It was only 20 per cent lower – the same percentage reduction that the European Union is targeting by 2020. Yet to have a reasonable chance of preventing the planet from dangerously overheating, it is reckoned that the world needs to halve its carbon emissions (relative to 1990 levels) by 2050 – with rich countries slashing theirs by 80 per cent. Does that imply the end of civilisation as we know it?

As concern about global warming mounts, governments, green lobby groups and journalists increasingly proffer advice about how to 'do your bit' to limit global carbon emissions.

This tends to range from the banal – switch off your television rather than leave it on standby – to the puritanical (ditch your foreign holidays) and from the plain ignorant (buy 'organic' produce from a small local farm) to the Luddite: turn off the lights and do things by hand rather than using household appliances. The eco-romantic vision of the good life would appear to be a return to the Dark Ages.

At the other extreme, a ragbag of 'climate-change sceptics' challenge the establishment scientific consensus that manmade carbon emissions are causing temperatures to rise, with potentially catastrophic consequences. They include reasonable sceptics who point out that our ability to understand – let alone forecast – the climate is inevitably shaky; assorted cranks, crackpots and conspiracy theorists with a variety of bizarre beliefs; liberals and libertarians with legitimate fears about the threat to individual freedom from misguided action in the name of combating climate change; and lobbyists in the pay of the oil and gas industries.

In between lie the vast majority of people: confused or ignorant about the science, reluctant to give up the convenience and comforts of modern life that they are used to (in rich countries) or aspire to (in poorer ones), overwhelmed by the scale of the problem and the potential changes it requires, and yet with a nagging fear that unless we do something, we could end up wrecking the world for future generations.

I am not a climate scientist. Like most people, I do not have the expertise to assess whether global warming is really happening, and if so whether it is manmade. The mainstream scientific consensus may be wrong. All scientific knowledge is imperfect, open to doubt and subject to revision – especially when it cannot be tested in controlled experiments in a lab. But the evidence that we are causing the planet to overheat seems convincing enough – and the breadth of scientists who believe it to be true impressive enough – that we should take the issue very seriously. Not because we can be absolutely sure that it is true, but because the consequences if we do nothing about it could be so calamitous. In such circumstances it is prudent and wise to take action to insure ourselves against a disaster – better safe than sorry. It is equally vital that we try to find the cheapest and smartest ways of tackling the problem – and that the costs of change are shared fairly.

Ending our addiction to oil would make the world a better place in other ways too. Western governments would no longer feel the need to go to war to attack (or defend) obnoxious regimes that threaten our supplies of black gold. Regions blighted by the scramble for oil by established powers and rising ones, such as China, would have a better chance to determine their own destinies. We would no longer be vulnerable to energy blackmail by the likes of Saudi Arabia, Iran, Russia and Venezuela, whose stranglehold over oil supplies dictates the price of nearly everything we buy, the pace of economic growth and the rate of joblessness – not to mention harming billions of poor people who eke out a precarious living. These are all good reasons to look beyond petroleum.

Zoom!

Few people want to live like Justin Rowlatt. But what if a low-carbon future was clean and alluring rather than bleak and medieval? One of the highlights of my trip around the world to research this book was taking an open-top Tesla Roadster for a spin in the summer sunshine of Palo Alto, California. It was bright red, styled like a Lotus Elise, accelerated from nought to 60 mph (97 kph) in less than four seconds and handled the road beautifully. You don't have to be *Top Gear*'s Jeremy Clarkson to appreciate the awesome power and sleek curves of these cutting-edge sports cars. I could have driven off into the sunset, but unfortunately I had another interview to get to (and the car wasn't mine). But what's truly amazing about the Tesla Roadster is that it is powered by lithium ion batteries like the ones used in laptop computers.

Driving one of these electric cars is not just great fun, it's clean and quiet too. You can breeze along a country lane without spewing out noxious fumes and hear birds singing over the gentle whirr of the battery-powered engine. The Roadster is also cheap – and convenient – to run: you can drive 244 miles (393 kilometres) on a single charge and then plug it into any ordinary electrical socket and charge it up overnight; a full charge will set you back a mere $4. (Unlike many rechargeable batteries, the Tesla's don't need to be fully discharged to maintain their staying power, so you can top them up every night.) In a country such as France, which generates 80 per cent of its electricity from nuclear power, or Brazil, where three-quarters comes from hydroelectric power, driving a Tesla produces hardly any carbon emissions. Even in America or Britain, which rely more on coal and gas, it is far better for the environment than getting behind the wheel of a clunky Toyota Prius hybrid. Not for nothing does Tesla Motors call it 'performance with a clean conscience'.

Granted, a Roadster will set you back $109,000 in the United States ($101,500 after a $7,500 federal tax credit). But that still works out $26,000 cheaper over ten years than a Porsche 911 thanks to savings on petrol and maintenance costs, according to Tesla's bubbly Rachel Konrad. Unlike conventional cars that require regular (and expensive) servicing, Teslas need only an annual inspection and a change of battery, coolant and oil every seven years. In Britain, the sticker price is £94,000; in the euro-zone, it is €89,000 plus value-added tax (VAT).

Ostensibly an American company based in Silicon Valley, Tesla is in fact a global product. Its chief executive and co-founder, Elon Musk, was born and raised in South Africa, then emigrated to his mother's native Canada. He went to university there, scraping by on as little as a dollar a day with part-time and summer jobs, before making his fortune in the US by developing PayPal, the online payments system sold to eBay in 2002 for $1.5 billion.[1] The chief financial officer comes from India, and the company currently employs over four hundred people (and the number is rising fast) from a wide range of other countries. The Roadster itself is assembled in Britain at the Lotus factory in Hethel from parts sourced around the world – motors from Taiwan, body panels from France, brakes and airbags from Germany and the lithium ion cells that make up the battery from East Asia. The transmission is made by Michigan-based BorgWarner, an automotive parts supplier that also sells to Chrysler, General Motors and others. Its future success surely depends not on the US government propping up clapped-out car companies that produce outdated gas-guzzlers but on expanding innovators such as Tesla.

Unfortunately, most of us cannot afford a top-of-the-range sports car – although after my test drive I was so enthused that I envisioned giving up food and other non-essentials in order to save up for one. A $100,000 car is also a non-starter for the vast majority of new car owners over the next twenty years – the millions of Chinese, Indians and other people in emerging economies who will be scrimping together to upgrade from a motorbike, scooter or bicycle. (China overtook the United States as the world's biggest car market in 2009.) But the good news is that car makers are scrambling to produce a wide range of different – and cheaper – electric vehicles, whose price will fall as technology improves and companies reap economies of scale. At the same time, governments are speeding up the transition through a host of regulations – such as higher fuel-economy standards – subsidies (to car producers and consumers) and taxes: on petrol and eventually on carbon emissions in general. Soon we could all be zipping down the road in a nippy electric car.

Tesla itself is developing a five-seater Model S saloon that is due to go on sale in 2012 for $57,400 (or $49,900 including the federal tax rebate). According to Tesla, it will work out cheaper over ten years than a saloon with a $35,000 sticker price, such as a fully equipped Honda Accord. The US government is providing $365 million in interest-bearing loans to help build an assembly plant for the Model S, and a further $100 million to build one for its powertrains. Tesla aims to sell these to other car makers, just as Honda sells conventional engines to other companies. It is also working with Daimler to produce an electric version of the German company's two-seater Smart car which went on sale in 2010.

Nearly every big Western car maker is rushing to get in on the act. At the 2009 Frankfurt motor show, Volkswagen showed off the E-Up!, Peugeot flaunted the iOn, while Renault unveiled the Twizy, Fluence, Zoe and Kangoo. Despite their quirky names, electric cars are likely to be far more common by 2020. Carlos Ghosn, the head of Renault and Nissan, which is launching its own, Leaf, reckons that by then they could account for 10 per cent of the global car market.

Switching to electric vehicles promises huge benefits not just for the global environment, but for the local one. Imagine cities that are eventually free of choking, poisonous fumes and all the associated respiratory and other diseases. Enjoy the peace and quiet of busy main roads and city centres. Picture buildings no longer stained by soot. We don't all need to cycle to make that dream a reality.

The bigger point is that there is no chance of convincing people in countries such as China and India that they should do without cars as they get richer. A Chinese contact told me a revealing story. An American environmentalist visiting Beijing commented that there were too many cars on the road and that the Chinese ought to ride bicycles instead. His host was too polite to point out that the Chinese had only recently got off their bikes and into their cars and had no desire to give them up. Besides, what right do rich Westerners have to tell the Chinese not to drive? Cars give you more freedom to go where you want when you want, a wider choice of jobs to which you can commute, a bigger range of shops you can reach and so on. That extra mobility benefits the wider economy too: it creates a larger and more flexible labour market, makes greater specialisation possible, boosts retail competition and bolsters the development of remote areas, among other things.

Non-Western companies are also big players in this electric shift. Amid all the hoopla about the Tata Nano – the 'People's Car' with a starting price of a mere 100,000 rupees (£1,360) – India's accomplishments in electric vehicles have attracted much less attention. Yet the best-selling electric car in the world is India's REVA, which is made in Bangalore. The basic model costs around $7,000 in India. A superior model retails in Britain as the G-Wiz i. This will set you back around £8,500, has a range of fifty miles and a top speed of 50 mph (80 kph) and is increasingly common on the capital's streets, not least because it is exempt from the congestion charge for driving in central London. How come REVAs are so cheap? 'They rethought the car,' explains Raj Atluru, the genial head of the clean-tech investment practice at Draper Fisher Jurvetson, a top American venture-capital firm. 'The average car has about 6,500 components; they [REVAs] have a third of that. And they're focused on the city: in the city you don't need to go two hundred miles. So you can have cheaper systems and fewer batteries. Come home and plug it in every day and it works well.'

China's BYD (Build Your Dreams), a rechargeable battery maker that manufactures over half of the world's mobile-phone batteries, is using its know-how to become an electric dynamo too. It already sells a plug-in hybrid, the F3DM, which uses battery power most of the time, with a petrol engine as a back-up. An all-electric car, the E6, was launched in 2010. A five-passenger saloon, it made a splash at the Detroit motor show, leaving Motown's much-hyped Chevrolet Volt (also known as the

Vauxhall or Opel Ampera) in the shade. BYD claims the E6 has a 250-mile (400-kilometre) range on as little as three hours of charging, reaches 60 mph in eight seconds and has a top speed of 100 mph (161 kph).[2] It will be sold first in China, primarily to fleet users. BYD also wants to make its batteries fully recyclable and has developed a non-toxic electrolyte fluid. Not bad for a company that was only founded in 1995, started making cars in 2003 and (unusually for a car maker) makes nearly all its components itself.

Warren Buffett, the canny billionaire investor, was so wowed by BYD that he bought a 10 per cent stake in the company for $230 million. 'There's no question that what's been accomplished since 1995 at BYD is extraordinary,' he says. His investment company, Berkshire Hathaway, initially tried to buy 25 per cent of BYD, but its founder, Wang Chuanfu, turned down the offer. Wang, now China's richest man, wanted to be in business with Buffett – to enhance his brand and open doors in the US, he says – but he would not let go of more than 10 per cent of BYD's stock. 'This was a man who didn't want to sell his company,' Buffett says. 'That was a good sign.' He thinks BYD has a chance of becoming the world's largest car maker, primarily by selling electric cars, as well as a leader in the fast-growing solar-power industry.[3]

What distinguishes Tesla, REVA and BYD is not just their technological prowess. They are also all upstarts, newcomers unencumbered by the old ways and attachment to petrol of traditional car makers – and their success (both commercial and environmental) depends on global markets remaining open. Even if they don't end up dominating the future market for electric cars, their competitive drive and innovative example are forcing existing car makers to put their foot down and go electric. For that, everyone should be grateful. It is regrettable that governments have muffled that international competition by lavishing subsidies on hidebound, loss-making car makers, seeking to protect yesterday's jobs – and padding today's boardroom salaries and investor returns – at the expense of tomorrow's green employment opportunities, clean cars and the climate.

Green living

The word 'eco-house' may conjure up images of a thatched cottage, a tepee or even a tree house. But you don't have to live in a mud hut in order to slash the carbon emissions from your home. These emanate partly from the building of the house and partly from your energy use while living there. Buildings are the fastest-growing source of Britain's carbon emissions – they are responsible for 46 per cent of them, with homes responsible for 27 per cent.[4] One way to reduce buildings emissions is simply to change the way electricity is generated: if it comes from nuclear power or renewable energy sources, you can use all you want without having much impact on the climate. Another way is to change the way buildings are built.

Making building materials has never been a glamorous business. Nor has it evolved much in recent decades. But that is now changing, as entrepreneurs try to cash in on booming demand for energy-efficient materials. Meet Kevin Surace, the hyperactive chief executive of Serious Materials, which makes eco-friendly walls, windows and doors. 'I'm on a mission to save the planet,' he shouts modestly. Throughout our interview his voice remains uncomfortably loud. When I tell him that I have just come from Tesla, he quickly interjects. 'Passenger cars account for only 9 per cent of global carbon emissions. The built environment accounts for 52 per cent – 40 per cent to operate and 12 per cent to build.' The other 39 per cent comes from industry (24 per cent) and transport (15 per cent). 'We can make the biggest dent on CO_2 [carbon dioxide] with buildings,' he booms. Despite his high volume, it's hard to concentrate on what he's saying. He seems all wound up and his manic facial twitching gets me thinking of Heath Ledger playing the Joker in *The Dark Knight*.

His products sound good, though. Serious Materials's EcoRock requires 80 per cent less energy to produce than plasterboard, the material used for most interior walls in the US. It is made using 80 per cent recycled industrial waste, and because it is naturally cured and dried, it eliminates the energy-intensive calcination and oven-drying used to make plasterboard. It can also be fully reused at the end of its life. Not only that, but it is resistant to termites and mould. These brilliant new products were developed largely by Chinese- and Indian-born materials scientists working in the US. There aren't a lot of US-born ones, Surace notes. He is adamant that 'nobody buys building materials because they're green'. His sales pitch is based on value – 'we give people their money back in short order' – and his products' other useful features; their green credentials are just a bonus.[5]

Serious Materials is creating hundreds of the green jobs that politicians are so keen on. It has bought three disused windows factories around the US – in Boulder, Colorado; Vandergrift, Pennsylvania; and Chicago – and is converting them for its own production, re-employing local workers who lost their jobs when the factories closed. Surace insists that it doesn't make sense for 'the business, the country or the climate' to produce overseas, because shipping bulky materials is expensive (and carbon-emitting) and labour accounts for only 5 per cent of the cost of making the company's high-value products. On the contrary, he envisages a greater localisation of production, even within America. While he plans to expand globally – his corporate mission is to reduce the world's carbon emissions by a billion tonnes a year (3 per cent of the current global total) – he would do so by establishing local production facilities around the world.

Surace is not your archetypal environmentalist. In fact, he freely admits that previously he wasn't green at all. He claims that it was Al Gore's movie *An Inconvenient Truth* and the reports by the

Intergovernmental Panel on Climate Change (IPCC) warning of the potentially catastrophic impact of climate change that led to his environmental awakening. 'This is not about saving a tree, or the spotted owl, it's about saving the planet,' he yells. 'I've got to step up and do something about it. What would my kids say if I didn't?'

Frankly, I have my doubts about his conversion to greenery. Surace seems more driven by ego than ecology. Helping to save the planet may be more about status and success – the corporate website shows him hobnobbing with Joe Biden during a visit by the US vice-president to Serious Materials's Chicago window factory – than ethics. But so what? Surace's manic lust for success is likely to drive him to do more to reduce carbon emissions than a roomful of earnestly worthy climate-change negotiators or indeed whole communes of holier-than-thou eco-radicals. In fact, it is precisely by channelling the huge energies of entrepreneurs who might otherwise be devising new financial instruments or internet programs into coming up with new low-carbon technologies that we stand the best chance of saving the planet. Larry Page and Sergey Brin, the founders of Google, have started an outfit called Google.org that is searching for a way to make renewable energy truly cheaper than coal. And it is only by keeping global markets open, allowing people and ideas to circulate and feed off each other, and enabling products and services to be disseminated quickly and cheaply around the world that the aim of halving carbon emissions by 2050 can be achieved. In doing so, new businesses will emerge that create millions of jobs, generate tax revenues, revitalise local communities and make lots of entrepreneurs and investors rich.

Efficiency has its limits

Homes and buildings are only one area in which energy efficiency can be increased. Power plants can be rejigged to reduce waste. Household appliances can be redesigned so as to use less power. New LED lights that produce a more pleasant glow than earlier models consume a tenth of the power of ordinary light-bulbs and last for thirty years. (The only drawback is that if changing a lightbulb becomes a thing of the past, so will all the many jokes about it.)

Sophisticated IT networks, such as those run by a company called EnerNOC, can be used to modulate energy use at times of peak demand – by switching off secondary lights in a building, for instance, or turning the air-conditioning down a notch. In effect, they act like a virtual power plant, saving the need for expensive additional generating capacity at peak times – and saving customers money. EnerNOC already manages 3,000MW – the equivalent of six large coal-fired power plants. In Britain such a system could be used to pay people to turn the heating down a bit at peak times.

Companies such as Silver Spring are at the forefront of creat-ing new 'smart grids' that could vastly improve the efficiency of electricity grids. Smart electricity meters in every home could tell you the price of power in real time. If it's high, you could decide to run your washing machine late at night, when power is cheaper instead. In the longer term, your fridge could be pro-grammed to let the temperature rise a degree at peak times. People with solar panels on their roofs could sell electricity to the grid when it's sunny and buy it back when it's dark. Consultants at McKinsey calculated that in the US alone an investment of $520 billion in efficiency savings would cut energy use outside the transport sector by 23 per cent of projected energy demand – and save the US economy more than $1,200 billion.[6]

These are all great ideas. They can certainly make a big dif-ference to our energy use. But there is a limit. As economies grow and people acquire new energy-using devices, energy demand inexorably rises. Computers, for instance, gobble up a lot of power – not just the ones you have at home or at work, but also the vast servers that store all the information needed to run Google or your internet banking. Homes and buildings are also getting bigger. Unless we decide to give up the huge benefits of television, the internet, washing machines and so on – and why should we? – the solution ultimately has to be to find alternative forms of green energy.

Limits to growth?

Why is life in modern societies so much better than life a generation, a century or a millennium ago? In essence, because we have learned how to harness two vast resources, human ingenuity and (largely) carbon-based energy, in creative ways that enable us to continually invent and deploy new and better means of satisfying our needs and wants. How? Through an ever-evolving framework of institutions and incentives which encourage innovation and investment and weed out bad ideas to leave good ones. Institutions range from property rights and the rule of law to universal education, competitive markets and social mechanisms that encourage cooperation. Incentives include profits, power, status, personal achievement, social recognition and security, as well as concern for others.

The good news is that there is no end in sight to human ingenuity. Far from slowing down, there is good reason to believe that the pace of progress will accelerate. Why? Because until recent times we were tapping the brainpower of only a tiny proportion of humanity. Most people were too poor, uneducated and constrained by traditional social norms, antiquated feudal systems and, more recently, communist central planning to contribute to their full potential. They needed all their wits just to survive. They were held back by class, gender, race, caste and ignorance. And they had every incentive to keep their head down, not look up to a brighter future. But over the past century in rich countries and more recently in poorer ones too, many of these barriers have fallen. While it is terrible that many limits remain, their lifting would unleash even greater opportunities.

Modern doomsayers who bemoan the world's many undeniable problems and injustices ignore the fact that in many respects things are much better than before. Over the past century, first primary and then secondary education has become universal in rich countries such as Britain – and nearly half of young adults now go on to college or university too. Women have been liberated, class barriers have fallen, racial discrimination has declined, homosexuality has been legalised. People's ambitions are much higher. Opportunities have also widened outwards, not least for the many immigrants who have moved to rich countries in search of a better life for themselves and their children.

In poor countries these changes are more recent, more rapid – and still have a huge way to go. Take China, home to 1.3 billion people, a fifth of the world population of 6.7 billion. A hundred years ago most Chinese people were illiterate, while for the literate few, opportunities for advancement depended on the imperial court in Beijing. Education was expanded massively after the Communist revolution in 1949, but the follies of Mao's Cultural Revolution caused a violent lurch backwards. But over the past thirty years, since the government began in 1978 to set people free to improve their lot and to open up the economy to the rest of the world, China's huge potential has been unbound. Hundreds of millions of people have migrated from subsistence farms to industrial cities. Wang Chuanfu, the founder of BYD, grew up on a farm in extreme poverty. His company's electric cars are now at the cutting edge of technology. Along the way, he has accumulated a net worth of $5.1 billion.[7]

Just think how much faster and further humanity could

progress if Africa emulated China's success, if women were liberated in the Arab world, if people were set free to live and work wherever they want in the world, if Silicon Valley's entrepreneurial magic cast its spell on Europe, and if every young person got a fair start in life. The combination of dynamic open markets and societies and progressive governments can be a huge force for good – and we must not squander it.

It's not just that a bigger proportion of humanity than ever is getting access to the tools of progress, there are also more of us. Contrary to the fashionable misanthropy which sees other people as a problem, every extra person is potentially the spark for a good new idea, big or small. I was once in a debate with a lady from the Optimum Population Trust, a green campaign group, who opposed immigration because she thought Britain's population ought to be halved to 30 million to make its 'ecological footprint sustainable'. That's fine, I said – you go first.

One of the patrons of the Optimum Population Trust is Jonathon Porritt – formally The Hon. Sir Jonathon Espie Porritt, 2nd Baronet – an environmentalist who advises Prince Charles and, until July 2009, chaired the Sustainable Development Commission, which was set up by Tony Blair to advise the British government on sustainable development. Porritt argues that people in poor countries in particular ought to have fewer children, with rich countries making 'massive investments in family-planning interventions in the poorest countries in the world . . . a driving programme for all our aid programmes'.[8] Translation: 'Poor people have this terrible habit of breeding – how dare they? We must stop them doing so.'

We have been here before. Two hundred years ago Thomas Malthus warned that the world couldn't feed a rising population. He was wrong: agricultural productivity more than outpaced population growth. Forty years ago Paul Ehrlich, also a patron of the Optimum Population Trust, wrote a best-seller called *The Population Bomb*, which compared population growth to a 'cancer' that required 'radical surgery' and warned that 'India couldn't possibly feed two hundred million more people by 1980.'[9] He was wrong too, although in the 1970s the Indian government briefly embarked on mass sterilisation programmes – of poor people, naturally – before seeing sense. Now, we have Porritt saying that Britain's population ought to halve – even though he himself has two children – and that rich countries ought to intervene to stop people in the poorest countries multiplying because of old fears about food compounded by new ones about running out of oil and global warming. It seems bizarre to be worrying about Britain not being able to feed itself at a time when record numbers of Britons are obese. Agricultural productivity also continues to grow. But is there any reason to think Porritt might be right?

Boundless energy

It all depends on the second element of the equation: can we find substitutes for carbon-based energy? Not because it is running out – it isn't; as we saw in Chapter 5, coal supplies remain plentiful and despite all the talk about 'Peak Oil', oil is unlikely to run out anytime soon, not least since as its price rises it becomes economic to extract petroleum from oil sands in western Canada and elsewhere, or to produce it from liquefied coal – but because of the threat of catastrophic climate change. The answer, surely, is yes. After all, coal, oil and gas are, essentially, fossilised organic material whose energy ultimately derives from the sun – so why not cut out the middleman (and millions of years) and tap the sun's unlimited energy directly?

If you travel sixty miles south-east from Jerusalem into Israel's Negev Desert, you will come across an amazing sight: more than 1,600 small mirrors that focus the sun's rays on to a boiler atop a tower to produce high-temperature steam. The steam is then piped to a conventional turbine, which generates electricity. In order to conserve precious desert water, the steam is air-cooled and piped back into the system in a closed-loop, environmentally friendly process. Unlike photovoltaic solar cells – the solar panels that have become increasingly common on roofs – 'solar thermal' plants are able to generate electricity at night or on cloudy days, by storing the heat they produce. The result is a large-scale solar system that delivers clean, reliable energy at a cost competitive with fossil fuels.

Luz, the Israeli company that devised this brilliant solar thermal technology, has three decades of experience in pioneering solar technology. In 2006 its technical leadership joined forces with a world-class finance and project development team to form BrightSource Energy, which is now based in Oakland, California. Yet again, it is that combination of foreign (and American) know-how and US venture capital operating across several countries that is making a difference. BrightSource is actively developing more than 4GW of solar-power projects in the south-western United States – enough to power 1.4 million homes.

Tapping the sun's energy offers the prospect of cheap, unlimited power.[10] It could also provide huge export earnings for poor countries with vast, uninhabited deserts. Munich Re, a German reinsurer, is trying to assemble a consortium called Desertec to build power stations in the Sahara and Arabia and connect them to Europe across the Mediterranean Sea using high-voltage direct-current cables. These, unlike conventional AC power lines, can transport energy over long distances and through water without big losses.[11] The ambitious plan envisages building enough solar-power stations to meet 15 per cent of European electricity demand in 2050, along with most of North Africa's and Arabia's, requiring an investment of €400 billion ($560 billion) at today's prices over the next forty years. Such big investments in solar technology could create huge economies of scale and stimulate further innovation, generating a virtuous circle of falling costs and increased output.

Another source of renewable energy is wind. The global leader is Vestas, a Danish company that makes, sells, installs and services wind turbines, and has 20 per cent of the world market. It began life after the Second World War as a small manufacturer of household appliances, then agricultural equipment and hydraulic cranes – hardly exciting stuff. But after beginning to make wind turbines in 1979, it is now at the cutting edge of the drive towards renewable energy. It has already installed 38,000 wind turbines across the world and by continually improving turbine technology it is bringing down the cost of wind energy. With revenues of €6 billion in 2008, and profits of €500 million, Vestas employs twenty thousand people around the world and has manufacturing plants across Europe as well as in the United States, Australia, China and India.[12] It is hiring and expanding fast, creating new green jobs even as the traditional manufacturing sector shrinks. Vestas could turn out to be Denmark's Nokia: an upstart from a small country that succeeds in dominating a huge new global market.

Wind power accounts for only 1 per cent of electricity generation in the US. It could 'easily' rise to 30 per cent, says Ditlev Engel, the boss of Vestas. America has plenty of wind blowing across the plains from North Dakota to Texas. Not harvesting it would be like Saudi Arabia not drilling for oil, he says.[13] Britain, where Vestas controversially closed a factory on the Isle of Wight in 2009, is pinning its hopes on offshore wind. The government is hoping to see 33GW-worth of maritime windmills – some five thousand turbines – built by 2020, up from 0.6GW in 2008.[14]

In both cases, finding ways to store the energy produced – so that solar and wind plants can feed the grid on cloudy, still days (and nights), as well as on sunny, windy ones – is vital. The good news is that large-scale storage capabilities are getting cheaper. Some use flow-cell batteries, others compressed air and still others salt storage.

As in other clean-tech industries, companies from emerging markets are among the leaders in renewable energy. The world's largest maker of solar panels is China's Suntech Power. It was set up by Shi Zhengrong, who studied at the University of New South Wales and became an Australian citizen before returning to China in 2001. Now one of the richest men in China – *Forbes* magazine estimated his personal net worth at $2.9 billion in March 2008 – he has repaid the favour to Australia by donating funds for renewable energy research to the University of New South Wales.[15] BYD, the Chinese battery and electric car maker, is developing a 'Home Clean Power Solution', basically a set of rooftop solar panels with built-in batteries to store power for use when the sun's not out. 'Solar is an endless source of energy,' BYD's Wang Chuanfu says. 'With better technology, we can reduce the costs.'[16]

India's Suzlon – which is based in Pune, where Baba Kalyani's Bharat Forge is also located – is Asia's largest (and the world's fifth-biggest) wind-power company. It is run by Tulsi Tanti, who discovered the benefits of wind after becoming frustrated with the high cost and unavailability of power for his earlier textiles business. Like many other Indian businesses, it is expanding internationally by snapping up Western companies, notably Hansen Transmissions, a Belgian manufacturer of gearboxes for wind turbines, and REPower, a German wind-turbine firm. It is also investing in facilities abroad, such as a rotor-blade factory in Minnesota and a $60-million plant in Tianjin, China, and thus creating new green jobs. It already employs over fourteen thousand people in twenty-one countries.

China's largest wind-turbine manufacturer – which is also in the global top ten – is Goldwind. It is based in an unlikely place: Urumqi, the capital of Xinjiang province, which was racked by ethnic unrest in July 2009. Most of China's manufacturers are located in its coastal regions, rather than in its remote north-west corner. China is already the world's second-biggest market for wind power, after the United States.

Replacing fossil fuels in electricity generation will require a huge expansion of solar, wind, hydro, geothermal, biomass and other renewable energy sources. In 2006 the world generated two-thirds of its electricity from fossil fuels (41 per cent from coal and peat, 20.1 per cent from gas and 5.8 per cent from oil) and the remaining third from hydro (16 per cent), nuclear (14.8 per cent) and other renewables (2.3 per cent).[17] Germany already generates over 15 per cent of its electricity from renewable sources – mainly wind, biomass and hydro.

Environmentalists will also need to swallow their hang-ups about nuclear power. Undeniably, atomic energy can provide a big chunk of the world's electricity safely and affordably – just look at France, where it generates 80 per cent of the country's power. Although nuclear energy is not strictly renewable, France's modern nuclear plants are so efficient that they use hardly any uranium and produce very little waste. Uranium is plentiful and available from stable, friendly countries such as Australia and Canada. In the short term, replacing old, dirty coal-fired power stations with new, clean, efficient gas-fired power stations can also deliver huge gains.

If a way is found to capture and store the carbon-dioxide emissions from coal-fired plants cheaply and reliably, coal could yet become 'clean' too. That would make a huge dent in emissions, since China generates 80 per cent of its electricity from coal, India two-thirds, America half and Britain nearly a third. Steven Chu, an American Nobel-prize-winning scientist (whose parents are Chinese) and now Obama's energy secretary, thinks carbon-capture technologies could be deployed commercially by 2019.[18]

Baba Kalyani, whom we met in Chapter 5, thinks emerging economies are well placed to leapfrog Western economies and jump straight to clean technologies – and that companies such as his can make the most of these new opportunities:

> Just as in the telecoms business we went directly to wireless without having to put a lot of copper lines across all of India, India is also likely to make this kind of technological jump in the energy sector. In the energy market everyone is at ground zero right now. So you have equal opportunities to a company in the US or Europe or anywhere else. And it's only your brainpower that's going to make things happen for you. I think this is where India has a unique advantage – the sheer quantity of brainpower is quite dramatic.

Pune is a growing hub for manufacturing innovation. A couple of hundred yards away from Bharat Forge's leafy headquarters, Tata has developed one of the world's most powerful supercomputers. The engineer who developed the Tata Nano is also from Pune. 'These things are starting to become possible. Ten years ago you would never even think of it,' Kalyani observes. 'In the energy business there are endless possibilities. People like us are beginning to say, "Let's use innovation as a lever to generate new businesses." And the good thing is, if you do succeed in some of these things, they're applicable globally.'

In developing countries, the technologies and approaches may sometimes be different. Whereas the US might try to make biofuels from food waste on a large scale, 'in India you can't, because the infrastructure's not there to transport feedstocks very well', Raj Atluru of Draper Fisher Jurvetson (DFJ) explains. 'So you need a technology that's smaller scale that can utilise waste rice husks or anything from the agriculture industry. There's a great company called Husk Power which is turning waste into electricity for villages. The electrification of Indian villages is still incredibly poor so we really need to scale the technology down for applications for rural India.' Another company called d.light uses LEDs and a solar cell to provide power in villages that do not have a reliable (or any) source of electricity. Technologies that rely on cheap solar power could be used in poor countries, in Africa and elsewhere, that get plenty of sun but don't have electricity.

There are many other possibilities too. Stephen Chu has suggested that a global 'glucose economy' might supplant oil. Fast-growing crops would be grown in the tropics, where sunlight is abundant, converted into glucose and shipped around the world much as oil is today, for eventual conversion into biofuels and bioplastics. It's a great idea. Brazil is already halfway there. It produces ethanol from sugarcane waste, supplying 40 per cent of the fuel used by cars in the country, all of which run on a blend of petrol and ethanol. If only the US abolished its absurd subsidies for ethanol made from maize and its hefty tariffs on cleaner Brazilian ethanol, Brazil could start filling up American cars too. Perhaps Chu should have a word with his boss about it. Chu has also observed that painting the roofs of buildings white and using light-coloured road surfaces would reflect a lot of sunlight back into space – possibly enough to have an effect on global warming as big as taking every car in the world off the road for a decade.[19] Who knows what other brilliant new ideas scientists will come up with over the next few decades?

Together with entrepreneurs, they can make it happen. Raj Atluru is enthusiastic:

We started investing in clean-tech in 2001. The first conferences we used to go to there were fifty people, ten investors and a handful of entrepreneurs. Now you go to a clean-tech conference and there's a thousand people. Which is great because this sector is massively underinvested. Even though billions of dollars have flowed in to clean-tech and there's going to be a bubble washout in some sectors, it's still way underfunded. Many people who are on the outside looking in would not agree at all. They'd say it's way too much money, it's a bubble, we shouldn't be putting money into renewables. They're totally wrong. The internet came along and you were looking at one-to-ten billion-dollar markets. That was about it, though. In renewable energy alone it's a trillion-dollar market. We've never seen markets this big. Water's gonna be next. That's an enormous market.

The global energy market is reckoned to be worth $6 trillion a year – around a tenth of the world's economic output.[20] In 2006 the world met four-fifths of its primary energy needs from fossil fuels – oil (34.3 per cent), coal and peat (26 per cent) and gas (20.5 per cent) – and the rest from biomass and waste (10.1 per cent), nuclear (6.2 per cent), hydro (2.2 per cent) and other renewables such as geothermal, solar and wind (0.6 per cent).[21] Changing to renewables is a huge challenge – and a massive opportunity.

Brazilian bounties

Cutting down forests contributes as much as 20 per cent of global carbon emissions. A big chunk comes from Brazil, home to most of the Amazon rainforest, the world's lungs. Deforestation accounts for 70 per cent of Brazil's carbon emissions.[22] Paying Brazilians not to cut down trees – or to manage their forests sustainably – is probably one of the cheapest ways of curbing emissions, although it requires careful monitoring to make it effective. The Brazilian government has already set up an Amazon Fund for this purpose, to which the Norwegian government has donated $1 billion.[23]

Roberto Smeraldi, the founder of Amigos da Terra, Brazil's Friends of the Earth, believes the best way to protect the Amazon is to nurture a successful forest economy. 'We have a living laboratory' that could generate all sorts of new products with proper investment in know-how, people and industrial chains, he enthuses. His studies show that clusters of medium-sized enterprises employing fifty to seventy families in niches such as harvesting Brazil nuts or native honey can be sustainable and competitive. 'It's a more competitive approach than just producing timber, which is already better than pasture.' While global finance for 'carbon sequestration' – payments for not cutting down trees – could help fund much-needed investment, he argues that it is a 'side activity that can be used to get extra financing for investment in other forest activities'.

'We are leaders both in forest destruction and in forest management,' Smeraldi observes. 'No doubt we might take a bigger share of the world timber market with investment in a sustainable forestry sector. But we need to look at the forest economy more broadly, in terms of the oils, resins, fruits, environmental services and biodiversity it can provide.' Natura cosmetics, for instance, are made with Amazonian products such as Brazil nuts or andiroba oil, a fruity-smelling essence that has all sorts of medicinal properties. Natura is a huge success: its sales now top £1 billion a year, and it has started exporting to Europe. Smeraldi points out that 'investing in natural capital also creates a Brazilian terroir and branding, blazing a trail for others'. Natura could become the new Body Shop.

Unfortunately, companies such as Natura are all too few. The problem, Smeraldi says, is that investment tends to go into subsidising traditional activities, rather than providing funding for innovators. In effect, what Brazil lacks is the venture-capital funded dynamism of Silicon Valley's innovating entrepreneurs.

Fabio Barbosa, the boss of Brazil's Banco Real, now owned by Spain's Grupo Santander, has long tried to act as a catalyst for change. 'The bank itself is not a major polluter,' he says, 'but we are indirectly responsible for what happens.' Once the bank had improved its own environmental record, it was in a position to require the same of prospective borrowers. Barbosa says the bank's business model has stood up well to the recession. Companies that comply with the bank's environmental criteria are normally well managed, he points out, and so pose a smaller risk. Many green measures also save costs. 'Society is coming along,' he says. 'It's not an issue of NGOs, it's bigger than NGOs. It's an issue of consumers.' The aim is not to be a green bank *per se*, it is to make profits while taking the environment into consideration. Where borrowers don't match the standards the bank requires, it can lend them money to help them comply. For instance, it might lend to a forestry company that wants to work with certified wood. 'It's not a victory to decline companies,' Barbosa says. 'It's a victory to attract them.'

What price to save the planet?

If the world is to embrace a low-carbon future, the price has to be right. In a nutshell, clean energy has to become cheaper than fossil fuels. The price of carbon has to rise to reflect its harmful impact on the climate; the price of clean-tech has to fall, mostly through technological innovation and economies of scale, but also where necessary through judicious government subsidies. The two are related: a rising carbon price will stimulate innovation and investment in clean-tech, pushing down its price.

The neatest solution would be a global carbon tax that ratcheted up gradually and predictably over time. That would give fossil-fuel users an incentive to switch to cleaner alternatives. It would also give clean-tech companies a good idea of the price target they need to achieve to be competitive, allowing them to raise funds and have a go at developing promising technologies. Many would fail; but successful ones would hit the jackpot. Importantly, governments wouldn't be trying to second-guess what the best technologies are or to pick winners among the many clean-tech companies. They simply don't know; nobody does – only trial and error (fostered by vigorous global competition) will tell.

The beauty of a carbon tax is that it is simple and transparent. Everyone knows what the price of carbon is and every user has to pay it. Any exceptions would also be clear: subsidies for some or lower rates for others would be readily apparent. It is also flexible: it could be raised (or lowered) quickly and easily if need be. And it would raise huge revenues that could be used to cut other harmful taxes and to compensate the poor and the vulnerable, notably in developing countries, for the cost of adjusting.

Al Gore supports a carbon tax. Sweden, Finland, the Netherlands and Norway all introduced one in the 1990s.[24] The IPCC, a United Nations-appointed group of scientific experts, reckons it should be pitched at $20–50 per tonne of carbon-dioxide emissions.[25] France is considering introducing one at an initial rate of €17 per tonne. The revenues will be used to trim other taxes, while the poor and vulnerable will be compensated directly.[26]

Nicholas Stern of the London School of Economics, author of a ground-breaking report into the economics of climate change, argues that global action has to be effective (at reducing emissions), efficient (in doing so cheaply) and equitable (with rich countries which have caused the problem bearing most of the costs). A carbon tax (plus redistribution) meets all three criteria.

Ideally, the climate-change negotiators who met in Copenhagen in December 2009 would have agreed to introduce an escalating global carbon tax. The poorest countries that hardly emit at all (and do not have the administrative capacity to levy such a tax) could be exempt for now, while emerging economies, such as China and India, would be offered financial – and, more importantly, technological – help to limit their emissions.

Unfortunately, politicians generally prefer 'cap-and-trade' emissions trading schemes instead. Whereas a carbon tax puts a price on carbon emissions directly, a cap-and-trade scheme does so indirectly. By putting a limit on annual emissions that falls over time, it drives their price up – the tighter the limit, the higher the price. Companies that can reduce their emissions for less than the carbon price have an incentive to do so, because they can earn a profit by selling some of their emissions permits to companies that need them. Conversely, whereas a carbon tax limits emissions indirectly – the higher the tax, the lower the emissions – a cap-and-trade scheme does so directly. This appeals to many environmentalists who value what they perceive as the added certainty of a fixed target. In practice, though, a tax could easily be adjusted to achieve any desired target.

In principle, a cap-and-trade scheme could work as well as a carbon tax, so long as at least four conditions are met. First, the initial emissions permits must be auctioned off to the highest bidders, making polluters pay and raising revenues for governments. Second, the total number of permits must be strictly limited, so that their auction price – in effect, the price of carbon – is reasonably high and the sums raised are large. Third, there must be a credible commitment for the cap to fall fast enough over time so that the price of carbon is high and rising. Fourth, the market for emissions permits – the 'trade' bit of cap-and-trade – has to operate efficiently. It has to be structured in such a way that trading is cheap, market manipulation difficult and speculative volatility rare. Four big ifs.

In practice, the main reason why politicians and lobbyists tend to prefer cap-and-trade schemes is precisely because they offer plenty of opportunities for handouts to special interests, plus the prospect of huge profits for financial speculators. They are opaque and inefficient by design. That means cap-and-trade is likely to be less effective, less efficient and less equitable than a carbon tax.

Assume, for the sake of argument, that politicians are saints and that they resist the temptation to hand out too many permits too cheaply. Why should we believe that the market for emissions permits will work better than other financial markets?

As Willem Buiter rightly argues, 'Such markets are costly to operate and can be manipulated. Even if they are competitive, they can, like all financial markets, be distorted by bubbles, herding and other forms of dysfunctional behaviour.'[27]

Just look at what has happened in Europe. The European Union blazed a trail by introducing its fledgling emissions-trading scheme (ETS) in 2005, with permits initially allocated for three years. Permits were handed out for free. Prices initially rose to around €30 per tonne, but then collapsed when it became clear that too many permits were to be handed out. The price of carbon eventually fell towards zero, giving companies no incentive to curb their emissions and wrecking the business plans of innovators relying on a higher price. Worse, emissions actually rose. So much for the certainty of cap-and-trade.

When the EU came to issue permits for a second period – 2008 to 2012 – it promised to do better. The number of permits was slashed and the price duly rose. A longer-term target – a 20 per cent cut in greenhouse-gas emissions by 2020 (relative to 1990 levels) – was also set to give companies greater certainty to invest. Most emissions permits were to be auctioned off from 2013 onwards.

Great. But then the recession and grubby politics intervened. Power companies warned that the cost of the permits would drive up electricity prices – precisely what ought to happen – and so were granted them on the cheap (or free). Heavy industries that face global competition claimed that they would lose out to rivals elsewhere that did not have to buy emissions permits, or have to move their operations overseas. Those that claimed to use the cleanest available technologies thus obtained up to 100 per cent of them for free. EU countries will also be able to buy in credits for (hard-to-verify) emissions reductions outside Europe to meet up to 90 per cent of their national targets – so that any decline in emissions may be more apparent than real.[28]

Thus, rather than raising revenues to cushion the impact on

the poor, cut taxes elsewhere or subsidise research into green technologies, the scheme has handed out valuable assets for free which will allow big emitters to make a fortune. In place of the 'polluter pays', the polluter profits. This inauspicious start raises serious doubts about whether the emissions cap, which is meant to start falling from 2013 on, will actually be binding.[29]

At least the EU has actually launched its ETS. Kevin Rudd's plans to introduce a carbon-trading scheme in Australia in 2011 with the aim of cutting emissions by at least 5 per cent by 2020 (from 2000 levels) were stymied when the country's Senate rejected them in August 2009. The opposition Liberals later ditched their leader, Malcolm Turnbull, who supported the scheme in favour of Tony Abbott, a diehard opponent of it. Rudd, who had called climate change 'the greatest moral, economic and social challenge of our time' then suddenly dropped his plans in 2010 – and soon after his party dumped him. His successor, Julia Gillard, has announced plans to put a price on carbon, but nothing has yet been implemented.

Will America do better? Candidate Obama raised hopes when he proposed a cap-and-trade scheme with all the allowances sold at auction.[30] Unfortunately, the bill approved by the US House of Representatives in June 2009 was rather different.[31] It makes a modest commitment to cut American emissions by 17 per cent by 2020. But instead of auctioning the permits, it doled them out to powerful special interests. The bill gives away 85 per cent of carbon permits for free and will only move to a system of full auctions in 2030! Gregory Mankiw of Harvard University calculates that the government could raise $989 billion from permit auctions over ten years, based on Congressional Budget Office estimates. But in the bill as written, the auction proceeds are only $276 billion.[32] The upshot is windfall gains for powerful producer lobbies at the expense of consumers, who will pay more for carbon-based products but not benefit from lower taxes elsewhere.

Border-tax battles

Worse, a clause was slipped into the legislation that would require the president to slap a tax on imports from countries that do not have comparable emissions caps, starting in 2020. France's Nicolas Sarkozy also wants Europe to impose its own carbon tax on imports.[33] Unsurprisingly, such proposals have sparked outrage in emerging economies.

Paul Krugman thinks such carbon tariffs are economically justified. He argues:

> If you only impose restrictions on greenhouse-gas emissions from domestic sources, you give consumers no incentive to avoid purchasing products that cause emissions in other countries; as a result, you have an inefficient outcome even from a world point of view. So border adjustments here are entirely legitimate in terms of basic economics. And they're also probably OK under trade law. The WTO has looked at the issue, and suggests that carbon tariffs may be viewed the same way as border adjustments associated with value-added taxes. It has long been accepted that a VAT is essentially a sales tax – a tax on consumers – which for administrative reasons is collected from producers. Because it's essentially a tax on consumers, it's legal, and also economically efficient, to collect it on imported goods as well as domestic production; it's a matter of levelling the playing field, not protectionism. And the same would be true of carbon tariffs.[34]

Yet Jagdish Bhagwati, the world's top trade economist, disagrees with his former pupil. If America wants India and China to pay for their current emissions so long as they do not apply identical carbon taxes, he argues, then the US must also pay for all its earlier emissions – to the tune of $250–300 billion a year.[35] Since 1850, it is estimated that China has contributed less than

8 per cent of the world's total emissions, while the US has been responsible for 29 per cent and Western Europe 27 per cent.[36] 'The US wants to walk on one leg, while raising its crutch aggressively against India and China because they reject the hypocrisy in the current US position,' he fumes.

India's environment minister, Jairam Ramesh, denounced the US proposal as 'pernicious'.[37] 'India has not polluted – we are bearing the brunt of global climate change caused by the developed countries and we are being asked to curb emissions,' he said. 'I find this ludicrous.' India's 1.1 billion people – roughly a sixth of the world's population – have among the lowest emission levels per person, with 1.2 tonnes per head, around 5 per cent of total global emissions. That compares with just over 20 tonnes per person in Australia, just under 20 in the US, 19 in Canada, around 10 in Japan, Britain and most other European countries (except nuclear France, where the figure is less than 7) and approaching 5 in China.[38]

China called it 'trade protectionism in the disguise of environmental protection'.[39] Simon Crean, then Australia's trade minister, also worries that green border taxes 'could become the new form of protectionism'. Victor Fung, the chairman of the International Chamber of Commerce, warns that they could trigger a huge trade war, just as America's protectionist Smoot–Hawley Tariff Act of 1930 prompted retaliation that caused world trade to collapse. 'It would set the developing block against the developed block,' he says. 'Is this the Smoot–Hawley of the twenty-first century?'

Fung is absolutely right. Fiddling with carbon tariffs is a very dangerous game. For a start, since the EU emits much less carbon than the US, in total and per person, and has enacted more stringent emission-reduction measures, it would – by the US logic – be entitled to slap border taxes on carbon-intensive US exports. Is that what the US Congress wants? In testimony to the US Senate finance committee, Gary Horlick, a trade attorney in Washington DC, suggested that 'If we reinterpret WTO rules to allow trade barriers based on how things are made, we open up a can of worms and might permit other countries to block our biotech exports, including major items such as corn, soybeans and other crops.'[40]

It's not just the principle of carbon tariffs that is dangerous. It's how they would most likely be applied in practice. Since almost every product generates carbon emissions, an innocuous-sounding 'border tax adjustment' would be open season for protectionists of every hue. Just as America and Europe slap whopping 'anti-dumping' duties on foreign products that they deem too cheap based on bogus calculations and sleight of hand, trade lawyers and lobbyists would doubtless find ways to justify huge taxes on imports from China, India and other emerging economies. It is devilishly complicated to calculate the carbon content of imports and the differential cost between a foreign carbon-control system and the US's – just the sort of issue protectionists can exploit to their advantage. Given the dismal spectacle of how the US and EU have succumbed to special interests in devising their cap-and-trade schemes, it is naive to think that such taxes wouldn't fall victim to protectionist abuse. The BEEs would not take this lying down: they would sting back. Cue a trade war that could fracture the fragile global economy – and preclude any chance of a global deal to cut carbon emissions.

The threat of US carbon tariffs has been avoided for now – because in July 2010 the Senate dropped its attempts to draft a carbon-cap bill and in November the Republicans seized control of the House. (Perhaps Paul Krugman will now call for carbon tariffs on American exports; or perhaps not.) Sarkozy's European mission may not succeed either. Obama himself has said, 'I think there may be other ways of doing it than with a tariff approach.' But the underlying problem will not go away. Rich countries do not want to incur the cost of curbing their emissions unless developing countries – in particular the big emerging economies (BEEs) – do so too, partly because they do not want to put local companies and workers at a competitive disadvantage, and partly because their efforts will fail to curb global emissions if the BEEs' emissions continue to rise rapidly.

Thea Lee, policy director for the AFL-CIO, America's biggest trade-union federation, is clear on this. 'We don't want the US to take dramatic action and impose additional steep costs on US manufacturing. Domestic production will either move to other countries or be undercut by foreign producers. If the US brings in emissions controls, they don't take steps in developing countries, and production moves to the dirtiest place, global emissions will actually increase,' she says. And she warns that if carbon tariffs are not part of a US climate-change act, some of her members will strongly oppose it.

But those threats may not be as great as politicians and trade-unionists think. Gary Hufbauer and Jisun Kim of the Peterson Institute for International Economics in Washington DC point out that US imports of carbon-intensive goods – such as steel, aluminium, paper and cement – come mostly from Canada and the EU, which have lower emissions than America, rather than from China and India.[41] Stefan Heck, a consultant at McKinsey, argues that while cap-and-trade might add 20–30 per cent to energy costs, which is a lot, it is not enough to spark a mass exodus to China.[42] Rising oil prices might also act as an unofficial carbon tax on imports that will hit bulky, low-value items shipped long distances particularly hard. Even so, the political perception in the US and Europe remains that the BEEs must do their bit to curb global emissions.

If the priority is stopping the planet overheating, the most important issue is not whether the remainder of America's and Europe's heavy manufacturing will relocate to China if the US and EU tax carbon and China does not. (Clearly, many big polluters, such as coal-fired power stations, cannot move.) It is whether cuts in American and European emissions will be offset by big rises elsewhere. China's emissions, which come largely from its coal-fired power plants, doubled between 1996 and 2006. It has now edged ahead of the US as the world's largest carbon emitter. (In the global rankings, Russia is third, India fourth and Japan fifth. Britain emits a tenth of what America does. Australia emits as much as France.) China says it plans to continue to rely on cheap coal as its main energy source and will increase coal production by 30 per cent by 2015. That decision alone will swamp any emission reductions elsewhere.

Closing the deal

What is to be done? Nothing, say many Chinese. When I raised the issue in China, I was often met with outraged declarations that it was unfair to expect China to limit its use of fossil fuels. Why, people said, should China accept constraints on its development when the West polluted its way to prosperity? While China may now be the world's largest carbon emitter, its per-capita emissions are still far below American levels; and besides, most of the problem is caused not by China's current emissions but by the previous emissions of today's wealthy countries. 'When Westerners criticise China about energy use, lots of Chinese people, especially young people, think that it's just an excuse, that America and Europe don't want China to develop, and want to put barriers on China's development,' says Victor Ren, whom we met in Chapter 5. 'They say that we can't lose our opportunities for development by adopting Western prescriptions.'

It is indeed unfair to expect China to pay for its current emissions when the West will not pay for the damage caused by its previous ones. But fair or not, we might all fry if nothing is done.

Bob Hawke, the former prime minister of Australia, argues that rich countries have to 'make very substantial funds available to basically China and India to encourage the use of more environmentally friendly methods of production'. That might seem politically impossible, but Hawke, a four-times election winner, disagrees. 'It's just a question of intelligent political salesmanship. In the end, morality always runs a poor second to self-interest. So you've got to explain to people that this is in their self-interest. We're not doing it to be nice to China, we're being nice to ourselves and to the world.' He is right. If offering financing and technology to reduce China's and India's adjustment costs could secure a global carbon-reduction deal, the planet, the American people *and* US businesses would all be more secure. Perhaps Obama's oratory could win people over.

But if Obama doesn't rise to the challenge, might it still be possible to find common ground? Perhaps. Although the failure of the Copenhagen summit was a big disappointment, the good news is that policy-makers in the BEEs increasingly accept the need for action on climate change. China does not want to be seen as a spoiler, according to one insider, it wants to be a big player. It has committed to cut carbon-dioxide emissions per unit of GDP by 40–45 per cent by 2020 from the 2005 level. It aims to generate 15 per cent of its total energy use from renewables by 2020.[43] It is adopting much tighter fuel-economy standards for vehicles than the US. Beijing has also set a target of 5 per cent of 'new energy vehicles' by 2011 and is offering $8,000 subsidies for buying electric vehicles.[44] India has launched an energy-efficiency drive.[45] It's a start. Such is the inefficiency of their energy use that there is huge scope for improvements that would cut costs, not raise them.

Since developing countries are likely to bear the brunt of climate change, curbing global emissions is also in their self-interest. India's agrarian economy, for instance, depends on water from Himalayan glaciers and monsoon rains. While their resistance to paying to solve the problem is partly a matter of fairness – why should the poor pay to clean up rich people's mess? – it is also a matter of timing. They don't want to pay now, when they are still poor, and when precipitate action could jeopardise their rapid growth. If living standards in China and India continue to grow at 8 per cent a year, they will double every nine years. Between 2010 and 2028 they could quadruple. Assuming the cost of them delaying their carbon curbs increases by less than 8 per cent a year, it makes sense to act later rather than sooner.

Acting later would not only be more affordable, it would also be more attractive, since the environment tends to matter more to people as they get richer. Put bluntly, when you're dirt poor, survival comes above all else; as you get richer, material comforts and basic needs such as better healthcare tend to take priority initially; when you are better off, it is easier to curb your lifestyle a little to improve the environment. Despite his doubts about Western motives, Victor Ren says he worries a lot about air pollution, energy consumption and climate change. 'If we go on like this, the whole world economy will be negatively affected, and there will be more droughts and floods in China.' Increasingly prosperous Chinese city-dwellers who are fed up of choking on filthy air could become an increasingly strong lobby for change.

So too could clean-tech companies such as BYD, Suntech Power and Goldwind in China and REVA and Suzlon in India. If they become global players in clean-tech, the BEEs will have a strong interest in championing their progress. China is already overtaking America as a market for wind turbines; its solar-cell industry is the world's largest; and Chinese 'clean coal' technology is attracting foreign customers.[46] It is also building its first commercial solar-power station. By the same token, Europe and America stand to gain by raising the domestic price of carbon earlier and further than others, because this will give their own clean-tech companies a better chance of becoming world-beaters.

Far-sighted politicians ought to realise that there is more to be gained from promoting tomorrow's well-paid jobs in the green industries of the future than from trying to protect polluting industries from the need to change.

Ultimately, the fairest way to allocate emission permits is an equal amount per person around the world. For a 50 per reduction in global emissions by 2050, the world average must drop from 7 tonnes per person to 2 to 3 tonnes (since the global population will also rise over that period). Emissions trading – not least rich countries buying permits from poor ones – would keep costs down and help compensate poor countries for cutting their emissions, making them more likely to sign up to a global deal.[47] But since it makes sense for poor but fast-growing economies to act later rather than sooner, China and India could make modest commitments now and progressively more ambitious ones from 2020 on. By then clean-tech may have improved so much that it is competitive even without putting a hefty price on carbon.

Standards and subsidies

A global carbon tax is by far the best way to tackle climate change. Failing that, a cap-and-trade scheme that is as fair, efficient and non-discriminatory as possible would be a second-best solution. But governments can also encourage change through a mixture of domestic (and regional) standards, subsidies and other policies. While private credit remains in crisis, government finance may be necessary. More generally, governments may wish to require companies to inform consumers about how much energy their products use, help the poor to invest in energy-efficiency measures (such as home insulation) that have a big upfront cost, and provide grants for basic scientific research into green technologies, among other things. Unfortunately, such government interventions can be inefficient and even counterproductive – as in the case of cloudy

Germany's huge subsidies for solar panels. In countries that tax carbon, standards, subsidies and other instruments should be used sparingly. In those that don't, they may need to be used more widely, but governments need to be careful not to do more harm than good.

The financial crisis hit the clean-tech industry hard. Globally, new investment in clean energy alone collapsed from $41 billion in the final quarter of 2007 to only $13.3 billion in the first quarter of 2009 – before bouncing back to $36.2 billion in the second quarter.[48] In Silicon Valley, Raj Atluru explains, finance dried up in the last three months of 2008 and the first three of 2009. Unsurprisingly, when the global financial system seized up, banks stopped lending and panicky investors dumped risky assets for safer ones, the capital available to take a punt on promising new technologies took a dive too. Investment in new companies – as opposed to ongoing financing for existing ones – was hardest hit. Even big power companies were no longer able to borrow and so froze investments in new plants, not least solar and wind ones. Thankfully, the government intervened. 'The market would have ground to a halt without the government stepping in,' Atluru says. Even Silicon Valley, perhaps the most entrepreneurial place in the world, is now on a government drip-feed.

The Obama administration's stimulus package and 2009 budget contained a flurry of green initiatives. First, hard cash. Around a tenth of America's $787-billion stimulus package was earmarked for energy and the environment. That includes $33 billion to green the country's electricity supply, $27 billion for energy efficiency and $19 billion for cleaner forms of transport. The budget also assigned $150 billion to improving green technology over the next decade.[49] Second, policy changes. Tax credits for investing in clean-tech have been extended, and the government is even offering cash rebates to investors who don't have any taxable profits. That last step was crucial, Atluru says, because in the depths of a crisis most investors are making losses and would have little incentive to invest in clean-tech otherwise. Third, loan guarantees. The Department of Energy has been given an extra $6 billion to backstop loans to the clean-tech industry. 'The loan guarantees are meant for the companies and technologies that are at the cutting edge that need to prove first commercial feasibility before the private markets step in,' Atluru says. Assuming one in ten defaults, that should allow the government to guarantee $60 billion in loans.

All of this is justifiable – albeit imperfect – so long as credit is crunched, carbon untaxed and clean-tech in its infancy. But as the financial crisis eases and demand recovers, it is far better to raise the price of carbon and let competing technologies fight it out. In general, the emissions cuts picked by politicians are far more expensive than those chosen by competitive markets. A study by the Peterson Institute for International Economics and the World Resources Institute, two think-tanks, puts the cost of every tonne of emissions avoided thanks to the provisions of the stimulus bill at somewhere between $69 and $137.[50] The cost using a carbon tax that initially priced emissions at, say, $30 a tonne would be much less.

Worse, governments often subsidise planet-polluting products and tax imports of eco-friendly goods and services. Absurdly, Germany – which prides itself on its green credentials – not only subsidises solar panels in sunless areas, it also gives handouts to its coal industry. It is planning to spend €21.6 billion in the decade to 2018 propping up an industry that employs a mere 34,000 workers to produce uncompetitive – and dirty – coal. Officially, the subsidies will then stop – but this will be reviewed in 2012. In 2002 Germany had promised to abolish its coal subsidies by 2010. Depressingly, many other countries, including America, Australia and Poland, also subsidise their domestic coal industries. Britain handed out a more modest £52.8 million to what remains of the UK coal industry between 2003 and 2009.[51]

America also gives huge handouts to its oil industry. It 'probably has larger tax incentives relative to its size than any other industry in the country', according to Donald Lubick, the US Treasury's former assistant secretary for tax policy.[52] One study estimates that whereas the effective tax rate on investing in, for instance, electricity distribution lines is 39 per cent, the tax rate on oil drilling (by non-integrated firms) is 14 per cent – that is, a subsidy of 14 per cent.[53] It is hard to measure the subsidies precisely. Greenpeace, the environmental campaign group, reckons they are worth $15–35 billion a year. James Woolsey, a former director of the Central Intelligence Agency (CIA), estimates that American oil companies receive preferential treatment from their government worth more than $250 billion a year.[54] While oil is not the only reason why the Bush administration went to war in Iraq, it is extremely unlikely that it would have bothered ousting Saddam Hussein if he'd been the tyrant of, say, Zimbabwe. So if one includes the cost of the Iraq war – at least $700 billion and mounting, not to mention all the lives lost – the fiscal cost of securing foreign oil supplies is astronomical.[55] Clean-tech looks like a bargain in comparison.

Many developing countries subsidise the consumption, rather than the production, of fuel. Half of the world's population is reckoned to get subsidised fuel.[56] Venezuela fixes the price of petrol in local currency at around 3 US cents per litre. Other oil producers also subsidise domestic petrol – while forcing foreigners to pay through the nose. Fuel subsidies are not only costly for governments and bad for the planet, they also benefit the rich (who tend to drive more) more than the poor they purport to help. An IMF study of five emerging economies found that the richest 20 per cent of households received, on average, 42 per cent of total fuel subsidies; the bottom 20 per cent less than 10 per cent.[57] According to the OECD and the IEA, eliminating fossil-fuel subsidies around the world by 2020 would reduce global greenhouse-gas emissions in 2050 by 10 per cent.[58]

Ostensibly green handouts are often nothing of the sort. As noted in Chapter 9, the US hugely subsidises ethanol, supposedly as an environmentally friendly substitute for petrol. But once the fertiliser and fuel used in corn production are taken into account, maize-based ethanol is not much greener than petrol (some say it is actually less green).[59] Importing bioethanol from Brazil would be cheaper, aid development and reduce carbon emissions. More broadly, protectionism in agriculture, which is responsible for around 30 per cent of global greenhouse-gas emissions, damages the environment, as was explained in Chapter 9.

Countries could make a big difference by renouncing environmentally harmful subsidies and tariffs, unilaterally as well as through a broader agreement at the World Trade Organization (WTO). But above all, they must avoid a green trade war, which would be catastrophic for the global economy and the global environment. It's simple, really. International agreement to limit carbon emissions requires the cooperation of China and India – and carrots are more likely to secure it than sticks. As Kishore Mahbubani, dean of the Lee Kuan Yew School of Public Policy in Singapore, observes, 'sanctions are the worst possible way of trying to win them over'.

Clean is cool

To make the shift to a low-carbon future, the world needs a mixture of four things: greater energy efficiency, smart government policy, a range of new technologies and lots of capital. But all too often public debate overemphasises the first two at the expense of the latter two. In the ultra-green view, the prescription morphs into abstinence by social pressure and government diktat. Policy-makers, naturally, place themselves centre stage, imagining that a blizzard of meetings, plans, initiatives, standards, regulations and so on will do the trick. They are also prone to try to micromanage people's lives in ways that are extremely costly to the economy and to individual freedom. But while governments' role is central – only they can enforce a price for carbon – they should concentrate on helping the poor to adjust and setting a framework that attracts bundles of finance into the clean-tech sector and enables technology entrepreneurs to experiment and find new solutions.

Given the complexities of climate change and global politics, an imperfect global deal is probably the best we can hope for. Enforcing it and ensuring any transfers between countries are well spent will be huge challenges. But that need not be a reason for pessimism. So long as governments provide sufficient incentives in the short term and a credible-enough commitment for the medium term, clean technologies are likely to make huge progress over the next ten to twenty years. If investment continues to pour into clean-tech research, with some of the world's brightest minds and sharpest businesspeople competing to clean up and save the planet, new and better solutions are highly likely to be found. Existing technologies can become much cheaper and new ones will emerge. The seemingly impractical or implausible can suddenly become possible, then probable. And as the market expands, individual companies and the industry as a whole will reap huge economies of scale.

Already wind power can compete with fossil fuels in some areas, as can solar. Tesla's Model S is predicted to work out cheaper to run than a top-of-the-range Honda Accord in the US – and will look even more attractive in Europe, where petrol prices are much higher. Serious Materials's EcoRock is better for the environment and your wallet. Rising oil and gas prices could help accelerate this switch. The spike in oil prices in 2008 had Americans dashing to ditch their Hummers. Pretty soon the switch to low-carbon technologies might be achieved even without a complex global climate-change deal. After all, it would be easy for countries, companies and people to jettison fossil fuels if clean-tech is greener *and* cheaper. Self-interest, not political bargaining still less abstinence, is our best hope.

We should treat the threat of catastrophic climate change as an opportunity to reshape the world economy in a cleaner, more secure, fairer and more efficient way. Carbon-based energy has been a fantastic engine for human progress. But it has always had big downsides – smog, war and dependence on nasty dictatorships – and now it endangers the planet. We should welcome the pressing need to accelerate the leap to better ways of life.

Oil, gas and coal are just means to an end. What is really valuable are the unprecedented opportunities of modern living – an escape from drudgery in the home, the mind-broadening delights of foreign travel, cool buildings in hot countries, the freedom to drive where we please. Their extension from a rich minority to the rest of the world is a cause for celebration, not despair. Don't campaigners for global justice really want poor people to be rich?

So the priority must be to find new sources of energy, not to reject modern lifestyles or to try to deny them to others. Imagine: breathable air, solar-powered electricity for rural Africa, no more wars over oil in the Middle East. Unlimited energy on tap. Progress indeed. But remember that clean-tech is a global industry, powered by people, money and markets that cut across national lines. What would really wreck the world would be a closing of borders, societies and minds. Localism, not globalisation, is the true enemy of the planet.

11

Big and Bust

Remodelling government

To be generically against markets would be almost as odd as being generically against conversations between people.

Amartya Sen, *Development as Freedom*, 2001

We are seeing a more fundamental regime change: the third in postwar history, starting with the Keynesian model, from the 1940s to the '70s; the neo-liberal ascendancy, from 1978 to 2008; followed by a new regime, which is currently being shaped. Perhaps this new regime will come to be called 'social capitalism' or 'social-democratic capitalism', or simply the term 'social democracy' itself. Whatever the nomenclature, the concept is clear: a system of open markets, unambiguously regulated by an activist state, and one in which the state intervenes to reduce the greater inequalities that competitive markets will inevitably generate.

Kevin Rudd, prime minister of Australia, 2009[1]

Impotent – that's what George Bush, Tony Blair, Gerhard Schröder and Lionel Jospin are, or near enough. Once, politicians could tax and spend with gay abandon, regulate at will and maybe even build a better world. No longer. Now, they have no choice but to cut taxes, pare back spending, deregulate. Global forces pen them in: when markets move, they quake. No wonder voters have no time for politicians.

In 2001, when I wrote the above in *Open World*, it was fashionable to claim that governments were either impotent or inexorably shrinking. I devoted a whole chapter to pointing out that writers such as Naomi Klein and Thomas Friedman were mistaken. A couple of wars and a bevy of bank bailouts later, governments seem in fighting form after all. Nobody would accuse today's leaders of being impotent. China has launched a huge stimulus to reflate its flagging economy. Barack Obama pumped $787 billion into America's flaccid economy. Silvio Berlusconi seems positively priapic.

So big and powerful do governments now seem that some have swung round 180 degrees, proclaiming the death of free markets and the return of all-mighty government. While some left-wingers have taken to dancing on capitalism's grave, right-wingers rage that socialism looms. More moderate voices, such as Kevin Rudd, Australia's prime minister from 2007 to 2010, think the crisis marks a shift from 'neo-liberalism' to social democracy. Continental Europeans herald the demise of the Anglo-Saxon – that is, Anglo-American – model.

But reality is rather different. The truth is big government never went away, nor did the world converge on a single economic model, Anglo-Saxon, neo-liberal or otherwise. And while government is now much bigger than before the crisis, it is also, paradoxically, weaker. When growth is strong and debt low, politicians can easily raise cash to pursue their objectives. But now that tax revenues have plunged and governments have already borrowed and spent so much, they will have to curb their ambitions. For sure, they can still regulate – and no doubt they will. They can also raise taxes if voters allow it. But in countries with gaping deficits, budget cuts loom. Austerity is never pleasant. It is vital that the axe be wielded wisely. But it is also an opportunity to rethink what governments should (and shouldn't) be doing and how they should be doing it. In particular, they need to find better ways to combine the flexibility that economies require with the security that people desire. They should also shake up the tax system to encourage desirable things, such as enterprise and effort, and discourage damaging ones, such as climate change and property bubbles.

Diet? What diet?

Contrary to what propagandists on both left and right claim, the last thirty years were not an era when free markets held sway in Britain or America, let alone everywhere else. Do not confuse politicians' rhetoric with reality. In a joint statement with Germany's Angela Merkel, France's Nicolas Sarkozy called for a new European model, proclaiming that 'Liberalism without rules has failed.'[2] But they are tilting at windmills. In France's case, the economy has long had plenty of rules and precious little liberalism. In an otherwise intelligent article for *The Monthly*, Kevin Rudd claimed that the financial crisis heralded the overthrow of neo-liberalism.[3] This apparently was the dominant ideology between 1978 and 2008. But later in the article, he boasts about how Labor prime ministers Bob Hawke and Paul Keating – who together ran Australia for fifteen of those thirty years – followed more leftish policies than John Howard's Liberals. 'Free-market fundamentalism' can hardly be an all-conquering global ideology if even a small economy such as Australia can deviate from it.

Rudd is quite right that social democrats should 'recognise the great strengths of open, competitive markets while rejecting the extreme capitalism and unrestrained greed that have perverted so much of the global financial system in recent times'. But by eliding the undeniable failures of financial markets in recent years with a sense that markets in general have failed and setting up a false dichotomy between the pre-crisis years of 'free-market fundamentalism' and post-crisis ones of 'social-democratic capitalism', he makes it more likely that social democrats will do what he urges them not to – 'throw the baby out with the bath-water' and 'retreat to some model of an all-providing state and . . . abandon altogether the cause of open, competitive markets both at home and abroad'. After all, if markets in general are at fault, why shouldn't they?

It would be more accurate – and politically wiser – to con-centrate his fire on financial excesses. He concludes that 'the social-democratic state offers the best guarantee of preserving the productive capacity of properly regulated competitive mar-kets, while ensuring that government is the regulator, that government is the funder or provider of public goods and that government offsets the inevitable inequalities of the market with a commitment to fairness for all'. That's fine, but it is hardly a 'fundamental regime change'. If you replace the words 'social democratic' with 'New Labour', that was precisely Tony Blair's economic philosophy while in office from 1997 to 2007 during the supposedly 'neo-liberal' era.

In the pre-crisis years, governments remained big and active, for good and ill. Far from the whole world aligning itself on a single 'Anglo-Saxon model' of liberalisation, deregulation and a small state, different countries continued to plough their own furrows. Swedish social democracy did not morph into American casino capitalism. France did not embrace *laissez-faire*. Germany's corporate state did not inhale Britain's entrepreneur-ial culture.

While it is true that a deregulated – often unregulated – financial sector went on the rampage in America, Britain and Iceland, that was hardly the case everywhere. Italy's shackled banking sector avoided America's excesses, while Germany's savings banks managed to speculate wildly while being partly state-owned. Yes, there has been (welcome) privatisation and deregulation in some areas – does anyone miss state-owned British Telecom or regret the deregulation of the EU airline market that has enabled low-cost airlines such as EasyJet to emerge?

But in other areas, the movement has been in the opposite direction. France introduced a maximum thirty-five-hour working week. George W. Bush presided over the biggest expansion of government since the 1960s. And while Japan's new prime minister, Yukio Hatoyama, hyperventilated during the 2009 election campaign about his country being 'continually buffeted by the winds of market fundamentalism', the notion that Japan is a country where free markets run wild is laughable.[4] In *Rivals*, Bill Emmott recounts a joke which was circulating in Tokyo about young Chinese studying at university there. 'The Chinese are asked why they spend so much of their spare time with other Chinese rather than with Japanese students. "Because we are afraid they might teach us communism," comes the answer.'[5]

Consider Britain, the epitome in Europe of the so-called Anglo-Saxon model. In 2007, at the height of the boom, when the state had supposedly shrivelled and markets had free rein, the government took nearly 40 per cent of national income in tax and spent a bit more than that, paid for and provided essential services such as healthcare and education, and regulated everything from employment rights to credit-card contracts. This was hardly a nightwatchman state. Nor had the public sector shrunk over the previous decade of New Labour rule. On the contrary: despite the introduction of market-based policies in some areas, the government's role in the economy had undeniably grown.

Examine the basics, tax and spending, first. In fiscal 1997–8, Labour's first year in office, the government's tax take was 35.1 per cent of national income, according to Treasury figures. By 2007–8 this had risen to 36.4 per cent.[6] After an initial fall, government spending rose even faster. From 38.2 per cent of national income in 1997–8, it dipped to 36.3 per cent in 1999–2000 as Labour kept to the previous Conservative government's exceedingly tight spending plans. But it then rose steadily to 41.1 per cent in 2007–8.[7] Far from tightening its belt, government was loosening the buckles.

In some areas, government spending soared. In inflation-adjusted terms, spending on health nearly doubled, from £56.4 billion to £102 billion, soaring from 5.3 per cent of national income to 7.2 per cent. Education outlays leaped from £48.9 billion to £78.1 billion, rising from 4.6 per cent of gross domestic product (GDP) to 5.5 per cent.[8] True, these big increases in public spending were accompanied by greater private-sector participation in providing services, notably in healthcare. But even so, it is hard to argue that the government's role in healthcare actually shrank. Whereas the National Health Service employed 1.2 million people when Labour took office, this had risen to 1.5 million people a decade later.[9] The NHS is the third-biggest employer in the world, after the Chinese army and the Indian railways. In education, the payroll swelled from 1.1 million to 1.4 million over the same period.[10] Overall, the number of people employed by the public sector rose from 5.2 million to 5.8 million.[11]

If anything, these figures underestimate the expansion of government. In many cases, investment in new schools, hospitals and transport schemes was financed and delivered by private companies, which were rewarded through juicy long-term government contracts. This is similar to buying a big-ticket item through a hire-purchase scheme, whereby the retailer provides you with, say, a sofa on credit and you pay for it in instalments.

While this tends to work out more expensive in the long term for both sofa-buyers and governments, it conveniently shifted the upfront spending off the government's books. In reality, then, the government incurred big new obligations – not just the ongoing payments to the private contractors, but also the need to step in if they folded – as in the case of Metronet, one of the companies working to upgrade (exceedingly slowly) London's crumbling Tube network. The collapse of Railtrack, the private company charged with the maintenance of Britain's rail network, and its quasi-nationalisation in 2002 by Network Rail also, in effect, enlarged the scope of government, but this is not reflected in the national accounts.

The government's role in other areas of the economy grew too. In the labour market, a minimum wage was introduced and steadily increased. For those aged over twenty-one, this started off at £3.60 an hour and had risen to £5.80 an hour by October 2009. Workers' rights were strengthened and a 'New Deal' – a set of policies to get first the young and then others back to work – introduced. Business regulation also increased. In July 2007 the British Chambers of Commerce estimated that the total cost of complying with seventy-seven new regulations introduced since 1998 on everything from data protection and working time to energy efficiency and building regulations was £55.6 billion.[12] So whether you look at tax, spending or regulation, the state was hardly in retreat in Britain in the decade before the crisis.

Nor was it in that other 'Anglo-Saxon' economy, the United States. Total government spending (federal, state and local) rose by 3.2 per cent of GDP in the pre-crisis years of George W. Bush's presidency, from 34.2 per cent of national income in 2000 to 37.4 per cent in 2007. The increased spending was not just on the two wars, but also on permanent measures such as prescription-drug benefits for pensioners. Despite Bush's tax cuts, government receipts (taxes and non-tax income) fell only a little, from 35.8 per cent of GDP to 34.5 per cent.

Ironically, Canada, which is widely seen as a country of big government – a source of pride for liberal Canadians and of disparagement for Republican Americans – has shrunk its state from a European-style 53.3 per cent of GDP in 1992 to an almost American 39.1 per cent in 2007, with the tax take falling from 44.2 per cent of GDP to 40.7 per cent. Naomi Klein must be tearing her hair out. Among rich OECD countries, the other hold-outs of smaller government are Australia, Ireland, Japan, South Korea and Switzerland.

In Europe, many governments tightened their belts through a mix of spending cuts and tax hikes in order to qualify for the euro, the common currency that was launched in 1999. The aim was to trim the budget deficit, not shrink the size of the state. After that, they let go a little. In France, for instance, government spending shrank from 55 per cent of GDP in 1993 to 51.6 per cent in 2000. It then expanded to 52.3 per cent in 2007. Government receipts rose from 48.5 per cent of GDP in 1993 to 50.8 per cent in 1999 and then dipped to 49.6 per cent in 2007. Italy followed a similar, but more pronounced pattern.[13]

Germany followed a different path. Spending was stable at a bit over 48 per cent of GDP from 1993 to 2003, before falling to 44.1 per cent in 2007. Receipts rose by 1.4 per cent of GDP between 1993 and 1999 and then fell by 2.8 per cent by 2007. Taking the euro-zone as a whole, government looked much the same in 2007 as it did in 2000, with both spending and receipts accounting for around 46 per cent of GDP.

Clearly, then, the state continued to loom large in Europe in the years before the crisis. Using comparable OECD figures, Britain converged up towards the euro-zone average in spending – from 36.6 per cent of GDP in 2000 to 44.1 per cent in 2007 – but not in receipts, which rose from 40.3 per cent of GDP to 41.4 per cent. At the onset of the crisis, Britain had a continental European-sized government, but with a considerably lower tax take.

Only in Scandinavia did the state shrink in the pre-crisis years, albeit from a very high base. After Sweden's banking crisis in the early 1990s, government spending briefly exceeded 70 per cent of national income. By 2000 it was back down to 57 per cent and it continued to fall to 51.3 per cent in 2007. The fall in government receipts was less dramatic, from 60.7 per cent in 2000 to 55.1 per cent in 2007. In Denmark, spending fell from 60.1 per cent in 1993 to 50.7 per cent in 2007, while receipts dipped by only 1.2 per cent of GDP over the same period, to 55.1 per cent. Economies where the government decides how over half of national income is spent are hardly ones where markets run riot.

In short, while poorly regulated financial markets ran amok in the pre-crisis years, markets in general did not. Governments shrank in some countries, but grew in Britain and America. But size isn't everything. One thing that governments could do better in coming years is help people cope with economic change.

Out with the Swedish model, in with the Danish

If governments are to be more active in the post-crisis years, perhaps they should take a leaf out of Scandinavia's book. For those of a social democratic bent, Sweden was for a long time the model of choice. It seemed to have it all: prosperity, equality and security – not to mention beautiful women. But the Swedish model has lost some of its lustre in recent years. Decades of slow growth have seen its living standards slip down the international league tables, while unemployment has crept up, lessening the allure of its labour market. Critics such as Johan Norberg have argued powerfully that the country's egalitarianism was a drag on growth, not the source of it. A banking crisis in the early 1990s didn't do much for Sweden's appeal either. And in 2006 voters ditched the long-ruling Social Democrats for a centre-right coalition.

Many left-wingers now lust after a different model, Denmark – although ironically it too has a centre-right government. Its economic growth has been perky and unemployment low. The Economist Intelligence Unit ranks it as the best place in the world to do business in the years ahead.[14] Its much-vaunted 'flexicurity' model is meant to combine the benefits of a flexible labour market with the security of a generous welfare system. This flexicurity goes hand in hand with a remarkable openness – to foreign trade, if not to foreign workers. Best of all, Danes seem comfortable with globalisation: even trade-union leaders speak approvingly of it. 'We're in favour of a global economy and globally competitive markets,' says Thorkild Jensen, the head of Dansk Metal, the Danish metalworkers' union. 'A small country like Denmark has to be able to distribute its products and knowledge all over the world.' So might Denmark be a model for other European countries, such as France, that are hostile to globalisation because they feel (incorrectly) that it threatens jobs and the welfare state?

On the face of it, Denmark's model has a lot to offer. Flexibility is vital in today's ever-changing economy, where people and capital need to be redeployed rapidly from one activity to another as new opportunities arise and old industries become uncompetitive. Flexibility has become a swear-word among inflexible left-wingers, who see it as a euphemism for cutting wages and eliminating job security. But in a dynamic and unstable world, economies need to adapt quickly in order to prosper. Those who oppose flexibility in the name of working people tend to be defending the entrenched rights of privileged insiders with jobs for life at the expense of outsiders who can't get a look-in. Less flexible economies – such as France, Germany and Italy – tend to have slower growth (which makes it difficult to pay for a welfare state) and high unemployment. Many people are excluded from the job market altogether, notably the young, the less-well educated and the children of immigrants. In other words, opposing flexibility is not progressive; it is a rigid defence of vested interests.

Denmark can scarcely be accused of being 'neo-liberal'. As we have seen, the government accounts for more than half of the economy. The country is highly unionised. Wages are generally very high. But Denmark is certainly flexible. Wages and working conditions are mostly set at a company level (rather than centrally) through negotiations between employers and unions, with scope to alter them as circumstances change. Most importantly, businesses can hire and fire workers easily. In a country of 5.5 million people, with 2.9 million people employed, 250,000 jobs are eliminated each year (and replaced by new ones). In all, some eight hundred thousand Danes change jobs each year.

Precisely because it is so easy to fire workers if they have to, businesses also hire them readily. So one reason why Danish workers feel secure is that if they lose (or quit) their job, they are likely to find another soon. In the summer of 2009, when the unemployment rate in most advanced economies was heading towards double digits, it was a mere 3.7 per cent in Denmark.

While Danes are in between jobs, they benefit from very generous unemployment benefits. People who have unemployment insurance are paid 90 per cent of their previous wages, up to a maximum of around €1,800 a month. A typical skilled worker who ends up unemployed would receive around three-quarters of their previous pay.

The third leg of the Danish model is extremely active government policies to help people retrain and find a new job. Even while they are in work, two in five Danes are engaged in lifelong learning. They are entitled to two weeks a year of education and training designated by their companies as well as a further two weeks of their own choosing within a similar field. If they lose their job, the government pulls out all the stops to help them find a new one.

All of this does not come cheap. The government spent nearly

3 per cent of GDP in 2007 on its labour-market policies.[15] Unemployment, while still very low by international standards, doubled between 2008 and 2009, so spending has doubtless risen even further. The second drawback of the Danish model is that the poor have few incentives to work, since wages are punitively taxed to pay for the generous welfare payments. Likewise, high taxes ought to deter people from working harder and acquiring new qualifications, because highly skilled workers don't take home much more money after tax than lower-skilled ones do.

Like a bumblebee, the Danish model looks like it shouldn't be able to fly – and yet somehow it does. One big reason for this is that Denmark is a small, tightly knit Protestant society where the social and cultural pressure to work hard is strong. 'If you have the capacity to work, it's not socially accepted not to,' says Kristian Jensen, the country's free-market-minded taxation minister, who is tipped as a future prime minister. 'Social pressure keeps the system going.' But he points out that high taxes spur some entrepreneurial Danes to go and work in countries where their efforts are better rewarded, while also deterring foreigners from coming to work in Denmark. In the longer term, he doubts whether the model is sustainable without continued reform.

Another reason for the Danish model's unlikely success is that the government forces job-seekers to attend rigorous job-placement interviews and cuts off their benefits if they don't. Even so, some people game the system. Around a quarter of the unemployed are reckoned not to be looking for work.

Last but not least, some of Denmark's success at keeping down unemployment is illusory. Over a tenth of the working-age population are off work owing to disability or early retirement, and the figure rises to more than a quarter among over-fifties.[16] Unemployment is also higher among young people, albeit still low by international standards. Immigrants and their children fare particularly badly. Strikingly, the daughters of immigrants who strive to obtain a university degree are much less likely to be employed than those of native Danish people: their employment rate is 57 per cent, compared with 87 per cent.[17] But for all its flaws, Denmark's economy works pretty well.

Might its model be exportable? Elements certainly ought to be emulated. Other European countries would do well to make it easier for businesses to hire and fire workers. True economic security comes from protecting people, not jobs. It is the only way to provide opportunities for the many people whom job-protection laws in other countries exclude. Instead big European countries have mostly reformed by tinkering around the edges. Many new workers, often migrants, have been hired on temporary contracts, while the privileges of those on permanent contracts have been left untouched. Unsurprisingly, people on temporary contracts have been the first to be fired in the recession, as letting go of permanent staff tends to be prohibitively expensive (in Spain) or even impossible (in France). In the French model of flexicurity, flexibility is for some, security for others. This is not only unfair; it is also inefficient.

Denmark's focus on lifelong learning and active policies to get people into new jobs are also admirable. As technologies change, people need to update their skills. Yet in France, fewer than one in five workers are enrolled in training courses, while in Germany the figure is only one in eight. In Spain and Italy, hardly anyone is. But in countries where joblessness is higher, Denmark's generous unemployment benefits would be prohibitively expensive. So flexibility must come first.

The relative success of the Danish model also relies heavily on the long tradition of partnership between employers and unions, which does not exist elsewhere. 'When foreign companies, particularly American ones, come to Denmark, we need to educate them about the Danish model,' Thorkild Jensen says with a smile. 'But when they realise what they get from working closely with union representatives, they appreciate its benefits.' Unions elsewhere might be more confrontational and less willing to accept necessary changes in wages and conditions.

One reason why unions are so accommodating is because they are aware that Denmark is a small, open economy that must compete in global markets. International competition prevents wages getting too out of line and deters unions from digging in their heels over issues such as asking employees to work longer hours when demand is strong. Denmark's openness, then, is a key element of its model. The model works much less well in the public sector, where unions are more intransigent. This suggests that it could not be copied wholesale in Europe's larger and less open economies unless it was accompanied by a sea change in industrial relations and reforms to bolster competition.

The broader lesson, though, is that globalisation need not threaten the European-style welfare state. On the contrary, by boosting economic growth, it helps to pay for it. The real challenge to the welfare state comes from sluggish growth and ossified employment structures that make it crushingly expensive and exclude the young and other minorities from work, and hence from society. If a high-wage, high-tax welfare society such as Denmark can prosper in international competition, then so too could France and Germany if they became more flexible. Rigid domestic laws and practices, not foreigners, are to blame for their problems. There is nothing progressive about slow growth and high unemployment.

One world, many models

More fundamentally, the notion that all countries are being forced – or ought – to converge on a single economic model is deeply flawed. Flexibility and openness are highly desirable, but they are not compulsory. They can also be achieved in different ways: Denmark's consensually negotiated flexibility is a world apart from Wal-Mart's non-unionised flavour of it. Since countries' circumstances differ, as do people's preferences, different models can happily coexist. If Europeans are willing to tolerate higher taxes to pay for a cradle-to-welfare state, then that is their choice. If they prefer to work (and earn) less and take longer holidays, that's fine. But it is vital that the welfare state promote flexibility, rather than hinder it, and encourage employment, rather than deter people from seeking work and employers from hiring. Those aims can better be achieved if their economies are open. Likewise, if Americans are warier of big government and more accepting of economic insecurity than Europeans are, they may choose to live with a threadbare social-safety net. Ideally, people could move to whichever country best suits their tastes and values if they wanted to.

In practice, though, many Americans seem torn between their ideology of individual self-reliance and the gnawing reality of pervasive insecurity. Despite their belief in free markets, Americans are more sceptical about free trade than most Europeans. A survey by the German Marshall Fund, for instance, found that whereas 83 per cent of Germans had a favourable opinion of international trade, only 71 per cent of Americans did. Just as many Europeans wrongly blame globalisation for threatening the welfare state, many Americans incorrectly blame trade for their insecurity. Although most Americans lose their jobs because of economic change other than globalisation – changing tastes, for instance, or productivity-enhancing new technologies – their fears tend to be focused on foreigners. Tariffs on Chinese imports are an easier sell politically than a tax on the internet.

Americans would feel less insecure, and thus more enamoured of globalisation, if they took a leaf out of Europe's book. Whereas European workers enjoy universal access to healthcare, Americans stand to lose their corporate health insurance if they lose their jobs. If their employer goes under, so does their pension. While Europeans enjoy generous unemployment benefits and plenty of help in retraining and finding a new job, Americans get little assistance. Fortunately, the US economy's dynamism usually enables most displaced workers to find another job quickly – but some don't, and many more fear that they won't, leaving them exposed not only financially but also to the vagaries of their families' health.

If unemployment remains high in the post-crisis years, the American model – and its openness to international trade – could come under severe strain. Making American workers feel more secure should therefore be a priority for everyone who believes in open markets and for every business with a stake in the global economy. Healthcare reform is a central part of that. Fears about foreign competition could otherwise tip into outright protectionism. Globalisation is not incompatible with government action to cushion the blow of adjusting to change; on the contrary, it may depend on it.

Bigger government?

As we have seen, governments were hardly svelte on the eve of the crisis. But since then they have swollen to gargantuan proportions. They have spent vast sums on bank bailouts, fiscal-stimulus packages, subsidies and other things. The recession has also depressed tax revenues, particularly in countries such as Britain and America where the housing and financial sectors were governments' golden geese in the bubble years. As a result, government borrowing has ballooned. The IMF estimates that the US will run a budget deficit of 11.1 per cent of GDP in 2010, with its gross debt rising to 92.7 per cent of GDP.[18] Britain's deficit is expected to be 10.2 per cent of GDP with government debt reaching 76.7 per cent of GDP. France and

Germany will run smaller deficits but reach similar debt levels.[19] Spain and Ireland are also set to run double-digit deficits. Italy's national debt will top 118 per cent of GDP, Japan's 225 per cent. Left unchecked, government debts will spiral out of control. The UK Treasury estimates that Britain has a £90-billion annual gap to fill – equivalent to 6.4 per cent of GDP.

It's not just governments' size that has grown, it's the scope of their activities. They now own stakes in banks and car companies. They are dishing out subsidies left, right and centre. They say they will act to curb carbon emissions and cage the banks. But unless they can persuade voters squeezed by the slump and struggling with their bubble-era debts to pay much higher taxes, their powers will be limited. They can regulate but not spend.

At some point, economic growth will fill some of the black hole in governments' books. The recovery will boost incomes and profits, and hence the government's tax take. Eventually, unemployment and hardship will lessen, and with it social spending. But since the recovery is likely to be slow and high unemployment prolonged, while revenues from housing and finance are likely to remain depressed, governments will have to tighten their belts. It is a mammoth task. But it is also an opportunity for governments to rethink what they should be doing and how they should finance their activities.

As the axe falls on public spending, governments would do well to remember that slashing much-needed investment is a false economy. It generates savings now, at the expense of slower growth and lower tax receipts in future. In particular, they should be careful to maintain investment in education and training, as well as infrastructure, both of which are essential not just for boosting economic growth, but also for ensuring that its benefits are shared across the society and across regions. Certainly, education systems need reform, and there is doubtless much waste that can be cut, but spending on poorer pupils in particular ought to rise, not fall. In Britain and America, whose rickety infrastructure is sometimes worse than that in developing countries, a failure to invest in better airports, roads and high-speed rail links is as short-sighted as not investing in high-speed internet networks would be. Again, there are doubtless huge savings to be made from injecting more competition into contracting for public-works contracts.

The wisest way to fill the gap in public finances would be to accelerate otherwise-desirable reforms. One obvious change is raising the official retirement age, along with removing the incentives for early retirement and the obstacles to working longer. It is natural for people to work longer now that they can be productive well past the age of sixty-five – and unaffordable for governments to burden young workers with paying to keep sprightly sixty-six-year-olds on the golf course. Now is the ideal time to keep older people in work longer. It would give a triple boost to government finances, reducing pension spending, increasing the tax take and boosting economic growth. Since many people have had their retirement savings devastated by the crisis, they should be open to working longer to replenish them. Governments could increase the retirement age by three months every year, so that between 2010 and 2022 it would rise by three years. Where public-sector pensions are much more generous than private-sector ones, they should also be looked at. At the same time, governments could boost growth and make society fairer through a broader rethink of tax policy.

Tax land, not labour

Consider these three facts. One: America and Europe are struggling to recover from a crisis caused in large part by a huge property bubble. Two: unemployment is high, workers are feeling the pinch and many people are worried about competition from countries with lower wages. Three: governments have a huge gap to fill in their finances. What would you raise taxes on?

Astonishingly, many governments are considering raising already-high taxes on labour. For instance, in the 2010 election campaign Britain's Labour government stoutly defended its planned increase in national-insurance contributions – and the incoming Conservative–Liberal Democrat coalition intends to implement some of that planned increase. Yet instead of penalising effort, governments should be cutting taxes on work and raising them on property instead. They raise hardly any revenues from taxing land. On the contrary, big rural landowners in Europe and America receive huge handouts from governments through their misguided farm subsidies, while in urban areas property taxes tend to hit (poorer) tenants, rather than (often very rich) landowners. At a time when governments are casting around for ideas on how to prevent another financial crisis, they could start by taxing the unproductive asset that has been at the heart of one bubble after another: land. Shifting the burden of taxation away from work and towards land values would not just help stabilise the economy, it would be efficient and fairer. By putting more money in workers' pockets and creating new jobs, it would also stimulate growth. An OECD study finds that shifting the tax mix away from income towards immovable property would give a big boost to growth.[20]

Considering most people think that work ought to be encouraged, it is perverse that governments tax it so heavily. On average in rich OECD countries, a quarter of governments' tax take comes from income tax and another quarter from social-security contributions (known as national-insurance contributions in Britain).[21] Together with payroll taxes, just over half (51 per cent) of tax revenue comes from taxes on personal income. A further 11 per cent comes from taxes on companies. Thirty per cent comes from taxes on consumption, such as sales tax or value-added tax (VAT). A mere 6 per cent comes from taxes on property, with the remainder from a variety of other taxes.

Taxes on labour cut pay and cost jobs because they drive a big wedge between the cost of employing people and how much people actually take home. In Germany, for instance, the cost to employers of hiring someone on average wages was more than double that person's take-home pay in 2008. The cost to employers was $61,600 a year, but 16.2 per cent of that went on social-security contributions paid by employers and a further 17.2 per cent on social-security contributions paid by the employee, while 18.6 per cent was gobbled up in income tax.[22] As a result, the average worker took home just $29,600 a year.

Imagine, for the sake of argument, that all those taxes were eliminated. The worker could take home an extra $32,000 a year and the employer would be no worse off. Alternatively, the worker's wages could rise by less than the full amount, and because the employer's labour costs had fallen, employment and output would rise. Germany is an extreme example. But in other countries the tax wedge is almost as large. In France, taxes double the cost of hiring workers. In Britain, they raise it by half. Even in relatively low-tax America, they raise it by 43 per cent. In every country, cutting taxes on employment would achieve the holy grail of raising wages *and* employment.

As well as slashing workers' pay and destroying jobs, high taxes on labour deter people from working harder. It is not just high-earners who are discouraged from working more, so are the poor. In many countries, the tax and benefit system is such that people with a low earning power may be scarcely better off working than on welfare, while it may not be economical for companies to hire them. A single person on two-thirds of average wages faces an effective tax rate of 34 per cent on every additional dollar they earn in the United States, 40.6 per cent in Britain and 66.3 per cent in France.[23]

By keeping poor people out of work, labour taxes not only

exacerbate welfare dependency and social exclusion, with all the psychological and social toll that go with these, they also add to government spending on unemployment and other social benefits. So the best way to cut taxes on work is to start from the bottom, raising the threshold at which people start to pay income taxes and social-security contributions. This would benefit everyone, but especially the poor. It would boost people's spending power, giving growth a lift. It would reduce welfare rolls. And it would create many new jobs, notably in the service sector. Cutting taxes on employment should be embraced by conservatives, liberals, progressives and pragmatists alike.

Many people think that lower taxes on workers should be paid for by higher taxes on companies. After all, they reason, companies make huge profits (at least in boom times), they pay their bosses outlandish sums and in any case they ought to be cut down to size. It's only fair: everyone knows that companies pay less tax than ever. Except that's not true. On average in rich OECD countries, the share of the total tax take raised from corporation tax has risen from 8 per cent in 1995 to 10.7 per cent in 2006.[24] It has increased in France, Germany, Britain and even in the United States.

More importantly, taxes on companies are in fact taxes on business activity – and thus on jobs and on the production of goods and services. They are also taxes on shareholders, often pension funds that have invested the retirement savings of millions of not-so-rich individuals. So taxing companies heavily is counterproductive. If you want to hit bosses hard, tax their incomes and capital gains more heavily, not the company they work for. If your target is wealthy shareholders, tax their dividends and capital gains. If companies are making excessive profits because they are abusing their market power, set competition watchdogs on them.

A better idea would be to tax things that you want to discourage. Top of the list is carbon emissions. OECD countries are expected to emit around 13 billion tonnes of carbon dioxide in 2010.[25] A tax of, say, $30 a tonne would raise $390 billion a year at current emissions levels. Pitched at $50 a tonne, it would raise $650 billion a year. Over time, of course, a carbon tax would reduce emissions – which is precisely why it is needed. But during the long transition to a low-carbon future, it would also provide much-needed extra revenue. If the tax rate rose as emissions fell, governments could be ensured a pretty steady source of revenue that could be used to cut taxes on working. Since OECD countries' GDP in 2010 is forecast to be $38.6 trillion, carbon-tax revenues of $390 billion a year would contribute 1 per cent of GDP to government coffers, while at a higher rate they would contribute 1.7 per cent of GDP. The contribution would be bigger in the US, where carbon emissions are particularly high, smaller in nuclear France, where they are pretty low. Instead, scandalously, most governments that are adopting carbon taxes are giving exemptions to big emitters, while those that are introducing cap-and-trade schemes to limit emissions are giving away permits to big polluters.

If you were feeling daring, another obvious source of revenue is drugs that are currently illegal. Legalising drugs and taxing them would provide a double whammy: huge savings on law enforcement and hefty revenues from taxing drugs. Tobacco and alcohol are big revenue raisers; cannabis (marijuana) could be too. The United States alone spends some $40 billion each year on trying to eliminate the supply of drugs. Globally, the United Nations reckons that the illegal drug industry makes around $320 billion a year. By legalising the trade and taxing it, governments could raise perhaps another couple of hundred billion dollars a year.

Another idea is a global tax on financial transactions, which Peer Steinbrück proposed when he was Germany's finance minister. A levy of 0.05 per cent on all financial trades within the G20, on or off an exchange – from which ordinary individual investors would be exempt – could yield as much as $690 billion a year, or some 1.4 per cent of global GDP, according to the Austrian Institute for Economic Research.[26] 'Evasive action would be almost impossible if the G20 stood united,' he argues. Trading volumes on G20 and EU exchanges account for roughly 97 per cent of total exchange-traded shares, and some 94 per cent of exchange-traded bonds. 'As the tax would be very low ... there would not be much of a distorting effect, either,' Steinbrück claims. 'I don't think such a tax would significantly affect market liquidity; even if it did, a nudge towards buying and holding would be no bad thing.' It is worth considering. People in Britain already pay stamp duty when they buy shares; why shouldn't banks' larger financial transactions also be taxed?

The single most important shift would be to cut taxes on work and raise them on land, more specifically the market value of land. Property speculation has huge costs: it diverts funds from productive investment during bubbles, then causes misery during the inevitable busts. As we know to our cost, it also causes havoc in the whole economy. If we are looking to shift the burden of taxation away from desirable things such as effort towards discouraging undesirable ones, property speculation should be top of the list. Taxes on land values would curb property bubbles and encourage greater investment in productive areas of the economy, such as new businesses. The tax rate could even be raised when land values are rising fast, thus taking the steam out of a bubble without affecting the rest of the economy, as a rise in interest rates would.

Taxes on work cause huge distortions and waste: their costs are far greater than the revenues raised. Tax effort and there is less incentive to strive; some people won't bother to work at all. But the supply of land is fixed – no matter how heavily you tax it, the amount available won't change. Taxing land values, rather than property or any improvements to it, would not penalise people who do up their home. Nor would it distort incentives to improve land. On the contrary, it would encourage the development of vacant and derelict land in areas where planning or zoning regulations permit it. Unlike stamp duty, a land-value tax would not be a tax on property purchases, so it would not discourage people moving. And unlike most property taxes, it would be paid not by tenants but by generally much richer landowners. Hong Kong and Singapore both derive a large share of their tax take from variants of a land-value tax and have very low income taxes as a result. Denmark also has a long tradition of land-value taxation.

Land taxes are also fair. Whatever you think of the merits of capitalism, there is nothing intrinsically desirable about the initial distribution of property rights. On the contrary, in most countries, it is highly unequal, owing to the unfortunate legacy of history. That is true in post-apartheid South Africa, as we saw in Chapter 9. But it's not only true in developing countries such as Brazil, where 1 per cent of the population owns 49 per cent of the land. It is even more so in Britain, where 0.3 per cent of the population owns 69 per cent of it.

The biggest landowner in Britain, the Duke of Buccleuch and Queensberry, owns 277,000 acres – that's around 277,000 football pitches – conservatively valued at €2 billion. He does so not because of any individual talent or endeavour, but because he descends from a man who seized vast swathes of Scotland by unsavoury means. Across Europe, 77,000 landowners – 0.022 per cent of the population – own 12 per cent of the total land area. In Spain, the Duchess of Alba owns at least 250,000 acres (and possibly as much as 2.5 million acres), while the once-royal Habsburg family own 500,000 acres across Europe. All of these facts are from *Who Owns the World: The Hidden Facts Behind Landownership*, an excellent book by Kevin Cahill.[27]

The value of that land increases each year not through their own striving, but that of others. As economic activity in London has soared through the ingenuity and toil of the masses of people who have flocked there, the value of the three hundred acres of fields bequeathed to the Duke of Westminster, now known as Mayfair and Belgravia, the priciest parts of central London, has skyrocketed. They are reckoned to be worth more than £5 billion. Wouldn't it be better to tax that windfall gain rather than the work that generates it?

Likewise, when a government builds a new railway line and the value of the surrounding property soars, surely it is right that this unearned wealth be taxed. When the Jubilee Line extension to London's Canary Wharf was built, property values adjacent to its stations rose hugely – by £2.8 billion at Southwark and Canary Wharf alone.[28] Land-value taxes would pay for – and thus encourage – public investment in valuable infrastructure and other amenities that increase land values. Conversely, landowners would be partly compensated for new developments that reduced the value of their land.

Land-value taxes have a fine pedigree. As David Ricardo, the founder of modern economics, pointed out, 'Rent is that portion of the produce of the earth, which is paid to the landlord for the use of the original and indestructible powers of the soil . . . The rise of rent is always the effect of the increasing wealth of the country, and of the difficulty of providing food for its augmented population. It is a symptom, but it is never a cause of wealth; for wealth often increases most rapidly while rent is either stationary, or even falling.'[29] Landowners contribute nothing to the productive economy through their ownership of land, yet they benefit from the productive efforts of others.

The case for a land-value tax was eloquently made by none other than Winston Churchill in 1909:

Roads are made, streets are made, services are improved, electric light turns night into day, water is brought from reservoirs a hundred miles off in the mountains – and all the while the landlord sits still. Every one of those improvements is effected by the labour and cost of other people and the taxpayers. To not one of those improvements does the land monopolist, as a land monopolist, contribute, and yet by every one of them the value of his land is enhanced. He renders no service to the community, he contributes nothing to the general welfare, he contributes nothing to the process from which his own enrichment is derived.

Since the distribution of land is highly unequal, taxing it would be highly progressive. Most poor people own no land at all, while the very rich own vast amounts of it. Since land values in rich countries are huge, even a relatively low tax rate could raise big sums of money. The tax take would also rise automatically with prosperity. The rate could be tapered so that small landholders pay very little, while large ones pay much more. Far from forcing a granny who lives in a big house out of her home, the tax could be deferred until her death if it was too burdensome.

Land-value taxes have other virtues too. They can be easily and cheaply collected. They cannot be evaded. Land cannot be spirited away to a tax haven or resident elsewhere for tax purposes. Where land registries are imperfect, the threat of seizure would persuade people to declare their ownership. The objection that land is hard to value is nonsense. Property changes hands all the time; estate agents and surveyors routinely value property as part of their work.

In short, taxing land values would be efficient, progressive, fair, stabilising and good for the economy. It would permit big cuts in taxes on employment, with all the huge benefits that would have. Over time, it would make sense to shift the burden of taxation progressively away from work and towards unearned land wealth. Now, before the next property bubble inflates, is the ideal time to introduce it.

12

The Future
is Open

Embrace progress

We can return to the beasts. But if we wish to remain human, then there is only one way, the way into the open society. We must go on into the unknown, the uncertain and insecure, using what reason we have to plan as well as we can for both security and freedom.

Karl Popper, *The Open Society and Its Enemies*, 1962

America has become a nation consumed by anxiety, worried about terrorists and rogue nations, Muslims and Mexicans, foreign companies and free trade, immigrants and international organisations. The strongest nation in the history of the world now sees itself as besieged by forces beyond its control.

Fareed Zakaria, *The Post-American World*, 2008[1]

> Up until recently the most optimistic societies of the
> world have been Western societies, but they seem to be
> losing their optimism, at a point in time when they should
> be celebrating the galloping modernisation of the world.
>   Kishore Mahbubani, *The New Asian Hemisphere*, 2008[2]

In São Paulo I saw an amusing T-shirt in a shop window. In a play on the World Social Forum's slogan, 'Another world is possible', it read: '*Fórum Anti-Social Mundial. Viver do mau humor é possivel.*' ('World Anti-Social Forum. Living in a bad mood is possible.')

Many people in rich countries are in an awful mood right now. The present is painful and the future seems bleak. Rage blends with fear and a sense of powerlessness – even despair – about their prospects. Confidence is shot. Americans as well as Europeans worry that their best days are behind them. People want to hide away from the world and hunker down. The cheerfulness of the Chinese, Indians, Brazilians and others only darkens the gloom. Their success seems to underscore our failings. How can we possibly compete?

Look up – and out. The world is still rich with opportunities for progress if we reach out and grab them. The boundless optimism of people in emerging economies should inspire, not frighten us. The Industrial Revolution raised the living standards of a fraction of humanity above the rest; now it is lifting up most people, although sadly not yet all. Celebrate – a fairer, safer, richer world beckons. And it can be greener too.

Dangers ahead

The future can be bright. But its huge promise can also be wrecked. The aftermath of the crisis, emerging economies' ongoing rise and climate change – the three big forces that will shape the global economy over the next decade – present huge challenges as well as massive opportunities. Resist the necessary changes and big dangers loom – another crash, a government debt crisis, the closing off of global markets and a climate catastrophe; embrace them and huge possibilities open up.

The immediate priority is fixing the Western banking system and nurturing healthier, more balanced sources of growth. It is a prerequisite for a sustainable recovery and essential to prevent another crisis that could devastate the global economy. Inflating another bubble is not the solution to our problems; it is the road to ruin. Make no mistake: the future of our Open World is at stake.

Whatever policy-makers do, advanced economies face difficult years ahead. This is not a normal recession caused by the authorities stamping on an overheating economy. Like Japan's bust in the 1990s, it is caused by a collapse in asset prices, exacerbated by excessive debt and complicated by a banking crisis. Weighed down by their past borrowing, consumers are not inclined to spend nor banks to lend until their balance sheets are healthier – so businesses that sell to them or borrow from them are suffering. Governments have stepped in for now, but cannot do so for ever. And while lending to sound borrowers needs to be restored, consumers and banks must not return to their reckless old ways. Production patterns therefore need to change too. In post-bubble economies, other industries must grow to fill the space left by housing and finance. In the rest of the world – notably emerging economies – consumers need to spend more while production is reoriented to servicing their own needs rather than Americans'.

Such an adjustment takes time. It also requires supportive policy decisions. But because policy-makers seem too craven to face down powerful corporate interests – especially in banking – and too blinkered to break out of the vicious cycle of bubble and bust, they are prolonging the pain and encouraging an unhealthy, unbalanced and unsustainable recovery. Instead of fixing broken banks, they are giving them licence to gamble their way out of trouble. Rather than letting bloated sectors such as the car industry shrink, they are propping them up with government handouts. Instead of investing in the future and encouraging enterprising new companies, governments stimulate overextended consumers to start spending again. Rather than propelling the economy towards a healthy recovery, governments are pushing it back towards its bad old ways.

As I argued in Chapter 1, the bad old banks rendered insolvent by their excessive borrowing and poor investment decisions should have been nationalised – or good new ones created in their stead. Wiping the slate clean and injecting fresh capital into them would have left the new banks well placed to lend. Instead the old banks were bailed out and their bad debts papered over with government guarantees. With free funding from central banks and iron-clad backing from governments, they can now make easy money as asset markets recover, shelling out undeserved bonuses to unrepentant bankers while cutting back on lending to companies and households. This is a monstrous racket. Rather than bust banks' shareholders and creditors carrying the can for their past mistakes, the rest of the economy is. While America and Europe suffer high unemployment, credit-starved companies and ruined public finances, the casino is rolling again and all the profits are for the banks.

Policy-makers' failure to clean up the banks is not only delaying the recovery. It is storing up huge risks for the future. Central bankers have their foot down on the monetary pedal, but because the banking transmission mechanism is broken and consumers are overstretched, the wheels of the economy are not responding. Instead the freshly printed money is pumping up asset prices around the world.

Note that balance-sheet problems can be resolved in several ways. Debts can be whittled down by saving more to pay them back. Borrowers can also default on part or all of them, either

individually through insolvency or collectively through inflation. But a third option is to reflate asset prices to restore
households' and banks' net worth. This may seem quick and
painless now, but it sows the seeds for the next crisis. Since
policy-makers have rejected the insolvency option for banks
and seem unwilling to postpone recovery until consumers pay
down their debts, they seem to have opted to inflate new bubbles instead.

In America, share prices could take over where real estate left
off, while in Britain people are raring to resume their property
speculation. An even bigger danger is that all the money slosh-
ing around the world will blow bubbles in emerging economies.
By driving up their currencies, boosting domestic consumption
and investment, and sucking in imports from America and
other advanced economies, this would appear to rebalance
global growth – but only until their bubbles burst, capital
drained out and they suffered a wrenching repeat of the 1997–8
crisis.

Super-loose monetary policy and rising asset prices will
doubtless eventually boost demand in the wider economy.
Banks will resume lending, companies investing and consumers
spending. But the economy will be even more dangerously
unstable than before. If household debts remain high, consumers will be more vulnerable to a subsequent downturn. If
banks are free to gamble with a taxpayer guarantee, they will
ruinously overextend themselves again. If public finances are
precarious, governments will be powerless to do much to cushion the eventual crash. Another vicious cycle of bubble, bust
and bailout could exhaust central banks' monetary powers and
stretch governments' borrowing capacity to breaking point. A
government debt crisis could occur even sooner if public borrowing gets out of hand. If investors suddenly lose confidence
in a country's finances, the consequences are brutal – spiking
interest rates, a collapsing currency, Iceland writ large.

Ultimately, if government debts become unmanageably large, the only two solutions are default or inflation. Confidence in capitalism would be shattered; the prudent would pay for the profligate's mistakes; and governments would be powerless to help.

To avert such nightmare scenarios, governments must act decisively now. Lending to small and medium-sized companies – the bedrock of the economy – must be restored as quickly as possible. If the old banks won't lend, create new ones that will, or use part-nationalised ones to that end. Government-backed banks should be banned from paying bonuses until they have amassed adequate levels of capital. Once the banking system is working better, central banks can start to withdraw the cash that they have pumped into it. Sooner rather than later, central banks (by raising interest rates), financial regulators (by raising banks' capital requirements) and governments (by taxing land values) should act together to pre-empt a future bubble and thus avoid a bigger bust. Emerging economies must be particularly vigilant. All the currency reserves in the world cannot prevent a cycle of bubble and bust; only controls on capital inflows and other prompt prudential measures can mitigate the risks.

While economies remain fragile, governments would do better to support them through fiscal measures than destabilising monetary ones. All their actions to boost demand should also promote economic adjustment rather than prolonging outdated ways. Support employment by cutting payroll taxes, not protecting specific jobs. Help create new ones by loosening the shackles that limit new job-creating businesses while making it easier for companies to fire – and therefore to hire – people. Protect the vulnerable while helping them to retrain and find new jobs. Invest in infrastructure and lifelong learning. Until private finance is restored and a price is put on carbon, help the green industries of the future rather than giving handouts to smokestack industries. Don't encourage overindebted consumers to spend. Don't prop up industries that have excess capacity. Confront the entrenched interests that seek to block reform. Break down the barriers that hinder innovation and enterprise.

Overhauling the financial system cannot wait. While the banks were on their knees, a golden opportunity to break finance's stranglehold over the economy and politics was missed. Now that finance is resurgent – a monstrous state-sponsored kleptocracy reminiscent of Yeltsin's Russia or Suharto's Indonesia – its grip will be much harder to break. Many policymakers appear too complicit, brainwashed or faint-hearted to cage the bankers. Yet this immoral and dangerous crony capitalism must be dismantled. Justice demands it, and so does the future prosperity and stability of the economy.

Better regulation is essential. To reduce the risk of banks failing, they must be compelled to hold much larger capital cushions. To stabilise the economic cycle, these capital requirements must rise in boom times to limit excessive risk-taking. To curb bankers' recklessness, bonuses should be paid in shares that cannot be sold for a long time so that they lose if their bets subsequently go wrong. To avert future bailouts, banks must be restructured so that they can be wound down quickly and safely if need be.

But even the best regulation is not fail-safe – and on past and present form politicians are all too likely to bend to the demands of big and complex banks in a crisis and bail them out. Even in good times, big banks are far too powerful. These government-licensed gamblers abuse their privileged position as gatekeepers of capital markets. Their monopolistic profits are a cost to companies, investors and the rest of the economy, not a contribution to society. To curb their power and ensure they are allowed to fail, they must be broken up. The European Commission's break-up of the Dutch behemoth ING sets a good example, which America and others should follow.

This crisis has caused the worst global recession since the 1930s, mass unemployment and an alarming rise in government debt. The next one could threaten governments' solvency, global capitalism and even liberal democracy. It need not be like this. The US government faced down and broke up J.P. Morgan in 1933. If Franklin Roosevelt did it, so could Barack Obama.

Emerging giants

Emerging economies are also an essential part of the solution to the crisis. Their resilience – and China's huge stimulus package in particular – limited the fall; the confidence of their investors and appetites of their consumers can help drive the recovery. China's vast demand for raw materials and foreign machinery to drive its new infrastructure boom is lifting growth around the world. Unleashing its consumers could help fill the gap left by America's. Already their spending is growing by 10 per cent a year – and with suitable reforms, they could account for as much as a quarter of global consumption growth over the next fifteen years. For that to happen, Beijing has to shake up its financial sector, unshackle service-sector companies so that they can grow and create new jobs, and establish a proper welfare state. It may sound like a tall order, but so too is the amazing transformation that China has achieved over the past thirty years. As China reforms, the renminbi needs to appreciate to accommodate and accelerate these changes – which would also limit Beijing's wasteful accumulation of depreciating dollar reserves. The prize is huge: a better life for the Chinese people, a more robust Chinese economy and more balanced global growth. Without these changes, growth in China and elsewhere will be slower and the risks of a protectionist backlash far greater.

The ongoing challenge for advanced economies is to adapt to the rise of emerging ones. Peer at countries' vital statistics and you could be forgiven for thinking the BEEs – China, India and Brazil – have already displaced the As (advanced economies) from the global leader board. While the As languish, the BEEs are growing strongly. Unemployment is higher in America than in Asia. Britain and America are printing money and racking up vast debts with gay abandon, while once-reckless Brazil is now a model of sobriety. With good reason, the world increasingly looks to Beijing, not Washington, for answers.

For sure, we should not get ahead of ourselves. America and Europe are still fantastically rich, while China and India remain poor. Average incomes in America are more than four times those in Brazil, six times those in China and fourteen times those in India.[3] But at current growth rates, living standards in China and India could quadruple within twenty years. Emerging economies are likely to account for the lion's share of global growth over the next decade and beyond. China looks likely to overtake America as the world's largest economy some time in the 2020s. While there will inevitably be setbacks along the way, the world economy will increasingly take its cues from Shanghai, Mumbai and São Paulo.

That will require adjustments – not least to Western attitudes. The West can no longer boss the rest around; nor can it presume that it always knows best. That may be a particularly big shock for America. For Europeans, the biggest loss may be their disproportionate voice in global institutions such as the IMF – although perhaps not, since they have cornered five of the twenty seats at the G20. Eventually, though, they must give way. A global economy with global problems, not least climate change, requires closer political cooperation. Stronger international institutions are essential – and they can only be effective if they are seen as legitimate, as EU members know all too well.

The G20 is a welcome improvement on the G8. It should coordinate the disparate efforts to regulate global finance, liberalise world trade, craft global investment rules, reform the IMF and World Bank and combat climate change. Such an enlarged role would, to some degree, extend the EU model of institutionalised cooperation on a global scale, as Gideon Rachman has perceptively pointed out.[4] Europeans might thus construe it as a victory after all. Fostering a sense of common purpose among government leaders is among the strongest safeguards against conflict, especially if complemented by stronger international rules.

While emerging economies' rise requires mental and practical adjustments, it should not be perceived as a threat. They are not to blame for rich countries' current misfortunes; the financial crisis is. Nor are the BEEs intent on overturning the global economic order; above all, they want their rightful place in it. In fact, emerging economies – notably the BEEs – could take over from America and Europe as the standard bearers of an open world economy. As Kishore Mahbubani, author of *The New Asian Hemisphere*, observes, the crisis has shaken Asians' faith in Western policies, but not in open markets. While many Western people have grown wary of free trade, 'most Asians want more, not less, globalisation'.[5] His words echo those of Luiz Fernando Furlan, Brazil's former trade minister, and of China's prime minister, Wen Jiabao, who is fond of quoting Adam Smith. Wen argues that his country 'would rather speed up reforms' to combat the crisis and should 'give full play to market forces in allocating resources'.[6]

'Asians want to replicate the West, not dominate it,' Mahbubani says. 'They want to create the same comfortable middle-class societies that the West has had.' That need not mean the planet cooking – our technologies need changing, not our lifestyles. And precisely because people in emerging economies have so many unmet needs, their growth opens up huge opportunities for Western exporters and investors. Instead of fretting that jobs are all destined to disappear to China and India, America and Europe should take a leaf out of Australia's book and seize the opportunities that Asia's growth offers. Don't growl like Joe Fehsenfeld of Midwest; emulate Darius Stenberg of AllDental and smile.

Inevitably, as the Rest rise, the West will decline in relative terms. But while its share of the global economy will shrink, it can prosper in absolute terms. Westerners' living standards will continue to rise – and will grow faster thanks to emerging economies' success. That's not such a terrible prospect, is it?

America profited handsomely from Western Europe's growth after the Second World War. They have both done well out of Japan's subsequent success. All three will benefit from emerging economies' dynamism – Brazilian food, Korean mobile phones, Chinese solar technology, Indian electric cars, cheap Vietnamese footwear – not just cheaper imports but better ones; not just imitated technologies but also innovative ones; people and ideas moving in both directions.

The protectionist peril

But only if world markets remain open. The immense pain that the crisis has caused has placed our Open World under huge strain – and the longer it lasts, the greater the risks. Despite the promises of G20 leaders, protectionism is on the rise. High unemployment, fear of China and greenery could combine to provoke an even bigger backlash – while another crisis would be devastating. The rollback is more likely to come from the anxious As than the buzzing BEEs, but it could easily cause a cycle of tit-for-tat retaliation. Protectionism and prejudice, in turn, could wreck the recovery, pit emerging powers against existing ones and jeopardise efforts to combat climate change.

Thankfully, global institutions such as the World Trade Organization and regional ones such as the European Union can limit backsliding. The threat of retaliation can also deter. Greater interdependence – whether through global supply chains that tie the interests of American and European companies to those of their subcontractors in Asia and elsewhere, or China's huge holdings of US Treasury bonds – also raises the cost of conflict.

Unfortunately, these safeguards are patchy and leaky. Interdependence does not preclude rash moves. If governments were guided solely by the common good, protectionism would not exist and there would be no need for the WTO. In practice, special interests often hijack governments to serve their narrow ends – and while many companies increasingly have global interests, immobile workers have local ones. At the behest of the unions, the Obama administration slapped hefty duties on Chinese tyres in September 2009 on the eve of the G20 summit in Pittsburgh despite the costs to American consumers and even though the US industry opposed the move. 'The trade decision was the president's first down payment on his promise to more effectively enforce trade laws, and it's very much appreciated,' said Thea Lee of the AFL-CIO ominously.[7] China responded by launching investigations into whether American chicken and car parts were being dumped in its market. As well as fears about jobs, voters may be swayed by a host of arguments that are prone to protectionist manipulation – from greenery to national security.

While WTO rules are much better than nothing, they are far from watertight. Most countries have plenty of scope to raise their import duties without breaking WTO rules because the tariffs they apply are well below the ceiling that they have pledged not to exceed. Other openings for protectionism include anti-dumping, countervailing and safeguard duties. Though 'legal', they are still economically harmful. In agriculture, WTO rules have little bite: if countries wanted to, they could choke off trade with tariffs and subsidies; export taxes and controls are completely unregulated. Governments' commitments in services – sectors such as transport, telecoms and tourism, which together account for the bulk of the global economy – are patchy. Nor do WTO rules curb officially tolerated monopolies, cartels and other anti-competitive practices – notably OPEC. There are no global restraints on protectionism that targets international investment or foreign workers.

Often WTO rules divert protectionism into more opaque forms, such as obscure regulations and standards. For instance, the US uses tougher inspections on its border with Canada, that notorious hotbed of Al Qaeda militancy, as a protectionist device. It employs bogus food-safety standards to keep out Brazilian food that even the pernickety Japanese will eat. Differing mobile-phone standards limit global competition. Even the internet can be segmented. The US government banned online gambling to stop foreigners encroaching on locally licensed betting monopolies.

In any case, the WTO cannot prevent countries from enacting protectionist measures if they really want to. If a country breaks the rules and another complains, the WTO cannot force the offender into line. It can only authorise retaliatory sanctions, which perversely restrict trade further. And if everyone breaks the rules, the rules break down. All the subsidies to car companies have so far gone unchallenged. Thus while WTO rules do deter some protectionism, their coverage is incomplete and their enforcement can be ineffective and even counterproductive.

If governments are not careful, protectionism could gather momentum. One risk is a salami-slicing of global markets that eats away at free trade. Another danger is an almighty trade war, most likely provoked by carbon tariffs. The damage could be

huge and lasting. After markets were closed off in the 1920s and
1930s, it took decades (and a world war) to open them up again.

Forward, not back

The fight back for open markets must begin with political leadership from the very top. After the Second World War, America
was instrumental in creating the multilateral trading system
through which world trade has been freed and regulated. This
was not a selfless act: Americans are $1 trillion richer, $9,000
per household, thanks to the liberalisation of world trade since
1945, according to a study by the Peterson Institute for
International Economics, a think-tank in Washington DC –
and they could be another $500 billion richer if remaining bar-
riers were torn down. Barack Obama has made rousing
speeches about restoring America's place in the world. Now he
needs to explain to anxious Americans why an open world
economy can make them safer as well as richer.

Americans appear terrified of trade even with Panama –
their unratified free-trade agreement lies gathering dust on
Capitol Hill. But their biggest fear is of China. Paranoia laced
with prejudice is fanning Sinophobia that Obama should try
to quell. The Chinese are not Americans' enemies; on the contrary, their fates are intertwined. America's recovery depends
on Chinese demand, while the US is still the main market
for Chinese exports. As the world's largest debtor, the US
depends on China, its biggest creditor, but Beijing's stockpile
of US Treasuries also makes it particularly vulnerable to decisions made in Washington. A trade war over the renminbi
would be self-defeating. Whether the issue is world trade
or climate change, progress is impossible without their cooperation. Just as when Britain was top dog it made the wise
decision to accept America's rise rather than resist it,

the United States would do well to adjust to China's peaceful rise.

Julia Gillard needs to convince Australians that closer links with China, and its investment in particular, are not a threat. Australians are lucky that the Chinese want to buy their mineral resources and provide a reliable source of capital to boot. Their economy, like Canada's, complements China's – and the growing personal ties that connect them are a huge asset that xenophobia devalues. If their current prime minister won't speak up, Australians should heed the wise words of their elder statesman, Bob Hawke, instead.

European leaders seem so paralysed by fears of their continent's decline that they fail to celebrate their immense achievements – the single market, the euro, the free movement of five hundred million people among twenty-seven countries, a continent that war and communism divided reunited within the EU. These are huge strengths that other regions can only aspire to. European leaders should have the courage and foresight to make the case for broadening euro membership and extending Europe's zone of peace, prosperity and stability more widely – to the Balkans, Ukraine, Turkey and North Africa, for starters. They should also reject the abject defeatism of those who want to hide from the world instead of embracing its many possibilities.

Words matter. But so do actions. The key to holding the line against protectionism and building a broader coalition in favour of open markets is domestic reforms to win over worried workers, pressing forward with freer trade at the WTO to mobilise export interests and global action on climate change.

Flexible and secure

Open markets work better in tandem with government policies that enable people to grasp their opportunities and help them adjust to economic change. Even though the internet is a bigger culler of jobs than China or India, many Americans wrongly blame their economic insecurities on foreigners. But they would find economic change in general less worrying if they had a proper safety net – not least guaranteed healthcare – and more help in finding new jobs. Trying to single out for special help workers who lose their jobs because of trade, as the trade adjustment assistance scheme does, is misconceived – they cannot be readily identified and it is not clear why they deserve more help than others who lose their jobs. It is far better to protect everyone.

Many Europeans also finger foreigners for many of their problems. They would find economic change less painful if they became more flexible. This would lower unemployment and boost growth, making their cherished welfare state more affordable. It would also help bring marginalised workers into the labour market, something than any progressive person should support. Combined with welfare reforms to encourage working, big cuts in payroll tax to reward effort and enhanced lifelong learning, this could revitalise Europe's hidebound economies. As Denmark's example highlights, flexibility and security are not substitutes, they are complementary. So too are globalisation and good government. It is not just about ensuring people get a fair deal, it is about enhancing economic performance and securing political consent.

Without the support of key interest groups, openness will always be precarious. Consumers and competitive companies can readily see its benefits; they need mobilising rather than convincing. The key constituency to win over is worried workers and their union representatives. While American trade unionists are often protectionist, unions can be a powerful force for openness. Britain's TUC is a strong supporter of the free movement of labour within the EU. Sweden's trade unions are vocally in favour of free trade. 'From a wage earner's perspective it's rational to be pro-free trade because it provides the potential for increased real wages,' says Lena Westerlund, chief economist for the Swedish Trade Union Confederation (LO). 'But productivity increases don't always translate into higher wages and that is an argument which supporters of protectionism can use.' Ensuring workers are properly rewarded today and equipping them for tomorrow's jobs could quell protectionist pressures. Making it easier for people to move – including abroad – to find a new job would also open up many new options. Since products and capital are mobile, labour gains from being mobile too. British workers may come to appreciate the freedom to work anywhere in the EU if jobs remain scarce and other EU economies recover more quickly than Britain.

Doing Doha and curbing climate change

At a global level, the surest way to resist protectionism is to push forward with efforts to free up world markets and curb climate change. With a global agreement to limit carbon emissions, governments would have no excuse to slap green taxes on foreign products. Ideally, such an agreement should provide financial and technological help to poorer countries to help them adjust – not just because it is fair, but because we are all in this together. China and India have plenty of scope to grow fast without harming the planet by using energy more efficiently and leapfrogging to low-carbon technologies. But since it makes sense for poor but fast-growing economies to act later rather than sooner, China and India could make modest commitments now and progressively more ambitious ones from 2020 on. By then, clean-tech may have improved so much that it is competitive even without putting a hefty price on carbon. Politicians everywhere should realise that there is more to gain from promoting tomorrow's well-paid jobs in green industries than from trying to protect polluters from the need to change. And a greener world would also be a more pleasant – and safer – one.

A new push to conclude the WTO's Doha Round could also mobilise export interests and deter governments from acting recklessly. Paradoxically, the Doha Round is a victim of its ever-shrinking ambitions. If it promised better access to fast-growing emerging markets, it could curb protectionist pressures in Western countries. That's why China's leadership – along with Brazilian enthusiasm and Indian acceptance – is essential. China's unilateral liberalisation has already worked wonders among its neighbours; now it should take the lead globally too. Since emerging economies now have a lot to gain from a global agreement on investment, this should also be a priority, either at the WTO or elsewhere. Patrick Messerlin of the Institut d'Études Politiques in Paris also proposes that the US and the EU press on with talks to free up trade in services, creating momentum that could see them quickly widened to other interested parties.[8]

Pressing on with multilateral liberalisation at the WTO would also help counter the pernicious spread of preferential trade agreements – deals involving two or more economies that are misleadingly known as 'free-trade agreements'. These provide signatories with privileged access to each other's markets and thus discriminate against others. While the WTO is blocked, these seem like the only game in town, although in reality countries always have the option to liberalise unilaterally (as many emerging economies have done). Preferential pacts have proliferated in Asia over the past decade, while

America and Europe have pursued their own deals around the world. This tangled web of discriminatory deals, each with its own complex and often contradictory rules, ties trade in red tape, to lawyers' delight and economists' despair. A priority for Asia is therefore to consolidate its overlapping deals into a wider pan-Asian free-trade area – and ultimately a European-style single market. But the only way to overcome the increasing fragmentation and segmentation of global markets is through a revitalised WTO.

Bolstering mobility

Enhanced mobility is an essential element of openness. It is often considered separately from trade and investment, but all three are in fact interconnected, as Chapter 8 explained. Mobile people create new connections that stimulate trade and investment, while trade and investment often require people to move too. A more mobile workforce is a key element of flexibility and thus increasingly vital to economic success in a fast-changing global environment. Migrants' different skills, attributes, experience and perspectives tend to complement those of native workers, boosting productivity and wages. And they are central to creating and disseminating new ideas and businesses that drive economic growth.

The success of Silicon Valley and other cosmopolitan regions and cities highlights the huge contribution diverse individuals can make – not least in developing the new clean technologies which are our best hope of stopping climate change. Now that Australia, Canada and also China are courting talented migrants, America and Europe cannot afford to turn them away.

Migrants' contribution is huge, but unpredictable. Nobody could have guessed, when he arrived in the United States as a child refugee from the Soviet Union, that Sergey Brin would go on to co-found Google. Had he been denied entry, America would never have realised the opportunity that had been missed. How many potential Sergey Brins do Europe and post-9/11 America turn away or scare off – and at what cost?

While prospects for freeing up migration may seem bleak for now, both the old and the young could act as powerful lobbies for change. Ageing – and soon-to-be shrinking – wealthy societies desperately need young workers, of which the developing world has an excess. As baby-boomers in America, Europe and Australia retire over the next twenty years, they will stop worrying about who might take their job and start fretting about who is going to look after them when they need care. At the same time, young people who have grown up in a culturally diverse environment tend to be more open to newcomers.

Pragmatism may also persuade. Far better, surely, that people cross borders legally and safely, than arrive covertly and live outside the law. A study by the Cato Institute, a think-tank in Washington DC, estimates that the US would gain $260 billion a year from allowing in more low-skilled workers instead of stepping up the crackdown against irregular migrants.[9] This is an underestimate, because it ignores the dynamic benefits of mobility. Humanitarian concern is another powerful argument – not least for the many environmental refugees that climate change could displace. Eventually, restrictions on people's freedom of movement might come to be seen as an unacceptable violation of their human rights.

Open to progress

Openness is not just a matter of tearing down border barriers, it is about breaking down barriers within society and changing people's attitudes. Open economies do best when they are also open societies made up of people with open minds.

The economic case for openness is usually made too narrowly. Cheaper imports help everyone's money go further, not least the poor's. Global markets enable cities and regions to specialise in what they do best while importing the rest for less. Uncompetitive industries shrink, freeing up resources so that more productive ones can grow. Yesterday's jobs are shed so that tomorrow's better ones are created.

All of that is true. But there is much more to it than that. Market economies are not computable machines that shift predictably from one steady state to another, they are dynamic, unfathomably complex organisms that are forever evolving – unsurprisingly, since they are made up of millions of human beings continually interacting with each other. Nor is economic growth a mechanical process oiled by new technologies that appear metronomically as manna from heaven. It is an ongoing voyage of discovery into an unknowable future, fuelled by ingenuity and energy, trialled by enterprising businesses and stimulated by competition within a framework of supportive institutions. That is why openness and flexibility are of such cardinal importance. Openness stimulates fresh ideas, disseminates technologies and fires up competition. Dynamic networks of businesses, capital and people create fertile new connections within economies and across them. Flexibility is essential not just to adjust to continual change, but to grasp new opportunities. It is a state of mind as well as a set of business practices.

When economies are open, foreign competition continually spurs companies – and governments – to up their game, while the prize for success is global rather than just local. When societies are open, newcomers and people of all backgrounds can fulfil their potential, with new ideas emerging from different people sparking off each other and new businesses from their desire to get ahead. When people's minds are open, they are receptive to better – or simply different – ways of doing things, they see opportunities before threats and they view the future as pregnant with positive possibilities.

Openness is not just a means of raising living standards, important though that is. It is about extending freedom, opportunity and peace. It is about combating discrimination, xenophobia and exclusion. It is about embracing difference, change and optimism.

Americans and Europeans once knew that. As Fareed Zakaria rightly remarks, 'America has succeeded not because of the ingenuity of its government programmes but because of the vigour of its society. It has thrived because it has kept itself open to the world – to goods and services, to ideas and inventions, and, above all to peoples and cultures.' Perhaps people in emerging economies can remind them of it. As Kishore Mahbubani observes, 'The real value of free-market economics is not just in the improvements in economic productivity. It is about how it uplifts the human spirit and liberates the minds of hundreds of millions of people who now feel that they can finally take charge of their destinies . . . People feel liberated when they have increased choices and access to all kinds of possibilities.'

Openness advances individual freedom. It breaks down barriers among societies and within them. It provides new opportunities to make contact with different people, places, products and ideas – a free choice over what we can consume, experience, eat, read, watch or listen to; whom we can work for or do business with; where we invest our savings; where we can live and whom we can love. Openness is thus a vital part of advancing human rights. It opens up a whole new world of possibilities that erodes the tyranny of geography whereby your birthplace and background dictate what you can do and who you can be. And because it also makes people richer, it gives them the capacity to make the most of those freedoms.

The flipside of increased individual freedom is greater variety and diversity within societies – not just a wider choice of products, but also a broader range of people, different ways of thinking, new opportunities for learning and exchange, the continual striving and cross-fertilisation of ideas that is the engine of progress.

Openness also widens opportunity, and thus promotes greater equality. When trade barriers make foreign things prohibitively expensive, only the privileged can afford them. When capital restrictions prevent people from taking their savings out of a country, only the wealthy can afford to hire accountants to get around them. When immigration controls stop most people living and working where they choose, only the rich and the educated can make the most of all the world has to offer. When social barriers hold the disadvantaged back, only the elites can reap the full rewards of growth.

Openness not only reduces the chasm between the opportunities available to rich and poor, it erodes the gap between prosperous places and poor ones. The world is anything but flat. The biggest determinant of your life chances is not how talented you are or how hard you work but where you were born and who your parents are. A hard-working entrepreneur born in a remote African village has far fewer opportunities to achieve her dreams than a lazy dimwit born in America. Even if the African seizes all her chances and the American none, the American is still likely to enjoy a more comfortable life. Enabling the African to obtain a decent education, sell overseas, receive foreign funding and go and work in America can help close the gap. Remember Joanne Chen and her son Jerry, whom we met in Chapter 4. Her parents starved; she now has a motorbike and a mobile phone; and when her son is grown up, she wants to travel the world. Openness helps to overcome the accident of birth. It is the opposite of discrimination, xenophobia and exclusion.

Openness can also promote greater understanding and peace.

Contact with unfamiliar people and ideas can broaden our horizons, dispel prejudice and make us aware of what we have in common, as well as what distinguishes us. Experiencing a new culture shows us that there are different – and sometimes better – ways of doing things. Learning a foreign language helps us understand how our own shapes how we think and view the world. Economic ties can give countries a shared interest in peace. Thanks to the EU, war in Europe is now inconceivable. China and the United States have a far stronger interest to stay on good terms because their economies are so intertwined. Links between people are especially important: Chinese students at American universities, American business-people in China and mixed marriages all bind their two countries together.

Of course, this is not an iron rule. Thomas Friedman's facile Golden Arches theory of international relations, whereby countries that have a McDonald's do not go to war, has repeatedly been proved wrong. The intimate integration of the global economy in 1914 did not prevent the First World War. Likewise, closer contact between people and ideas can sometimes cause misunderstanding and even conflict. But in general, closer economic, political, social and cultural ties tend to bind people and countries together, rather than set them apart.

Openness goes hand in hand with progress. It is, to use the words of Amartya Sen, about expanding 'the power to do things' – the freedom and the capacity to realise your dreams. To make the most of its possibilities requires progressive governments that enforce fair laws, combat discrimination, promote social mobility, equip people for change, catch them when they fall and break down the monopolistic bastions of landownership and finance. And it requires optimism. The optimism to try to improve things, invest in the future and embrace change. The optimism that views challenges – even crises – as opening up new possibilities.

Crises don't come much bigger than the recent one. The pain is undeniable, the injustice flagrant. But the world is still full of promise. We would be mad to close ourselves off to its possibilities. Individual effort, collective enterprise and a helping hand from government can lift us up. We should believe in ourselves – and give our future a chance.

Notes

Introduction: Back from the Brink

1 Fortune Global 500. http://money.cnn.com/magazines/fortune/ global500/ 2010/
2 Calculations and references are in Chapter 5.
3 Martin Ravallion, 'The Developing World's Bulging (but Vulnerable) "Middle Class"', World Bank Policy Research Working Paper 4816, January 2009
4 Personal calculations based on figures for gross domestic product per capita at constant prices in national currency from IMF, *World Economic Outlook* database, April 2009
5 *Ibid.*
6 http://www.globaltradealert.org/
7 It did so under the previously unused Section 421 of US trade law. This does not require Washington to prove that goods are underpriced or subsidised – merely that they have been rising quickly.
8 http://www.ft.com/cms/s/0/04228662-a9fd-11de-a3ce-00144feabdc0.html

1 Meltdown

1 IMF, *Global Financial Stability Report*, April 2006
2 http://www.ft.com/cms/s/0/97cb78ba-a3ea-11de-9fed-00144feabdc0. html
3 http://www.ft.com/cms/s/0/825cf2ea-09b9-11de-add8-0000779fd2ac. html
4 http://blogs.ft.com/maverecon/2008/11/how-likely-is-a-sterling-crisis-or-is-london-really-reykjavik-on-thames/
5 http://www.economist.com/opinion/displaystory.cfm?story_id= 4079027
6 http://en.wikipedia.org/wiki/Japanese_asset_price_bubble
7 The combined value of all the land in Japan, a country the size of California and only 50 per cent bigger than Britain, reached $18 trillion – almost four times as much as the value of all property in the United

States at the time. http://www.nytimes.com/2005/12/25/business/
yourmoney/25japan.html?pagewanted=print

8 http://en.wikipedia.org/wiki/Chemdex; http://www.economist.com/
surveys/displaystory.cfm?story_id=E1_GVQDSD

9 http://en.wikipedia.org/wiki/Boo.com

10 S&P/Case-Shiller House-Price Index, Composite 10, CSXR

11 Nationwide House Price Index, http://www.nationwide.co.uk/hpi/
historical.htm

12 http://www.cotizalia.com/cache/2008/07/03/46_europa_preocupa_
mucho_ajuste_inmobiliario_espana.html

13 http://www.fotocasa.es/indice-inmobiliario__fotocasa.aspx

14 Australian Bureau of Statistics, http://www.abs.gov.au/AUSSTATS/
abs@.nsf/DetailsPage/6416.0Jun%202009?OpenDocument

15 http://www.esri.ie/irish_economy/permanent_tsbesri_house_p/

16 Permanent TSB ESRI House Price Index, http://www.esri.ie/ irish_
economy/permanent_tsbesri_house_p/

17 http://www.economist.com/opinion/displaystory.cfm?story_id= 4079027

18 Charles Roxburgh et al., *Global Capital Markets: Entering a New Era*,
McKinsey Global Institute, September 2009

19 As John Maynard Keynes put it, 'We devote our intelligences to antici-
pating what average opinion expects average opinion to be. And there
are some, I believe, who practise the fourth, fifth and higher degrees.'
John Maynard Keynes, *The General Theory of Employment, Interest
and Money*, 1936

20 Charles Kindleberger, *Manias, Panics and Crashes*, Wiley, 1978

21 This helpful summary comes from Hugo Dixon's excellent *The Penguin
Guide to Finance*, Penguin, 2000.

22 United States Federal Reserve, Flow of Funds Accounts of the United
States, Second Quarter 2009, September 2009, Table D.3

23 Calculations from flow of funds and national accounts produced by
United States Bureau of Economic Analysis, Table 2.1. Personal Income
and Its Disposition.

24 http://www.economist.com/specialreports/displaystory.cfm?story_id=
14530085

25 http://www.thenewamerican.com/index.php/economy/economics-main-
menu-44/1641-william-white-of-the-bank-of-international-settlements-
predicted-the-economic-crisis

26 http://www.guardian.co.uk/business/2007/sep/30/5

27 http://www.sifma.org/uploadedFiles/Research/Statistics/SIFMA_
USMortgageRelatedOutstanding.pdf

28 http://www.sifma.org/uploadedFiles/Research/Statistics/SIFMA_
USMortgageRelatedIssuance.pdf

29 http://www.sifma.org/uploadedFiles/Research/Statistics/SIFMA_
GlobalCDOData.pdf

30 http://www.fsa.gov.uk/pubs/speeches/at_21jan09.pdf

31 Financial Services Authority, *The Turner Review*, March 2009

32 Calculations from flow of funds and national accounts.

33 http://www.fsa.gov.uk/pubs/speeches/at_21jan09.pdf

34 http://www.ft.com/cms/s/0/868473d0-ad28-11de-9caf-00144feabdc0.html

35 http://www.theatlantic.com/doc/200905/imf-advice

36 http://www.hm-treasury.gov.uk/press_68_07.htm

37 http://www.theatlantic.com/doc/200905/imf-advice

38 http://www.voxeu.org/index.php?q=node/2900

39 IMF, *International Financial Statistics*, August 2009

40 Yin-Wong Cheung, Menzie David Chinn and Eiji Fujii, 'The Overvaluation of Renminbi Undervaluation', June 2007. CESifo Working Paper Series No. 1918; HKIMR Working Paper No. 11/2007. http://ssrn.com/abstract=965402

41 As Stephen Roach put it in an article in the *Financial Times*, 'Mr Bernanke was the intellectual champion of the "global saving glut" defence that exonerated the US from its bubble-prone tendencies and pinned the blame on surplus savers in Asia. While there is no denying the demand for dollar assets by foreign creditors, it is absurd to blame overseas lenders for reckless behaviour by Americans that a US central bank should have contained. Asia's surplus savers had nothing to do with America's irresponsible penchant for leveraging a housing bubble and using the proceeds to fund consumption. Mr Bernanke's saving glut argument was at the core of a deep-seated US denial that failed to look in the mirror and pinned blame on others.' http://www.ft.com/cms/s/0/a2ba2378-9186-11de-879d-00144feabdc0.html

42 Bank for International Settlements, *79th Annual Report*, 2009

43 IMF, *Global Financial Stability Report*, October 2009

44 Charles Roxburgh et al., *Global Capital Markets: Entering a New Era*, McKinsey Global Institute, September 2009

45 http://www.economist.com/surveys/displaystory.cfm?story_id= 14530093

46 http://online.wsj.com/article/SB125509067304175871.html?mod=WSJ_hps_LEFTWhatsNews

47 Barry Eichengreen and Kevin O'Rourke, 'A Tale of Two Depressions', 1 September 2009. http://www.voxeu.org/index.php?q=node/3421

48 http://www.ft.com/cms/s/0/ed968d70-a07f-11de-b9ef-00144feabdc0.html

49 UNCTAD, *World Investment Report 2010*, 2010

50 IMF, *Global Financial Stability Report*, April 2009

51 Bank for International Settlements, *79th Annual Report*, 2009

52 http://www.theatlantic.com/doc/print/200905/imf-advice

53 http://online.wsj.com/article/SB123371182830346215.html

54 http://blogs.ft.com/maverecon/2009/01/the-good-bank-solution/

2 Too Big to Fail?

1 http://www.ft.com/cms/s/0/2fec6426-9674-11de-84d1-00144feabdc0.html
2 Greenspan famously preferred to 'mitigate the fallout when it occurs and, hopefully, ease the transition to the next expansion'. Testimony for the Committee of Government Oversight and Reform, 23 October 2008
3 http://www.ft.com/cms/s/0/c045384e-a322-11de-ba74-00144feabdc0.html
4 Bank for International Settlements, *79th Annual Report*, 2009
5 http://www.ft.com/cms/s/0/84ab191e-a3d3-11de-9fed-00144feabdc0.html
6 http://www.ft.com/cms/s/0/a830fcf6-aed1-11de-96d7-00144feabdc0.html
7 http://www.ft.com/cms/s/0/4f857c8c-4a2a-11de-8e7e-00144feabdc0.html
8 http://www.ft.com/cms/s/0/76e13a4e-9725-11de-83c5-00144feabdc0.html
9 http://www.ft.com/cms/s/0/0666adfe-ffb6-11de-921f-00144feabdc0.html
10 http://blogs.ft.com/maverecon/2009/06/too-big-to-fail-is-too-big/
11 http://www.ft.com/cms/s/0/47403c68-698f-11de-bc9f-00144feabdc0.html?nclick_check=1

3 Money Matters

1 http://www.ft.com/cms/s/0/a324a9b0-51f2-11de-b986-00144feabdc0.html
2 The world also lacks a bankruptcy regime for insolvent governments.
3 IMF, *World Economic Outlook* database, April 2009
4 IMF, *International Financial Statistics*, September 2009
5 IMF, *Currency Composition of Official Foreign Exchange Reserves (COFER)*, September 2009
6 China, Japan, Indonesia, Malaysia, Philippines, Singapore, South Korea and Thailand
7 http://www.imf.org/external/np/speeches/2009/100209.htm
8 http://www.pbc.gov.cn/english/detail.asp?col=6500&id=178
9 Zhou also proposes an SDR-denominated fund, managed by the IMF, into which dollar reserves could be exchanged for SDRs. Countries could then reduce their dollar exposure without pushing down the dollar (although it is unclear who would bear any exchange-rate losses).
10 http://online.wsj.com/article/SB125053694840237795.html
11 http://www.ft.com/cms/s/0/671a76ec-a950-11de-9b7f-00144feabdc0,dwp_uuid=9c33700c-4c86-11da-89df-0000779e2340.html
12 http://www.economist.com/businessfinance/displaystory.cfm?story_id=13988512

4 Where Next?

1 http://www.economist.com/businessfinance/displaystory.cfm?story_id=14124376

2 http://www.ft.com/cms/s/3/e1de3324-a819-11de-8305-00144feabdc0.html

3 Personal calculations based on McKinsey Global Institute, *If You've Got It, Spend It: Unleashing the Chinese Consumer*, August 2009. McKinsey's figures have been converted from 2000 renminbi to 2008 US dollars.

4 Personal calculations based on McKinsey Global Institute, *The 'Bird of Gold': The Rise of India's Consumer Market*, May 2007. McKinsey's figures have been converted from 2000 rupees to 2008 US dollars.

5 Peter Mandelson, 'Living with China', speech at the China-Britain Business Council, 15 April 2008. http://www.springerlink.com/content/q0343g36g4r73912/

6 Razeen Sally, *New Frontiers in Free Trade: Globalization's Future and Asia's Rising Role*, Cato, 2008

7 Martin Ravallion, 'The Developing World's Bulging (but Vulnerable) "Middle Class"', World Bank Policy Research Working Paper 4816, January 2009

8 Fareed Zakaria, *The Post-American World: And the Rise of the Rest*, Penguin, 2008

9 http://english.peopledaily.com.cn/90001/90778/90860/7161844.html

10 http://www.ft.com/cms/s/0/1054574c-ae0a-11de-87e7-00144feabdc0.html

11 Asked why he chose China over India, Stenberg replies: 'I know China now, so it's easy. Chinese people are also better placed to produce a search engine for the Chinese market. There are more barriers to entry than in India, where everyone speaks English. And targeting China is more of a unique concept for investors.'

12 IMF, *Direction of Trade Statistics*, August 2009

13 *Ibid.*

14 http://www.ft.com/cms/s/0/16041848-ad11-11de-9caf-00144feabdc0.html

15 *Ibid.*

16 *Ibid.* Britain's exports to China rose from $2.0 billion in 1999 to $9.0 billion in 2008; America's increased from $12.9 billion to $71.5 billion over the same period; and Germany's swelled from $7.4 billion to $50.1 billion. Note that there are discrepancies between Chinese import figures and other countries' export figures, notably because China counts imports that transit through Hong Kong as trade with Hong Kong.

17 OECD, *Employment Outlook 2009*, 2009

18 http://www.imf.org/external/pubs/ft/weo/2009/02/pdf/c4.pdf

19 IMF, *World Economic Outlook*, October 2009

20 http://news.bbc.co.uk/1/hi/8221540.stm

21 IMF, *World Economic Outlook*, October 2009
22 IMF, *World Economic Outlook* database, April 2009
23 Bank for International Settlements, *79th Annual Report*, 2009
24 Oil/gas exporting countries are Algeria, Angola, Azerbaijan, Bahrain, Ecuador, Equatorial Guinea, Gabon, Iran, Kazakhstan, Kuwait, Libya, Nigeria, Norway, Oman, Qatar, Russia, Saudi Arabia, Turkmenistan, United Arab Emirates and Venezuela.
25 IMF, *World Economic Outlook* database, October 2010
26 *Ibid.*
27 Alan J. Auerbach and William G. Gale, 'An Update on the Economic and Fiscal Crises: 2009 and Beyond', Brookings, July 2009, http://www.brookings.edu/papers/2009/06_fiscal_crisis_gale.aspx
28 Interview in *Prospect*, September 2009
29 http://www.nytimes.com/2009/07/21/business/economy/21manufacture.html?_r=1&scp=1&sq=doug%20bartlett&st=cse
30 OECD, STAN Database for Structural Analysis, June 2009 update
31 Erin Lett and Judith Banister, 'China's manufacturing employment and compensation costs: 2002–06', Bureau of Labor Statistics, *Monthly Labor Review*, April 2009. http://www.bls.gov/opub/mlr/2009/04/art3full.pdf
32 http://www.labour.org.uk/peter-mandelson-speech-conference
33 WTO, *International Trade Statistics*, 2008
34 Ingo Borchert and Aaditya Mattoo, 'The Crisis-Resilience of Services Trade', World Bank Policy Research Working Paper 4917, April 2009, http://www-wds.worldbank.org/external/default/WDS ContentServer/IW3P/IB/2009/04/28/000158349_20090428090316/Rendered/PDF/WPS4917.pdf
35 McKinsey Global Institute, *If You've Got It, Spend It: Unleashing the Chinese Consumer*, August 2009
36 http://www.doingbusiness.org/economyrankings/
37 IMF, *World Economic Outlook*, October 2009, Table A16
38 http://www.ft.com/cms/s/0/25708658-b41f-11de-bec8-00144feab49a.html
39 http://www.ft.com/cms/s/0/94314bde-91a3-11de-879d-00144feabdc0.html
40 Nicholas Barr and Peter Diamond, *Reforming Pensions: Principles and Policy Choices*, Oxford University Press, 2008
41 http://www.economist.com/businessfinance/displaystory.cfm?story_id=14124376
42 McKinsey Global Institute, *If You've Got It, Spend It: Unleashing the Chinese Consumer*, August 2009

5 Awakening

1 Fareed Zakaria, *The Post-American World: And the Rise of the Rest*, Penguin, 2008

2 From 1984 the maglev train at Birmingham airport took passengers (much more slowly) to the railway station until 1995, when the line was closed because it was unreliable.

3 'Shanghai Buys Itself a Makeover Before a Fair', *New York Times*, 31 May 2009

4 IMF, *World Economic Outlook* database, October 2010. In 1998 UK GDP in current prices was $1,456 billion; China's was $1,019 billion and India's $428 billion. In 2010 UK GDP was an estimated $2,259 billion; China's was $5,745 billion and India's $1,430 billion.

5 *Ibid.*

6 *Ibid.* Advanced economies are as per IMF definition, excluding the newly industrialised Asian economies of Hong Kong, Singapore, South Korea and Taiwan.

7 *Ibid.* In 2000 world exports were $7,892 billion, with advanced economies (excluding the newly industrialised Asian economies) accounting for $5,196 billion. In 2010 world exports were an estimated $18,334 billion, with advanced economies accounting for $10,023 billion. In 2000 world imports were $7,904 billion (the figures don't tally with world exports because of measurement problems), with advanced economies accounting for $5,396 billion. In 2010 world imports were an estimated $17,929 billion, with advanced economies accounting for $10,090 billion.

8 WTO, Statistics database

9 http://www.ft.com/cms/s/0/2fa8f09a-90db-11de-bc99-00144feabdc0.html

10 Tim Harcourt, *The Airport Economist*, Allen & Unwin, 2008

11 IMF, *Direction of Trade Statistics*, September 2009

12 Greg Linden, Kenneth L. Kraemer, Jason Dedrick, *Who Captures Value in a Global Innovation System? The Case of Apple's iPod*, Personal Computing Industry Center, June 2007. http:// pcic.merage.uci.edu/papers/2007/AppleiPod.pdf

13 Advanced economies are OECD countries; emerging ones are non-OECD countries. IEA, *World Energy Outlook 2008*, 2008

14 Jeffrey Rubin and Benjamin Tal, 'Will Soaring Transport Costs Reverse Globalization?', *StrategEcon*, CIBC World Markets, 27 May 2008

15 World GDP was $54,841 billion and world exports were $17,149 billion. IMF, *World Economic Outlook* database, April 2009

16 48.9 per cent of East Asia's trade in 2007 was intra-regional, where East Asia is sixteen countries: Brunei, Cambodia, China, Hong Kong, Indonesia, Japan, Laos, Malaysia, Mongolia, Myanmar, Philippines, Singapore, South Korea, Taiwan, Thailand, Vietnam. Source is Asian Development Bank Institute, *Infrastructure for a Seamless Asia*, 2009, Table 2.3, http://www.adbi.org/files/2009.08.31.book.infrastructure.seamless.asia.pdf

17 50.7 per cent of North America's trade in 2007 was intra-regional,

where North America is Canada, Mexico and the United States, the three members of the North American Free Trade Agreement (NAFTA).

18 67.7 per cent of the European Union's trade in 2007 was among its twenty-seven member countries.

19 http://online.wsj.com/article/SB125314622440117989.html#mod= WSJ_hps_sections_news

20 http://www.economist.com/businessfinance/displayStory.cfm?story_ id=E1_RDPVRSR

21 Fareed Zakaria, *The Post-American World: And the Rise of the Rest,* Penguin, 2008

22 OECD, *Information Technology Outlook,* 2008

23 Pankaj Ghemawat and Thomas Hout, 'Tomorrow's Global Giants', *Harvard Business Review,* November 2008

24 http://www.channelregister.co.uk/2009/10/15/idc_pc_figs/

25 http://en.wikipedia.org/wiki/Chery_Automobile

26 UNCTAD, *World Investment Report 2010,* 2010. http://www.unctad.org/ en/docs/wir2010_en.pdf

27 *Ibid.*,Table I.7

28 http://www.economist.com/businessfinance/displayStory.cfm?story_ id=E1_TDQJGGRQ

29 UNCTAD, *World Investment Report 2010,* 2010. Annex Tables 1 and 2. http://www.unctad.org/en/docs/wir2010_en.pdf

30 UNCTAD, *World Investment Report 2009,* 2009. Annex Tables B.4 and B.5. http://www.unctad.org/en/docs/wir2009_en.pdf

31 Bill Emmott, *Rivals: How the Power Struggle Between China, India and Japan Will Shape Our Next Decade,* Penguin, 2008.

32 $60.7 trillion according to IMF, *World Economic Outlook* database, April 2009

33 The calculations are based on the IMF's *World Economic Outlook* database, April 2009. Advanced economies are the European Union, the United States, Japan, Canada, Australia, Norway, Switzerland, Israel, New Zealand and Iceland. Emerging economies are all other economies, including the newly industrialised Asian economies.

34 http://www.ft.com/cms/s/0/8fc9df9c-a991-11de-a3ce-00144feabdc0.html

6 Facing the Dragon

1 United States Bureau of Economic Analysis, 'Value Added by Industry'. http://www.bea.gov/industry/iedguide.htm#gpo

2 http://www.epi.org/publications/entry/ib235/

3 Christian Broda and John Romalis, *The Welfare Implications of Rising Price Dispersion,* University of Chicago mimeograph, July 2009

4   Robert Lawrence, *Blue-Collar Blues: Is Trade to Blame for Rising US Income Inequality?*, Peterson Institute for International Economics, 2008

5   Paul Krugman, *Trade and Wages, Reconsidered*, Brookings Papers on Economic Activity, April 2008. http://www.brookings.edu/economics/bpea/~/media/Files/Programs/ES/BPEA/2008_bpea_papers/2008_bpea_krugman.pdf

6   B. Hoekman and L.A. Winters, 'Trade and Employment: Stylized Facts and Research Findings', World Bank Working Paper, 2005

7   Bureau of Labor Statistics, 'International Comparisons of Hourly Compensation Costs in Manufacturing, 2008'. http:// www.bls.gov/news.release/ichcc.pdf

8   *Ibid.*, Table B

9   Figures are from IHS/Global Insight. http://online.wsj.com/article/SB124927488392500809.html

10 Steven Dunaway and Xiangming Li, 'Estimating China's "Equilibrium" Real Exchange Rate', IMF Working Paper 05/202, October 2005. http://imf.org/external/pubs/ft/wp/2005/wp05202.pdf

11 http://www.economist.com/businessfinance/displaystory.cfm?story_id=14124376, http://www.economist.com/node/17420096?story_id=17420096

12 http://www.economist.com/businessfinance/displayStory.cfm?story_id=E1_JTRQDVP

13 http://blogs.cfr.org/setser/2009/07/22/two-trillion-and-counting-%E2%80%A6/#more-5958

14 *Ibid.*

15 J.C. McCarthy, 'Near-Term Growth of Offshoring Accelerating', Forrester Research, 2004, and A. Parker, 'Two-Speed Europe: Why 1 Million Jobs Will Move Offshore', Forrester Research, 2004

16 J.F. Kirkegaard, 'Outsourcing – Stains on the White Collar?', Institute for International Economics, Working Paper Series WP 04-3, 2004

17 McKinsey Global Institute, 'The Emerging Global Labour Market', 2005

18 D. Van Welsum and G. Vickery, 'The Share of Employment Potentially Affected by Offshoring – An Empirical Investigation', DSTI/ICCP/IE(2005)8/FINAL, OECD, 2005

19 OECD, *Staying Competitive in the Global Economy: Moving Up the Value Chain*, 2007

20 Alan Blinder, 'How Many US Jobs Might Be Offshorable', *World Economics*, 10 (2, April–June): 41–78

21 N. Gregory Mankiw and Phillip Swagel, 'The Politics and Economics of Offshore Outsourcing', NBER Working Paper No. 12398, 2006

22 *European Restructuring Monitor Quarterly*, Issue 3, Autumn 2010 quarterly. http://www.eurofound.europa.eu/emcc/erm/templates/displaydoc.php?docID=57

23 Mark Kobayashi-Hillary, *Who Moved My Job?*, Lulu, 2008.

24 Mark Kobayashi-Hillary, *Talking Outsourcing*, Lulu, 2009.

25 OECD, *Staying Competitive in the Global Economy: Moving Up the Value Chain*, 2007

26 http://www.voxeu.org/index.php?q=node/3950

27 McKinsey Global Institute, 'Offshoring: Is It a Win-Win Game?', 2003

28 OECD, *Information Technology Outlook 2008*, 2009, Fig. 2.12. OECD and major emerging economies' computer and information services trade, 2006

29 Runjuan Liu and Daniel Trefler, 'Much Ado about Nothing: American Jobs and the Rise of Service Outsourcing to China and India', NBER Working Paper No. 14061, June 2008

30 It is true that trade collapsed for several reasons, including falling demand. But protectionism greatly amplified the damage. According to a study by Jakob Madsen of Monash University ('Trade Barriers and the Collapse of World Trade During the Great Depression'), world trade declined 14 per cent in inflation-adjusted terms between 1929 and 1932 because of declining incomes, 8 per cent because of policy-induced tariff increases, 5 per cent because of deflation-induced tariff increases (when prices are falling, a tariff of, say, £1 per item rises in real terms) and a further 6 per cent because of the imposition of non-tariff barriers. So, most of the collapse in trade was due to rising protectionism rather than falling demand. Nor did protectionism save American jobs. Research by Doug Irwin of Dartmouth College, a leading US trade historian, concludes that 'The Smoot–Hawley tariff of 1930, for example, significantly reduced imports but failed to create jobs overall because exports fell almost one-for-one with imports, resulting in employment losses in those industries.' (Douglas Irwin, *Free Trade Under Fire*, Princeton, 2002)

31 Ha-Joon Chang, 'Jobs, not shopping', *Prospect*, March 2009

32 Australia's exports to China increased from $2.6 billion in 1999 to $27.1 billion in 2008.

7 Panda Panic

1 Bill Emmott, *Rivals: How the Power Struggle Between China, India and Japan Will Shape Our Next Decade*, Penguin, 2008

2 http://www.dfat.gov.au/trade/focus/081201_top10_twoway_exports.html

3 http://www.dfat.gov.au/geo/fs/chin.pdf

4 OECD, *International Migration Outlook 2008*, 2008, Table B.1.4

5 http://en.wikipedia.org/wiki/Chinese_Australian

6 The Lowy Institute for International Policy, *Australia and the World: Public Opinion and Foreign Policy*, 2008

7   Australian Bureau of Statistics, 'International Investment Position, Australia: Supplementary Statistics', 2009. http://www.abs.gov.au/AUSSTATS/abs@.nsf/DetailsPage/5352.02008?OpenDocument Stocks quoted are for 2008

8   http://www.barnabyjoyce.com.au/Issues/Thisweekinpolitics/tabid/56/articleType/ArticleView/articleId/741/Keep-Australia-Australian.aspx

9   90 per cent of Australians agree (61 per cent 'strongly') that 'the government has a responsibility to ensure Australian companies are kept in majority Australian control'. The Lowy Institute for International Policy, *Australia and the World: Public Opinion and Foreign Policy*, 2008

10 For instance, Sinosteel was limited to a minority stake in Murchison Metals, an iron-ore developer.

11 David Marchick and Matthew Slaughter, *Global FDI Policy: Correcting a Protectionist Drift*, Council on Foreign Relations, June 2008, http://www.cfr.org/publication/16503/

12 John Cranford, 'Defining "Ours" in a New World', *CQ Weekly*, 3 March 2006, p. 592

13 Richard Cookson, *For a Few Sovereigns More*, HSBC Global Research, February 2008

14 McKinsey Global Institute, *The new power brokers: How oil, Asia, hedge funds, and private equity are faring in the financial crisis*, July 2009

15 http://www.economist.com/businessfinance/displayStory.cfm?story_id=E1_TDDGQVDT

16 T. Makin, 'Capital Xenophobia and the "National Interest"', paper prepared for symposium on 'Australia's Open Investment Future', Institute of Public Affairs, Melbourne, 4 December 2008, p. 11

17 OECD, 'OECD's FDI Regulatory Restrictiveness Index: Revision and Extension to More Economies', Working Papers on International Investment 2006/4

18 http://www.ft.com/cms/s/0/bef2177a-a924-11de-9b7f-00144feabdc0.html

19 ITS Global, *Foreign Direct Investment in Australia*, 21

20 Giuseppe Nicoletti, Stephen Golub, Dana Hajkova, Daniel Mirza and Kwang-Yeol Yoo, 'The Influence of Policies on Trade and Foreign Direct Investment', OECD Economic Studies 36:1, p. 66

21 Calculations from UNCTAD, *World Investment Report 2008*. http://www.unctad.org/sections/dite_dir/docs/wir08_fs_au_en.pdf

22 http://online.wsj.com/article/SB125244863511393619.html#mod=WSJ_hps_LEFTWhatsNews

23 Flows of foreign direct investment into China were $83.5 billion in 2007, while outward flows were $22.5 billion. The stock of inward investment in China was valued at $327.1 billion, while the outward stock was $95.8 billion. UNCTAD, *World Investment Report 2008*. http://www.unctad.org/sections/dite_dir/docs/wir08_fs_cn_ en.pdf

24 David Marchick and Matthew Slaughter, *Global FDI Policy: Correcting a Protectionist Drift*, Council on Foreign Relations, June 2008. http://www.cfr.org/publication/16503/

25 http://online.wsj.com/article/SB125244863511393619.html#mod=WSJ_hps_LEFTWhatsNews

8 Don't Stop

1 http://www.chinadaily.com.cn/china/2009-01/02/content_7360348.htm
2 http://www.chinadaily.com.cn/bizchina/2009-07/13/content_8420117.htm
3 http://www.chinadaily.com.cn/cndy/2009-07/02/content_8345115.htm
4 http://www.chinadaily.com.cn/bizchina/2008-09/27/content_7066904.htm
5 http://www.chinatravel.net/forum/Guangzhou-Guangzhou-Chocolate-City-Africans-Seek-Their-Dreams-in-China/1499.html
6 http://www.elpais.com/articulo/espana/inmigracion/toca/fondo/elpepuesp/20090917elpepinac_12/Tes
7 http://www.cso.ie/releasespublications/documents/population/current/popmig.pdf
8 Khalid Koser, 'The Global Financial Crisis and International Migration: Policy Implications for Australia', Lowy Institute for International Policy, July 2009
9 http://web.worldbank.org/WBSITE/EXTERNAL/NEWS/0,,contentMDK: 20648762~menuPK:34480~pagePK:64257043~piPK:437376~theSitePK:4607,00.html
10 http://yaleglobal.yale.edu/content/angolan-riches-lure-new-wave-workers
11 The skilled immigration intake for 2009–10 will be cut to 108,100, from 133,500 in 2008–09. Quotas for working holiday-makers are also under review.
12 http://news.bbc.co.uk/1/hi/business/8025089.stm
13 http://www.chinadaily.com.cn/cndy/2009-07/02/content_8345115.htm
14 http://online.wsj.com/article/SB124424701106590613.html
15 http://www.chinadaily.com.cn/bizchina/2009-07/13/content_8420117.htm
16 National Venture Capital Association, 'American Made: The Impact of Immigrant Entrepreneurs and Professionals on US Competitiveness', 2006
17 http://www.soc.duke.edu/GlobalEngineering/pdfs/media/losingtheworlds/nam_usexperiencing.pdf
18 http://www.chinadaily.com.cn/bizchina/2009-07/13/content_8420117.htm
19 OECD, *Education at a Glance 2009*, Indicator C2. http://www.oecd.org/document/24/0,3343,en_2649_39263238_43586328_1_1_1_374 55,00.html
20 *Ibid.*, p. 172

21　Dhananjayan Sriskandarajah and Catherine Drew, *Brits Abroad: Mapping the Scale and Nature of British Emigration*, Institute for Public Policy Research, 2006

22　Tim Finch, Maria Latorre, Naomi Pollard and Jill Rutter, *Shall We Stay or Shall We Go? Re-migration Trends among Britain's Immigrants*, Institute for Public Policy Research, 2009

23　Naomi Pollard, Maria Latorre and Dhananjayan Sriskandarajah, *Floodgates or Turnstiles? Post-EU Enlargement Migration Flows to (and from) the UK*, Institute for Public Policy Research, 2008

24　Office of National Statistics, 'Increased Emigration of Central and Eastern Europeans', 20 May 2009, http://www.statistics.gov.uk/pdfdir/ppmgnr0509.pdf

25　Home Office, 'Accession Monitoring Report: May 2004 – March 2009 (A8 Countries)', May 2009 updated with Home Office, Control of Immigration: Quarterly Statistical Summary, United Kingdom, July–September 2009, November 2009

26　New Zealand Department of Labour, *Migrations Trends and Outlook 2007/2008*, 2009

27　*Ibid.*

28　While 213,000 foreigners moved to settle in New Zealand between 2001 and 2006, its foreign-born population rose by only 162,000 over that period. This implies that at least 51,000 foreign-born people who were in the country in 2001 had left by 2006. Thus departures are equivalent to nearly a quarter of new arrivals. This understates the two-way flow because some migrants no doubt came and left between 2001 and 2006 and thus were not counted in either census. New Zealand Department of Labour, *Migrants and Labour Market Outcomes*, August 2008, Table 3.5, p. 21, http:// www.dol.govt.nz/PDFs/migrants-and-labour-market-outcomes.pdf

29　Australian Department of Citizenship and Immigration, *Immigration Update: July to December 2008*, 2009, Table 4.2, http://www.immi.gov.au/media/publications/statistics/immigration-update/update-dec08.pdf

30　*Ibid.*, Table 4.1

31　*Ibid.*, Table 4.5

32　*Ibid.*, Table 2.9

33　*Ibid.*, Table 2.11 and calculations from Table 2.12

34　Citizenship and Immigration Canada, 'Facts and Figures 2008', Canada – Temporary residents by yearly status, 1984 to 2008, p. 48

35　A. Aydemir and C. Robinson, 'Global Labour Markets, Return and Onward Migration', Working Paper No. 2006-1, University of Western Ontario, 2006

36　OECD, *International Migration Outlook 2008*, 2008, Table I.4, p. 49

37 *Ibid.*, Box I.3, p. 33
38 G. E. Bijwaard, 'Modelling Migration Dynamics of Immigrants: The Case of the Netherlands', IZA Discussion Paper No. 2 891, Institute for the Study of Labour (IZA), 2007
39 Statistics Norway, 2007
40 *Ibid.*, Table III.1, p. 171
41 The OECD estimates indicate that the exit rate of Mexican migrants entering in 1999 was 18 per cent after five years, while it was 24 per cent for people from South America, 43 per cent for immigrants from Canada and 54 per cent for those from a country of the EU-15.
42 http://online.wsj.com/article/SB124424701106590613.html
43 Jeffrey Passel and D'Vera Cohn, 'A Portrait of Unauthorized Immigrants in the United States', Pew Hispanic Center, 2009, http://pewhispanic.org/reports/report.php?ReportID=107
44 http://online.wsj.com/article/SB124424701106590613.html
45 http://www.ft.com/cms/s/0/2ef546bc-8c17-11de-b14f-00144feabdc0.html
46 European Integration Consortium, 'Labour mobility within the EU in the context of enlargement and the functioning of the transitional arrangements', 2009, http://ec.europa.eu/social/BlobServlet?docId=2506&langId=en, *see also* http://www.ft.com/cms/s/0/3fd57e9a-34e5-11de-940a-00144feabdc0.html
47 Christian Dustmann, Tommaso Frattini and Caroline Halls, 'Assessing the Fiscal Costs and Benefits of A8 Migration to the UK', CReAM Discussion Paper No. 18/09, July 2009, http://www.econ.ucl.ac.uk/Cream/pages/CDP/CDP_18_09.pdf
48 http://news.bbc.co.uk/1/hi/england/london/8035293.stm
49 Jonathan Levie, 'Immigration, In-Migration, Ethnicity and Entrepreneurship in the United Kingdom', *Small Business Economics*, 2007, 28:143–69
50 Jonathan Levie and Mark Hart, 'Global Entrepreneurship Monitor: United Kingdom 2008 Monitoring Report', 2009
51 http://www.ft.com/cms/s/0/17dc6c94-8da7-11de-93df-00144feabdc0.html
52 *See*, for instance, Scott Page, *The Difference: How the Power of Diversity Creates Better Groups, Firms, Schools, and Societies*, Princeton, 2007, and Agnieszka Aleksy-Szucsich, *Economic Benefits of Ethnolinguistic Diversity*, Amherst, 2008.
53 David Law, Murat Genç and John Bryant, 'Trade, Diaspora and Migration to New Zealand', NZIER working paper 2009/4, 2009
54 Giovanni Peri and Francisco Requena, 'The Trade Creation Effect of Immigrants: Testing the Theory on the Remarkable Case of Spain', CReAM Discussion Paper No 15/09, June 2009

9 Food Fight

1 http://www.guardian.co.uk/business/2009/may/15/tesco-south-africa-living-wage
2 http://www.ft.com/cms/s/0/cb3fdc8e-1f86-11dd-9216-000077b07658.html
3 http://www.economist.com/displaystory.cfm?story_id=E1_ TDNVDQND
4 *Ibid.*
5 http://www.economist.com/displaystory.cfm?story_id=E1_ TDNVDQND
6 OECD, *Agricultural Policies in OECD Countries: Monitoring and Evaluation*, 2009, Table 5.2: European Union: Estimates of support to agriculture (EU25)
7 This is 1.2586, http://www.hmrc.gov.uk/exrate/european-union.htm
8 The figures are for the EU-25 whose population is 468.5 million according to Eurostat.
9 OECD, *Agricultural Policies in OECD Countries: Monitoring and Evaluation*, 2009, Table 14.1: United States: Estimates of support to agriculture
10 *Ibid.*, Table III.4: OECD: Total Support Estimate by country
11 http://www.oxfam.org/en/news/pressreleases2005/pr051212_cap
12 http://news.bbc.co.uk/1/hi/uk_politics/4374655.stm
13 http://www.oxfam.org/en/news/pressreleases2005/pr051212_cap
14 http://www.telegraph.co.uk/finance/newsbysector/retailandconsumer/5586541/Sainsburys-v-Tesco-the-rumble-in-the-supermarket-aisles.html
15 The study for the European Commission is available from http://ec.europa.eu/agriculture/analysis/external/scenar2020ii/summary_en.pdf. The Duke of Buccleuch estimate is from Kevin Cahill, *Who Owns the World: The Hidden Facts Behind Landownership*, Mainstream, 2006
16 *Ibid.*
17 http://www.economist.com/world/americas/displaystory.cfm?story_id=E1_VTDSRQJ
18 http://www.nytimes.com/2007/08/06/opinion/06mcwilliams.html?_r=2&oref=login&oref=slogin
19 http://www.guardian.co.uk/environment/2008/mar/23/food.ethicalliving
20 *Ibid.*

10 Clean is Cool

1 Michael Belfiore, *Rocketeers*, HarperCollins, 2007, from http://en.wikipedia.org/wiki/Elon_Musk
2 http://en.wikipedia.org/wiki/BYD_e6
3 http://money.cnn.com/2009/04/13/technology/gunther_electric.fortune/
4 Defra
5 SeriousWindows are marketed as 'the most energy-efficient residential

windows on the market today. Homeowners could save tens of thousands of dollars over the life of their home.' ThermaRock greatly improves the insulation of existing walls.

6 http://www.ft.com/cms/s/0/1812bffe-8da4-11de-93df-00144feabdc0.html
7 http://www.ft.com/cms/s/0/348e5d02-ac56-11de-a754-00144feabdc0.html
8 http://www.youtube.com/watch?v=0Ds3l3Nv_xQ
9 http://en.wikipedia.org/wiki/Paul_R._Ehrlich
10 For now, Spain and Germany are among the world leaders in solar power.
11 http://www.economist.com/displaystory.cfm?story_id=13982870
12 http://en.wikipedia.org/wiki/Vestas
13 http://www.economist.com/specialreports/displaystory.cfm?story_id=13686538
14 http://www.economist.com/world/britain/displaystory.cfm?story_id=14177328
15 http://en.wikipedia.org/wiki/Shi_Zhengrong
16 http://money.cnn.com/2009/04/13/technology/gunther_electric.fortune/
17 IEA, *Key World Energy Statistics*, 2008
18 http://www.ft.com/cms/s/0/3ec020f6-b770-11de-9812-00144feab49a.html
19 http://www.economist.com/people/displaystory.cfm?story_id= 13941982
20 http://www.economist.com/specialreports/displayStory.cfm?story_id=11565685
21 IEA, Share of total primary energy supply in 2006. http://www.iea.org/Textbase/stats/pdf_graphs/29TPESPI.pdf
22 http://www.nytimes.com/2009/08/22/science/earth/22degrees.html
23 http://www.economist.com/displaystory.cfm?story_id=13824446
24 http://en.wikipedia.org/wiki/Carbon_tax#cite_note-defranl-27
25 http://www.economist.com/specialreports/displayStory.cfm?story_id=11565685
26 http://www.ft.com/cms/s/0/a5fb6084-9e32-11de-b0aa-00144feabdc0.html
27 http://blogs.ft.com/maverecon/2009/07/does-poverty-give-a-country-the-right-to-pollute-the-atmosphere/
28 http://www.economist.com/world/international/displaystory.cfm?story_id=12815686
29 As *The Economist* has remarked, the ETS is 'focused on the short term, vulnerable to gaming and plagued by hugely fluctuating prices', http://www.economist.com/opinion/displaystory.cfm?story_id=14167834
30 When asked about a carbon tax in an interview in July 2007, he said that 'depending on how it is designed, a carbon tax accomplishes much of the same thing that a cap-and-trade program accomplishes. The danger in a cap-and-trade system is that the permits to emit greenhouse gases are given away for free as opposed to priced at auction. One of the

mistakes the Europeans made in setting up a cap-and-trade system was to give too many of those permits away.'

31 H.R. 2454:111th Congress, American Clean Energy and Security Act of 2009

32 http://www.nytimes.com/2009/08/09/business/economy/09view.html ?scp=1&sq=mankiw&st=cse

33 'We need to impose a carbon tax at [Europe's] borders,' Sarkozy says. 'I will lead that battle.' He argues that 'A carbon tax at the border is the natural complement to a domestic carbon tax. More importantly, a carbon tax at the borders is vital for our industries and our jobs. This has nothing to do with protectionism. This is about fair play.' http://www. ft.com/cms/s/0/a5fb6084-9e32-11de-b0aa-00144feabdc0.html

34 http://krugman.blogs.nytimes.com/2009/06/29/climate-trade-obama/

35 'If the US wants India (and China) to assume "flow" obligations for current emissions, and these too in the same degree as implied by the current legislative provision that if these countries do not have identical carbon taxes then they should be subject to border tax adjustments, then it is clear that the US should want to accept "stock" obligations for a century of carbon emissions in the manner of the domestic US Superfund for past damages ... the moneys to be spent on environmental mitigation and accommodation ... But one looks in vain for any serious acceptance of such an obligation in US discourse.' http:// www.ft.com/cms/s/0/653771c4-7654-11de-9e59-00144feabdc0.html

36 Kishore Mahbubani, *The New Asian Hemisphere: The Irresistible Shift of Global Power to the East*, PublicAffairs, 2008, p. 189

37 'We reject the use of climate as a non-tariff barrier,' he said. 'And we categorically reject any attempt to introduce climate change as an issue at the [WTO].' http://www.ft.com/cms/s/0/22a06cc0-6593-11de-8e34-00144feabdc0.html

38 http://www.ucsusa.org/global_warming/science_and_impacts/science/each-countrys-share-of-co2.htmlLocl

39 'It has always been China's position that the international society should fight climate change together, but the proposal of some developed countries to slap a carbon tariff on some imported products violates the WTO's basic principles and is trade protectionism in the disguise of environmental protection,' said Yao Jian, spokesman for China's ministry of commerce. http://www.ft.com/cms/s/0/76f0e4b0-67fc-11de-848a-00144feabdc0.html

40 http://www.ft.com/cms/s/0/da6df660-6c1e-11de-9320-00144feabdc0.html

41 http://www.voxeu.org/index.php?q=node/2456

42 http://www.economist.com/specialreports/displaystory.cfm?story_id=13686538

43 http://online.wsj.com/article/SB126192809041606467.html

44 http://www.ft.com/cms/s/0/ff08faec-8cdf-11de-a540-00144feabdc0,dwp_uuid=9c33700c-4c86-11da-89df-0000779e2340.html
45 http://www.ft.com/cms/s/0/18deffb8-ab88-11de-9be4-00144feabdc0.html
46 http://www.ft.com/cms/s/0/d566f76c-8a8b-11de-ad08-00144feabdc0.html
47 http://www.voxeu.org/index.php?q=node/757
48 http://www.ft.com/cms/s/0/1780bf20-8b3b-11de-9f50-00144feabdc0.html
49 http://www.economist.com/displaystory.cfm?story_id=13272099
50 http://www.iie.com/publications/pb/pb09-3.pdf
51 http://www.guardian.co.uk/environment/2009/aug/23/coal-wave-power-energy
52 http://cleantech.com/news/node/554
53 Gilbert E. Metcalf, 'Taxing Energy in the US: Which Fuels Does the Tax Code Favor?', New York: The Manhattan Institute, 2009. Tellingly, Western Capital, a Houston-based drilling and finance firm, sets out the tax benefits of investing in the oil industry: 'The tax benefits generated by a direct participation in oil and/or natural gas are substantial. The immediate deduction of the intangible drilling costs or IDCs is very significant, and by taking this up front deduction, the risk capital is effectively subsidised by the government by reducing the participant's federal, and possibly state income tax.' http://www.oilandgasjointventures.com/tax-benefits.html
54 http://www.economist.com/specialreports/displayStory.cfm?story_id=11565685
55 http://articles.latimes.com/2009/apr/11/nation/na-iraq-vietnam11
56 http://www.economist.com/businessfinance/displayStory.cfm?story_id=11453151
57 http://www.economist.com/businessfinance/displayStory.cfm?story_id=11453151
58 http://www.oecd.org/dataoecd/62/38/43707019.pdf
59 http://www.econbrowser.com/archives/2007/02/ethanol_subsidi.html

11 Big and Bust

1 http://www.themonthly.com.au/monthly-essays-kevin-rudd-global-financial-crisis—1421
2 http://www.economist.com/world/europe/displaystory.cfm?story_id=13782546

3 http://www.themonthly.com.au/monthly-essays-kevin-rudd-global-financial-crisis—1421?page=0%2C0

4 http://www.nytimes.com/2009/08/27/opinion/27iht-edhatoyama.html?_r=1&scp=1&sq=hatoyama%20a%20new%20path&st=cse

5 Bill Emmott, *Rivals: How the Power Struggle between China, India and Japan will Shape Our Next Decade*, Penguin, 2008

6 HM Treasury, Public Sector Finances Databank, 22 July 2009, Chart C2, http://www.hm-treasury.gov.uk/psf_statistics.htm

7 *Ibid.*, Table B2, http://www.hm-treasury.gov.uk/psf_statistics.htm

8 HM Treasury, Public Expenditure Statistical Analyses 2009, Tables 4.3 and 4.4, http://www.hm-treasury.gov.uk/d/pesa09_chapter4.pdf

9 UK National Statistics, C9LG, Public Sector Employment by Industry; NHS; UK; HC; NSA; Thousands

10 UK National Statistics, C9LF, Public Sector Employment by Industry; Education; UK; HC; NSA; Thousands

11 UK National Statistics, C9KD, Public Sector Employment by Sector; Total Public Sector; UK; HC; NSA; Thousands

12 British Chambers of Commerce, 'Burdens Barometer 2007', http://www.britishchambers.org.uk/policy/pdf/burdens_barometer_2007.pdf

13 In Italy, government spending was cut by 10.3 per cent of GDP between 1993 and 2000, but then rose by 1.7 percentage points again by 2007. Contributions from Italy's notoriously reluctant taxpayers remained roughly stable. Spain slashed spending by nearly 10 per cent of GDP between 1993 and 2000 and it then stabilised at around 39 per cent of GDP. Receipts were a similar share of national income in 1993 and 2007.

14 http://www.economist.com/markets/rankings/displaystory.cfm?story_id=11697971&source=login_payBarrier

15 OECD, *Employment Outlook 2009*, 2009, Table J

16 OECD, *Economic Survey: Denmark*, 2008, Table 3.2: Transfer payment recipients, 2005

17 OECD, *International Migration Outlook 2007*, 2007, Annex Table I.A1.4

18 IMF, *World Economic Outlook* database, October 2010

19 Germany is forecast to run a budget deficit of 4.5 per cent of GDP in 2010 with a gross debt of 75.3 per cent of GDP, France a deficit of 8 per cent with a debt of 84.2 per cent.

20 Åsa Johansson, Christopher Heady, Jens Arnold, Bert Brys and Laura Vartia, 'Tax and Economic Growth', Economics Department Working Paper No. 620, OECD, 2008

21 OECD, *Revenue Statistics 1965–2007*, 2008, Table C

22 OECD, *Taxing Wages 2007–2008*, 2009, Table 0.2: Income tax plus employee and employer social security contributions, 2008

23 Marginal rate of income tax plus employee and employer contributions less cash benefits, by family-type and wage level (as percentage of labour costs), 2007. OECD, *Revenue Statistics 1965–2007*, 2008, Table I.6

24 *Ibid.*, Table 13

25 http://www.eia.doe.gov/oiaf/ieo/emissions.html

26 http://www.ft.com/cms/s/0/25afd1d4-a905-11de-b8bd-00144feabdc0.html

27 Kevin Cahill, *Who Owns the World: The Hidden Facts Behind Landownership*, Mainstream, 2006

28 Dominic Maxwell and Anthony Vigor, *Time for a Land Value Tax?*, Institute for Public Policy Research, 2005

29 David Ricardo, *On the Principles of Political Economy and Taxation*, 1817

12 The Future is Open

1 Fareed Zakaria, *The Post-American World: And the Rise of the Rest*, Penguin, 2008

2 Kishore Mahbubani, *The New Asian Hemisphere: The Irresistible Shift of Global Power to the East*, PublicAffairs, 2008

3 GDP per capita at purchasing power parity. IMF, *World Economic Outlook* database, October 2010

4 http://www.ft.com/cms/s/0/a47079b2-b1e6-11de-a271-00144feab49a.html

5 http://www.ft.com/cms/s/0/5cfd7324-762b-11de-9e59-00144feabdc0.html

6 http://www.economist.com/world/international/displaystory.cfm?story_id=13610801&source=login_payBarrier

7 http://www.nytimes.com/2009/09/15/business/15labor.html?_r=1&hp

8 Patrick Messerlin and Erik van der Marel, *Leading with Services: The Dynamics of Transatlantic Negotiations in Services*, Sciences Po policy brief, June 2009

9 http://www.reuters.com/article/pressRelease/idUS154272+10-Aug-2009+PRN20090810

Index